Revolution Around the Corner

T0244292

EDITED BY
JOSÉ E. VELÁZQUEZ,
CARMEN V. RIVERA, AND
ANDRÉS TORRES

Revolution Around the Corner

Voices from the Puerto Rican Socialist Party in the United States

TEMPLE UNIVERSITY PRESS
Philadelphia • *Rome* • *Tokyo*

TEMPLE UNIVERSITY PRESS
Philadelphia, Pennsylvania 19122
tupress.temple.edu

Library of Congress Cataloging-in-Publication Data

Names: Velázquez, José E. (José Emiliano), 1952– editor. | Rivera, Carmen V.
(Carmen Vivian), 1949– editor. | Torres, Andrés, 1947– editor.
Title: Revolution around the corner : voices from the Puerto Rican Socialist Party in the
United States / José E. Velázquez, Carmen V. Rivera, and Andrés Torres.
Description: Philadelphia : Temple University Press, 2021. | Includes bibliographical
references and index. | Summary: "Revolution Around the Corner is the story of the
Puerto Rican Socialist Party-U.S. Branch from the late 1960s through the mid-1990s.
It combines historical accounts, personal stories, interviews, and retrospective
analysis to describe mass campaigns, the inner workings of a revolutionary
organization, and key ideological tensions over time"— Provided by publisher.
Identifiers: LCCN 2020019230 (print) | LCCN 2020019231 (ebook) | ISBN 9781439920541
(cloth) | ISBN 9781439920558 (paperback) | ISBN 9781439920565 (pdf)
Subjects: LCSH: Partido Socialista Puertorriqueño. Seccional de Estados Unidos—
History—20th century. | Socialism—United States—History—20th century. |
Puerto Ricans—Political activity—United States. | Puerto Rico—History—
Autonomy and independence movements.
Classification: LCC JL1059.A57 R48 2021 (print) | LCC JL1059.A57 (ebook) |
DDC 324.27295/074—dc23
LC record available at https://lccn.loc.gov/2020019230
LC ebook record available at https://lccn.loc.gov/2020019231

Printed in the United States of America

9 8 7 6 5 4 3 2 1

For our children:
Gabriel, Javier, Talisa, Rachel, and Orlando

For our grandchildren:
Isabella, Ava, Emma, Jaclyn, David,
Jonathan, Abigail, and Omar

For all former members of the MPI-PSP,
including those no longer with us

Contents

PART III COALITIONS AND ALLIANCES

PART IV CONCLUSION

List of Figures

Note: Photographs courtesy of José R. "Pucho" Charron and *Periódico Claridad*. Info graphic designed by Sandra Rodríguez, Hechizos Gráficos.

Acknowledgments

T he editors are deeply grateful to the individuals who contributed
chapters to this book. From the start, we believed that participants in
the actual history should be invited to relate their memories and perspectives. Without their sense of mission and passionate collaboration, this
project would never have been completed. Thanks also go to former members of the Puerto Rican Socialist Party (PSP) who agreed to be interviewed
for this anthology. Their names are mentioned in the text and in the list of
interviews. As well, we sincerely appreciate the involvement of focus group
participants who shared recollections of growing up as "PSP children."

The photo images are the product of various photographers, mostly
affiliated with *Claridad* newspaper. We especially thank José R. "Pucho"
Charrón and *Claridad* director Alida Millán Ferrer for photographs of the
early years of the PSP. There was no better person to design the book's cover
and info graphic than Sandra Rodríguez, who joined the PSP as a high
school student. By then, she was already showing her creative talent for
graphic design. We appreciate the work of Olga Iris Sanabria Dávila, who
transcribed most of the interview material. Emily Blais Alemany and Yes-
enia López contributed logistical and technical assistance.

Various *compañeras* and *compañeros* helped with their recollections
of events, controversies, and debates. These include José Alberto Álvarez
Febles*, Sigfredo Carrión, Alfredo del Valle, Jesús López, Melba Maldonado,

---

* in memorium

Carmen Méndez, Florencio Merced, Luis Negrón, Franklyn Pérez, Europa Piñero, Doris Pizarro, Jenaro Rentas, Arturo Rivera, Margie Santiago, and José Soler*. These conversations were indispensable for a comprehensive description of the PSP story.

This book would not have been possible without the work of the *¡Despierta Boricua!* Recovering History Project and its archival collection on the PSP's U.S. Branch. The archive, compiled under the direction of Carmen V. Rivera, served as a primary source for the writing of several chapters. Besides the editors, many individuals donated documents, posters, books, and other memorabilia. We take this opportunity to thank Fred Álvarez, Alice Simon Berger, Denis Berger*, América Sorrentini Blaut, Maggie Block, Judy Cohen, Eduardo "Pancho" Cruz*, William Cruz Alicea, Armengol Domenech, Bobby Greenberg, Jill Hamberg, Jorge Hernández, Alan Howard, Bomexí Iztaccihuatl, Hector López, Isabel Malavet*, Carmen López Martinez, Nelson Merced, José-Manuel Navarro, Franklyn Pérez, Pedro Reyes, Philip Rivera Jr., Virginia Rodríguez, Alberto Salas, Olga Iris Sanabria Dávila, Digna Sánchez, Margie Santiago, and Denis Urrútia*. (Apologies to any individuals we may have omitted!) We appreciate the support of María E. Pérez y González of the Brooklyn College Department of Puerto Rican and Latino Studies for providing an institutional home to the Recovering History Project. We also thank the Center for Puerto Rican Studies (Centro) Archives and Library at Hunter College, City University of New York, and in particular Pedro Juan Hernández, for contributing the first supply of archival boxes and folders. For their assistance in acquiring and processing archival material, our thanks go to Jorge Matos and Andrew Luecke. We also benefitted from the assistance of Chandler Davis and the special support of Gerald J. Meyer.

Aaron Javsicas at Temple University Press warmly welcomed this project and assisted us through its several phases. We are immensely grateful for his support and advice. Ashley Petrucci's diligent and cheerful monitoring of workflow and deadlines made for efficient collaboration. Many thanks to the two anonymous reviewers who, by challenging our earlier drafts, considerably improved the final product. Finally, we acknowledge Gary Kramer, Kate Nichols, and Jon Dertien, who helped steer this publication to its conclusion, and especially Heather Wilcox, copy editor, who skillfully enhanced our story and amiably responded to our inquiries with precision and patience.

---

* in memorium

Revolution Around the Corner

I
Histories

Introduction

José E. Velázquez, Carmen V. Rivera,
and Andrés Torres

Revolution Around the Corner

Revolution Around the Corner is the story of the U.S. Branch of the Puerto Rican Socialist Party (PSP), whose years of activism were the late 1960s through the mid-1990s. Also discussed is the *Movimiento Pro Independencia* (MPI), which was founded in 1959 and was the precursor to the PSP. This volume provides the first complete account of the rise and decline of the PSP's U.S. Branch. Combining historical accounts, personal stories, interviews, and retrospective analysis, *Revolution Around the Corner* offers readers an in-depth view of various mass campaigns, the inner workings of a revolutionary organization, and the drama of ideological tensions over time.

Beyond the literature written by Puerto Ricans themselves, this story has remained hidden from most accounts of radical social and political movements in the United States. The editors hope this book will help broaden the knowledge of the PSP's history. We also hope it will bring more attention to Puerto Rico's present crisis of austerity economics and extreme climate change.

The PSP sought to tear down the "curtain of silence" concealing U.S. colonialism in its Caribbean territory. Its members also led and participated in numerous social justice campaigns throughout the United States where Boricuas (Puerto Ricans) had formed communities. The U.S. Branch, called *La Seccional*, was organically tied to the national PSP, based in Puerto Rico.[1] Its members perceived themselves as simultaneously part of a national liberation movement and the U.S. Left. This double role was at once a source of vibrancy, success, and exhaustive internal conflict. The effort to fulfill this double role partially contributed to the PSP's decline.

We believe the PSP experience has been underappreciated in the scholarly literature about the U.S. Left and social movements. In part, this lack of attention is due to the general neglect of radical movements of racialized minorities. Perhaps scholars also feel some confusion over the organization's mission: a common misperception is that its exclusive mandate was to attract solidarity for Puerto Rican independence from Boricuas in the United States and North American anti-imperialist sectors. Anyone familiar with the full scope of its activity, however, recognizes the PSP's deep involvement in the daily life and struggles of the diasporic community and its aspirations for self-determination *in the United States*. A somewhat binary view emerged among observers of the time: your mission may be to rouse up solidarity for Puerto Rican independence or to be part of the Puerto Rican "minority" struggle—but not both. They did not recognize the impracticality of this vision. Rather, they disputed the PSP's claim to a double role, *as a political prerogative*. The PSP asserted that the role of its U.S. Branch would not be confined to this either/or vision and that it would pursue both goals.[2]

Furthermore, members of the PSP's U.S. Branch argued that organizing Puerto Rican workers and community residents was not strictly about advocating for democratic rights; rather, doing so would induce Boricuas to participate in the revolutionary transformation of U.S. society. This notion meant engaging directly with the U.S. Left and with social movements inside the "belly of the beast."

The PSP was partially complicit in the confusion over its identity. Its theoretical statements suffered from some inconsistency. Its practical work tended to alternate haphazardly between the roles espoused as its leadership searched for proper balance among performing solidarity work, fighting for democratic rights, and forging revolutionary alliances. In the early phase, this confusion was not always evident or even consequential, as so much was done on both fronts. In time, though, the strength that came from a creative approach, largely a result of the PSP's view on the "national question," became a weakness that exhausted the organization. The explication of this tension is one of the hallmark themes of this book.

Revolution Around the Corner serves as a sequel to *The Puerto Rican Movement: Voices from the Diaspora*, an anthology that looked at organizations and individuals instrumental in the movements that emerged in the late 1960s. Several pieces on the PSP in general and its work in Boston and Hartford are published therein.[3] The present book exclusively discusses the PSP. Since the 1990s, other works have also been published.[4]

The title for this book came to us through testimonies and interviews. It refers to a perception that the political conjuncture in the early 1970s promised independence for Puerto Rico in the short run. This sense of immediacy emboldened militants to perform acts of passionate activism and enormous sacrifice. It also undermined the capacity for adopting new approaches once reality sunk in.

The personal testimonies—and excerpts from interviews interspersed throughout various chapters—are at the center of this book. As such, they offer a range of views and interpretations of people's PSP experiences. As the editors of this volume, we did not seek consensus or an overarching coherence from the contributing authors—only clarity of expression. Neither did the authors seek to suppress testimonies that some readers may find problematic (i.e., articulations that may come across as hyperbole, rhetoric, dogmatism, or political jargon). Some readers may even interpret certain testimonies as advocating for supporting leaders, movements, or governments they consider indefensible. We did not see our editorial role as contesting assessments or conclusions with which we differed. Our opinions are voiced in the Introduction, the Conclusion, and the chapters we individually authored. As for the testimonies—these are life stories and political views. They are truthful, passionate statements from genuine activists for social change, worthy on their own terms.

Finally, a separate and independent enterprise that has assembled much of the primary source material included in this book is the ¡Despierta Boricua! Recovering History Project. This extensive archival collection of primary documents, posters, photographs, and oral histories dealing with the PSP is organized by coeditor Carmen V. Rivera and several former PSP members, including some contributors to this book.[5]

Some Historical Context

Most people in the United States were unaware until recently that the country possesses a colonial territory in the Caribbean. Fewer still were aware that Puerto Ricans are fellow U.S. citizens, whether they live on the island or in U.S. communities. It took the monumental catastrophe of Hurricane María in 2017 to bring this point home. Some readers of this book may therefore benefit from a brief review of Puerto Rico's history under the United States, the state-sponsored migrations to which it has been subject, and the political and social struggles of Puerto Ricans in U.S. communities. It will be useful for readers to keep in mind that the Puerto Rican diaspora has a long history of social and political movements, both radical and reformist. The movements that started in the late 1960s did not arise out of thin air.

Puerto Rico has been subject to U.S. imperialism since the early nineteenth century as part of the Monroe Doctrine. A small community of Cuban and Puerto Rican merchants and political exiles were already organized in the United States, before the Spanish-American War led to the military and political occupation that ended the short-lived Autonomist Charter granted to Puerto Rico by the Spanish authorities. Puerto Ricans in this first wave of migration advocated for the independence of Cuba and Puerto Rico, with some even hoping that the U.S. invasion would be a prelude to independence. The first Puerto Rican organizations, such as the Puerto Rican section of the Cuban Revolutionary Party, had the struggle in Puerto Rico as their primary frame of reference. Exile leaders, including Sotero Figueroa Hernández, Julio J. Henna, Juan de Mata Terreforte, and Antonio Vélez Alvarado, formed such organizations as the *Club Borinquen* and the *Liga Antillana*, a racially mixed group of working-class women.[6]

The Foraker Act of 1900 initiated the process of Puerto Rico's incorporation into the U.S. political and economic domain, increasing the number of people migrating to and settling on the mainland. Migration increased after the Jones Act of 1917 conferred citizenship, despite objections by Puerto Rico's House of Delegates. Puerto Rican organizations in the United States began to address what have been historically the two major concerns in the diaspora: the colonial situation of Puerto Rico and the political, social, and economic conditions of those who live in the "Metropolis."[7]

Increased migration and presence in American cities also meant that Puerto Ricans faced head on the issues of racism, discrimination, and racial identity. News reports about the Harlem riot of 1935 identified the main protagonist, Lino Rivera, a Puerto Rican, as simply "Negro," revealing the sometime invisibility of Puerto Ricans. America's so-called one-drop rule for racial identification meant that Puerto Ricans would be classified as "Negro" or "nonwhite" and therefore second-class citizens of color as well as newcomers. During the Harlem Renaissance, many black Puerto Ricans immersed themselves into the African American community and its struggles, as in the cases of Arturo A. Schomburg, Pura Belpré, Sammy Davis Jr., and others. This multicultural syncretism continues in the present and is often overlooked.[8]

During the 1930s and 1940s, many Puerto Ricans viewed increased migration as a consequence of U.S. colonialism, and the general tendency of progressive working-class Puerto Ricans was to join already-established socialist formations that also supported independence for Puerto Rico. By 1920, New York City's Puerto Rican population numbered 7,364, centered around Harlem, the West Side, Chelsea, Lower East Side, and Red Hook, Brooklyn.

Although they formed local civic organizations of their own, Puerto Ricans also joined the Communist Party (CP) and the Socialist Party. Jesús Colón, arriving in 1918, became the chair of the Puerto Rican Commission of the CP. He was a major contributor to its newspaper and the leader of the *Alianza Obrera Puertorriqueña* (Puerto Rican Workers Alliance), which called for Puerto Rican–Negro labor unity. Other well-known Puerto Rican leaders joined him in the CP, such as Clemente Soto Vélez, Homero Rosado, and Bernardo Vega. Colón ran for office on the American Labor Party ticket and is credited with founding more than twenty community organizations.

The CP-inspired *Centro Obrero Español* (Spanish Workers Center) helped found the Hotel Workers Union, which had a large Puerto Rican membership and pushed for Puerto Rican–Negro labor unity. It is estimated that during 1918–1920, the Socialist Party received 40 percent of the Puerto Rican vote. The International Workers Order (IWO), founded in 1930 by the CP, had more than ten thousand members in its Hispanic Section by 1947. In addition to socialist formations, such groups as *La Liga Antiimperialista*, *La Asociación Pro-Independencia de Puerto Rico*, and *El Congreso Pro-Independencia de Puerto Rico* focused on the struggle in Puerto Rico.[9]

The post–World War II era initiated a second wave of migration from Puerto Rico often called "the Great Migration (1946–64)," a movement that was still predominantly focused on New York City but also included cities in New Jersey, Connecticut, Pennsylvania, Massachusetts, and Chicago. The "push" and "pull" factors for migration were accompanied by recruitment on the part of U.S. companies, government-sponsored migration, and Operation Bootstrap development policies. This migration spurred growth of distinct Puerto Rican communities throughout the continental United States. This new development meant greater influence of Puerto Rican radicalism, as seen in the support for the American Labor Party and Congressman Vito Marcantonio in New York City. Marcantonio, an Italian American, was a long-time and stalwart advocate for Puerto Rico's independence and the defense of Puerto Rican rights in New York.[10]

The 1950s ushered in a period of mass repression of the Nationalist Party in Puerto Rico, while the rise of McCarthyism weakened the Left and Socialist movements in the United States. The 1954 Nationalist attack on the U.S. Congress also led to a culture of fear and anti–Puerto Rican sentiment. Support for the American Labor Party waned, and it was dissolved in 1956. Colón ran for office in 1953 and 1969, with a platform that emphasized Puerto Rican rights. The politically active sectors, without ignoring the colonial situation, began to focus on Puerto Rican rights and empowerment on the mainland, although not always from a radical perspective. The repression of the Left led to what has been referred to as a "fragmenting of memory."[11]

The Great Migration led to a sharp population increase, from seventy thousand in 1940 to almost nine hundred thousand in 1960, with the great majority still living in New York City. Many of the first social service agencies in the late 1950s and 1960s, such as the Puerto Rican Association for Community Affairs (PRACA), the Puerto Rican Community Development Project (PRCDP), the Puerto Rican–Hispanic Leadership Forum, and the Puerto Rican Family Institute, provided second-generation Puerto Ricans with access to resources, public policy advocacy, and professional development. Generally, they did so without overtly challenging the U.S. systems of racism and capitalism.

Until 1964, New York City and other cities required potential voters to pass a literacy test in English before they could register. The elimination of this requirement by the Voting Rights Act of 1965 launched the rise of political power brokers, such as Herman Badillo, elected in 1970 as the first Puerto Rican congressional representative; Ramón S. Vélez; and Robert García.

Grassroots organizations, such as United Bronx Parents (1966), led by Evelina Antonetty, and the *Congreso de Pueblos*, took a more militant stance in the struggle for Puerto Rican rights. Especially important was the *Congreso de Pueblos*, organized by Gilberto Gerena Valentín, previously a member of the American Labor Party. He was a pro-independence activist who had previously led a campaign in defense of political prisoner Oscar Collazo. The *Congreso de Pueblos* brought together the many local grassroots organizations hosted in towns where Puerto Ricans lived; more than twelve hundred delegates attended its second congress in 1957.

The National Association for Puerto Rican Civil Rights formed in 1963, led by Gerena Valentín and others, had a national and progressive perspective that used the terminology of the civil rights movement. Gerena Valentín supported the 1963 March on Washington for Jobs and Freedom, where he was an invited speaker; was a leadership member of the 1964 New York City school boycott; and later participated in the 1968 Poor People's Campaign. Manny Diaz was another important figure who won the confidence of black leaders, including Dr. Martin Luther King Jr., Bayard Rustin, and Ralph Abernathy.[12]

A renewed Left also focused attention on the labor movement and pressured New York City's Central Labor Council to form a Hispanic Labor Committee in 1969. New York's District 65 withdrew from its parent union and the American Federation of Labor and Congress of Industrial Organizations (AFL-CIO) to protest the lack of organizing among Black and Puerto Rican members. The Puerto Rican Welfare League sought to organize farm workers in Lorraine, Ohio, and similar campaigns took place in New Jersey and Connecticut.

By the mid-1960s, Puerto Rican youth were becoming inspired by the struggles of African Americans, the Cuban Revolution, the anti–Vietnam War movement, the women's movement, and the upsurge of support for Puerto Rico's independence. Reacting to police brutality and socioeconomic oppression, Puerto Ricans were involved in uprisings in Chicago (1966) and joined African Americans in uprisings in 1968 in New York City, Philadelphia, Hartford, and New Haven. ASPIRA, formed in 1961 by Antonia Pantoja and others, became a hub of cultural affirmation and Puerto Rican Left formation.[13]

Bypassing the prior tendency to join existing movements on the Left, young Puerto Ricans with a radical perspective began to talk about launching a "Puerto Rican movement." Existing Nationalist and Leftist groups, such as the Nationalist Party, the MPI, and the Puerto Rican Independence Party (PIP), were now joined by the Young Lords Organization (Chicago); Puerto Rican student organizations, such as the Puerto Rican Student Union (PRSU); Puerto Ricans Involved in Student Action (PRISA); the Young Lords Organization in New York City; the PSP, newly transformed from the MPI; El Comité–MINP (Movimiento de Izquierda Nacional Puertorriqueño [Puerto Rican National Left Movement]); and subsequently such groups as the Latin Women's Collective and the National Congress for Puerto Rican Rights. Opposing the anti-poverty, reformist, and assimilationist philosophy of earlier Puerto Rican organizations, these groups all centered on an anti-capitalist, anti-racist, and anti-colonial perspective.[14]

This Introduction has been focused on New York organizations because, prior to the 1960s, that is where the Puerto Rican community and political developments were overwhelmingly centered. But subsequently, community and political formations developed in other cities and regions, such as Chicago, Philadelphia, northern New Jersey, New England, and suburban New York. Indeed, by 1980, the majority of diaspora Puerto Ricans lived outside New York City.

Part I: Histories

The PSP's history is marked by several contentious issues. The membership tried to resolve several ongoing questions: What is strategy, and what are tactics? Is there an inescapable contradiction posed by the "double role" of the party? In the relationship with the national PSP, how much autonomy is desirable? Similarly, what should the base-leadership interaction look like? What are the criteria for determining the relationship with the North American Left? What is the proper balance between centralism and democracy in party functioning? What is the real significance of the "national question" as traditionally understood? These and other stress points are embedded in the history of the PSP. In the Puerto Rican diaspora, other organizations—before, during, and following the era covered by this narrative—were obligated to handle several of these tensions, whether these groups were revolutionary or reform-oriented. And beyond the Puerto Rican experience, numerous groups and movements—whether Left or progressive—faced aspects of these tensions. The PSP experience is relevant beyond its confines.

Parts I, II, and III of this book are each grouped by general theme. Part I focuses on history. Part II is a collection of "testimonies" written by PSP members. Part III covers the coalition work of the PSP, written by nonmembers. The contributors had no hard and fast rules, so readers will notice varying degrees of narrative history and personal reflection across the chapters.

Part I, the main history section, includes chapters dealing with the overall U.S. Branch (written by Andrés Torres) and the two largest PSP organizations, in New York (written by José E. Velázquez Luyanda) and Chicago (written by José E. Velázquez Luyanda, América Sorrentini, and Pablo Medina Cruz). These chapters trace the narrative arc of an organization's rise and decline. Indispensable to an understanding of the U.S. Branch of the PSP is the story of the national PSP, based in Puerto Rico. Coverage of the national PSP is woven into key junctures in the story of the organization in the United States.

Major events and activities of the MPI-PSP are outlined in Part I's three chapters. A partial list includes internal transitional assemblies (1969, 1970, 1971); the First Congress (1973); the National Day of Solidarity with Puerto Rico (*El Acto Nacional*) in Madison Square Garden (1974); the Save Hostos struggle (1975–1976) and other democratic rights struggles, beginning in the late 1960s (see next paragraph for examples); the Hard Times Conference in Chicago (1976); the release of the Nationalist prisoners (1979); the Vieques campaigns (late 1970s); the People's Convention in the South Bronx (1980); electoral participation (1980s); and advocacy at the United Nations throughout the 1960s, 1970s, and 1980s.

From the late 1960s through the early 1980s, the MPI-PSP led or supported numerous democratic rights, labor, and social justice campaigns. Some of the most well-known events include anti–Vietnam War protests; the Young Lords church occupation in El Barrio, New York; the Newark, New Jersey, uprising against police brutality in 1974; farm worker organization in New Jersey, Connecticut, and Massachusetts; resistance to community displacement in Boston, Chicago, and Hartford; Local 1199 Hospital Workers Union; and the campaign to end sterilization abuse in New York. These and other issues are referenced or discussed by the contributors to this book.

Other accounts describing the work of local chapters in Hartford, Boston, and California have been published elsewhere.[15] Still other aspects of the PSP experience have also been discussed by writers and scholars elsewhere.[16]

Part I describes crucial moments in the evolution of the organization, including the gradual emergence of a core group of the MPI in New York City (early to late 1960s), participation in the PSP's Founding Congress in Puerto Rico (1971), the First Congress of the U.S. Branch (1973), post-election crisis and rectification (1976–1978), the Second Congress of the U.S. Branch (1978), engagement in electoral campaigns (1978 through the 1980s), the Third Congress of the U.S. Branch (1983); and the PSP's final decline and dissolution (mid-1980s through 1993).

A chronology of essential theoretical statements of the *Seccional* is dispersed throughout Part I, including *Proyecto de Declaración General* (1970), *El Partido en Estados Unidos* (1971), *Desde Las Entrañas* (1973), *One Nation, One Party* (1975), *Tesis Política de la Seccional del Partido Socialista Puertorriqueño* (1978), and *Suplemento de Tésis (Tercer Congreso*; 1983). Other important documents of the national PSP discussed in Part I include *La Hora de La Independencia, Presente y Futuro*, and *La Alternativa Socialista*.

Part II: Testimonies

Part II presents the personal testimonies of PSP activists. Some central themes emerge in these testimonies. Here in this Introduction, we discuss five: (1) diversity of the membership as a resource and as a source of tension, (2) engenderment of loyalty and *compañerismo* (comradeship), (3) transnational political practices of the PSP, (4) management of the "double role," (also termed *dos vertientes* in Spanish) and (5) lessons learned.

The editors encouraged contributing authors to address five categories of topics: (1) their origin stories, including birthplace, coming of age, sources of their ethnic and racial identity, and sources of their political and social consciousness; (2) their MPI-PSP experience, including their reasons for joining, their roles in the organization, and their involvement in specific campaigns; (3) their reflections on various facets of the experience, including the PSP's strengths and weaknesses, their perception of the internal conflicts and external factors that led to its eventual decline, and its contributions to the Puerto Rican community and to the aspiration for Puerto Rican independence; (4) lessons learned from PSP activism relating to personal development and other issues; and (5) their post-PSP life, including their present political beliefs, activism or involvement in later years, career choices, and assessment of the current struggle for independence and, generally, Puerto Rico's future and that of the diaspora.[17]

The contributing authors touched upon the following themes of particular interest.

Diversity as Resource and as Tension

Notwithstanding the heavily working-class background of *Seccional* members (and not just of U.S.-born members), significant differences in identity and political perspective among PSP members sometimes stirred up cultural tensions and affected their sense of belonging. Yet a deep bond of loyalty and comradeship prevailed among them.

The PSP's base and leadership, like that of the diaspora in general, comprised many bilingual/bicultural individuals. Members of different backgrounds were constantly interacting with one another:

> My upbringing in two worlds of language and culture prepared me for the role of editor and writer. . . . *Claridad*, as well as life in the PSP, provided me with continuous enrichment in Spanish. . . . [I]t was another unanticipated benefit, if you will, of being engaged in revolutionary struggle. (José-Manuel Navarro, Chapter 9)

The joke of *Claridad "Trilingüe,"* coming from Puerto Rico–based members and sometimes even accepted self-mockingly by U.S.-based members, was evidence of internal language oppression. And it was hurtful, if rarely challenged openly:

> We laughed . . . , and yet we felt humiliated. We were one, but there were cracks in the unity. (Maritza Arrastía, Chapter 4)
>
> Many PSP colleagues in Puerto Rico believed that members whose dominant language was English were not as Puerto Rican. . . . I witnessed many debates among members in New York and other U.S. cities as to who was more "Puerto Rican" than another. . . . I found the whole debate superficial; what mattered to me was that we were exploited equally as a people and oppressed as colonials whether we lived in San Lorenzo or Jersey City, Barranquitas or the Bronx, Ponce or Philadelphia. (José-Manuel Navarro, Chapter 9)
>
> For a Puerto Rican militant whose life was formed on the island, to hear Puerto Ricans speaking English was a reminder of the potential cultural genocide that is the ideological nutrient of imperialism and colonialism. (Alfredo López, Chapter 7)

Other fissures had to do with individual political backgrounds or orientations: some members were grounded in Marxism, others were oriented toward nationalism or radical community activism, and still others were not grounded in any specific ideology:

> There had always been fundamental differences in our leadership and organization. . . . Each of the members of the Political Commission during the bulk of the 1970s had a different perspective that, behind the drive of our community and independence work, never really came up in the early years. (Alfredo López, Chapter 7)

Loyalty and Compañerismo

Several PSP initiatives were central to enhancing loyalty and comradeship, including the newspaper *Claridad bilingüe*, political education classes, and family-based social activities. Others had to do with party theory itself, such as the very fact that the PSP's view on the national question served to unite all Puerto Ricans, whether in the United States or the diaspora. Not to be underestimated was an official philosophy of *compañerismo* that emphasized mutual respect and support. One contributor reminisces about experiencing this feeling as a child:

> I remember one time floating in a sea of hundreds of people at a rally against the Vietnam War. I was about three or four at the time, and although I had no idea where my parents were, I simply went up to strangers and opened my arms for them to carry me. I felt loved and protected in rallies, like I could trust anyone. Being raised red and Boricua inspired this faith in people. (Lenina Nadal, Chapter 8)

Claridad bilingüe was a powerful vehicle for bridging language differences in the PSP as well as within the community. The newspaper was also a workplace of intense activity and interaction among the staff, which was recruited from the base and its diverse membership. *Claridad* reported on events and trends in Puerto Rico, often serving as the main source of such information in the more far-flung chapters of the PSP, and it covered what was going on in the diaspora with a political edge, going beyond what was available via mainstream and Spanish-language newspapers. Sharing this information created opportunities for bonding among party members.

If *Claridad* was often the gateway to recruitment, political education was the principal mechanism for following up on initial interest. The PSP had no official policy on language use. For the most part, classes were conducted in Spanish, but certainly some were conducted in English, especially those for students and younger Boricuas from the diaspora. Classes were oriented toward the preferences of the majority. Many English-dominant participants chose to stay in Spanish-language classes, a form of rapid immersion for those ready to take on the challenge. There was give-and-take when it came to the discussion of reading material, although bilingualism was the typical mode. Materials were often bilingual, with a prime example being *Desde las Entrañas*.

Political education programs enhanced unity. Members received an introduction to Puerto Rican history and culture, benefiting U.S.- and Puerto Rico–born members. Discussions about Puerto Rican migration and settlement told of the multigenerational experience inside the "belly of the beast." Across languages and across generations, members read about and discussed their backgrounds and heritages, even those aspects that did not perfectly overlap:

> The discussions were animated, and I loved that they included younger twenty-somethings such as I along with the middle-aged ones who never went to college or even high school. (Digna Sánchez, Chapter 11)

> The first undertaking [in the Los Angeles nucleus] was to set up weekly study group meetings. For me, the study group opened a world of investigation and intellectual inquiry. (Zoilo Torres, Chapter 12)

Other ways in which social bonds were cemented across generations and diverse backgrounds were through social activities (e.g., picnics, basketball and baseball games, and parties) and cultural events (e.g., concerts and dances) that were often tied to fundraising. Inclusion of the children of PSP members was typical:

> The annual summer outing, *Jiras de Verano*, was one of many party fundraising efforts. . . . In 1972, eight buses left from the Bronx, Manhattan, and Brooklyn, filled with members, sympathizers, and their families, all heading to Arrow Park in Monroe, New York. These outings served as a recreational outlet and moment of respite from the demands of political work for PSP members and their families. (Teresa Basilio Gaztambide and Carmen V. Rivera, Chapter 5)

Transnational Practice and Experience

The PSP saw itself as a force for the liberation of a colonial people who had one foot in the colony and the other in the metropolis. In asserting that the diaspora was part of the Puerto Rican nation, the PSP was engaging in a range of transnational practices well before that notion became popular in academic discourse. The strategy, structure, and program of action of the U.S. Branch concretized the field of action for these transnational practices. The testimonies in Part II as well as the histories rendered in Part I describe myriad forms of these practices.

These include, for example, the constant flow of *Seccional* members who attended meetings, seminars, and congresses on the island and, simultaneously, the multiple visits and tours of PSP national leaders to the United States. Other interrelationships involved the transmission of island-originated campaigns, such as the defense of the copper mines, support for labor struggles, sterilization abuse, the Organization of the Petroleum Exporting Countries (OPEC) crisis, and opposition to the "Super-Port"; these campaigns became opportunities for the *Seccional* to build the organization.

One example of a cause that bridged the island and the mainland United States was the case of José Soler, who was an active member in the U.S. Branch and in Puerto Rico. Raised in the United States, he became politicized during the 1960s and eventually joined the *Seccional*. He moved to Puerto Rico with his family in the early 1970s, maintaining his membership in the PSP. At one point, he was recruited to run as the party's candidate for the Puerto Rican Senate from Mayaguez in the 1976 election. Shortly after, he returned to the United States to take care of his ailing father, but he remained very actively involved with the PSP. Other contributors in Parts I and II relate their experiences; see Chapters 2, 9, 10, and 11.[18]

The very nature of a colonial people in constant motion has spawned a number of descriptors, including *"va y ven"* (going and coming), "circular migration," and *"la guagua aérea"* (air bus). For many, the transnational life is concretized in the act of returning to the island, in middle age or as an elder, in pursuit of the *"sueño del retorno"* (dream of return). Or it may be a decision made in young adulthood to explore one's heritage and test the idea of permanent residency in Puerto Rico. It may even reflect a desire to establish roots in both locations. Among PSP members, this dream was not uncommon; see Chapters 3, 9, 10, and 11.

Managing the Double Role

The issue of the double role continues to be relevant beyond the confines of the PSP context. Even today, activists in the diaspora face the question of prioritization. Here are the words of just two contributors regarding this subject:

> I firmly believe that for progressive Puerto Ricans in the United
> States, the dual nature of the struggle remains and will continue

until Puerto Rico is a sovereign nation. The struggle for national liberation cannot be set aside while the struggle for democratic rights is waged. We must do both! The balance of how much effort is given to one versus the other will, of course, depend on the conditions that exist at a given time. (Digna Sánchez, Chapter 11)

As Puerto Ricans here, we need to continue to link our struggle to the broader Latinx diaspora and the African diaspora, and we need to seek support and help in solidarity efforts with empowering the resistance groups on the island while educating them on the issues we face here.

And we need to be openly and unapologetically fabulous socialists. Because the more we project our vision, the more we will feel the impulse not just to participate but to lead. (Lenina Nadal, Chapter 8)

Lessons Learned

In their testimonies, contributors point to lessons they learned from PSP activism, including those relating to personal and political development:

My experience in the MPI, and later the PSP, was very rich in terms of learning and personal growth. . . . We created a stimulating environment of political debate and decision making; these were fast-paced learning experiences that built our resistance and resilience. . . . To devote ourselves to bringing our country to freedom is . . . worthy of an entire life. . . . It is a great honor. (Olga Iris Sanabria Dávila, Chapter 10)

My time in the PSP was a determining factor in my ideological formation, which I define as critical Marxism. It was fundamental to my organizational and Spanish-language skills, to the expansion of my "Puerto Rican national consciousness," and to the deep relationship I maintain with Puerto Rico and family members who returned there. (José E. Velázquez Luyanda, Chapter 2)

The PSP taught us how to look at the bigger picture, break it down into its component parts, and get a handle on understanding events and proposing solutions large and small. . . . It instilled an empowering self-confidence. My hope is that my children and the young people of today will experience similar life-changing events born from participation in a mission-driven organization like the PSP. (Zoilo Torres, Chapter 12)

Yet there could also be negative lessons for anyone who experienced separation as a loss:

> My membership in the PSP was, other than leaving Cuba, the most formative experience of my life. My five years or so with the party prepared me for everything else I have done in my life. And at the same time, or maybe because it was so formative and generative and central, losing the party was a big hurt, a big loss, a multiple divorce. I do not think I have fully grieved it—maybe writing this account will be healing. (Maritza Arrastía, Chapter 4)

While perusing the various chapters in this volume, the interested reader will identify several more themes beyond those highlighted here. As argued earlier, the voices heard here are not exclusive to the PSP and its members; they resonate, to a larger or lesser degree, with the experiences of other activists, organizations, and movements in Puerto Rico and beyond.

Part III: Coalitions and Alliances

The PSP understood that North American support for Puerto Rican independence or for multinational unity on behalf of transformational change in the United States would require a measure of reciprocal action: if you wanted the support of people and organizations for your cause, you had to deliver when they came with their own requests for help or collaboration. Mutual support was essential not only for achieving specific ends but also for building widening relations of trust. The forms of reciprocity were manifold, including mobilizing PSP members and supporters to attend an antiracism rally, sending participants to reinforce a direct action or occupation, assigning a speaker for an International Women's Day forum, providing security for a march in support of Palestinian liberation, and offering strike support at a factory or hospital. In each of these instances, the struggle was not primarily centered on Puerto Ricans, yet socialist principles of solidarity and class unity demanded a *quid pro quo* response.

Part III is devoted to the PSP's policies relating to coalitions and alliances.[19] The PSP counted on and worked with numerous activists and organizations that were generally aligned with its goals and campaigns. They were indispensable to the success of various major efforts that the PSP was known for, including *El Acto Nacional*, the Hard Times Conference, the U.S. Bicentennial, the People's Convention, the United Nations case, and several electoral campaigns. They were also instrumental to other struggles of the larger Puerto Rican movement, providing solidarity for the causes of Puerto Rican independence, freedom for the Nationalist prisoners, and the expulsion of the U.S. Navy from Vieques. They were in the mix of forces that coalesced around projects for the revolutionary transformation of U.S. society, such as the Mass Party Organizing Committee (MPOC) and the People's Alliance. These were multiracial cooperative projects with their own agendas, and each required significant commitments by member organizations and individual activists.[20]

Some examples of unity processes involving other forces are described in Part III, written by three individuals who were not members of the PSP, although Borenstein and Glick were involved for years in collaborative projects. Ribeiro is a young scholar who has researched and written about the Puerto Rican community in the Philadelphia area.

Borenstein opens Chapter 13 with the winding road that led to her eventual connection with the PSP. She provides thorough coverage of two key solidarity groups of which she was an activist and leader: the Committee for Puerto Rican Decolonization (CPRD) and the Puerto Rican Solidarity Committee (PRSC). Remembering the beginning days of planning for the Madison Square Garden event, she recalls:

> I believed that I was at the heart of a colossal military-like operation, although I knew nothing about military mobilizations except what I had seen on movie and television screens.

In her recounting, as in the chapters by Glick and Ribeiro in Part III, the reader finds a virtual honor roll of the people of leftist and progressive movements who were involved in Puerto Rico solidarity work. She describes the meetings, decisions, and debates that took place in the background of the major successes referenced above. But as the 1980s approached, these coalitions fell apart, as did so many other radical political journeys of the time. She interprets the causes of the fraying as well as its personal effects on her.

Glick opens Chapter 14 by proclaiming, "I was not planning to be a revolutionary." Yet many courageous young men and women put their lives on hold, and on the line, to oppose anti-imperialism. He describes such pivotal moments in his life, including his prison term for an anti-war protest, a collective late-night action that destroyed the records of a draft board in New York. His politics eventually conveyed him to the Puerto Rico solidarity movement and the PSP, at a point when the party was connecting with such vital figures as Arthur Kinoy. During the 1970s and early 1980s, Glick's political energies partially overlapped with those of the PSP. Beyond solidarity activities, other campaigns that received his commitment included the MPOC, the Bicentennial, the Dellums Resolution, the People's Alliance, the People's Convention in the South Bronx, and independent electoral campaigns. He witnessed not only the successes but also the difficulties of sustaining broad, multiracial, multi-class coalitions for transformational change.

In Chapter 15, Ribeiro offers a historian's deep dive into the U.S. Bicentennial campaign. Relying on extensive press accounts and internal documents of the July 4th Coalition (J4C), she recounts the preparations in the lead-up to the mobilization, the forces holding the coalition together, and the tender spots threatening unity. The event itself is judged as successful for its propagandistic impact, for the turnout exceeded that of the official Philadelphia event promoted by the U.S. government. The organizing coalition was able to surmount several obstacles imposed by the city of Philadelphia, some local community groups, and the Federal Bureau of Investigation (FBI), not to mention a virtual boycott by the media. Ribeiro evaluates the cost to coalition sponsors of the People's Bicentennial, including to the PSP, and comments on the inability of the "fragile coalition" to endure over the long haul.

Part IV: Conclusion

In the Conclusion, we summarize our reflections on the PSP's achievements, contributions, and mistakes. We reconsider the national question, which was at the heart of the organization's distinctiveness. In claiming that Boricuas in the diaspora formed part of the Puerto Rican colonial nation, it created a political space in which the PSP could thrive, at least for a time.

Revisiting the national question in its contemporary meaning, we consider whether U.S.-based Boricuas continue to identify as Puerto Ricans in substantive ways and the degree to which islanders may reciprocate such ties. Evidence on this question is examined through reports on recent developments in Puerto Rico. Is the diaspora viewed as a strategic resource in building the future Puerto Rico, following the Puerto Rico Oversight, Management, and Economic Stability Act (PROMESA) and Hurricane María? If so, this perspective would appear to be further affirmation of the national question as originally posed by the MPI-PSP. Finally, what is the status of today's Puerto Rican Left in the diaspora? We briefly speak to these questions.

NOTES

1. The term *Seccional* is used interchangeably with U.S. Branch.

2. An example of this view is found in César J. Ayala and Rafael Bernabé, *Puerto Rico in the American Century: A History since 1898* (Chapel Hill: University of North Carolina Press, 2007), 243–244. A similar implication is found in Lorrin Thomas and Aldo A. Lauria-Santiago, *Rethinking the Struggle for Puerto Rican Rights* (New York: Routledge, 2019), 3–4. Edna Acosta-Belén and Carlos E. Santiago, *Puerto Ricans in the United States: A Contemporary Portrait*, 2nd ed. (Boulder, CO: Lynne Rienner Publishers, 2018), is another example of what we would term a "blind spot" in the treatment of

Puerto Rican radical movements in the United States; for example, Chapter 6 ("Social, Civil Rights and Empowerment Struggles") in this comprehensive work omits coverage of the PSP's activism. We believe that these passages underplay the PSP's push for democratic rights and for social the transformation of U.S. society.

3. Andrés Torres and José E. Velázquez, eds., *The Puerto Rican Movement: Voices from the Diaspora* (Philadelphia: Temple University Press, 1998). See the chapters by Ángel A. Amy Moreno de Toro (on Boston), José E. Cruz (on Hartford), and José E. Velázquez (on the PSP nationally).

4. Eric Larson, "José Soler: A Life Working at the Intersections of Nationalism, Internationalism, and Working-Class Radicalism," *Radical History Review*, no. 128 (2017): 63–76; Miranda J. Martínez and Alan A. Aja, "Democratic Rights and Nuyorican Identity in the Partido Socialista Puertorriqueño," in *Latino(a) Research Review* 8, nos. 1–2 (2011/2012): 101–123; Frederick Douglass Opie, *Upsetting the Apple Cart* (New York: Columbia University Press, 2015), 99–104; and Victor M. Rodríguez, "Boricuas, African Americans, and Chicanos in the 'Far West': Notes on the Puerto Rican Pro-Independence Movement in California, 1960s–1980s," in *Latino Social Movements: Historical and Theoretical Perspectives*, ed. Rodolfo D. Torres and George N. Katsiaficas (New York: Routledge, 1999), 91–109.

5. Steps are currently underway to place the archive in an institutional home. Interested individuals and researchers may contact the editors for further information.

6. Virginia E. Sánchez Korrol, *From Colonia to Community: The History of Puerto Ricans in New York City*, 2nd ed. (Berkeley: University of California Press, 1994), 13, 167–172.

7. Thomas and Lauria-Santiago, *Rethinking the Struggle for Puerto Rican Rights*, 7–38; Victoria Nuñez, "Remembering Pura Belpre's Early Career at the 135th Street New York Public Library: Interracial Cooperation and Puerto Rican Settlement during the Harlem Renaissance," *CENTRO Journal* 21, no. 1 (Spring 2009): 36–51; Rubén Berríos Martínez, Francisco Catalá Oliveras, and Fernando Martín García, *Puerto Rico: Nación Independiente Imperativo del Siglo XXI* (San Juan: Editora Corripio, 2010), 21–32; and David J. Vazquez, "Jesús Colón and the Development of Insurgent Consciousness," *CENTRO Journal* 21, no. 1 (Spring 2009): 78–99.

8. Lorrin Thomas, "Resisting the Racial Binary? Puerto Ricans' Encounter with Race in Depression-Era New York City," *CENTRO Journal* 21, no. 1 (Spring 2009): 4–35.

9. Roberto P. Rodriguez-Morazanni, "Linking a Fractured Past: The World of the Puerto Rican Old Left," *CENTRO Boletin* 7, no. 1 (Winter 1994/Spring 1995): 20–30; Sánchez Korrol, *From Colonia to Community*, 172–200; and Linda C. Delgado, "Jesús Colón and the Making of a New York City Community: 1917–1974," in *The Puerto Rican Diaspora: Historical Perspectives*, ed. Carmen Theresa Whalen and Victor Vázquez-Hernández (Philadelphia: Temple University Press, 2005), 68–87.

10. Clara E. Rodriguez, *Puerto Ricans: Born in the U.S.A.* (Boulder, CO: Westview Press, 1991), 3–19; Roberto P. Rodríguez-Morazzani, "Puerto Rican Political Generations in New York: Pioneros, Young Turks, and Radicals," *CENTRO Journal* 4, no. 1 (1991/1992): 97–116; Edgardo Meléndez, "Vito Marcantonio, Puerto Rican Migration, and the 1949 Mayoral Election in New York City," *CENTRO Journal* 22, no. 2 (Fall 2010): 198–234; Sánchez Korrol, *From Colonia to Community*, 147–153; Vazquez, "Jesús Colón and the Development of Insurgent Consciousness"; and Gerald Meyer, *Vito Marcantonio: Radical Politician, 1902–1954* (Albany: State University of New York Press, 1989).

11. Rodríguez-Morazzani, "Puerto Rican Political Generations in New York," 20–30; Thomas and Lauria-Santiago, *Rethinking the Struggle for Puerto Rican Rights*, 7–38.

12. Sánchez Korrol, *From Colonia to Community*, 211–236; C. Rodríguez, 3–19; Joseph P. Fitzpatrick, *Puerto Rican Americans: The Meaning of Migration to the Mainland*, 2nd ed. (Englewood Cliffs, NJ: Prentice-Hall, 1987); Carmen Theresa Whalen, "Colonialism, Citizenship, and the Making of the Puerto Rican Diaspora," in *The Puerto Rican Diaspora: Historical Perspectives*, ed. Carmen Theresa Whalen and Victor Vázquez-Hernández (Philadelphia: Temple University Press, 2005), 35–42; Rodríguez-Morazzani, "Puerto Rican Political Generations in New York," 97–116; Gilberto Gerena Valentín, *Soy Gilberto Gerena Valentín: Memorias de un Puertorriqueno en Nueva York* (New York: Center for Puerto Rican Studies, 2013), 65, 86–95; Thomas and Lauria-Santiago, *Rethinking the Struggle for Puerto Rican Rights*, 7–75; and Sonia S. Lee and Ande Diaz, "'I Was the One Percenter': Manny Diaz and the Beginnings of a Black-Puerto Rican Coalition," *Journal of American Ethnic History* 26, no. 3 (Spring 2007): 52–80.

13. Sánchez Korrol, *From Colonia to Community*, 224–236; and Fitzpatrick, *Puerto Rican Americans*.

14. Andrés Torres, "Introduction: Political Radicalism in the Diaspora—The Puerto Rican Experience," in *The Puerto Rican Movement: Voices from the Diaspora*, ed. Andrés Torres and José E. Velázquez (Philadelphia: Temple University Press, 1998), 1–22.

15. Torres and Velázquez, *The Puerto Rican Movement*, contains three chapters: Ángel A. Amy Moreno de Toro, "An Oral History of the Puerto Rican Socialist Party in Boston, 1972–1978"; José E. Cruz, "Pushing Left to Get to the Center: Puerto Rican Radicalism in Hartford, Connecticut"; and José E. Velázquez, "Coming Full Circle: The Puerto Rican Socialist Party, U.S. Branch." Journal articles and book chapters include Larson, "José Soler"; Martínez and Aja, "Democratic Rights and Nuyorican Identity in the Partido Socialista Puertorriqueño"; and Rodríguez, "Boricuas, African Americans, and Chicanos in the 'Far West.'"

16. Opie, *Upsetting the Apple Cart*, 99–104; Carmen V. Rivera, "Our Movement: One Woman's Story," in *The Puerto Rican Movement: Voices from the Diaspora*, ed. Andrés Torres and José E. Velázquez (Philadelphia: Temple University Press, 1998), 192–209; and Meg Starr, "'Hit Them Harder': Leadership, Solidarity, and the Puerto Rican Independence Movement," in *The Hidden 1970s: Histories of Radicalism*, ed. Dan Berger (New Brunswick, NJ: Rutgers University Press, 2010), 135–154.

17. The contributors were at liberty to address the topics of interest to them; not every chapter speaks to each topic. Chapter 6 by Ramón J. Jiménez was written prior to the rest of this book. The chapters written by Rosa Borenstein (13), Ted Glick (14), and Alyssa Ribeiro (15) respond to a modified set of questions.

18. Larson, "José Soler."

19. The differences between the two forms could be murky at times, but generally the former were of an ad hoc, issue-oriented nature, while the latter involved longer-term coalescing around strategic goals. Either of these approaches could be Boricua-focused or involve a range of intersectional dimensions (e.g., race, class, gender).

20. For discussion of an African American's experience in this process, see James Early, "An African American–Puerto Rican Connection," in *The Puerto Rican Movement: Voices from the Diaspora*, ed. Andrés Torres and José E. Velázquez (Philadelphia: Temple University Press, 1998), 316–328.

1

A Brief History of the Puerto Rican
Socialist Party in the United States

ANDRÉS TORRES

Independentistas in the Diaspora: The Sixties

In the late 1950s, the state of the Puerto Rican independence movement
was at a historic low. Since the nineteenth-century anti-colonial struggle
against Spain, and after the U.S. takeover in 1898, Puerto Rico had endured
peaks and valleys. This was a valley.[1]

A new political status had been devised, the Commonwealth of Puerto
Rico, that had effectively co-opted the impetus toward self-determination
by promising social and political reforms. The hard power of the Federal
Bureau of Investigation (FBI) and U.S. military forces attacked, assassinated, and jailed the militant nationalists. This was the Cold War era, and
the United States was determined to retain its Caribbean territory.

Nevertheless, in the aftermath of World War II, third-world countries
were in the spotlight, dislodging themselves from subjugation. In 1959, the
Cuban Revolution offered new inspiration to the moribund Puerto Rican
movement. In this context, it would not be surprising to detect a glimmer-
ing of renewed activity by the anti-colonial forces. Signs of life were stirring
in Puerto Rico—and in the Puerto Rican diaspora, where close to a million
Puerto Ricans lived:[2]

> More than a year ago the Movement For Independence of Puerto
> Rico planted a new seed of hope in New York in the struggle to
> obtain the independence of our country. At last the MPI was orga-
> nized and in a meeting held at the home of Jimmy Negron it was

named the Vito Marcantonio Mission, in memory of the only voice
that *independentistas* and the Puerto Rican people have had in the
North American Congress.[3]

With these words, Carlos Maldonado opened a public event hosted in
1962 by the *Movimiento Pro Independencia* (MPI). He proceeded to describe
various activities and campaigns that the group had undertaken: commemoration of dates in the patriotic calendar, including the seventieth birthday
of Don Pedro Albizu Campos; a picket denouncing Columbia University's
"Citizen of the Year" award, given to Arturo Morales Carrión; celebration
of the anniversary of the abolition of slavery in Puerto Rico; and others.
These efforts, he explained, were achieved despite criticisms from within
and without the MPI and even from other independentista groups.

During the 1950s, Maldonado had been a member of the Nationalist
Party, the organization led by Pedro Albizu Campos, a Harvard-educated
lawyer and the fiery leader of Puerto Rico's militant wing of the independence forces. He had recently joined the MPI, which hoped to pick up the
baton of the struggle. At the time, the Nationalist Party had lost much of
its influence due to U.S. repression, and Campos himself was languishing
in federal prison. Maldonado's address expressed appreciation for the hard
work by the mission, pointing out the contributions of four valued *compañeras*: Carmen Miranda, a teacher; Panchita Santos; Ada Morales, whose
apartment was decorated like "a piece of Puerto Rico"; and Raquel Rivera,
who recorded the minutes and who, when absent from meetings, made it
feel as though "the star in our flag is missing." This documentation is the
earliest known of the MPI in New York City.

In early 1964, the MPI published its first edition of *Carta Semanal*, the
internal newsletter of the organization.[4] By then, the head of the group was
Victor "Marcianito" Santiago, an auto mechanic in his forties, who had
joined in 1962. Previously he had been active with the Nationalist Party in
Puerto Rico and then in New York, to which he had migrated in 1943.[5] In
the years to come, many individuals would walk through the portals of the
MPI (and later the Puerto Rican Socialist Party [PSP]), the majority active
for a few fevered, intense years, others for a decade or two. Marciano was the
connecting thread through all the ups and downs, ever loyal and disciplined,
ever available for the roles and tasks that the moment required, ever the
inspiration to the *vieja guardia* (old guard) and to the *jovenes* (young ones).

Carta Semanal reported on the recent tour of MPI missions (*misiones*) in the New York area made by Pedro Baigés Chapel, a member of the
national political commission. Baigés Chapel was a top lieutenant of Juan
Mari Brás, MPI's Secretary General. The newsletter's assessment was positive: "Our membership is growing geometrically in Manhattan as well as in

Figure 1.1 Misión Vito Marcantonio MPI, with Juan Mari Brás (front row center) New York City, 1967.

the Bronx and Brooklyn. There is greater participation of the youth and a better understanding of local and international issues."[6] Further commentary echoed a concern of Baigés Chapel's on the need for "a total reorganization of the missions and a better coordination of the struggle. He [Baigés Chapel] also recommended that the political education of the New York leadership be increased through seminars and discussion groups."[7]

The following year, MPI mobilized protests of the war in Vietnam and on behalf of the anti-draft case of Sixto Alvelo, a member living in Puerto Rico. Alvelo was one of the first Puerto Ricans to refuse induction into the U.S. military, which caused him to face five years in federal prison. At the same time, the anti-war movement was gaining mass support in the United States. The MPI in New York joined up with the Fifth Avenue Parade Committee, which was organizing a mass march for August 1965. Alvelo was invited to be a speaker at the closing event in Times Square. Members and supporters were instructed to provide "financial and political support" to Alvelo's legal case (handled by the Emergency Civil Liberties Committee) and to the anti-war effort. Always open to the opportunity to infuse political organizing with a social component, the organization scheduled a fundraiser as part of a Circle Line boat ride around Manhattan. Supporters were also strongly encouraged to attend a presentation by Mari Brás on July 29 at Casa Puerto Rico.[8]

Voices

Dixie Bayó was one of the first to become active in the New York MPI. She was a young woman who had come in 1960 to join her family, who had previously migrated to eastern New York. For a time, she had studied at the University of Puerto Rico (Rio Piedras)—and been involved with the University Federation for Independence (FUPI)—before dropping out to join her family in Brooklyn. Separation from the family was unbearable, and the lack of money made student life impossible. Bayó remembers some of the MPI's activities in the 1960s:[9]

> Since I had been with the FUPI, Juan Mari Brás communicated with me and asked that I join the MPI in New York. They had a tiny basement office on 125th Street and Broadway. This was 1960, and I had just arrived.

As the years progressed, MPI members got involved in rallies against the U.S. intervention in Vietnam and other issues, including housing and police brutality against Blacks and Puerto Ricans. One incident was particularly formative:

> In those days, they had killed a Puerto Rican taxi driver, and when it was reported in the news that the abuse had been by the police, our group went to picket the police precinct in El Barrio . . . and I remember the demonstration was enormous. . . . [S]uch was the militancy that we displayed in support of the incensed Puerto Ricans that the MPI grew incredibly. [Bayó]

MPI's Beginnings in Puerto Rico

The MPI, a precursor to the PSP, was constituted officially on November 22, 1959, in the city of Ponce. The First General Assembly capped a nearly year-long process of discussion and debate among a group of activists.[10] The founders aspired to revive a dormant independence movement that had lost the impetus of earlier years, when such groups as the Nationalist Party and the Puerto Rican Independence Party (PIP) were dynamic presences in the political life of the island. The prime movers of the new effort were an intergenerational and multi-ideological cohort: former members of the PIP; university activists from the FUPI, founded in 1956; former leaders and combatants of the Nationalist movement; and cadre from the old Communist Party of Puerto Rico. It was a united front of the seasoned and youthful, the Left and Nationalist sectors, a multi-class formation bound up in a new effort to spark La Nueva Lucha (The New Struggle).[11]

The 1960s were to be a decade of consensus building through internal debate and intervention in crucial issues and struggles of the times. In the ideological arena, a gradual assertion of socialist principles and ideas took shape, much influenced by the example of the Cuban Revolution and the many movements for third-world liberation. In Marxist terminology, the MPI was an alliance of the working class, the national bourgeoisie, the petty bourgeoisie (what today we would refer to as the self-employed middle class), and other dispossessed sectors. The multi-class nature of the MPI allowed for a strategic role of the national bourgeoisie, as indicated in the key document, *La Hora de la Independencia* (1963).[12] For example, under an independent Puerto Rico, sectors of the economy controlled by U.S. capital would be nationalized and potentially passed to Puerto Rican capitalists. A more socialist conception, not yet formulated, would have transitioned these assets to state ownership, controlled by the people.[13]

The MPI pursued a militant spirit of struggle, breaking from the PIP's more traditionalist approaches. It organized cultural and educational forums to restore the example and historical legacy of Pedro Albizu Campos, the imprisoned leader of the Nationalist Party. It led an effective electoral boycott in 1964. It aggressively denounced U.S. colonialism on the international scene, especially at the United Nations (UN). And it mobilized resistance through direct action and civil disobedience on several fronts.

During the mid-1960s, it organized opposition to selling mining rights to Kennecott Copper and American Metal Climax to extract minerals, under the slogan "Puerto Rican mines or zero mines," resulting in the cancelation of negotiations between the Commonwealth government and the U.S. companies. It spearheaded a boycott of the 1967 plebiscite on status, which led to a significant abstention of the electorate (one-third of enrolled voters). Within the public university and beyond, the MPI organized protests of the Reserve Officers' Training Corps (ROTC), the military draft, and the Vietnam War, leading to the radicalization of a new generation of youth. All this activity contributed to the U.S. government's eventual decision to abandon the military draft in Puerto Rico and the United States.

Responding to the growing insistence on a more robust labor orientation by sectors within the MPI, the organization committed to a major intervention in the historic General Electric (Palmer) labor strike of 1969. The MPI coordinated strike support activities with the employees and a broad trade union group that had coalesced around the strike. Activists were able to expose the anti-worker and anti-independentista bias of the media and elicit support from the larger public. As workers and labor leaders engaged more directly with the organization, and as MPI cadre, many of whom were university students, developed greater experience in labor struggles, the gap was narrowed between the anti-colonial and anti-capitalist visions, evident in *La Hora de la Independencia*.[14]

Transitions and Theoretical Intricacies

By 1968–1969, after years of internal debate and intense engagement in political and social struggles, the organization sought to refine its ideological underpinnings. The outcome was a new document, *Presente y Futuro de Puerto Rico: La Doctina de la Nueva Lucha de Independencia* (Present and Future of Puerto Rico: The Doctrine of the New Struggle for Independence).[15]

The new statement, seventy-five pages of fine print, updates *La Hora de la Independencia* with a magnificent overview of the history and current conditions facing the island. It contains a deep class analysis of the economic, cultural, and social forces in Puerto Rico and demonstrates the many ways in which U.S. imperialism had thwarted the possibilities for autonomous development. The Commonwealth status, established in 1952, was a rubber-stamp entity that simply facilitated continued U.S. domination.

Presente y Futuro enunciates the group's new direction. Going forward, the MPI would acknowledge the working class as the primary social base of the struggle for national independence. The notion of conquering independence is envisioned as organically linked to the daily conditions and lives of ordinary people. It would be necessary to fuse the anti-colonial project with the concrete, real demands (*reivindicaciones*) of the masses, always being aware of the need to go beyond the push for reforms or the betterment of living conditions. From the revolutionary perspective:

> Every economic struggle of the workers is important, but is not an end in itself. It is just a beginning, because the ultimate [goal] is to raise the struggle to higher and higher levels. In that way the economic and social struggles will merge with the struggle for independence and national liberation.[16]

The section on international solidarity includes discussion on the United States. It distinguishes between the ruling elites and its people and between its capitalists and workers. Subject to more severe exploitation are the principal minorities: Afro-Americans, "neo-Mexicans," and Puerto Ricans. It is among the working class in general and among racial minorities that the cause of Puerto Rican independence will find its strongest allies. The liberation of its colony will have another effect:

> The breaking [*quebrantamiento*] of imperialist power will bring as a result, not only the independence of Puerto Rico and other colonial and semi-colonial peoples of the world, but also the liberation of black people and other national minorities [*minorías nacionales*]

who are racially discriminated against, economically exploited, and politically oppressed, as well as the emancipation of [all] the people of the United States.[17]

In the last part (*Perspectiva Futura*), the document outlines a series of longer-term objectives, which briefly mentions Puerto Ricans in the United States. A future Republic of Puerto Rico would

look after [*velará*] the condition of the numerous population of Puerto Ricans based in the United States. Double citizenship [would] be accepted for those born in the country [Puerto Rico] and their descendants in the second generation.[18]

These initial comments relate to a question of vital importance for the MPI. On the one hand, the organization ratifies the traditional nationalist discourse relating to the condition and role of Puerto Ricans in the United States. *Presente y Futuro* represents no appreciable advance in analysis compared to *La Hora de La Independencia*. On the other hand, the MPI is not yet prepared to engage in the debates within the world of radicalized and progressive Puerto Ricans in the metropolis.

Not alluded to in this document were several questions already being discussed by radicals in U.S. Puerto Rican communities. What was the nature of the vast post–World War II community? Was it an exile community, such as the Cubans of Miami, still clinging to the idea of going back home (*el sueño del retorno*)? Was it a population on the path toward "assimilation"? Was it part of the Puerto Rican nation or a "national minority" within the United States? Was there such a thing as a Puerto Rican diaspora? Were revolutionary Puerto Ricans (independentistas and leftists in the United States) called to a special role in catalyzing solidarity among U.S. peoples? Or should they focus on dealing with the day-to-day problems faced by workers and barrio residents? Or perhaps they should perform double duty? Some of these questions are only partially alluded to in *Presente y Futuro*, and the island-based MPI was not yet in possession of the experience or perspective to develop a full analysis. But even as these gaps were left unaddressed at the national level, the MPI activists in the diaspora were developing their thinking on these issues.[19]

Starting in the summer of 1969, the MPI began conceptualizing a strategy for how to more systematically apply the vision of *Presente y Futuro* to Puerto Rican communities in the United States: *Proyecto de Declaración General*, the first major statement to emerge from the internal process of strategy development, was completed in the summer of 1970.[20]

This statement communicates the consensus position of the *militancia* of the *Misión Central Vito Marcantonio*, based in New York, the central body overseeing all members of the MPI in the diaspora at the time. In it, the members affirm several key points: completely adhering to the perspective outlined in *Presente y Futuro* and the by-laws of the MPI; committing to building the organization throughout the United States; spreading the anti-colonial message; and achieving the independence of Puerto Rico, the greatest contribution to social change in the United States.

Elsewhere in the statement, marking a new development, is the assertion of a more expansive position regarding the MPI's role in the United States:

> The revolutionary potential of the Puerto Rican community in this county is great: besides accelerating the conquest of liberation of our homeland, we have the obligation to contribute to making the revolution here, struggling for our demands [*reivindicaciones*] and constituting a revolutionary organization of the most exploited sectors of this people to bring down the structures of power that subjugate us.[21]

Referring to the revolutionary left in the United States, the document reads:

> With the truly revolutionary parties that fight to change this system of exploitation for a dignified and just one, we will enter in alliance toward advancing the revolutionary struggle in the heart of North American society.[22]

This statement was the MPI's first official reference to direct participation in a U.S. revolution. Previously, the organization had envisioned itself as cultivating support, from Puerto Ricans and other U.S. communities, for the independence project. Now it was seeing itself as part and parcel of the revolutionary process *in* the United States. In keeping with the new emphasis laid out in *Presente y Futuro*, the MPI's focus was to be the sector with the capacity to actually propel a social transformation: the Puerto Rican working class. "Our first responsibility in the U.S. is to organize Puerto Rican workers"[23] who are concentrated in low-wage jobs and often find themselves in weak or corrupt unions. The demands associated with this focus were identified: "equal pay for equal work"[24] and opportunities for promotion into better jobs as well as for leadership in unions in which Puerto Ricans had large membership.

The statement also directly links low-wage employment to social demands beyond the workplace:

As a result of the miserable salaries we receive and housing discrimination, we Puerto Ricans see ourselves obligated to live in
the giant slums of the city. We will struggle for decent housing,
raising the demand, "better housing conditions or zero rent." In
this way, our work in Puerto Rican communities . . . [will orga-
nize] our compatriots so that they demand of the landlords and
the city adequate sanitation, clean-up, heating, repairs, and other
essential services.[25]

Community work also entailed making demands in the areas of health
services and putting pressure on the educational system to respond to the
needs of Puerto Rican youth. The MPI's call for decent socioeconomic conditions was not issued without caution. As in the organization's national
documents, the pursuers of these demands had to be aware of the minefield
of reformism:

[We] repudiate the multiple manifestations of reformism that take
place in this society, that seek only to save the capitalist system from
its inevitable collapse, bringing confusion and false hopes to the
exploited masses. We therefore alert the people to be wary of those
organisms that, using a supposedly revolutionary rhetoric, serve
imperialism by trying to deviate the masses toward those distinct
roads of participation in the system that follow imperialism's structures of power.[26]

The *Proyecto* of August 1970 served as the first chapter, a brief but potent
statement, in the development of the MPI-PSP's thinking on strategy and
tactics in the United States. Later, the decision was made to keep the document for internal consumption rather than publish it.

In early 1971, the MPI in the United States was tasked with coming up
with a position paper that would update its analysis of the Puerto Rican
reality. The new analysis would also provide a perspective on strategy and
tactics in the United States. In the next months, members hashed out a
consensus paper, *El Partido en Estados Unido*, four pages of single-spaced,
mimeographed text.[27] Certain parts reflect advancements from prior position statements:

Aside from the class divisions inherent in capitalism, North American society is fragmented by racism. Puerto Ricans, like other
minorities, are doubly affected by these systems of subjugation. The
challenge of real transformation is complicated by the absence of a
great vanguard party of the Left. Nor is there a mass vanguard party

among the exploited minorities capable of "precipitating the revolutionary struggle and pushing the unity of sectors in the struggle against imperialism."[28]

The conclusion being advanced is obvious: Puerto Ricans needed to form their own revolutionary party in the diaspora, and, in so doing, they would inevitably perform a dual role:

> The Party understands that the Puerto Ricans based in the United States form an integral part of the Puerto Rican nation; that the struggle for independence and socialism contributes to the development of the revolutionary struggle in the United States. At the same time, it understands that, being a part of the most exploited strata in the United States, Puerto Ricans residing in the United States have to struggle for revolutionary change right here.[29]

Further wording apparently is intended to reassert the prominence of the group's first goal (independence and socialism in Puerto Rico):

> Therefore, in the struggle for immediate demands of Puerto Ricans in the United States and for the revolution in the United States, the struggle for independence and socialism in Puerto Rico constitute a priority [una prioridad].[30]

But this statement is softened by a following sentence:

> Both struggles [i.e., for Puerto Rico's independence and socialism and for revolutionary change in the United States] are one and the same, against the same enemy, and for both, the Party commits itself with all its strength to the organization of Puerto Ricans in the United States.[31]

This double phrasing articulates a serious commitment to the direct organizing of the Boricua diaspora around an agenda transcending strictly solidarity functions.[32] But it may also have planted the seeds of future confusion about the interrelationship between national liberation, democratic rights, and revolutionary change in the United States, and in particular the weight to be attached to each aspect.[33]

El Partido en Estados Unidos, a short but dense treatise, would be a turning point in the MPI-to-PSP trajectory in the diaspora.

Meanwhile, the New York–based MPI had begun to extend its organizational network, following the tracks of Great Migration Boricuas who had settled in New England, the Mid-Atlantic, and the Midwest. These areas were populated by three migrant flows. Some had tested life in New York City and then decided to try elsewhere. Some had moved directly to non–New York City hubs of Puerto Rican population, such as Chicago, Hartford, Bridgeport, Holyoke, Springfield, Boston, Philadelphia, Newark, and a score of other enclaves. Finally, seasonal farm laborers (tens of thousands of contract workers during the 1950s and 1960s came from and returned to Puerto Rico) worked along the Atlantic coast, picking crops. After the harvest season ended, some stayed behind and settled in a nearby enclave. Within every city, town, and enclave lived politically aware Puerto Ricans, independentistas of various stripes—workers and professionals, *jibaros* and second-generation young people, recently arrived and veteran residents. It was among these politically aware Puerto Ricans that the MPI sought to grow.

Voices

Among the arrivals from the island were two young men, Rafael "Rafín" Baerga and Ismael Barreto. Despite their different backgrounds, they shared similar political feelings:

> I'm from Guayama, Puerto Rico. I graduated high school in '65 and entered the UPR [University of Puerto Rico] that same year and graduated in '69, when I decided to go to the United States. During that period, there were many people that began to leave [PR], professionals started leaving, people that had studied in the university. Actually my leaving was really an adventure . . . like a change. . . . I boarded a plane and left for the U.S. to New York, because I was offered . . . a chance to get a teacher's license, and I worked for the first seven, eight months with a temporary teacher's license at PS 25 in the Bronx. [Baerga]

> [It was] 1968 when I migrated, on August 28, 1968, when I arrived with a shopping bag with two pants, two shirts, and *aguacátes* [avocados] for my aunt. . . . I was fifteen, I was fifteen when I arrived, you see? A kid who didn't know the language, who came from farm country, from a [different] culture . . . to clash with all of that there. . . . Well, I committed my first crime, which was to falsify my birth certificate, making me eighteen years old, and I bought my first job for $20. That was the practice . . . and they gave me a job. . . . I got a job working in a factory that made women's belts. [Barreto]

A New Infusion, a New Activism

By the late 1960s, the Vito Marcantonio Mission in New York City was participating in a number of campaigns, including the anti-war protests that had enveloped the U.S. Left. A number of MPI-affiliated students and intellectuals, who had been suspended or displaced from the University of Puerto Rico during the 1968 and 1969 conflicts, found positions teaching in the public schools and the City University of New York (CUNY). These played a significant role in radicalizing Puerto Rican students. When the radical Young Lords led a church takeover to open the facility to community programs, MPI's director at the time, José Antonio Irizarry, mobilized the organization to support this occupation. Along with other members, he also assisted by interpreting for the occupiers and the public.

As political awareness among second-generation Puerto Ricans heightened, the MPI found a growing receptiveness among many of them for its projects. The organization participated with other groups, such as the Young Lords, *El Comité*, and the Puerto Rican Student Union (PRSU), in a series of campaigns. In the autumn of 1970, a political prisoner conference held at Columbia University drew hundreds of young people who listened to revolutionary speakers from across the burgeoning movement, including Flavia Rivera Montero, a FUPI and MPI leader. Later that fall, the Young Lords and the PRSU initiated a mass march to the UN to emphatically memorialize the twentieth anniversary of the Nationalist uprising in Jayuya.[34] That same year, the nationalist leader Carlos Feliciano was arrested in New York on weapons charges, galvanizing a movement for his freedom. Activists from various groups formed the Carlos Feliciano Defense Committee, which was instrumental in his eventual release. Another united front effort, initiated by El Comité in 1971, was the Committee to Defend and Free Political Prisoners.[35] The MPI was involved in all these interorganizational drives.[36]

Building a Party of Puerto Rican Socialists in the United States: The Early Seventies

On a cold Sunday in late 1971, the leaders and key activists of the organization met in Casa Puerto Rico. The fifty or so individuals were there by invitation only and had come from throughout the Northeast, but primarily New York City.[37] The purpose of the meeting was to agree on a vision that would make the embryonic PSP a force within the diaspora. This goal meant finding a way to appeal to the two main radical currents within that population: (1) nationalists who viewed themselves as an exiled community and

(2) radicalized second-generation Boricuas, born (or raised primarily) in the United States. It could be assumed that the nationalists, most of whom were MPI members or followers during the 1960s, would follow Mari Brás's call for a socialist party. But it was crucial that the new organization become relevant to the many young Puerto Ricans who had been politicized during the late 1960s. The success of the Young Lords and other U.S.-based groups caused the island-oriented, older members of the PSP to rethink their mission in the United States.

For several months leading up to the meeting at Casa Puerto Rico, discussion groups had hashed out the outline for a new political formula that would expand the group's scope in cities where Puerto Rican communities were rapidly growing. Members started to realize that more attention had to be directed toward the day-to-day concerns of Boricuas in diaspora communities. With members having already decided to transform the group into a socialist organization, with a greater focus on class exploitation in Puerto Rico, it stood to reason that the same blueprint should be applied in the diaspora.

It made no sense to ask the young Puerto Ricans, most of who were in the United States to stay, to denounce colonialism, poverty, and social injustice on the island while ignoring the same problems in their own neighborhoods. In dealing with immediate problems like unemployment, discrimination, and lack of housing, people could be educated on the ills of capitalist society and imperialism. Many members believed that the connections to the colonial situation of Puerto Rico could be made. After all, the U.S. government was behind the mass migration that had literally exiled so many native sons and daughters from their homeland during the 1940s.

That December afternoon, the political debate that had absorbed the base's attention during the previous months was to culminate in a vote. Two basic views were put forth. The first, voiced mostly by island-based "veterans," favored a focused conception of the new *Seccional* as a vehicle for solidarity work, including such issues as the fight to liberate the Nationalist prisoners. The second view, supported most actively by second-generation Boricuas, argued for an additional role, that of organizing in local communities and workplaces around a program of democratic rights and contributing to a socialist transformation in the United States. In retrospect, posing this double agenda might come across as the height of ambition, to say the least. Yet such was the historical moment and such was the level of self-confidence that members believed themselves capable of monumental achievements.

The more veteran members, those deeply attached to the homeland, feared that the second proposal would dilute the organization's mission.

They worried that taking on the struggle in the mainland *and* the colony was simply too much for the organization. Others said that the organization would get drawn into the contentious debates and rivalries with the U.S. Left. To accentuate their point, they recalled an incident that had happened a year earlier, when the PSP was still the MPI.

A group called the Progressive Labor Party, notorious for provoking clashes within the Left, had attempted an "invasion" of Casa Puerto Rico. Members had previously condemned the MPI in their newspaper for "bourgeois nationalism," saying that Puerto Ricans should organize directly for proletarian revolution in the United States.

One Friday night, about twenty members of the Progressive Labor Party had entered the street-level doorway of the building where Casa was located, at 106 E. Fourteenth St. The ultra-leftists had come charging up to the second floor, bent on disrupting the weekly public program. That had turned out to be a big mistake. They had gotten as far as the front door, where members were stationed. The second-floor landing had filled up with tensed bodies, and then raised voices, and then a bilingual barrage of political sloganeering from both sides. About a half dozen *MPIistas* had stood outside the entrance to Casa, blocking the leftist extremists from entering the main hall. As tensions had escalated, suddenly screams of pain had been heard, and the intruders had abruptly backpedaled. Several of them had received knife wounds, causing them to retreat hurriedly down the narrow stairway and disappear onto Fourteenth Street.

The following day's *New York Times* had reported the melee, saying this skirmish was evidence of the violent nature of the Puerto Rican independence movement. Incidents such as these were cited by the veterans as reasons for the PSP to have a narrowly focused mission in the United States. Others distrusted those of the younger generation. In their eyes, the younger members were ambitious new recruits trying to take over the organization. They had little knowledge of Puerto Rico and were more comfortable speaking the language of the colonizer. The veterans were reserved in their enthusiasm for the Nuyorican influx.

After hours of ideological debate, the question was called to a vote. Despite resistance from some of the old guard, the outcome was clear: two-thirds of those present raised their hands to affirm a new direction for the PSP. Although the organization was still dominated by "islanders," most of them were savvy enough to realize that the future of the organization lay in its potential to bring in second-generation Boricuas.

In April 1973, after a year and a half of intense organizing throughout the Northeast and Midwest, the Seccional harvested the fruits of its labor. Fifty group members had attended the 1971 meeting at Casa Puerto Rico; at Manhattan Center, located on Thirty-Fourth Street off Eighth Avenue,

Figure 1.2. PSP U.S. Branch First Congress, Manhattan Center, New York City, April 8, 1973.

three thousand members and supporters attended the opening and final sessions of the First Congress of the U.S. Branch of the PSP. The Seccional issued its landmark publication, *Desde las Entrañas* (From the Belly of the Beast), and introduced its leadership. The first *Comité Seccional* (Seccional Committee [CS]), made up of thirty individuals, was elected by delegates to the Congress. Later, the Political Commission was formed.[38]

From fifty individuals to three thousand: it might have seemed unreal. Yet there was no mystery to the PSP's success, which was borne of old-fashioned, painstaking organizing—along with occasional dramatics and publicity. The jubilant enthusiasm and raucous chanting that filled that historic meeting hall confirmed members' belief that a new radical movement, based on scientific socialism at that, could be aroused by uniting the issues affecting the community in the diaspora with the demand for Puerto Rican independence.

The event at Manhattan Center was an impressive outcome to the fevered pace of the previous year and a half. It established the PSP as the dominant force in the Puerto Rican Left, as a visible entity within the Puerto Rican community at large, and a rising influence within the U.S. Left. The PSP was consciously attempting to build a classic vanguard political organization,

Figure 1.3. First Congress Political Commission, 1973. *Far left at microphone:* Ramón Arbona; *top row, left to right:* Alfredo López, Digna Sánchez, and José "Ché" Velázquez; *bottom row, left to right:* José Alberto Álvarez Febles, Jesus López, and Andrés Torres.

following the model of Marxist-Leninist groups throughout the world. These groups had spread like wildfire among third-world countries. Their goal was to effect revolutionary social change in a direct challenge to imperialism, colonialism, and capitalism.

In the preceding and ensuing few years, the fledgling Seccional built a vibrant political organization. Members took on numerous campaigns in the growing network of cities where chapters (*núcleos*) were established: Boston and Springfield, Massachusetts; Hartford, Waterbury, and New Haven, Connecticut; Hoboken, Newark, Jersey City, Camden, and Trenton, New Jersey; and Philadelphia, Pennsylvania. As far as Gary, Indiana; Chicago, Illinois; and eventually in Los Angeles and the Bay Area in California, Puerto Ricans joined up to build the vanguard party. And, of course, in the New York City area, home to a million Boricuas, the PSP found fertile terrain.

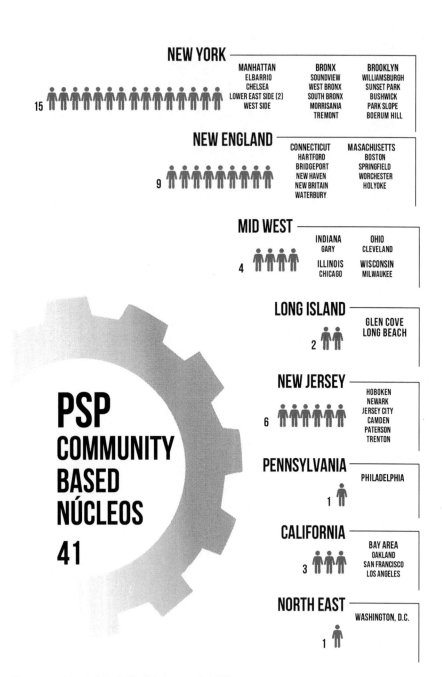

NEW YORK

MANHATTAN	BRONX	BROOKLYN
ELBARRIO	SOUNDVIEW	WILLIAMSBURGH
CHELSEA	WEST BRONX	SUNSET PARK
LOWER EAST SIDE (2)	SOUTH BRONX	BUSHWICK
WEST SIDE	MORRISANIA	PARK SLOPE
	TREMONT	BOERUM HILL

15

NEW ENGLAND

CONNECTICUT	MASACHUSETTS
HARTFORD	BOSTON
BRIDGEPORT	SPRINGFIELD
NEW HAVEN	WORCHESTER
NEW BRITAIN	HOLYOKE
WATERBURY	

9

MID WEST

INDIANA	OHIO
GARY	CLEVELAND
ILLINOIS	WISCONSIN
CHICAGO	MILWAUKEE

4

LONG ISLAND

GLEN COVE
LONG BEACH

2

NEW JERSEY

HOBOKEN
NEWARK
JERSEY CITY
CAMDEN
PATERSON
TRENTON

6

PENNSYLVANIA

PHILADELPHIA

1

CALIFORNIA

BAY AREA
OAKLAND
SAN FRANCISCO
LOS ANGELES

3

NORTH EAST

WASHINGTON, D.C.

1

PSP COMMUNITY BASED NÚCLEOS 41

Figures 1.4 and 1.5. PSP *Núcleos* and Affiliates.

LABOR NÚCLEOS AND
UNIVERSITY AFFILIATES 21

LABOR NÚCLEOS

5

HOTEL WORKERS UNION
POSTAL WORKERS (NJ)
ASOCIACION DE TRABAJADORES AGRICOLAS
META
CAMP

UNIVERSITY NÚCLEOS

3

BROOKLYN COLLEGE
HOSTOS COLLEGE
JOHN JAY COLLEGE

STUDENTS: FEDERACIÓN UNIVERSITARIA
DE SOCIALISTAS PUERTORRIQUEÑA (FUSP)

6

NEW YORK
HOSTOS COMMUNITY COLLEGE (BRONX)
BROOKLYN COLLEGE
LEHMAN COLLEGE (BRONX)
JOHN JAY COLLEGE (MANHATTAN)
CITY COLLEGE (MANHATTAN)
HUNTER COLLEGE (MANHATTAN)

2

CONNECTICUT
UNIVERSITY OF CONNECTICUT
YALE

4

ILLINOIS
NORTHEASTERN ILLINOIS UNIVERSITY
UNIVERSITY OF ILLINOIS COMMUNITY COLLEGE
YMCA COMMUNITY COLLEGE
LOYOLA UNIVERSITY

1

WISCONSIN
UNIVERSITY OF MADISON IN WISCONSIN

Voices

Recollections from a few members are descriptive of the period from the late 1960s to the early 1970s in the transition of MPI to the PSP, leading up to the First Congress in 1973. A sizeable cohort of U.S.-raised Boricuas joined during this period.

Freddie Rodríguez remembers his early years in Brooklyn. His father was a soldier stationed in Panama in the mid-1940s. There was a nationalist influence in his family, and shortly after completing army service, he became involved with the Nationalist Party in Puerto Rico. He was on the verge of being arrested at the time of the *Jayuya* uprising in 1950, when his family alerted him to escape. He eventually found himself in New York, where relatives lived and where Freddie was later born. Brooklyn figures largely in Freddie's coming of age, as does a certain rebellious streak in his makeup that could account for his susceptibility to the militant spirit of the 1960s.

He was a teenager when he joined with other youths to form a quasi-karate/political street group. They were aware of the Black Panthers and a few times went to Manhattan to check out the Young Lords. But Freddie's group still lacked a clear purpose, as he recalls:

> It was hard with no money for the group to go to El Barrio and to relate with the Young Lords, so that summer, I think it was '68, or maybe the summer that followed, the karate group got more and more political and we would hang out. . . .
>
> We'd play stickball. . . . [W]e would go into the projects to play handball. But we got involved in, like, copying everything that was going on. There was a garbage drive where the garbage wasn't being picked up, so we figured, well, let's get involved. Let's put the garbage in the middle of the street. . . . [W]e turned over two cars, gasoline started pumping out, we would put them on fire. We would all go to the roof, [and] as soon as the firemen came, we would throw bottles at them.
>
> You know, crazy shit, just totally crazy, not knowing what we were really doing, except that it was exciting. It was so exciting that we got together, and we used to have stencils of the Black Panther T-shirts, so we would make Black Panther T-shirts. But then we felt . . . that we should do our own thing, so we created a group called the Young Warriors Party.
>
> But that gave us an opportunity to move the Black Panther newspaper and the Young Lords newspaper. Eventually, I would walk with my mother, shopping, we're talking about maybe '69. Graham Avenue was a major, major commercial [street] . . . so

going shopping with my mother on Graham Avenue, I noticed that there was a bunch of people selling *un periódico* called *Claridad*. . . . [T]here was a barbershop, and right next to the barbershop, there was a *comité* of the MPI, you know. . . . [S]ince I knew the area so well, we started going to Varick Street, and eventually we got into the comité, which at that time they were called *misiones* . . . I think it was La Misión Carmen Miranda. . . . I think it was '69. . . . I was very young, I was what, 14 years old? . . . [W]e would start hanging out with them [members of the MPI]. I would help out, it was David Quiñones. I remember him, with his big mustache. . . . I was already . . . participating in the meetings.

Milga Morales was born in Guayanilla, near Ponce. She says of her hometown that it "has always been poor . . . but the best people in the world come out of Guayanilla." She was only two years old when she came to New York in the late 1940s. Her extended family of uncles and cousins all lived in downtown Brooklyn, having pooled their money to buy a house. In Puerto Rico, her parents never got much schooling, but she says they were "both very smart people":

[M]y mom was very much of a union activist, my father also, he was a steward of the union; my father was very much a *simpatizante de los nacionalistas*, and my mother was very much a community civic involvement person. . . . I think it was in high school that . . . I started to make connections with civil rights and issues of colonialism, Puerto Rican independence. . . .

So [in high school], I became active in going to demonstrations and going to Washington, D.C., and going with a friend of mine from the neighborhood and just . . . making our own placards and just getting on the bus. They were pretty much all civil rights demonstrations. And I think that just very early on, I remember writing an essay when I was in my social studies class . . . on brotherhood. So, the concept that we all learned early on was about brotherhood. And it was something that I felt very strongly about. . . . I think that set the basis for me to understand all the other things that were going on and make those connections.

So, anyway, I wound up going there [Casa Puerto Rico], and I was super excited because they were pretty much a lot of people talking in Spanish, which I was like, "Umm, I wonder about this and being a part of this." But it was very mixed, and there were professors and there were workers; you could tell it was a very good mix of people, and there were older folks, and they reminded me of people in my family. . . . For me, it was always a struggle trying to figure out how do I meld that with the civil rights stuff, which was the first stuff that was in my mind, but I felt that there were connections with things there.

So, I think the MPI was also . . . not only good for the brain, but it was also good socially because you did meet a lot of different people, and it was a very comfortable environment, very challenging environment, and lots of times there would be debates and discussions where I wasn't quite clear what they were talking about, but it gave me food for thought. . . . For me, it was always the education, it was always the independence movement, education and civil rights. Those were the three cornerstone pieces for me. And if you were doing that, and that was the environment, it was a very comfortable environment for me, and I felt like, "Okay, these people have the same goals that I have."

And yet she experienced moments when relations were not always so smooth:

It depended on socially who you were around because in some cases, I got turned off by what I felt was a holier-than-thou attitude by some folks. . . . It was sometimes rough during those times, trying to be part of that but also having to swallow some of that as well.

Eduardo "Tito" Delgado grew up in the Lower East Side in a mixed community of mostly Puerto Ricans and Blacks. So to a great extent, he related to the Black experience, dancing to soul music, like James Brown and the Temptations. He was tall, skinny, and targeted by bullies. It did not help that his poor vision necessitated wearing thick eyeglasses. Expelled from high school for fighting, he enrolled in an alternative program, the Academy of the Streets, where he was exposed to radical politics. He gravitated to the Nation of Islam. He went to see Malcolm X speak in Harlem once and got to shake hands with him, remembering that Malcolm greeted him, "How you doing, brother?" Although he had a close black Muslim friend who was active and encouraged him to join, he believed that he would stand out too much with his white skin. But he continued to seek ways to express his political beliefs:

So, my next experience was with the Young Lords. I had heard about them taking over the church, and I went up there. But I had a very short experience with them. I was there about a year when my father saw me on TV in the news, and he beat the shit out of me, he beat me, and he didn't want me, blah, blah, blah, blah, so that was the end of my Young Lords career.

And then, my next experience—and this is where I became Puerto Rican—was with the Puerto Rican Socialist Party. For me, that was a cultural awakening of who I was, what my history is, where my parents come from, what their struggles had been, and basically learning Spanish, because at some point, many of us that were born here were kind of shy about speaking the language. But the PSP really took that away and gave me something that I [will] cherish all my life—they gave me my "Puerto Ricanness."

Sandra Rodríguez was born in Manhattan in 1954, raised by a single mother who worked two jobs, determined to send her daughter through Catholic schools. Her father was not in her life, and she did not see him for the first time until she was twenty-one years old. Summers were spent with her grandmother in Puerto Rico, where she absorbed her Puerto Rican culture. At Cathedral High School, she was active in the ASPIRA club and inevitably crossed paths with independentista students and counselors:

I identified with the Puerto Rican power movement, yes, but I didn't identify with the Young Lords. . . . I think it was that they were more New York, [but] there was something about the MPI that made the connection with Puerto Rico that I liked more, I think it was basically that.

Her mother vehemently opposed her involvement in the MPI-PSP. Sandra, at the time a rebellious sixteen-year-old, confronted her mother to the edge of a physical encounter, demanding the right to attend a study group reading Vladimir Lenin's *What Is to Be Done?* When her mother finally relented, she discovered that her grandfather was a *Nacionalista*. She remembers feeling a special connection:

So when she told me that about my *abuelo*, I got even more proud. Oh yeah, I have it in the blood, you know. So that was really a big turning point for me. . . . [T]he discussions in the study groups was a very rich thing. For me, I think I was just a sponge. I was, like, bring it on. And I felt good belonging to this movement. I didn't know. I think I thought that the revolution was right around the corner. Oh yeah, I think you had to believe that to do it with such passion and all that.

Other testimonies and perspectives representative of members in Hartford and Boston have been published elsewhere. As with the testimonies from the above interviews, these members reflect a diversity of backgrounds, different pathways to membership in the PSP, a variety of experiences within it, and a range of interpretations regarding the contributions and shortcomings of the organization.[39]

El Acto Nacional

In late 1973, the PSP's national leadership in Puerto Rico decided that the time was ripe for a major event: a National Day of Solidarity with Puerto Rico. *El Acto Nacional* (The National Action) would rally people to denounce U.S. colonialism and capitalism. It would coincide with the UN discussion about Puerto Rico's colonial status, and it would fully involve the North American Left. Puerto Rican independence should be the cause célèbre of the progressive and anti-imperialist forces in the United States, now that the war in Indochina was winding down. The world's oldest democracy was hanging onto the oldest colony, and this crime had to end.

The activists in the Seccional were put in charge of organizing the solidarity event. The challenge was clear: the Acto had to attract thousands of Boricuas, third-world community members, and progressive white folks. It had to involve as many people from the Left as possible; it had to be held in New York City, where it would be noticed by national and international media; and it had to deliver a hard-hitting message to the U.S. government. It

Figure 1.6. National Day of Solidarity with Puerto Rico, Madison Square Garden, New York City, October 27, 1974.

would also be the moment to make important announcements about future goals. The big question: Could the venue for the event, Madison Square Garden, be filled to capacity? Full capacity meant twenty thousand people.

To some members, the whole idea of the Acto sounded much too ambitious. But their reservations were swept aside by the charismatic speeches and political columns of PSP leaders, especially Mari Brás. On Sunday, October 27, 1974, the Puerto Rican movement, in coalition with many allies and friends, scored a major achievement and scaled a new peak when it filled the Garden to capacity.[40]

It took weeks to wind down from El Acto Nacional. The PSP's members were thoroughly spent after a mighty effort, but they had the luxury of only a brief respite before resuming their frenzied pace.[41]

Voices

It could be said that Armengol Domenech was neither a traditional Puerto Rican, born and raised on the island, nor a Nuyorican, a product of the metropolis. Born in Santurce, his coming of age was passed as an "army brat" stationed in Camden, New Jersey, and then in Alaska, and then in Maryland; eventually, he found himself in New York City, approaching adulthood and looking for work. His upbringing would have included a stint in Germany were it not for the fact that his father had declined to have the entire family stationed there. Curious about the history and politics of the United States and of Puerto Rico, he met several MPI members in the late 1960s and quickly got involved with the organization. By 1969, he had been recruited by Ramón Arbona and Rafín Baerga to be an organizer with the MPI. Armengol was perfectly bilingual, a gregarious personality who could engage with both sides of the Boricua cultural spectrum. He was another key cadre in the period leading up to the First Congress and then El Acto Nacional. Domenech recalls:

> At the beginning, we had doubts . . . that we were going to be able to move that many people. But, again . . . I think Mari Brás even had doubts, and I think that Jenaro [Rentas] had doubts, but the dreamer in this whole group, the dreamer was Ramón Arbona. . . . Ramón Arbona, if you let him, he would fill up Yankee Stadium. He would sell you on that idea that we could do it.

Pedro Reyes's parents came from the country towns of Moróvis and Barceloneta. His father was a sugarcane-cutter who had reached the fifth grade, and his mother had had one year of schooling. After his parents met and married, his father served a tour in the army at the tail end of World

War II. Following his return to Puerto Rico, they began a family, had three kids, and in a few years found themselves in the Lower East Side of New York City. Pedro was the fourth child and the only one not born in Puerto Rico. They lived on the fifth floor of an "old, old tenement" at 80 Monroe St. that the family nicknamed *la nevera* (refrigerator) for its lack of heat in the winter. Next, they moved to another fifth-floor apartment, at 224 Delancey St. After bouncing around for a few more years in congested living quarters in Manhattan, the Reyeses triumphantly landed an apartment in the projects of the West Side. Reyes recalls that "when you moved to the project[s], you made the middle class, you'd made it. . . . [W]e all hugged."

For many PSP activists, memories of workplace situations were foundational to their sense of injustice and their later politics. Even to a seven-year-old boy, accompanying his father on payday, impressions had a lasting impact, as Reyes recalls:

> [M]y father worked at the Waldorf Astoria. . . . My father used to drink . . . [and] he always drank on Fridays. Friday was payday. [One day], my mother told me, "Pedro . . . go with your father to get paid," [and] then I went with him. We walked into this train station, Grand Central, beautiful ceiling, wow I'd never seen such a beautiful ceiling like this, and we walked through toward the Waldorf and came in through the side entrance, and there were beautiful rugs and tables and lamps, everything; it was fantastic. . . .
>
> I see him going into a room, and I hear shouting and somebody saying, "No, you have to work today, because someone didn't come in," and I remember him saying, "No, but I have my son," and the other one said, "I don't care if you have your son, you have to work today." And my father comes out, pale, watery eyes, dry mouth, and he looks at me, and I look at him, and we didn't have to talk, I knew exactly what was happening, and he says, "Do you know how to go home by yourself?" and I said, "Yeah." Because, of course, we were always pretending. I guess I knew. He says, "I'm going to take you down to the train station, and all you have to do is take this train and get back and get off at West 4th Street." . . . I understood from there on in why he drank, and I never asked him again why he drank, I understood. If he had to face that every day, then that was rough, and I just admired him for the fact that he woke up every day with a newspaper in his pocket and went to work and made sure we had food on the table.

Baerga, a key organizer, has more to say about the period from 1969 through El Acto Nacional at Madison Square Garden:

The PSP had a lot of creativity, but the experience [and] the genius of Ramón Arbona helped put things in their proper perspective . . . then Mari Brás, who helped with that whole project [building the Seccional], the idea that we had to have autonomy to do what we wanted to do. Like, he used to say, "Do what you think is right. . . . I can't tell you how you are going to do things because you have different conditions [in the United States], and you have to develop your own leadership, your own structures, your own finances; you can't expect that anyone else is going to finance it, the very struggle itself has to be financed."

So, the biggest contribution of the PSP and the MPI was the development of the discussion about the existence of a single nation, a political-ideological issue that is still discussed. We Puerto Ricans have comprised a single nation until now. This might change within twenty, thirty, forty years. There are civilizations that have disappeared completely . . . but today we form a single nation, by our own positive decision.

Another contribution . . . is the organizational experience. In other words, we developed methods of work that today should be used by people. . . . [W]e had tremendous relations with the Left . . . the people from the Communist Party, Workers World, Socialist Workers Party . . . then the New Left. . . .

I believe we were sectarian, but we were young. . . . We had to defend the organization. We were under attack also, but we should have given the opportunity to others to participate. . . . The student movement, perhaps there was another way to have done the student work . . . instead of developing an organization [the FUSP] tied to our party. . . . [We should have helped] strengthen the student organizations [the PRSU and other groups] that already existed.

Antonio (Tony) Nadal's parents were an interesting duo, possibly a case of opposites attracting. His father was a teacher, his mother a *jibarita* (country girl) with a third-grade education; he was dark-skinned, she was light-skinned. Her family owned some land, "so that she was really better off than [Nadal's] father economically." Her family was also "rather racist" and would not accept him; but she was "somewhat of a rebel," according to her son, and the two eloped. All of this happened in the town of Manatí, on Puerto Rico's northern coast. Eventually, they ended up in Brooklyn's South Side, with their brood of five children.

Nadal was just three-and-a-half years old when his family arrived in the United States. Their Williamsburg home was a beehive of activity. His mother "was really the one who built up the family. . . . [She was] a go-getter

even though she had little education . . . and she always had business flair."
She opened a bodega on South Third Street, where she ran a numbers operation (*bolita*) and was a spiritualist (*espiritista*). His father was a gentle man,
"a quiet Nationalist," in contrast to his mother, a *Popular* devoted to Muñoz
Marín. He helped in the bodega, but at night worked at his true passion:
teaching English to veterans. Nadal remembers his father as being "strictly
a scholar" but never able to get a regular teaching job in the New York City
system because his accent was considered too strong. The family never
spoke English at home, as Nadal explains:

> You have the Puerto Rican culture at home and in the community,
> and then you have your instruction in school [in English] and—you
> might say—that dichotomy of living literally in two different worlds.

Nadal came up through the public schools and then entered Brooklyn
College, where he met his future wife, Milga Morales. An extended journey
of graduate studies and part-time teaching and counseling in a variety of
programs ultimately led to his becoming part of the Brooklyn College faculty in the early 1970s, specializing in Puerto Rican and Caribbean studies.
He also gravitated toward the MPI-PSP during this time. Not to be confined to a strictly academic life, he had another side: he was a musician, a
songwriter, and the leader of a Latin band, Orchestra *Bembé*. He recalls the
politics of academia:

> This was the time of the clamor by Boricua youth for access to the
> City University of New York [CUNY]. From the beginning, Brook-
> lyn College officials—and many faculty—resisted the perceived
> invasion of students of color. Among the students and faculty clus-
> tered around the college's Puerto Rican milieu were a fair number of
> *independentistas* and progressives. Soon, the PSP created a nucleus
> and became enveloped in the defining struggle for Puerto Rican
> Studies at the college.

As Nadal remembers, the battles at the college were over a struggle for
the "self-determination" of Puerto Rican studies at the famed campus. One
fight centered around the right of the Department of Puerto Rican Studies
to select its own chairperson, a battle that lasted through 1974 and 1975 and
in which the PSP ultimately played an instrumental role. The college administrators intended to assign their own person as chair rather than a member
of the faculty, none of whom was tenured. The administration's designated
chair came from the University of Puerto Rico and was unknown to anyone

but was suspected of being part of a plan to eventually dismantle—or at least control—the department's faculty. One department member, Sonia Nieto, was sent to Puerto Rico to learn more about the candidate and found out that she had misrepresented her qualifications and only planned to stay at Brooklyn College during her husband's medical residency at St. Vincent's Hospital in New York. Despite sharp opposition from the faculty, the campus president forced her in as department chair. Naturally, the faculty and students erupted in protest. What ensued was a long conflict between Puerto Rican/Latino faculty and students and entrenched administrative officials, between faculty governance and top-down bureaucratic control.[42] Nadal recalls:

So, from that moment on, it was war. We declared war. We started the takeovers, we took over the Registrar's Office twice, and we had any number of demonstrations. We picketed the president's house. We went into . . . Faculty Council meetings, and we would make presentations, and we'd have to be removed. This lasted for about a year and a half. . . . The *New York Times*, the *Daily News*, the Justice Department became involved . . . the FBI came in . . . and we had organized the Vietnam Veterans Against the War to join our struggle. These were mostly Vietnam-era vets and their director, who was very sympathetic to our position—he organized the veterans to do security and to organize the demonstrations and to even go to the rooftops and all that because they were trained.

And it became so big. It became what some people called *el gran peo* (the big fart) of the college, and it was ruining the standing of the college. . . . [M]any white professors said, "We have to do something to get rid of these people." While there were others, the more liberal of course . . . and there was a group of radical professors that went out there, among them the historian Hobart Spalding, of course; Loida Figueroa [Mercado] went on speaking engagements to talk about what was going on. During that time also, there was the whole struggle to keep Hostos [Community College] open.

So, *el partido* was involved with any number of issues that had to do with Puerto Ricans in the United States, and this was all work *de la* Seccional. So, the struggle at Brooklyn College became the work *que el partido* was doing. So, we had to go on with *ese trabajo* [that work]. We had to organize the *simpatizantes*. We threw dances where we played [music] and everything else to get funds to be able to do the kinds of activities that were necessary to widen that struggle.

Eventually, the college could not deal with what we had done. It had become too embarrassing. We never allowed [their appointed person] . . . for that whole year, early '75, to come into our office, into the chair's office.

There was a student contingent guarding the offices. Mind you, this was with college security and all that knowing, we would not allow her to go in there. . . . And the whole thing was, "*Ya no podemos con estos boricuas* (we can't go on like this with these Boricuas)" . . . and we ignored them [the administration] because María [Sánchez] was our "People's Chair." And they didn't dare remove María or remove any of us because they had already arrested us twice.[43]

Graciano Matos was a long-time Bronx leader of the PSP. A "field day" was being celebrated at his high school in Puerto Rico when students from another high school went by his school. Somehow, a fight broke out between the two groups. The disturbance drew the riot squad, which caused hundreds of students to pour out into the schoolyard. Bottles and rocks were hurled, bringing out the heavy-handed repression of the police. This was in 1968, when student protests were at a high pitch in Puerto Rico. When the police arrived, they directed shots toward the school, leaving bullet holes all over the façade. Fortunately, no students were wounded.

Matos was surprised at how the events were covered by the media the following day: all the blame was heaped on the students for what had been a minor scuffle. The police's abusive show of force was treated as normal. The police response and subsequent media treatment radicalized Matos. Over the next few years, Matos's political views gravitated toward the independence movement. Then he moved to New York City, where before long he enrolled in the PSP just as it was transitioning from the MPI.

His years of activism, including as a leader of Bronx local chapters (or *núcleos*), benefited an organization embedded in the struggles of the diaspora, as he recalls:

The accomplishments of the Puerto Rican Socialist Party were many. It was both a pro–Puerto Rican independence party as well as a socialist organization. Despite the fears and apprehension one might think would arise . . . [toward] an organization identified as such, it became a large organization. It was organized in communities as well as in workplaces. It had a newspaper that for a while became a daily newspaper. It also developed a bilingual section. . . . This level of organization runs counter to the belief that our people would be scared off by both the words *socialism* and *independence*. . . . [T]he

Seccional . . . was also able to keep the subject of Puerto Rican independence . . . on the radar of the U.S. Left.

A party nucleus engaged in a number of activities. Some were local issues, such as tenant organizing or the fight to preserve a bilingual school. In the early seventies, Dr. Antonio Silva [known in Puerto Rico as a sterilization supporter] was appointed director of obstetrics of the Lincoln Hospital. The opposition to his appointment organized immediately. The West Bronx nucleus designated Carmen Vásquez to represent the nucleus in the coalition that came together to oust him.

Besides selling [issues of] *Claridad*, another responsibility was fundraising by ensuring all members, "militants" and "affiliates," pa[id] their membership dues and creating a network of *cotizantes*, or sympathizers, who would donate money to the organization.

One of the campaigns the U.S. Branch was involved in was the struggle first to save Hostos Community College and later to get a [new] building across the street on Grand Concourse called *el quiniento*, or the five hundred, referring to the number of the building address.

At the time, I lived on the Grand Concourse . . . not too far from Hostos. My father, Graciano Matos, and my sister, Lucy Matos, who at the time was a Hostos student, joined the struggle. My father cooked for them; since the buildings had been taken over by the students, he would also sleep over sometimes and joined the rallies. Our house became a center for the struggle, where the FUSP members would meet socially but also occasionally for strategizing.

I recall this struggle as very positive because there were a lot of young people joining in the fight to get the 500. Many were party members or were interested in the party. There were study groups, and the potential for the party to grow was ever more tangible. The PSP Branch had assigned experienced members to work directly with the FUSP. Hence, the role of the West Bronx núcleo was a supportive one; we lent the house as an office when needed, provided food, and some of our members slept . . . in the building that was taken over by the students.

At a personal level, joining the Puerto Rican Socialist Party and becoming a *militante* with the *carnet rojo* [red membership card] was quite an accomplishment. It was proof of hard work, discipline, and integrity. It served as a great schooling experience. I learned to analyze the reality around me and to operate in murky political waters.

A Bicentennial Without Colonies

The idea for conducting a *Bicentenario Sin Colonias* (Bicentennial Without Colonies) was to install the Puerto Rican cause as a central piece of the progressive social justice agenda in the country. As with the Acto, the PSP would help build a broad coalition from the Left and liberal movements. There would be room for everyone concerned about the conservative shift in American politics and the crass commercialism that had come to dominate the official Bicentennial activities. A national political group, the "July 4th Coalition" (J4C), would be formed to include leftist political organizations, civil rights and labor groups, organizers involved in anti-racist and environmental work, and international solidarity activists. Activists perceived the numbers were there for a significant propagandistic coup, for a radical critique of American politics. Even though there was no thought of competing on the same scale as the official festivities taking place in Philadelphia, the J4C calculated that the counter-celebration could draw significant media attention by taking place close to the main event.

On March 27, 1976, the First Secretary of the Seccional, José Alberto Álvarez Febles, addressed the opening session of the J4C's founding conference, held in New York City. Álvarez Febles had been an activist and leader during the protests that had rocked the University of Puerto Rico in the late 1960s. In the early 1970s, he had come to New Jersey and joined the PSP as it was transitioning from the MPI; he would become a lead organizer in New Jersey and then eventually for the entire Seccional, serving as the organization's First Secretary from early 1975 through the early 1980s.

In late 1974, a chain reaction of change had been triggered by the untimely death of *Claridad*'s national director in Puerto Rico, Raúl González. Arbona was called upon to return to Puerto Rico to fill the vacuum, and Álvarez Febles was named to replace him. Shortly thereafter, José La Luz, the lead organizer for the party's New England zone, was pulled out of his Hartford base to serve as Secretary of the Organization for the Seccional.

In his March 1976 speech to the J4C, Álvarez Febles emphasized the importance of a successful counter-mobilization, especially as an opportunity to foster a regrouping of U.S. Left and progressive forces. The key to an effective critique, he argued, was that it be an anti-imperialist formation: "In that way we will take important steps toward the insertion of our politics—anti-imperialist—in the national politics of this country. . . . The independence of Puerto Rico has to be one of the pillars of our campaign."[44]

That same month, terrifying news hit the airwaves in Puerto Rico: Santiago Mari Pesquera, the twenty-three-year-old son of the Secretary General, was shot and killed under mysterious circumstances. Chagui, as he was known, had followed in his father's footsteps. He had been an anti-war activist, one of many who had refused to serve in Vietnam. He was murdered by a young man who was known to Chagui and, it turned out, had connections to right-wing Cuban exiles. These were anti-Castro zealots who operated in Puerto Rico and had links with local police, the FBI, and the Central Intelligence Agency (CIA). Although the killer was eventually convicted and imprisoned, officials denied he was part of a conspiracy. Independentistas and civil rights groups denounced the government's seeming cover-up, including its refusal to release police and FBI records on the case.[45]

No one on the Left doubted that Chagui was the target of a political assassination. The killing was meant to provoke the independence movement into vengeful reaction. It appeared that the police or the FBI was trying to bait the PSP into a violent confrontation designed to destroy the party and to frighten voters in the middle of an electoral contest. In Puerto Rico and the United States, selected cadre were quietly sent underground in anticipation of mass arrests. Mari Brás instructed the PSP militants to refrain from violence.

From early to mid-1976, the Seccional stayed immersed in preparations for the Philadelphia demonstration. Everything learned in the previous years, all the resources that had been accumulated, all the structures that had been established, were put to the service of the mobilization. It would be the greatest test yet of the PSP's skills and capacity. The J4C had been established throughout the East Coast and the Midwest, and reports from local chapters predicted a major turnout. By early spring, it was apparent that progressive forces would pull off a successful action.

In May 1976, the FBI entered the scene. The agency announced it would investigate the J4C, citing the leadership roles of the PSP and other leftist groups. Exhibit A in its message of alarm was a congressional report on terrorist activity titled *The Cuban Connection in Puerto Rico*,[46] which had been compiled obviously by experts at the FBI with the help of paid informants. The pages contained organizational charts and the names of many PSP members, clearly designed to intimidate supporters, and claimed that the group was acting on the orders of Fidel Castro.

Yet none of these events—Chagui's killing, the FBI report, or a request by Philadelphia mayor Frank Rizzo to mobilize the national guard— deterred the J4C's plans.

Finally, the big day arrived. By early afternoon, tens of thousands were disembarking from assembly points in North Philadelphia to begin the two-hour march through primarily black communities toward Fairmount Park. The signs of success were evident: long columns of protester-celebrants, strident but disciplined. Marchers chanted political mantras and shouldered message-laden banners, accompanied by all sorts of percussive instruments. Five hundred busloads of participants had arrived from along the Eastern Seaboard and across the Midwest. Many more came from the immediate area by public transportation or simply walked. Young people joined the parade as the march passed their homes. Led by two parallel lines of Native American and African American militants, people weaved and switched-back through streets and avenues under overcast skies. The Boricua imprint was indelible. Dozens of contingents from the cities where Puerto Ricans lived were organized, spearheaded by sound trucks and waves of Puerto Rican flags. Sprinkled throughout were flags containing a white star on a red field, the PSP's emblem. As at the Madison Square Garden rally in October 1974, Mari Brás was a featured orator. Once again, he delivered a soaring message to the crowd. Only a few months before, he had lost his son.

According to the leftist press, roughly fifty thousand people participated in the Bicentennial Without Colonies event, counting the Philadelphia and West Coast rallies. The *New York Times* was less impressed, reporting an overall turnout of thirty thousand. Regardless, in the eyes of the J4C and the PSP, it was as a total success. Organizers had reason to believe that the J4C could emerge as a unifying force within the radical or progressive wing of the U.S. political spectrum. Members anticipated that the coalition could be converted into a permanent organization, with Puerto Rican decolonization as one of its central tenets.[47]

It should be stated at this point that the PSP did not hold an exclusionary attitude about who "qualified" for membership in the party. Recruitment was directed at Puerto Ricans, but this effort did not preclude bringing in others who supported the PSP's goals and ideological stances. Latin Americans joined—Cubans, for example—as did North Americans.[48] Throughout the Seccional's history, multinational coalitions around solidarity for Puerto Rico's independence and for democratic rights were abiding principles; in these contexts, unity with African American individuals and organizations was prioritized, as it was with Chicano and Native American movements. But the direct recruitment of individuals was not emphasized. Several North Americans became active militantes and leaders of the U.S. Branch, principally among them, *el compañero* Denis Berger.[49]

Democratic Rights and National Liberation: An Experiment in Organizing

In the crucial period leading up to the First Congress of the Seccional, from 1969 to 1973, the militants of the organization framed what would become their vision of their role in the United States. It was most commonly described as a "dual" or "double role," with the idea of melding two aspects of a grand liberation project into one:

> Its primary role in the United States is to unleash that national liberation struggle, in all its fury, in the very hearts of North American cities to which a significant portion of our colonized population was forced, and to link that national liberation struggle to the struggle for the revolutionary transformation of North American society.[50]

Central to the idea of the double role was that the Seccional would engage in the day-to-day social and class struggles of Puerto Ricans in the United States. This formulation mirrored the new position taken by the MPI at the national level (as expressed in the 1969 document *Presente y Futuro*): it would be necessary to systematically fuse the anti-colonial project with the concrete, real demands (*reivindicaciones*) of the masses. In the diaspora, organizing around *reivindicaciones*—construed as democratic and cultural rights—was the gateway to the two overall strategic objectives: (1) national liberation and socialism in Puerto Rico and (2) social revolution in the United States. This goal meant that organizing for liberation required transcending the traditional mode of commemorating patriotic events (e.g., relating to national heroes, the uprisings of *Lares* and *Jayuya*, and so forth) and that organizing for social revolution in the United States required going beyond securing North American solidarity for Puerto Rico's independence. In 1973, the Seccional's document *Desde Las Entrañas* spelled this out.

Optimizing this vision of a double role required identifying those moments when the effects of colonialism in Puerto Rico were clearly linked to oppression in Puerto Rican communities in the diaspora. Where the simultaneous effects of imperialism and capitalism on the lives of Boricuas *in both places* were apparent, the PSP could be the most effective. Where this synergy of purpose was less readily achievable, the PSP's practice would be less productive.

In several instances, linking the two roles was effective in educating and mobilizing people, leading to the organization's growth.

The Military Draft

One such early instance, anticipating the "dual role" thesis, was the MPI's campaign denouncing the military draft in Puerto Rico, during which hundreds of youth defiantly burned their draft cards. Beginning in the mid-1960s, the Vito Marcantonio Mission participated in several anti-war and anti-draft campaigns and protest marches. Later, the MPI supported the resistance of such young men as Pablo "Yoruba" Guzmán, of the Young Lords. Then came the case of José "Che" Velázquez, a PSP activist and leader in the United States. The simultaneous enactment of anti-imperialist opposition in Puerto Rico and in the United States was a unifying factor in the activities of the MPI as it transitioned to the PSP.

Farmworker Organization

Migrant workers who labored in the fields of the Northeast were subject to severe exploitation. The problem was that the Commonwealth government, for fear of alienating U.S. farmer associations, did not vigorously enforce the protective provisions of labor contracts. By the late 1960s, ecumenical groups in Puerto Rico and in the United States had begun a reform effort to expose egregious contract violations. They assigned organizers to interview workers in the fields, often trespassing onto the camps. They set up support centers in nearby towns, populated by Puerto Ricans, to instruct workers on their rights. Organizations such the Association of Agricultural Workers (ATA) were created to speak for the workers. Young people on the island and in the mainland joined the effort, as did MPI-PSP members. Community support centers were based in such towns as Springfield, Massachusetts; Hartford, Connecticut; and Camden, New Jersey, where MPI activists lived and were able to connect with these workers.

Figure 1.7. Selling *Claridad* in Hartford, Connecticut.

The Organization of the Petroleum Exporting Countries "Crisis"

Another example involved the federal government's manipulation of the so-called oil crisis of 1974–1975, involving the Organization of the Petroleum Exporting Countries (OPEC). Because OPEC's decision to freeze production led to a "shortage" of crude oil and a spike in energy prices, major cities, including as New York, were strapped for heating oil and began cutting back on fuel for their public housing. In New York and other cities, the PSP conducted petition drives, in coalition with other groups, denouncing the cuts and exposing the government's refusal to draw on the vast oil reserves maintained for contingencies such as these.

This campaign coincided with an organizing offensive in Puerto Rico that opposed the creation of a *Super-Puerto* (Super-Port) off the northwest coast near Aguadilla, a proposal designed precisely to reduce energy dependence on foreign countries by increasing U.S.-based capacity for refining oil. By appealing to economic, environmental, and moral arguments, the PSP and other organizations in the United States helped force Commonwealth officials and Big Oil (in this case, Exxon, owned by the Rockefeller family at the time) to abandon the project.

The Fiscal Crisis

In the days of New York City's fiscal crisis (1975–1976), a movement arose to save Hostos Community College and to galvanize protesters of the state's Emergency Financial Control Board (EFCB). During this period, the PSP threw its energies into coalition efforts, offering the support of its organizers, *Claridad* coverage, and the mobilization of its base for key events, such as campus occupations and public rallies and marches. The victory preserved the school for future generations of students of color, including immigrants. While the immediate struggle was over the demand to preserve a college with a bilingual curriculum, an important aspect of the fight resonated with pro-independence aspirations: the college's namesake was a principal patriotic figure for Puerto Ricans in the diaspora and in Puerto Rico. At stake was not only a prime community institution and resource but also a cultural and historic symbol for the nation. The island media gave thorough coverage to the contentious struggle, and the anti-colonial sectors shared in the celebrated outcome.

Sterilization Abuse

During the early to mid-1970s, a campaign against sterilization abuse resulted in a hard-won victory for women's reproductive rights. The fact that a medical doctor had been brought from Puerto Rico to head a steriliza-tion program in New York's Lincoln'Hospital, located in the South Bronx, sharply accentuated the links between the colony and the barrio. Here, the course of interaction was reversed: a population control program initi-ated on the island was now being imported to a Puerto Rican (and African American and Latino) site in urban America. Opposition, led and inspired by such PSP allies as Dr. Helen Rodríguez-Trías, was fierce enough to cause the implementation of new regulations in New York prohibiting the steril-ization of women under the age of twenty-one and requiring waiting peri-ods between advice and consent.

Such organizations as the Committee to End Sterilization Abuse (CESA), in which the PSP was heavily involved, illuminated how people can be victimized when they lack control over levers of self-determination. Yet grassroots organizing and policy advocacy achieved an important reform: the right to informed consent. These organizations continued their cam-paigns through multiple challenges into the late 1970s.

The above are some key examples of campaigns in which the MPI-PSP successfully melded the two dimensions of its double role: connecting the fight for Boricua rights in the diaspora to the fight for the independence of Puerto Rico. In the midst of these efforts, it should be emphasized, the organization was simultaneously organizing large mobilizations for its First Convention (1973), El Acto Nacional (1974), and the Bicentennial Without Colonies (1976).

Difficult Questions

The PSP's goals for a robust turnout at the Bicentennial were achieved, bringing significant attention to the Puerto Rican cause and expanding networks of unity with North American progressive forces. The Seccional leadership held high hopes, despite grumblings among members, that the organization could surpass the pinnacle of success represented by the Phila-delphia mobilization. Yet events would soon prove these expectations to be unreasonable. A few months later, the Puerto Rican elections of 1976 revealed how inaccurately the PSP had judged the public's receptivity to its message. Not only did the electorate choose the pro-statehood party (the New Progressive Party [PNP]); the PSP received less than 1 percent of all integral ballots.[51] The PIP secured 5 percent. Adding salt to the wound was the fact that the new governor, Carlos Romero-Barceló, represented the extreme right wing of his party and had ties to the Cuban exile community in Puerto Rico and Miami.

For the rest of 1976 and into the spring of 1977, much time was expended in reassessing the state of the organization and debating the way forward.

Tensions had been accumulating for more than two years, since the achievement of El Acto Nacional in the fall of 1974. After the results of the elections in Puerto Rico, party activists turned inward to address difficult questions.

Reports were prepared by the various work areas (Organization, Press and Propaganda, Finances, *Claridad*, Labor, Student, and so forth), which were consolidated into an overarching document issued by the Secretariat for the CS.[52] A parallel report, sixty-five pages long and produced by the Political Commission, covered the full range of political and organizational issues: the present Puerto Rican reality (including that of the diaspora) and a thorough evaluation of the degree to which the Seccional had or had not achieved, its six principal objectives of 1976.[53] The report also analyzed the flaws in the Seccional's political practice, largely agreeing with the defective "isms" that had been found to permeate the party nationally. A litany of such deviations was acknowledged: bureaucratism, authoritarianism, gigantism, volunteerism, immediatism, liberalism. Only lightly touched upon was the non-working-class origin of many of the very top leaders (for example, of the National Political Commission) and how this circumstance underlay the problematic "isms." More fundamental and contentious matters would surface from the subsequent discussions held at the base of the organization.[54]

One thing could not be denied: the seriousness with which Seccional members approached the challenge of self-evaluation. For weekends on end, starting in February 1977, the CS met to respond to the two reports. Local leaders from throughout the organization traveled to Seccional headquarters on East Thirteenth Street in Manhattan to hash out a draft accord, often with children in tow, often on their weekend breaks from full-time jobs.

This report was then submitted to the various chapters. Militants and affiliates in New York City, Boston, Connecticut, northern and southern New Jersey, Chicago, and California, and others in the areas of labor and student work participated as well. In an era devoid of emails and teleconferencing, there were lapses and delays in reporting back with amendments and proposals for change. Yet the majority of chapters and members complied with the sobering task of understanding the past to better chart their future.

Before the process was completed, a draft of a consensus statement was debated within the CS. Sentences were revised; nouns and adjectives were parsed for exact meaning. The documents were in Spanish but had to be orally translated on the run—at times in the middle of heated discussions—for those whose primary tongue was English.

The result was a document issued by the CS in April 1977.[55] Preliminary drafts of the statement had been developed by the Political Commission and the Secretariat, discussed in the CS, and then reviewed by the base across the chapters. Amendments were then proposed by the base and submitted to the CS for final approval. It was the first time since the discussions leading to the First Congress of the U.S. Branch (1973) that formalization of a political consensus was undertaken.

The nine-page April resolution began by contextualizing the state of the Seccional within the problems faced by the party nationally:

> [We] recognize that the *Seccional* shares the grave defects of bureaucratism, authoritarianism, gigantism, volunteerism, the low ideological level and other deviations that have been developing in the entire party. This is so because the *Seccional*, although operating in a front that is outside our national territory, forms an integral part of this Party. It is governed by the same organizational structure, programmatic proposals and organizational line. It is subordinated to the same bodies of national leadership as all other party organisms.[56]

The weaknesses were associated with several practices. The flow of information was deficient, primarily emanating from the top leadership, who expected the membership to implement directives with rapid response. There was a tendency to exaggerate the organization's capacity; in particular, the goals set for 1976, which focused on the Bicentennial and the elections in Puerto Rico, were outlandish and blocked any chances for patient base building.

Compounding the grandiose goals set by the CS for the base were the expectations of the national leadership for the U.S. Branch. The CS accepted and pushed the tasks assigned by the Central Committee without "examining the implications for the development of the party in the US." The problem wasn't the organizational line (building a revolutionary working-class party) but the act of putting it into practice: "The CS understands the grave separation between what the party says it is and what it proposes to do, and what it does in truth."[57]

The concluding section stated the projections for the rest of the year: (1) to celebrate the Second Congress of the U.S. Branch; (2) to develop a major response to the new statehood offensive represented by Governor Romero-Barceló in Puerto Rico; (3) to tighten up the organizational apparatus and continue the work in the various fronts that had been developed, the work in the democratic rights campaigns, and the struggle against repression; and (4) to evaluate all levels of the Seccional leadership and report conclusions to the base for their feedback and recommendations for change in the CS, the Comisión Política (Political Commission; CP), and the Secretariat.

In tone and content, the resolution of April 1977 was self-critical and prescriptive. In the effort to seal party unity, however, it showed signs of a false compromise and evidence that mistakes of the past had not been fully absorbed. Several passages toward the end hinted at the same mentality that gave way to the *gigantismo* and *voluntarismo* denounced in the opening paragraphs.

According to the document, the new threat of statehood (point #1) created an "enormous potential for organizing patriotic unity and pushing the solidarity of the North American people in the face of imperialist maneuvers in Puerto Rico."[58] Yet a crisis is only an opportunity if you have the wherewithal to engage it, and members may have imagined that another campaign of the scale of the Bicentennial was in the works. Organizing the U.S. Branch's Second Congress (priority #2) certainly was not to be taken lightly, especially with the base's insistence on a thorough process of theoretical development. The resolution emphasized that working toward the aforementioned priorities did not mean that other "important aspects" (points #3 and #4, which contained several more pages of tasks) were to be abandoned. Finally, it went unremarked—although the membership was fully aware— that the Seccional was expected to participate fully in the National Congress slated for the end of 1978 in Puerto Rico: "In the final analysis, the Party and its leadership bodies have to know to coordinate these tasks so that they relate dialectically in a sure politics of concentration of efforts."[59]

A present-day reader could reasonably wonder whether the CS had really grasped the fragile state of the party.

No time was wasted in planning for the rest of 1977, with the hope of ending the year on a high note with a successful Second Congress. The CS met in May, with the double purpose of discussing a Political Report submitted by the Political Commission[60] and defining organizational priorities based on a number of new reports from the various areas of work (compiled by the Secretariat).[61] The Political Report defined the principal task for the year as putting into practice the work methods that would rectify the various "isms" suffered by the party. This reference was to the need to implement a more reasonable pace of activism, to emphasize the political development of members, to respect the need for greater balance between personal and political life, to deal with male chauvinism, and generally to have a longer-term perspective on the struggle.

The document followed with a reminder of the tasks external to party practices: "On the other hand [we have] to get the party apparatus—which has been relatively paralyzed in the last months—functioning again to organize the Puerto Rican revolution."[62]

In the next sections, several tasks were prioritized (basically reiterating the points expressed in the April 24 resolution), but the main focus was the need to respond to the new Annexation Offensive. It is noteworthy that the first draft of the Political Commission's report discussed in depth the question of the struggles for social demands or reforms (*luchas reivindicatívas*).[63] Between the first draft and the second draft, the discussion of organizing around the social and economic needs of the Puerto Rican diaspora was reduced from five pages to *three sentences* and appeared only as a reminder that this area of work had its own "importance and urgency [and] demand[ed] our immediate attention."[64]

The discussion about the Annexation Offensive dominated the second version, taking up four pages out of seven-and-a-half pages of political analysis. The report argued for making a broad effort to counter the statehood forces, encompassing work in Boricua communities, mobilizing people toward the UN discussions, and pushing North American left and progressive sectors to build solidarity with the self-determination of the Puerto Rican people.[65] Less than a year had passed since the Bicentennial campaign.

Rectification and Compromise: 1977–1978

The unrealistic nature of these plans became evident in the summer and fall of 1977. This realization occurred in part because the rectification process at the national level began to rupture the top leadership, including the Political Commission. Few Seccional members were privy to these conflicts, until they surfaced in December and January (1976–1977) with the resignation of the Secretary of Organization, Jenaro Rentas.

Rentas was a leader from the early MPI years and had risen to direct the core apparatus of the PSP. He was a former high school history teacher, a formidable ideologue, and a taskmaster responsible for making sure that the various levels of the party structure—from nuclei to zone committees to the national Secretariat—implemented the work plans approved by the Central Committee. His role required him to be regularly in contact with many cadre in Puerto Rico and in the United States. When the term *Stalinist* was used to critique party practices, he caught the brunt of the flack; even Mari Brás leveled this claim. But, in fairness, Rentas was only carrying out the directives ratified by the Central Committee and the Political Commission. He had warned, to no avail, that leadership had to be clear about its priorities. During the spring of 1977, Rentas submitted a one-sentence letter of resignation to the organization. Because he had multiple personal links with Seccional leaders and the base cadre, his departure was a blow to Seccional morale.

Another key leader, Ángel M. Agosto, resigned in the summer of 1977. Agosto had served as the Secretary of Labor Affairs and briefly as the Deputy Secretary General to Mari Brás. He was also tasked with other roles dealing with the party's "infrastructure."[66] Although not exactly aligned in perspective with Rentas, Agosto shared his conviction that the PSP's main priority should be the construction of a revolutionary workers' party and that the goal of independence was not achievable without a mass base in the working class. The immediate issue that led to Agosto's leaving had to do with the gnawing problem of establishing priorities.

The poor election results of the previous November had pushed the party to a fork in the road: should its leaders (1) attend to the challenge of building the working-class (proletarian) organization and stick to this project with discipline or (2) develop a response to the new statehood push by forming a united front of independence and anti-statehood forces? Mari Brás and the majority of the Political Commission and Central Committee members argued for the latter, saying the two goals were not mutually exclusive; it was a matter of sequencing them properly and ensuring that the access to the mass sectors attracted to the united front would help the party recruit new members. Agosto, and Rentas before him, countered that the two goals were incompatible given the state of the organization. He also argued that the Annexation Offensive was not as serious as described by Mari Brás and others and that to forestall the necessary course correction (#2) was to indefinitely postpone the development of a working-class party.

In the summer of 1977, this question of priority came to a head when Mari Brás and the majority proposed a leadership seminar to discuss the new political reality of the Annexation Offensive. Agosto countered in the strongest language, saying that the party needed to organize as soon as feasible an emergency Congress to iron out its differences.[67] This divide formed the backdrop to the party's national crisis, yet the full picture was opaque to the vast majority of Seccional members, who sought to focus their work in the diaspora.

As national tensions in the party were coming to a head, repercussions were being felt in the U.S. Branch. Several leaders resigned from their positions for political reasons. Others in the Political Commission were dealing with serious health conditions that limited their participation. In the base nuclei, yet others began formally leaving the organization or simply withdrawing from activity.[68] The toll of uncertainty and overwork was too much for many. Members from different nuclei complained that clear information had not been forthcoming from the Political Commission or the CS.[69]

To address these issues, the CS decided first to improve information flow by creating a group, the *Comisión de Centralismo Democrático* (CCD), to be responsible for publishing the discussions and decisions of the CS; second, the CS moved to elect new members to fill vacant slots. These new recruits would be chosen according to an evaluation of potential candidates recommended by all organisms within the party's structure. One of the problems blocking a true "renovation" of Seccional leadership was the fact that nearly a third of its members had been brought in during the recent past by the CS itself to replace people who had left.[70] In replacing leaders without a selection process involving the base organisms, the CS was violating a central principle of democratic centralism. Later, criticism would arise that the CCD was more concerned with enforcing party discipline than with anything else. In practice, the "centralism" side was being privileged over the "democratic" side of the equation.

These matters were taken up in a CS meeting held in late September. The meeting also revisited the perennial issue of the relationship between the goal of independence (national liberation) and the goal of organizing for the democratic rights (reforms or *luchas reivindicativas*) of Puerto Ricans in the United States. Some CS members posed the concern that in recent months, some base nuclei had relegated the former goal to a secondary level. What should be the clear priority, they argued, was the struggle for independence—specifically in the current moment, the anti–Annexation Offensive campaign, as emphasized by the party nationally.[71] Those who held this view stated that the struggle for reforms was a tactical question, whereas independence was a strategic matter and therefore of greater priority. Formulated in this manner, one could imagine that organizing around basic needs in the diaspora would be left on a secondary plane until independence was achieved.[72] The meeting attendees agreed that this debate would be discussed in the upcoming Seccional's Second Congress. Shortly after the meeting, though, it was decided the Congress would have to be delayed until 1978.

In late February 1978, the CS met on two consecutive weekends. The Political Report prepared for these meetings updated the state of the organization. The party's numbers were stagnant: membership had stayed flat during the previous year, the proportion of militants to affiliates had risen (a negative indicator of future recruitment), the financial picture was weak, sales of *Claridad* had declined by a quarter, and the scale of public activities at the núcleo/chapter level had diminished.[73]

How could the tension between the weak state of the party organization and the need to revive the PSP's contact with the masses be resolved? The Political Report was unable to articulate a clear formula or viable plan of action. It itemized the principal objectives until the next U.S. Branch Congress: (1) holding a Congress in September; (2) organizing in workplaces; (3) strengthening *Claridad*; and (4) maintaining solidarity with advocates for independence, especially ensuring the PSP's presence in local chapters of the Puerto Rican Solidarity Committee (PRSC) and pushing the anti-annexation campaign.[74]

With the last point, PSP leaders hoped that engaging in the current status conflict would lure back former members and followers who had been alienated by the party's internal doldrums. In practice, though, this goal would mean assigning experienced organizers to attend to these initiatives. But many of these were the very same people tasked with following up on the plans for the Congress, workplace organizing, and *Claridad*. Less importance was placed on other areas of work, including democratic rights and political education. Indeed, eleven other objectives were identified.[75] As in the past, these were conceived of as synergistically tied to the overarching priorities of the moment. However, the party organization of mid-1978 was a distant cry from that of mid-1975.

One bright spot in the CS Political Report was that efforts to build a base in workplaces and unions had expanded, especially in New York. Three industries had been targeted: hotels, health care, and retail. In the context of a total private-sector workforce of more than two million workers, the numbers were miniscule. But at least there was growing influence within the American Federation of Labor and Congress of Industrial Organizations (AFL-CIO) Hispanic Labor Committee (HLC), which could potentially serve as a platform for solidarity work. A main obstacle to attaining solidarity from U.S. unions was the PSP's labor policy in Puerto Rico. Its critique of the AFL-CIO's "labor imperialism" and its strategy of organizing independent unions on the island was anathema to U.S. labor officials.[76]

At the same time, political discussions were intensifying as party members were taking a more active role in expressing critiques and alternatives. With the Seccional's Second Congress being planned for the end of 1978, base members did not feel as though they had a deep understanding of the issues on the table. Some believed that the Draft Thesis prepared in the summer and fall of 1977 needed to be rigorously reviewed instead of debated via informal "discussions" that had been programmed. One militant decried the lack of formal political education:

> In recent years our party experience in political education has been nil or in one way or another castrated. . . . [There has been a] disregard for the actual state of the party. . . . The political development of our membership has to be constant until the taking of power, and thereafter in the construction of socialism. Any other thinking repeats the practice we had in relation to the *Acto* in the Garden and the Bicentennial, during which time our political education had no proportionate relation to the objectives we laid out.[77]

A new publication, *Teoría y Práctica*, became a platform for members to air their views on a variety of topics, including the national question, organizational policy, and styles of communication. The first issue contained submissions from party members in Chicago, southern New Jersey/

Pennsylvania, New York, and northern New Jersey. For example, the submission from members of the northern New Jersey chapter argued the need to revisit the party's notion of "cellular multiplication." The organization had emphasized rapid growth over sustainability, and quantity over quality, by forcing smaller chapters (cells or nuclei) to divide prematurely. This directive had resulted partially from the constant pressure from higher leadership (the Political Commission and the Secretariat)—the maladies of *inmediatismo* and *voluntarismo*. But it had also ensued from an inverted application of Leninist organizational convention. When dealing with large urban areas (such as Newark, New Jersey), the priority should have been on placing developed cadre (strong organizers who could serve as spokespersons and policy makers) at an intermediate level (between the city and the "national" center in New York) rather than at the local community/barrio level:

> Under these circumstances the tendency develops for cells to either isolate themselves in a spirit of self-sufficiency and competition or they become satellites of the main cell and thus cannot develop. This situation occurs, in our opinion, when the cells create the committee instead of the opposite. We in Newark have had two experiences with this process.[78]

By the end of the year, U.S. Branch members had participated in *two* congresses: in September, the Second Extraordinary Congress in San Juan, and in December, the Seccional's Second Congress in New York (some two years overdue). Both addressed the debates over the rectification process, and both represented efforts to revise political strategy, based on understandings of new realities in Puerto Rico and the United States. The national organization approved an updated *Programa Socialista*, a 110-page assessment of the situation in Puerto Rico, and new by-laws. The U.S. Branch produced the Tésis Política de la Seccional del Partido Socialista Puertorriqueño (MPI) (Political Thesis of the U.S. Branch of the Puerto Rican Socialist Party [MPI]), a ninety-three-page follow-up to 1973's *Desde Las Entrañas*.

The 1978 *Programa Socialista* signified a major change, charting a new orientation on a variety of positions. In general, it recognized that Puerto Rico did not face a pre-revolutionary situation, which required the PSP to develop a new vision of how to proceed. The reality was that the statehood forces had increased their strength as the independence and socialist forces had lost momentum, and the working classes suffered from a low political conscience (with the exception of unionized public workers).[79] Drawing from Gramscian notions of consensual hegemony, the future required a more sophisticated strategy that would overcome the "old independence ideology that only knew how to respond on the terrain of force and that underestimated the specific weight of mass political struggle and its *eventual* conversion into armed mass struggle" (author's emphasis).[80]

The theme of the San Juan Congress, "Towards a Workers' Party for the Puerto Rico of Today," encapsulated the PSP's new focus. Yet the party faced a special challenge, according to the *Programa*: the lack of a national liberation front that could assume the international terrain:

> The double character of a movement for liberation and the role of a worker's party. . . . [U]nquestionably the theoretical-political base for this double role resides . . . only in the proletariat.[81]

Only the working class had the capacity to give leadership to the struggle for independence, which, in a colony, was the shortest and most powerful path to socialism. With this formulation, the PSP was still clinging to a protagonist role in two major strategic functions. This stance was, in effect, a new compromise by which the PSP hoped to respond to the two perceived demands: independence and socialism. Could a single organization do this?[82]

Returning from San Juan were three dozen militante delegates who had participated actively in the National Congress. They found it well organized, were pleased with the quality of political discussion, and were impressed by the party's renewed commitment to rectifying past practices. But one member was bothered by the changes in Puerto Rico itself, which he had not visited in ten years: "Puerto Rico is being filled with cement where before there were fields. There are many signs in English. . . . I think that our children will not have a place to live."[83] For these delegates the trip meant more than a meeting.

Along with the rest of their compañeras and compañeros, who had stayed behind in the United States while the National Congress met in Puerto Rico, they set forth in the late fall to organize the Second U.S. Branch Congress, which was to take place two months later in New York City. The first day of the three-day conclave, December 8, 1978, was dedicated to Bernardo Vega and Lorenzo Piñeiro—early MPI leaders who had lived many years in the United States—and to the remaining four Nationalists who were still in prison.[84]

The Seccional's challenge was to produce an updated analysis of the Puerto Rican reality in the United States and adjust the party's organizational policy, strategy, and tactics. In contrast to the slogan for the San Juan Congress ("Toward a Workers' Party for the Puerto Rico of Today"), the New York meeting's theme was "For National Survival, Independence and Socialism! Statehood, No Way!"[85] The principal document emanating from

Figure 1.8. U.S. Branch Second Congress at Washington Irving High School, New York City, 1978.

Figure 1.9. Second Congress Political Commission and PSP national leaders.

the congress was a new Political Thesis from the U.S. Branch, which had been in the works since mid-1977.[86]

Unlike *Desde Las Entrañas*, the new document (hereafter referred to as the *Thesis of 1978*) was not distributed widely, nor was it bilingual. The U.S. Branch Congress of 1978 attracted perhaps five hundred people to the closing event at Washington Irving High School; the original goal, first set in early 1977, was for a turnout of two thousand. At the First Congress, held in April 1973 at Manhattan Center, three thousand people had attended the closing event.[87]

Women in the MPI-PSP

From the party's beginning, the role of its women members was fraught with stereotype and tradition. Leadership was heavily male dominated. The compañeras were typically assigned to supportive work areas—taking minutes at meetings, providing nourishment, and so forth. They were not expected to be spokespersons or ideological leaders. The sources of this discrepancy are found in the very structure of all societies; national liberation movements are not immune to the workings of patriarchy.

The symptoms of gender inequality were varied and numerous, but lack of representation in leadership roles was the most obvious. In 1963, the MPI's central leadership (*La Misión Nacional*, in Puerto Rico) was composed of eighteen individuals. Of these, three were women, including Carmen Rivera de Alvarado, in charge of *Acción Femenina* (Women's Action). In 1969, the top leaders were restructured into a smaller group, the twelve-member Political Commission; no women were elected to this body. By the time the MPI had transformed into the PSP, in the founding Congress of late November 1971, the newly elected Political Commission consisted of twelve members, only one of whom, Flavia Rivera Montero, was a woman. In summary, in forty-two leadership "openings" over the first decade, only five women served. During the 1978 Extraordinary Congress in San Juan, Lucía Romero was elected Deputy Secretary General, the highest position held by a woman to that point; the other seven members of the Political Commission were men.[88] In the mid-1980s, Doris Pizarro was named Deputy Secretary General of the PSP.

As for the Seccional, although women were very instrumental in the transition from the MPI to the First Congress of the U.S. Branch in 1973, only one compañera, Digna Sánchez, was part of the first Political Commission, which comprised seven individuals. One positive effect of the rectification period was an increase in women within the Political Commission, as two more—Shelley Karliner and Carmen V. Rivera—were added to that body during the Second Congress.

Patterns of top leadership do not tell the party's whole story. Throughout its history, women were indispensable to the organization. They filled numerous positions, from the Central Committee (and the CS of the U.S. Branch), to the intermediate levels, to the base organizations. Women filled roles in a wide array of functions, including at *Claridad* and in the Secretariat. But their leadership was felt mostly outside of the Political Commission, at the intermediate and base levels.

Another symptom of gender inequality was inconsistency in the performance of entities that were designed to address this problem. A Women's Commission was established on more than one occasion, but follow-through was sporadic. Spokeswomen were delegated to represent the PSP at events commemorating International Women's Day and other occasions. Yet when push came to shove, and resources were stretched by multiple demands, the women's initiatives were relegated to a secondary plane in the work plans.

Differentiation of roles can be seen when the Political Commission and the Secretariat are compared: the former was dominated by males, the latter with a relatively greater presence of females; members of the former were presumed to be the visionaries and strategists; the latter were the implementers. Yet a third center of power, the thirty-member CS, contained an even larger female presence. CS members often criticized the other two bodies of usurping control over party decisions, and in the late 1970s, they gained more direction over the organization, as was the goal stipulated in the 1978 Congresses. The revival of the CCD was largely responsible for this change.

Traditional gender roles led to women's having to cut back their activity levels once they entered motherhood. Child-rearing obligations were assumed to be the domain of the compañeras. Interruptions in activism were more likely for women than men, thus curtailing their potential for advancement.[89]

There was no shortage of statements on the women's question and of Puerto Rican women's essential part in the revolution.[90] Still, there was much to be desired in the implementation of policies and practices that would concretize these words into action.

The idea that sexism was a petit bourgeois defect, rooted in colonialism or capitalism, was enshrined in the party's DNA:

In the defense of the national culture, the Party will maintain, besides, a critical and combative policy against the vices inherited from the colonial-capitalist culture, such as machismo.[91]

As part of the development of proletarian culture, the Party will struggle for the emancipation of the Puerto Rican woman within

the struggle for the emancipation of our nation. For this, it will combat within the Party, as well as within the people, the petit bourgeois
ideas about the role of woman in society and will struggle for the
immediate needs of our women as workers and as women and as
Puerto Ricans.[92]

The possibility that the sources of sexism were transhistorical and not
particular to a specific mode of production (capitalism) or to a particular
class (petit bourgeois) did not seem to be the case, according to these statements. A similar statement could be made about racism in Puerto Rican
society.

Carmen V. Rivera was a leading PSP member throughout the 1970s
and later. In her activism memoir, published in 1998, she speaks critically
of her experience as a woman in the organization. Male leaders' attitudes
toward promoting women's leadership could be rhetorically impressive, but
in practice, they often failed badly. Women who did reach leadership roles
were challenged and tested by men in the base as well as by leading male
cadre. Rivera expresses deep frustration with being stereotyped as *la femi-
nista nuyorquina* (New York feminist), too influenced by the U.S. feminist
movement.

She distinguishes between the overt sexism of PSP members from the
island and the covert sexism of militants from the Seccional: the latter felt
greater pressure to present themselves as a more advanced *hombre nuevo*
(new man). When it came to their personal lives, "many of them talked the
talk but couldn't walk the walk." Household chores and child rearing were
relegated to wives, even if they were active in the organization. Political
education on sexism and the history of women in liberation struggles were
part of the curriculum in study groups, but this inconsistently implemented
effort was not enough to overthrow the culture of machismo. The women
were presumed to be responsible for following through on the detailed
plans; the men specialized as the ideologues, the strategic thinkers.[93]

A feminist consciousness grew gradually in the late 1970s and 1980s,
making way for a rising participation of women in Seccional leadership.
Unfortunately, this achievement of sorts was realized in the context of a
declining organization.[94]

Labor Organization

To describe the working-class character of the PSP's social base, one need
only list the various jobs that members and supporters held. A partial list
of occupations included manual laborers, mechanics, plumbers, service
and maintenance workers of all kinds, social service workers, office clerks,

paraprofessionals, counselors, educators, farmworkers, postal workers and others. They were distributed along a range of industries, but two tendencies dominated: (1) in manufacturing, few were found in unionized, heavy-manufacturing categories and (2) relatively few were found in the public (government) sector, where Puerto Ricans were still just beginning to make inroads. In time, the latter trend changed, as higher education and English-language levels enabled people to enter professional jobs in the private and public sectors.

As the urban economies succumbed to deindustrialization and globalization, more jobs shifted from the private to the public sector, and from manufacturing to service industries. The high residential mobility of Puerto Ricans—whether from movement to other parts of the United States or the result of the *va y ven* (going and coming) between Puerto Rico and the diaspora—complicated organizing efforts. The PSP's capacity for community-based organizing far exceeded that of its capabilities regarding workplace organizing. The Puerto Rican labor force in the diaspora was a far cry from the German industrial proletariat of Karl Marx's day. And in many ways, it even differed from the island's labor-force profile. Nevertheless, the PSP committed to attending to the condition of workers wherever their members were. Following are testimonies from a small sample of the members involved in this area.[95]

Figure 1.10. Puerto Rican Day Parade, PSP contingent, Hoboken, New Jersey.

Voices of Labor Organization

Armengol Domenech started working as a drug counselor at Bronx State Hospital and became active as a union delegate with Local 1199. The most active of the progressive forces in the union was the Communist Party U.S.A. (CP). At the time, the CP and the PSP had established a certain working relationship, following a period during which the CP had not accepted the PSP's legitimacy to organize Puerto Ricans in the United States. Subsequently, Domenech was recruited as an organizer for the International Furniture Workers of America, led by Ennio Carrión, a progressive and a member of the HLC:

> The Hispanic Labor Committee was an organization of presidents and vice presidents . . . that were an advisory council to the New York City Central Labor Council under Harry Van Arsdale. . . . So, we were the experts advising Harry Van Arsdale on Latino issues, Latino organizing. If we're organizing *una fábrica* where there were a lot of Latinos, it was the Hispanic Labor Committee that was there to give support to organize.

The HLC, with Domenech's experienced input, also helped unionize workers at Yale University, New Haven community centers, and a few factories in Connecticut and Massachusetts. PSP nuclei in those areas contributed support.[96]

The party was also active in Local 1199 of the Health-Care Union at a critical moment in its history. In 1982, after long-time president Leon Davis stepped down, the union experienced a struggle for leadership. At the time, many rank-and-file members from the English-speaking Caribbean were of a more conservative bent. They had not been supportive of Davis's leadership, which had been backed by more progressive members, including African Americans and Latino/as, among them PSP members. They enabled the election of Doris Turner, who later removed the more progressive organizers and staff.

Dennis Rivera challenged Turner in the next election. Working from a storefront office that was owned by El Comité–MINP, the opposition ultimately regained the leadership of the union in 1986, with Rivera as the new president. A coalition of rank-and-file members, including leftists and progressives, kept the union in its traditionally progressive stance. Back in the 1960s, 1199 had been described by Dr. Martin Luther King Jr. as his "favorite union."[97]

Employment in the hospitality industry left little room for romantic ideals about labor organizing. It was a sector that presented itself as a luxury product for tourists from around the world, but another reality existed on the inside. Prostitution rings and abusive bosses were not uncommon, and anti-Communist ideology was a norm, thanks to anti-Castro Cubans in the labor force. Whereas the community is a public space protected by a web of political rights, the workplace is a realm of private property, protected by capitalist interests. Protesting conditions in the barrio is quite different from politicizing workers on the shop floor or in the hotel kitchen. There, the worker is acting on the owner's turf.

Hilda González Barreto met her husband, Ismael Barreto, while he was organizing tenants in Bushwick. Eventually, she got involved in the PSP's labor organizing. Her training and socialist commitment led her to become a union delegate in the Hilton Hotel, where she confronted reactionary supervisors and coworkers. On several occasions, her life was threatened, until finally she had to quit her job—as the mother of two boys, she was not taking chances. Hilda recalls the difficulty of activating workers to be involved in the union:

> What happens is that the worker doesn't want to organize or is afraid of losing their job or doesn't realize that organizing is how you liberate yourself, to at least demand more rights. So then [the worker] goes to the union representative, to the delegate [Hilda], but when the [situation] gets hot, they leave you alone—they sell out. Me, for example, what I did was tell the girls, "Come on, let's go—what do you think?" I'[d] look out for our rights, but when it came to making a grievance, it was for me to raise the complaint, but then I'[d] say, "No, *you* tell them!"

José Soler describes some of his labor organizing in a published oral history:[98]

> To me unions were another arena of struggle. . . . We discussed Lenin's writings and the role of the trade unions, and also the whole issue of Gramsci on organic intellectuals in the labor movement.
>
> In building the PSP Labor Committee in New York, we worked with Hotel Workers Local 6. It was mobbed up, but there was one Puerto Rican who was a Vice President, and he opened up doors for us. . . . Some of us worked in hotels, and others worked in the clubs. You know, these were ruling-class clubs. It was interesting. I organized a club and organized the Puerto Ricans and some of the Latin Americans into a workers' movement. We did a little newsletter that we called *Arroz y Habichuelas* [Rice and Beans] every week. We did all kinds of shit, walkouts and all that, and I was also the assistant shop chairman.

[We] saw the Hispanic Labor Committee as a vehicle to get rank-and-file members active in the struggle and as a way to insert issues from the Puerto Rican struggle and democratic right struggles into the U.S. labor movement. . . . We were able to get the Hispanic Labor Committee to sign on for the liberation of the nationalists, like Lolita Lebrón, Rafael Cancel Miranda, Andrés Figueroa Cordero, Irving Flores, and Oscar Collazo, all in U.S. jails.

Myself, Dennis Rivera, and a number of other Puerto Rican, Dominican, and Honduran trade unionists were able to open the doors for rank-and-file union members to be part of the Hispanic Labor Committee of New York, Central Labor Council, which was controlled by Cold Warriors. But we opened the door for trade unionists from Guatemala to talk about the aggression against the Pepsi-Cola workers, as well as workers from Colombia and El Salvador to present their experiences as workers in their national struggles.

Attempts at Renewal

September 1979 occasioned a celebration of freedom and victory for the Puerto Rican movement at large following the release of the four remaining Nationalist revolutionaries who had been incarcerated in federal prisons since the 1950s. Starting in 1970 with a national conference in New York City, initiated primarily by El Comité–MINP, a decade-long campaign had unfolded, culminating in a pardon by President Jimmy Carter. The campaign was a central priority of the Puerto Rican Left in the diaspora, becoming a point of collective unity in action among the different groups.

This multidimensional crusade encompassed a variety of steps, tactics, and coalitional politics. Periodic conferences were held to coordinate publicity and educational activities. In 1972, *Claridad bilingüe* published a surprise, unauthorized interview and photos of Lolita Lebrón in federal prison by reporter Sonia Marrero. This scoop was the first time in two decades that the public had seen Lebrón's image and words. Delegations to the UN and protest marches in Washington, D.C., and major cities were organized. The North American Left and many progressive groups became integral to the solidarity effort. In 1977, a dramatic takeover of the Statue of Liberty was carried out with former members of the Young Lords. An appeal on humanitarian grounds was effective in convincing elected officials, such as Congressman Bobby García, and religious leaders to lobby for the prisoners' freedom.

On their journey home from prison, they were received by jubilant crowds in Chicago; in New York, where a standing-room-only audience of

Figure 1.11. Campaign to free the Nationalist political prisoners.

three thousand in St. Paul the Apostle Church welcomed them; and at San Juan Airport, where five thousand people embraced them as they disembarked from their plane. For PSP members and supporters, and for everyone in the entire movement who had worked tirelessly for the cause of freedom, it was a tremendously satisfying conclusion to a hard-fought cause.[99]

The CS deliberated twice during 1979. In March, a reorganization plan was submitted to follow up on the agreements reached in the Second Congress. With the loss of several experienced members, existing cadre had to be reallocated to principal areas of work (organization, commission on democratic centralism, finances, political education, *Claridad*, and so forth). Others were designated to assist in the development of núcleos. At this time, the PSP had official groups in New York City (in three specific communities), Chicago, New Jersey, Philadelphia, Boston, Hartford, and the Bay Area. Small clusters of supporters also met in areas where no official organization existed but *Claridad* was circulated. The hope was to rebuild the party from this diminished base. The immediate task was to

> evaluate the state of the *núcleos* of the Party. Our priority for this year will be the growth, development and strengthening of the *núcleos*. As well, to reactivate the periphery, and to identify the issues . . . [that] . . . most affect our community.[100]

Other objectives were laid out for the rest of the year: carry out a new census of PSP membership; disseminate programmatic documents; amplify the *Viernes Socialistas* (Socialist Fridays), political-cultural gatherings that often presented political discussion followed by cultural and musical performances and even dances, across all the geographic regions; and activate the special commissions on women, housing, and political education. In keeping with the national priority of building the workers' party, the labor area would focus on the hotel industry in New York.

When the CS met on October 20–21, 1979, it was evident that the restructuring plan developed in March had not accomplished its goals. Work areas still faced unstable leadership, triggering a new round of musical chairs. The Secretariat needed replacements in the areas of organization, political education, labor, and propaganda. *Claridad* was in the throes of a financial crisis. The accumulation of work had revealed "organizational deficiencies." At no point did the Political Commission (which had approved the Political Report submitted by First Secretary Álvarez Febles) voice awareness that the organization was simply being overextended. In the Political Report (*Informe Político*), the committee merely reiterated the priorities that had been approved in the Congress of 1978:

> At all moments we have been guided by [these] priorities—the development of the Party; anti-colonial unity; unity around democratic rights; anti-imperialist, anti-capitalist, and revolutionary unity of the North American people, and solidarity with Puerto Rico. . . . [T]he Political Commission reaffirmed that these represent a correct level of prioritization, [and] decided to not cut the number of areas [of work] but rather to adapt the structure and organization accordingly. It points out the need to balance everything with the development of the revolutionary Party. We have to guarantee the ability to respond adequately to the events that arise day to day. We have to ensure that the Political Commission and Commission of Organization exercise their function.[101]

Once again, it appeared that leadership was falling victim to denial. It took time for some PSP members to recognize their own complicity in this problem.[102]

Voices

Decades later, several PSP members reassessed these events in interviews. Freddie Rodríguez recalls:

In 1976, right after the elections . . . a lot of *compañeros* were hit with the reality of failure, and also it was more real for a lot of people in the base, I think. . . . [The PSP in] Puerto Rico had this major argument that I remember talking to *compañeros* . . . [who argued] for armed struggle [or] . . . developing . . . the party of [the] dictatorship of the proletariat . . . but we were far from thinking like that in New York. And it's not that we questioned the national question. We were questioning the actual activities of how to create roots and to make those roots work.

Others shared thoughtful remarks on the reasons for PSP's shortcomings. Some militants had seemingly contradictory feelings about their experiences. Their assessments were simultaneously positive and negative. That these mixed feelings could be sustained over many years is a sign of how a deep sense of duty could command one's loyalty alongside sharp criticism. PSP base leader Graciano Matos, who earlier described a positive and fulfilling political life in the organization, embodied this sentiment.

As the Bronx Comité president, at one point overseeing several nuclei, Matos was unhappy with the way the PSP handled internal processes and echoed the criticisms levied by other members. Even early on, while active in the East Tremont nucleus, he was troubled by the tendency of upper-level leaders to limit discussion and *planchar las cosas* (steamroll things). As time went on, he became more concerned about the increasingly unrealistic demands of major campaigns. He recalls:

Members were disillusioned and dropped out of the party after the end of every campaign. New members would join, but eventually the exodus became greater than the recruitment of new members. The scenario would repeat itself over and over and over again, to the point where it was impossible . . . to develop a permanent base superstructure. . . . [T]he slow, hard, patient process of building an organization, creating an infrastructure, and developing cadres always took the back seat.

Matos was angry enough that, by 1978, he was starting to wonder:

Why would the organization constantly get involved in campaigns that wore people out, that only burned up human and material resources without getting positive results?

It is true that the *Desde Las Entrañas* clearly stated the need to be involved in social justice struggles. . . . Many of our members were involved in these types of struggles already. What I objected to was the push without consideration as to what the party was going to gain from a given campaign—how was it going to grow ideologically, politically, and organizationally?

Elsa Ríos points to the PSP's difficulty in adjusting to the actual political juncture. Ríos's family came from the farm country of Quebradillas. Her parents found work as factory laborers at the same Brooklyn company, after they came to the United States in the 1940s and 1950s. Her mother was a seamstress, and her father manufactured lamps. She recalls visiting her mother at work as a teenager:

> [I]t was like something out of a Charles Dickens novel. When I walked into the building, it was those large cinder blocks, and they were black of soot . . . and there was this endless sea of women sewing on these large mounds of fabric throughout. It was pretty dark actually. It really sounded like, it really looked like something from the 1800s—it really did.
> [W]e moved around, like most Puerto Ricans . . . we moved around a lot, but always in Brooklyn. So I got to live in Brownsville, Williamsburg, [the] Ridgewood section—Knickerbocker Avenue, that kind of thing—but always in Brooklyn.

The Williamsburg area was a PSP stronghold, and it wasn't long before the precocious Ríos got political and connected with the local nucleus. She "literally grew up in the PSP" and was told that she was the "second-youngest militant" when she joined. Membership was a "rigorous process," with people having an "incredibl[y] high level of analysis." After years of involvement and reflection on why the PSP did not attain its goals, she describes her thinking:

> The revolution around the corner—I'm not sure what could have changed in terms of that because having that sense of urgency provided a real impetus; we're in the middle of change, we're gonna make this happen, it's gonna happen soon, we better be ready, that whole mind-set kind of generated this incredible electricity, energy, and dedication; like, oh my God, if we could just bottle that, we'd be in great shape! But, when the revolution did not come, I think there needed to be a faster pivot to [the idea that] this is long term; we need to address the changing reality of Puerto Ricans . . . in the U.S. and address a more longer-term view of this work, that I don't think it really happened, I don't think it happened.

I remember a lot of our activities being less about what was going on here and more about what was happening in P.R. And after a while, that may have been because the folks in Puerto Rico were insisting upon that, I don't know, but that tension didn't resolve itself in a way that seemed particularly relevant to folks here.

William Cruz was born in Aibonito, a mountain town that sits in the southeastern region of the island. His father was a veteran of the Korean War; his mother worked in a glove factory and was the center of a household that included seven children. After finishing high school in 1969, he enrolled at the Cayey campus of the University of Puerto Rico and joined up with the FUPI. Before long, he was living on the West Side of Manhattan and active in the PSP. He recalls:

Looking back, we were twenty-three or twenty-four years old, and probably because we were so immersed in the movement and in wanting to achieve our goals, we didn't evaluate the situation. We evaluated, but not . . . with the maturity that we have now. Now, we're more mature. There's a question out there now about what were the problems that existed that led to the Seccional's ending. I can talk about that now because it's part of this conversation, that yes, we were young with huge responsibilities that we were obligated to complete because we had developed a strong political consciousness, and we understood the magnitude of what we were doing, that was how we understood it.

Later, we can say no, we weren't able to achieve this or that, but it could have been that when Fidel left Mexico with others, on the *Granma*, and they arrived at the southern part of Cuba, they said, "Us? How did we, being so young do this?" And I imagine you would put your hands on your head in disbelief because that remains marked in history, and we can't deny that period, that work which formed us so incredibly. . . . It formed us and continues to form us. We have not changed. You know what I mean.

For Cruz, his involvement in the struggle within the diaspora signified something other than what the typical members raised in the United States experienced:

[W]henever I think about what we went through, I think—what would have become of me, and probably of other people like me, if I hadn't found myself in New York, where I had raised my political consciousness . . . where I arrived *nuevecito* [brand new]. . . . [W]ell, that was a great experience. For I can say to you [the interviewer] . . . that these days when I meet up with you guys [members from the Seccional] . . . thank you!

The Early Eighties

The year 1980 was projected to be extremely busy, judging by the campaigns and initiatives set out for the party base in late 1979. But the organization's reach far exceeded its grasp, if by grasp we mean the successful translation of activism into organizational growth. This assessment was made at an expanded CS retreat on November 9–10, 1980. The revived CCD reported on the contentious meeting.[103]

It began with a Political Report prepared by the Political Commission officially but in reality authored solely by First Secretary Álvarez Febles. According to the Political Report, the analysis that led to the general vision of the moment and the associated objectives for the year was basically correct. In 1979, there were two main opinions about the political moment:

> In the first place, was the fact that we were facing an annexionist conspiracy in full development, and that this constituted the principal challenge to the Puerto Rican people as far as the patriotic struggle was concerned. . . . [T]he priority [as determined by the Central Committee of the Party] was to detain the annexionist conspiracy. In the second place was the sharpening [*profundización*] of the rightward move on the part of the North American bourgeoisie which had achieved a greater support among significant sectors of the North American people [and that] ha[d] coalesced in the election of a new extremely reactionary president [Ronald Reagan].[104]

These views led to the approval of five objectives for the year. Despite the accuracy of the political analysis, the report emphasized the party's shortcomings in achieving the objectives. The PSP's real problem lay in the difficulty of executing those objectives, mostly due to lack of resources.[105] Yet, on the whole, the organization had a positive year.

Therein followed a tense discussion initiated by a few members, most prominently José E. Velázquez. They critiqued the report for being overly optimistic about the current and future state of the party and for lacking self-criticism by the Political Commission. Further criticism was leveled at the oral presentation of the report, which left members with little time to digest it and prepare for discussion. A vocal minority of the CS argued that top leadership was dancing around the real question: why did the party lack resources? Why was it not growing those resources—meaning human resources—in the form of more members and cadre?

Critics also pointed to the very content of the Political Report, which identified as the greatest challenges during this period the creation of study groups, scanty recruitment, the stagnant number of financial supporters (*cotizantes*), and the distribution of *Claridad*.[106] These were precisely the tasks involving day-to-day party organizing that required their own attentive follow-up, independent of the mass campaigns articulated in the main objectives of 1980. These were also the very tasks that relied on the base núcleos, the organisms that had the most direct contact with communities and workplaces. Yet another complaint was the glaring failure of leadership, after almost two years, to publish the *Thesis of 1978*. It had not been issued until November 1980, and only two hundred copies had been produced. How was the mandate to launch a new recruitment drive around the creation of study circles to take place without having in hand this essential document of political education? This situation made untenable the process of building on the momentum of the Congress of 1978.

Critical members also questioned the report's objectivity when it stated that the Political Commission "ha[d] functioned effectively during the year in terms of its basic tasks, although with great problems due to changes in composition"[107] The retreat ended with unresolved problems and an uneasy lack of unity. As if to underscore the organization's problems, the actual minutes of the proceedings (i.e., the report of the CCD) were not disseminated to the base of the organization until February 1981, a full three months after the gathering.[108] But by then, events in the national PSP had once again overtaken dynamics in the U.S. Branch.

A Short-Lived Compromise

The attempt at Seccional renewal that began in early 1979 was for all intents and purposes aborted in early 1981. This shift occurred when the national party leadership effectively raised doubt about the accords of the National Congress of 1978, saying that privileging the "Workers Party" was too narrow an objective for the PSP and that the political conjuncture called for a strategic opening to encourage non-Marxist sectors to join the PSP. Several factors fed into this calculus: (1) the relative success of the PSP candidates in the 1980 election (Juan Mari Brás and Carlos Gallisá received robust support for their legislative candidacies, even though neither won a seat; Luis Lausell, a labor leader at the top of the PSP slate, also did not do well), "success" being measured in the context of having propagated a socialist platform in the mainstream media and discourse; (2) the realization that building party units in workplaces (especially in the industrial sectors) required long-term, patient organizing with substantial resources; and (3) an assessment that the moment was ripe for a regrouping of independence forces, assuming that the PSP could redefine itself in less ideological (i.e., non-Marxist-Leninist) terms and refrain from electoral ambitions, ceding this terrain to the PIP.

The plan appeared to be to loosen the party's ideological frame and invite a broader membership (for example, being open to adherents of Liberation Theology and to activists in various new social movements). This reformulated PSP, larger and more flexible, would then call for a new anti-colonial united front that could potentially draw in the PIP. In the 1980 election, the PNP governor Carlos Romero-Barcelo' had been reelected, but the *Partido Popular Democrático* (Popular Democratic Party; PPD) had won both legislative houses, signaling a waning of the statehood forces, in the eyes of the PSP.[109]

From the beginning, in early 1981, the proposal provoked opposition, and the internal debates dragged on. Then, on January 11, 1982, Mari Brás announced the PSP's plans to push for a "socialist regrouping." This official proposal was the culmination of the previous year's internal debate.[110] Needless to say, members of the U.S. Branch were caught up in the maelstrom, and the debates consumed much of the U.S. Branch's attention.[111]

Striving for Renewal in the Seccional

The CS convened for six meetings in 1981 and another critical session in the winter of 1982. A new Commission on Seccional Coordination (*Comisión de Coordinación Seccional*) had been charged with gathering data from various internal units and núcleos and assembling reports outlining the fragile state of the organization. Discussions were designed to propose a way forward.

The resolution of April 18, 1982, represented a major moment in the history of the Seccional.[112] The opening section of the nine-page document summarized previous internal reports on the state of the organization. After the last Congress in December 1978, the party had experienced a big drop in membership; this decline continued until mid-1979, after which numbers began to stabilize. Uneven growth levels followed, with areas outside New York characterized by general decline, the base in New York City less so. Between December 1978 and February 1982, *more than a third* of the members had moved, with the largest single flow ending up in Puerto Rico. There was no information on how many of these migrants had continued their involvement in the organization. *Claridad*'s situation was described as "alarming": since November 1978, the paper's circulation had dropped by 35 percent, and outside New York (including such areas as Chicago and Boston), it had fallen by 54 percent. The resolution warned,

"Not reversing this situation will endanger the very existence of the U.S. edition."[113]

The "why" of this dismal picture was multipronged: the effects of the party crisis (national and Seccional) that had seriously weakened the organization during 1978 and 1979; the lack of attention to areas outside New York City; the decline in financial resources, which made it impossible to cover salaries for full-time cadre and *Claridad* staff; the breakdown in consensus among leadership, especially over different conceptions of the precise relationship between party building and mass work; and the problems of subjectivism within various leadership bodies. Recognizing that some of these factors were not under the control of the party, and cognizant that most of the areas of weakness were interconnected (e.g., declining membership and declining resources), the CS could not agree on which problems were more significant than others.

Straining to put a positive spin on the situation, the CS accentuated other points: (1) the party had maintained a certain "visibility and influence in our communities," but this presence varied from place to place, being "very present" in some areas and "almost nil" in others; (2) it had retained a good part of its experienced cadre, many of whom were recognized leaders in the community; and (3) whereas the number of full-time organizers had declined, those who had left had gone on to find jobs in places that enabled them to continue their socialist organizing, which "represent[ed] an achievement and implie[d] a potential that should not be underestimated."[114]

The priority going forward was identified as "the ideological and organizational strengthening of the party." This task was to involve two stages of implementation: (1) participating in the National Congress, scheduled for October 1982; and (2) conducting the Third Seccional Congress, to take place in the spring of 1983. Numerous aspects of this strengthening process were delineated, from organizing internal forums for debating views on strategy and tactics, to assigning CS members to specific base núcleos to assist in the rebuilding process, to providing clearer guidance on how local núcleos should engage in mass work around concrete issues. Four such issues were specified: (1) responding to the Reagan-inspired attacks on economic conditions; (2) answering the recent annexationist maneuvers; (3) addressing the rise in repression against the independence movement (alluding to the case of *Fuerzas Armadas de Liberación Nacional* [Armed Forces of National Liberation; FALN] activists); and (4) supporting the universal struggle for nuclear disarmament and the solidarity movement for Central America, especially El Salvador.

An overarching theme was a commitment to rooting the party's direct work in Puerto Rican communities and labor and university spaces with a strong Puerto Rican/Latino presence; to maintaining an independent and robust profile within coalitions; and to conveying messages that were consistently anti-imperialist, anti-capitalist, and pro-independence. The resolution included an updated articulation of the always contentious link between the goals of national liberation and democratic rights:

> The potential for mass struggle against Reagan's socio-economic policies and political influence that this struggle can generate makes it possible to broaden the support for the Dellums Resolution, for Vieques and other related issues, in the Congress and other government forums. Congressman Dellums has indicated to us on numerous occasions that it is necessary that members of Congress feel pressure in their local districts [*bases políticas*] to support the resolution if the resolution is to acquire greater resonance and support. This applies especially to those congressmen with Puerto Rican bases, and we Puerto Ricans are one of the factors they need to take into account to get re-elected. . . . The same vision can be applied to municipal and state governments.[115]

It would be a mischaracterization to depict the U.S. Branch as being secluded from mass work during this period of attempted renewal. After its Second Congress (1978), the organization had a weakened profile, all the more evident when compared to its growing scale of operations from 1969 to the mid-1970s. Yet it was still able to exert a socialist presence in several arenas, whether in solidarity work, concerns regarding democratic rights, or, eventually, the mainstream electoral process.

Through núcleos, special commissions, and *Claridad*, PSP members were active protagonists or supporters in an array of campaigns and projects. At the risk of simplification, an inventory (covering 1979–1984) may suggest the validity of this point. Examples in areas dealing with solidarity work and Puerto Rico's independence include support for Puerto Rico's case at the UN Decolonization Committee; mobilizations on behalf of the struggles in Central America; the campaign to free the Nationalist prisoners and their victorious release (1979); support for Fidel Castro's visit to New York (1979); anti-repression protests and defenses; the Vieques Solidarity Network; and support for the PSP's electoral campaign in Puerto Rico (1980). Examples in the area of democratic rights include advocacy for housing conditions and community reinvestment through the South Bronx People's Convention (1980), protests at the Democratic National Convention (1980), and participation in the National Congress for Puerto Rican Rights (1981 onward). Part of the PSP's increasing participation in electoral work, first as an independent force and then within the left wing of the Democratic Party, included campaigns in support of Frank Barbaro, Gilberto Gerena Valentín, and José Rivera (in New York City); Harold Washington (in Chicago); and Mel King (in Boston).[116]

The Third Seccional Congress

The Third Seccional Congress was held in May 1983 in El Barrio, Manhattan.[117] Six months earlier, in San Juan, the national PSP's Extraordinary Congress had failed to resolve the ideological differences within the organization. The ripple effects of this congress on the U.S. Branch were immediate: many members resigned in the lead-up to the Third Seccional Congress, and at least four ten-year veterans had withdrawn from the PSP by the end of the year.[118]

Members approved a new theoretical/programmatic document, *Partido Socialista Puertorriqueño: Suplemento de Tesis* (hereafter referred to as the *Thesis of 1983*), that was intended to update the *Thesis of 1978*.[119] It analyzed anew the contemporary conjuncture and redefined the party's role in the United States. (The final version of the *Thesis of 1983* was released later in the year, after feedback from Congress discussions had been incorporated.) It also reviewed the history of the Seccional from the MPI days. In tone and messaging, it reassured the reader that despite the crises of recent years (in the Seccional and in the PSP nationally), the organization was committed to a vision of "inclusion" for Boricua struggles in the diaspora, beyond the traditional focus on solidarity.[120] Within the thirty-six-page document, however, the message was not that clear, if by "inclusion" one expected to encounter specific and unambiguous guidance on the strategic importance of democratic rights.[121] Two examples, selected from several similar passages, illustrate this confusion:

> The Second *Seccional* Congress culminated a discussion process . . . that achieved a greater emphasis on the importance of the democratic rights and social demand struggles of Puerto Ricans in the US *within the context* of our revolutionary struggle and of the priority of struggle for independence *above* that of the struggle for revolutionary change in the U.S. (author's emphasis)[122]
>
> The seccional of the PSP in the US exists *above all* to organize the participation of Puerto Ricans in the struggle for independence and socialism in Puerto Rico. Our strategic function is to develop in the "belly of the beast" the struggle for national liberation of the Puerto Rican people in its full breadth. This *implies* that our work will also embrace the struggles of Puerto Ricans in the US for their democratic rights. (author's emphasis)[123]

Another source reported on discussions in the base prior to approval at the Congress itself. According to several pre-Congress documents, members provided feedback conveying numerous concerns about the Seccional's vision for the future:

> [The] conclusion that the principal idea [*eje principal*] should be the national liberation struggle should not be applied mechanically, without taking into account the needs of Puerto Ricans in the US. . . . There's no consistency across the document; too many things are brought up in the abstract. The proposal about democratic rights varies in emphasis in different parts of the document. What's lacking is a coherent vision of work, setting guidelines that have ideological coherence. . . . We should specify that democratic rights are a priority in our work, in what we concentrate. . . . [I]ndependence is [also] a democratic right. . . . Even though [the document] says there is no contradiction between the democratic rights struggle and the strategic struggle for independence, the tone implies some contradiction. . . . Projecting democratic rights as reformist tends to focus the goal on independence and national liberation in an unbalanced way.[124]

Shortly after the Third Congress, José Soler writes in *Claridad*:

> The Third *Seccional* Congress of the PSP that culminated last month established that there is no more important task for Puerto Rican socialists in the US than the reconstruction of the Party and assuring the growth of our *Claridad*. . . . The Congress also discussed the campaign for Lares in the United Nations as the principal Party [campaign] until September. . . . [I]t is important to emphasize in this context . . . [that] we are not talking about closing ourselves off and abandoning mass work. On the contrary we propose retaking the street, being present in the Puerto Rican struggles against the outrages of the Reagan administration.[125]

Toward the end of 1983, Mari Brás resigned from the PSP, which he had led since the early days of the MPI in 1959. During the crisis period, he had hinted about his desire to step down as Secretary General; now he was leaving the organization altogether. He declared his intention to help build a united independentista front and said that his identity as the long-time spokesperson of the PSP would hamper these efforts.[126] It appeared that the PSP was returning to the original MPI vision of a multiclass united front.

Figure 1.12. U.S. Branch Third Congress and new leadership. *Left to right:* José Alberto Álvarez Febles, Olga Iris Sanabria Dávila, Digna Sánchez, José Soler, and María Vázquez (José Berrios, MC at the microphone).

Mari Brás insisted that the PSP would still have a vanguard role to play, although not as a Marxist-Leninist entity. The organization forged ahead under the leadership of Carlos Gallisá, who had been elected Secretary General in the National Congress of 1982.

Last Plans, Last Efforts

Through the rest of the 1980s and into the early 1990s, a devoted, but diminishing, core of members pressed on, following the shifting paths determined at the national level.

A new round of solidarity activities was planned around the traditional celebrations of *El Grito de Lares* (the Cry of Lares), the educational and lobbying work at the UN, and a new effort to create a Latin American Committee for solidarity with Puerto Rico. These tasks were accompanied by the party's commitment to stay involved in the National Congress of Puerto Rican Rights and to explore electoral avenues in Brooklyn and the Bronx.[127]

In the fall of 1984, the new CS took up the topic of electoral policy with regard to the approaching U.S. presidential elections. By that time, the Jesse Jackson campaign had successfully tapped into a wealth of progressive and left activism, although it was ultimately a losing cause. The "Latinos for Jackson" campaign had recruited many radical activists into its fold, including some PSP members. Once Jackson was no longer a candidate, the

PSP had to figure out a position consonant with its historical resistance to voting for bourgeoise candidates. Ultimately, it decided on a two-pronged approach: (1) mount a campaign to denounce Reagan and his policies through education and voter registration and (2) support progressive anti-imperialist candidates at *the local level* rather than encourage people to vote for the Walter Mondale/Geraldine Ferraro ticket. By implication, the PSP was not calling on Puerto Rican voters to actually vote for the Democratic candidate for president, even though most voting Puerto Ricans saw supporting the Democratic candidates as "the only viable electoral method of defeating Reagan."[128]

In 1985 and 1986, activists in anti-imperialist and solidarity movements in the United States turned their attention to supporting the Nicaraguan revolution. The PSP joined this effort, calling on Puerto Rican and Latino communities to denounce the U.S. attempt to overthrow the Sandinista government. Of particular concern was a Reagan administration proposal to militarize Puerto Rico as a base of operations to support the "Contras," which included a plan to install nuclear arms on the island, as reported by the *New York Times*.[129]

Toward the end of the 1980s, the island was once again thrust into the mire of plebiscite debates, and the Seccional was inevitably drawn into the fray. Although the organization had always decried plebiscites as a distraction from the real questions, it could not ignore the contest, which was only an opinion poll as far as the U.S. Congress was concerned. The PSP organized events in several cities to revive connections with former members, with the goal of securing statements on the "right to self-determination and decolonization of the people of Puerto Rico that will be taken to [a] congressional hearing in July . . . [and] [i]n addition, at the United Nations Decolonization Committee Puerto Rico Hearings."[130]

In the fall of 1991, PSP members set up a forum in Manhattan to have Gallisá speak about a potential regrouping of independence forces. Called the *Nuevo Proyecto Político*, it was a last-ditch effort at constructing a PSP-driven umbrella entity. A list of "21 programmatic bases" would serve as a starting point for discussion.[131]

While these activities offered proof of life, the reality of shrinking resources, human and material, could not be denied. Declining membership, partly due to members who relocated to Puerto Rico, led to the de facto elimination of the CS, which had been reduced from thirty to fifteen elected militants at the Third Congress. In its stead was formed a Coordinating Committee (*Comité Coordinador*) that supervised all tasks, including *Claridad*. Personal obligations and leaves of absence undercut the Political Commission, which had been reduced from seven to five members at the 1983 Congress. Debts piled up, rent was overdue, and the modest storefront headquarters in El Barrio had to be abandoned.[132] A work plan for 1990 proposed two events focusing on democratic rights: a conference on the status of Puerto Ricans in the diaspora and a "People's Tribunal" on the economic crisis. Neither was realized.[133]

As long as the PSP positioned itself as the convener and protagonist for a *Nuevo Proyecto Político*, it was unable to arouse significant interest among independentistas, even from Mari Brás and the followers of his new project. But in 1993, a broader and less-ideological entity did emerge as a new compromise. The organization was called the New Movement for Puerto Rican Independence (*Nuevo Movimiento Independentista* [NMI]). The PSP backed it all the way and, as evidence of its commitment, announced that it would *dissolve itself* in favor of the new formation. On October 5, 1993, at its Constituent Assembly in San Juan, the NMI was established, and the PSP immediately ceased to exist.[134] The remaining Seccional members and informal supporters followed suit, some (in Newark and Chicago, for example) later saying that they had never left the PSP—the PSP had left them. The singular thread that tied the new formation with its origins was *Claridad*, which persevered as a weekly publication and as a discussion point for many independentista activists.[135]

As they approached the millennium, the remnants of the former PSP, along with all the independentistas and *socialistas* who had ever participated in it and all the other anti-colonialists who had ever differed with it, faced a challenging future for the liberation of Puerto Rico. But to this day, neither the flame of hope nor the spirit of resistance has been tamed.

NOTES

1. This book focuses on one organization, the MPI-PSP, and its history within the United States. Well before the time period covered here, since the era of Spanish rule, pro-independence groups were organizing among the Puerto Rican population in the United States. See, for example, Jesús Colón, *A Puerto Rican in New York* (New York: Mainstream Publishers, 1961); Joaquín Colón López, *Pioneros Puertorriqueños en Nueva York, 1917–1947* (Houston: Arte Público Press, 2002); César J. Ayala and Rafael Bernabé, *Puerto Rico in the American Century: A History since 1898* (Chapel Hill: University of North Carolina Press, 2007), 113–116; and Roberto P. Rodríguez-Morazzani, "Linking a Fractured Past: The World of the Puerto Rican Old Left," *Centro Boletin* 7, no. 1 (Winter 1994/Spring 1995): 20–30.

2. In 1960, 877,000 Puerto Ricans resided in the United States. U.S. Commission on Civil Rights, *Puerto Ricans in the Continental United States: An Uncertain Future* (Washington, DC: U.S. Commission on Civil Rights, 1976), 19.

3. Mimeographed copy of typed speech with handwritten notation, "Por Don Carlos Maldonado, 1962." Archives of the ¡*Despierta Boricua!* Recovering History Project, hereafter referred to as "PSP Archives." All translations from Spanish to English are by the author, unless otherwise indicated. Arturo Morales Carrión was a historian and defender of the Commonwealth government; he was appointed by President John F.

Kennedy to the U.S. State Department in the area of Inter-American Affairs. Gordon K. Lewis, *Puerto Rico: Freedom and Power in the Caribbean* (New York: Harper Torch-books, 1968), 24.

4. *Carta Semanal*, March 7, 1964, PSP Archives.

5. Tamara Ferrer, "Firme tras 40 años de lucha," *Claridad*, May 1973.

6. *Carta Semanal*, 1.

7. Ibid.

8. "A La Communidad Puertorriqueña en Nueva York," July 25, 1966; mimeo correspondence, signed by Pedro Juan Rúa, Secretary of Organization, MPI, Vito Marcantonio Mission, PSP Archives.

9. The Voices sections in this chapter include excerpts from interviews conducted by the editors and other contributors. All interviews are in the PSP Archives.

10. *Movimiento Pro Independencia* (MPI), *La Hora de la Independencia de Puerto Rico* (San Juan, Puerto Rico: Misión Nacional del MPI, 1963), 9.

11. See Wilfredo Mattos Cintrón, "Breve historia del MPI y del PSP," *En Rojo, Claridad*, January 12–18, 1979, 2–14; and Juan Mari Brás, "Informe del Comité Central," *Colegio de Abogados*, San Juan, October 22, 1982.

12. *Movimiento Pro Independencia, La Hora de la Independencia de Puerto Rico.*

13. Mattos Cintrón, "Breve historia del MPI y del PSP," 6. Mattos Cintrón also notes that *La Hora* acknowledges that it is "not Marxist-Leninist and that it is inserted in the frame of Christian tradition"; ibid.

14. Ibid., 6–9.

15. *Movimiento Pro Independencia, Presente y Futuro de Puerto Rico* (Rio Piedras, Puerto Rico: Misión Nacional del MPI *Movimiento Pro Independencia*, 1969). In April 1968, the MPI celebrated its Seventh National Assembly, approving the basic points of what would become *Presente y Futuro*, published in July of the following year.

16. Ibid., 37–38. Mattos Cintrón argues that the document really postulated a less than rigorous commitment to the idea of working-class preeminence. Under an independent Puerto Rico, workers "in the national interests" might have to adopt "conciliatory measures between workers and industrialists" regarding salary demands. In Mattos Cintrón's view, this language hinted at future problems. Mattos Cintrón, "Breve historia del MPI y del PSP," 7.

17. *Movimiento Pro Independencia, Presente y Futuro*, 58–59.

18. Ibid., 73–74.

19. In April 1969, Mari Brás went on a tour of the United States to gain North American support. Speaking at Harvard University, he appealed to the radical left: "It is our vehement message to the North American friends that want to cooperate with the cause of our independence, that this reality be transmitted to more and more North Americans that we know are not part of the imperialist structure that dominate this country." Juan Mari Brás, *The New Struggle for Puerto Rico's Independence* (Boston: New England Free Press, 1969), 6.

20. *Movimiento Pro Independencia, Proyecto de Declaración General* (New York: MPI, 1970). From the mid-1960s to about 1970, leadership of the MPI in the United States consisted of a succession of coordinating teams. Some of the known figures include Angelo Alicéa, Rafael Baerga, Arlene Bayó, Dixie Bayó, Ramón Cintrón, Armengol Domenech, José Antonio Irizarry, Carmen Ortíz, Victor "Marcianito" Santiago, and Isolina "Cuca" Vargas.

21. Ibid., 2.

22. Ibid., 3.

23. Ibid.

24. Ibid.

25. Ibid., 2.

26. Ibid., 3.

27. Partido Socialista Puertorriqueño, Comité de Nueva York, "El Partido en Estados Unidos," November 14, 1971. Elements of this four-page position paper were incorporated into *La Declaración General* of the new PSP.

28. Ibid., 2.

29. Ibid.

30. Ibid.

31. Ibid., 3.

32. Between 1969 and 1971, other position papers and statements were discussed by MPI's membership in preparation for the impending change. They included (1) "Declaración Política . . . Borrador" (probably written mid-1970); mimeo, 4 pp.; (2) José A. Irizarry, "Ponencia Sobre los Objetivos a Corto Plazo y a Largo Plazo" (probably 1970), 8 pp.; (3) "Política Organizativa del *Movimiento Pro Independencia* en Nueva York" (probably 1970), mimeo, 4 pp.; and (4) MPI, "Borrador de la Declaración General a ser sometida a la Octava Asamblea Nacional del MPI, el 19 de Noviembre, 1971" (New York, November 14, 1971), 5 pp. These fed into the two official statements discussed in this section.

33. This is a personal interpretation of the author.

34. Iris Morales, *Through the Eyes of Rebel Women: The Young Lords: 1969–1976* (New York: Red Sugarcane Press, 2016), 39.

35. Rose Muzio, *Radical Imagination, Radical Humanity* (Albany: State University Press of New York, 2017), 129–132.

36. More examples of intergroup collaboration are described in Basilio Serrano, "*¡Rifle, Cañón, Escopeta!:* A Chronicle of the Puerto Rican Student Union," in *The Puerto Rican Movement: Voices from the Diaspora*, ed. Andrés Torres and José E. Velázquez (Philadelphia: Temple University Press, 1988), chap. 7.

37. The following paragraphs are partially drawn from Andrés Torres, *Signing in Puerto Rican: A Hearing Child and His Deaf Parents* (Washington, DC: Gallaudet University Press, 2009), chap. 10; and Andrés Torres, "Juan Mari Brás y los comienzos de la Seccional del PSP en Estados Unidos," *Claridad*, November 29–December 5, 2007, 52–53.

38. Delegates to the CS were selected by base nuclei and work areas (such as the Secretariat and *Claridad*) that had been formed in the prior period. Members of the Political Commission were Ramón Arbona (First Secretary), José Alberto Álvarez Febles, Alfredo López, Jesús López, Digna Sánchez, Andrés Torres, and José E. Velázquez. There was no direct election of the Political Commission. Although no criticism was voiced at the time, Arbona simply presented a slate of candidates to the CS for ratification. Author recollection.

39. See the chapters by Ángel A. Amy Moreno de Toro (Boston) and José E. Cruz (Hartford) in *The Puerto Rican Movement: Voices from the Diaspora*, ed. Andrés Torres and José E. Velázquez (Philadelphia: Temple University Press, 1998). While Amy Moreno de Toro's work is a generally positive recounting, Cruz presents a more skeptical and critical evaluation of the PSP's history in Hartford.

40. Peter Khiss, "20,000 Rally Here for Puerto Rican Independence," *New York Times*, October 24, 1974, 35.

41. See Chapter 13 by Rosa Borenstein and Chapter 7 by Alfredo López in this volume for more discussion on El Acto Nacional.

42. Another account of the clash is offered in Sonia Nieto, "The BC 44, Ethnic Studies, and Transformative Education," in *Latino Civil Rights in Education: La Lucha Sigue*, ed. Anaida Colón-Muñiz and Magaly Lavadenz (New York: Routledge, 2016), 72–87.

43. The victory of the Puerto Rican/Latino Studies Department at Brooklyn College has endured for decades. The department became a mainstay institutional center for the academic field and for Boricua communities throughout Brooklyn. It has also been a crucial resource to the Puerto Rican Studies Association (PRSA), which is still active.

44. José Alberto Álvarez Febles, *Proyecto de País vs Proyecto de Estado* (Editorial Luna Llena, 2016), 126, 127. After returning to Puerto Rico in the mid-1980s, Álvarez Febles remained active in the independentista movement, seeking a broader unity among anti-colonial sectors. In 2017, he died tragically, a casualty of Hurricane María.

45. To this day, efforts to obtain classified information on police investigations have been blocked by the U.S. Department of Justice.

46. A congressional classified hearing was actually held in July of the previous year. U.S. Committee on the Judiciary, TERRORISTIC ACTIVITY: *The Cuban Connection in Puerto Rico; Castro's Hand in Puerto Rican and U.S. Terrorism* (Washington, DC: U.S. Government Printing Office, July 30, 1975).

47. For more on the Bicentennial campaign, see Chapter 14 by Ted Glick and Chapter 15 by Alyssa Ribeiro in this volume.

48. Cubans who were active for several years included Tomás Azcuy, Dagmaris Cabezas, Jorge Capote, Mauricio Gastón, and María Valdoquín. Other members hailed from the Dominican Republic, Nicaragua, and Peru.

49. The late Denis Berger was a staunch supporter of the Cuban Revolution and a volunteer in the first Venceremos Brigade in 1969. In 1972, while living in Springfield, Massachusetts, he and his wife, Alice, came in contact with PSP organizers from Hartford, Connecticut. They soon joined local residents Raquel Rodríguez and Ramón Cruz Santos to form a núcleo in Springfield. In the summer of 1974, Denis and Alice relocated to New York City (where they were from originally) to work in the main offices of the Seccional. Denis was instrumental in the development of various business projects, such as the bookstore Libro Libre and the speakers' bureau Voices of the Third World. He also organized several tours of cultural performers from Puerto Rico. He was elected to the CS and as a delegate to two National PSP Congresses. Alice worked with the PRSC and was in charge of press relations for El Acto Nacional. She also acted for several years as an administrator for *Claridad bilingüe*. Other North Americans who became militantes included Jeff Perry, Jill Hamberg, Toby Bergman, and Larry Garvin. Two outstanding scholar-activists, James Blaut and Richard Levins, were connected with the independentista struggle in Puerto Rico and in the United States. They provided vital intellectual resources to the Seccional.

50. Puerto Rican Socialist Party, *Desde Las Entrañas—Political Declaration of the United States Branch of the Puerto Rican Socialist Party* (New York, April 1973), 47.

51. As a candidate for governor, Juan Mari Brás received eleven thousand votes. Other island-wide PSP candidates did better: Carlos Gallisá garnered forty-three thousand votes while competing for an at-large Senate seat, and well-known labor leader Pedro Grant received twenty-two thousand votes for an at-large representative position. *Manual de Afiliados*, 41, PSP Archives.

52. "Informe Secretariado Presentado al Comité Seccional—Enero 1977," PSP Archives.

53. "Informe Político al Comité Seccional," January 29, 1977, PSP Archives. Other internal documents capturing the discussions in this period were drafted: "Resolution

Approved by the Comité Seccional del PSP, en el día 10 de febrero de 1977" and "Informe de la discusión de la membresía sobre la Resolución del Comité Seccional," both in the PSP Archives.

54. Also muted, for the time being, were concerns about the *caudillismo* (charismatic, often autocratic, leadership style) that was typical in Latin American and Puerto Rican politics and that critics said should have been eliminated in the MPI's transition to the PSP.

55. "Resolución, Documento de Consenso Aprobado por el Comité Seccional del Partido Socialista Puertorriqueño, el 24 de abril, 1977 despues de ser discutida y enmendada por la base de la Seccional," PSP Archives.

56. Ibid., 1.

57. Ibid., 2.

58. Ibid., 8.

59. Ibid.

60. "Informe Político—Comité Seccional, Reunión del 14 y 15 de Mayo, 1977" (second draft), PSP Archives.

61. These various reports were submitted on May 14–15, 1977, and are available in the 1977 Secretariat records in the PSP Archives.

62. "Informe Político—Comité Seccional, Reunión del 14 y 15 de Mayo, 1977" (first draft), 1.

63. "Informe Político—Comité Seccional, Reunión del 14 y 15 de Mayo, 1977" (first draft); the comment here refers to the section "Prioridades Tácticas en el plano de las luchas reivindicatívas."

64. "Informe Político—Comité Seccional, Reunión del 14 y 15 de Mayo, 1977" (second draft), 3.

65. An ancillary memo proposed a work plan to prepare for the Second Congress: "Hacia el Segundo Congreso Seccional, Esbozo de un Plan de Trabajo para el Congreso, Sometido 14 y 15 de mayo del 1977 al Comité Seccional," PSP Archives. Among the tasks: producing a new Seccional Thesis to update *Desde Las Entrañas* and creating a new set of by-laws. A goal of two thousand attendees was set as the turnout for the closing (public) session of the Congress. A tentative date was proposed for late November of 1977.

66. This language was code for the clandestine operations of the organization, as Agosto details in his riveting and remarkably frank description of his experience. Ángel M. Agosto, *Lustro de Gloria* (Rio Grande, Puerto Rico: LaCasa Editora de Puerto Rico, 2009).

67. "I will not lend myself to participation in a farce that has no purpose other than to distract the attention of our militants from the grave ideological problems . . . that shakes party life this moment. These problems, at this point, can be faced satisfactorily only through the celebration of party congress within a few weeks, convened and organized in a form that guarantees, without a doubt, true socialist democracy. . . . I accuse in this moment the present Central Committee—excepting several members of this body—and very specially the Political Commission of breaking up [*destrozando*] our party." Ibid., 176.

68. José La Lúz and Shelley Karliner, both militants since 1971, and both members of the Political Commission, resigned from their posts; La Lúz resigned for political reasons, and Karliner resigned for health reasons. Two other long-standing CS members also resigned from that body. "Memo: Con el presente informe . . . ," CS, October 1977, 1, 4, PSP Archives.

69. *La Carta Roja* was the internal communication newsletter. Normally published biweekly by the Secretariat, it had fallen into an irregular printing schedule.

70. "Memo: Con el presente informe . . . ," 4.

71. Ibid., 5.

72. The matter was complicated by a situation that arose during the year when an affiliate member of the party decided to run for the Hartford City Council on the Democratic Party line, violating official policy. Letter to Edwin Vargas from Andrés Torres, September 25, 1977. PSP Archives.

73. "Informe Político del Comité Seccional, Reunión del 18, 19, 26 de febrero del 1978," 26–29.

74. Ibid., 36. Later in the spring, the U.S. Branch Congress was postponed until December, *after* the National Congress, which was to be held in October.

75. Ibid., 36–37.

76. Ibid., appendix on Labor Report.

77. "Political Education and the Apparent Contradiction with Discussions toward the National and U.S. Branch Congress," William Cruz, letter to the CS, February 22, 1978, PSP Archives.

78. "The Committee as a Possible Starting Point," Northern New Jersey Zone, in *Teoría y Práctica*, February 1978, PSP Archives. The piece went on to narrate a detailed account of recent experience.

79. *Breve historia del Partido Socialista Puertorriqueño*, San Juan, Puerto Rico, n.d., 54, PSP Archives.

80. Ibid., 47.

81. *Programa Socialista*, San Juan, Puerto Rico, November 1978, 63–64.

82. There was, of course, the PIP, larger and with a longer history. But the PIP had rejected all overtures for a broad front, although it sought independentista-socialist support at the ballot box. Other leftist and nationalist groups were resistant to accepting PSP leadership on a continuing basis, preferring ad hoc collaboration.

83. Milga Morales Nadál, "Delegados al Congreso Opinan," *Claridad*, October 6–12, 1978, 12.

84. Olga Sanabria, "El *Movimiento Pro Independencia* en Nueva York (II): Entrevista a Marciano Santiago y Tomás Ascuy," *Claridad*, November 17–23, 1978. The fifth Nationalist, Andrés Figueroa Cordero, had been released previously, ill with cancer. He died in March 1979.

85. In Spanish, "¡Por La Supervivencia Nacional Independencia y Socialismo! ¡La Estadidad No Va!"

86. *Tésis Política de la Seccional del Partido Socialista Puertorriqueño (MPI)*, New York, U.S. Branch, PSP, 1978, PSP Archives.

87. Elections for the CS led to turnover in its membership. A change also took place in the Political Commission; its new composition consisted of José Alberto Álvarez Febles (First Secretary), Andrés Torres (Deputy First Secretary), José "Dukey" Gonzalez, Alfredo López, Carmen V. Rivera, Digna Sánchez, and José Soler. Since 1975, two others had served on the Political Commission: José La Luz and Shelley Karliner. Both had resigned before the Second Congress. It should also be noted that two militantes who had strong ties to the national leadership made significant contributions to the Seccional at different junctures of its history. One was Rafael Anglada, who was essential to its international work, and the other was Antonio Gaztambide, a former national Secretary of Finances and member of the national Political Commission, who came to the United States to pursue doctoral studies.

88. *Breve historia del Partido Socialista Puertorriqueña*, Wilfredo Mattos Cintrón, pamphlet issued under the auspices of Manuel de Afiliados, second in a series; no date, but known to appear during 1979; published by PSP, San Juan, Puerto Rico; 15, 19, 24–25, 58.

89. See Chapter 4 by Maritza Arrastía in this volume. Chapter 13 by Rosa Borenstein, who worked closely with the PSP although she was not a member, describes a similar situation.

90. For example, *Declaración General Asamblea Constituyente* (Rio Piedras, Puerto Rico, Ediciones Puerto Rico, 1972), 64–65; "Resolution on Puerto Rican Women," in Resolutions Section, *Desde Las Entrañas*, 1973; *Tesis Politica de la Seccional del PSP*, 1978, 36–37, 83–85; and *Suplemento de Tesis, Partido Socialista Puertorriqueño, Tercer Congreso Seccional*, 1983, 26–27.

91. "El Partido en EEUU," mimeo, November 1971, 3, PSP Archives.

92. Ibid., 4.

93. Carmen V. Rivera, "Our Movement: One Woman's Story," in *The Puerto Rican Movement: Voices from the Diaspora*, ed. Andrés Torres and José E. Velázquez (Philadelphia: Temple University Press, 1998), 204–206.

94. Fast-forwarding to current times, it is noteworthy that social justice movements in Puerto Rico and in the diaspora are accompanied by several women-led and women-focused formations. The rise of autonomous female organizations is perhaps a main lesson learned from the decline of independence organizations of the past.

95. The PSP's labor work was directed from the Secretariat of Union Affairs (*Secretaría de Asuntos Sindicales*), and a number of militants were assigned to this area beginning in 1970, during the MPI's transition to the PSP. A long line of cadre had been involved in coordinating this work, including Angelo Alicea, Ramón Cintrón, Armengol Domenech, Shelley Karliner, David Santiago, José Soler, and Andrés Torres, to name a few.

96. The New Haven nucleus included community residents and students from Yale University and other campuses: Carlos Juliá, Palmira Ríos, José Rodríguez, Judith Berkan, and Roberto Cantú.

97. Armengol Domenech interview; "Leon Davis, 85, Head of Health-Care Union, Dies," *New York Times*, September 15, 1992.

98. Eric Larsen, "José Soler: A Life Working at the Intersections of Nationalism, Internationalism, and Working-Class Radicalism," *Radical History Review* 128 (May 2017): 63–76. Sadly, José Soler passed away in 2020.

99. Muzio, *Radical Imagination, Radical Humanity*, 129–136; José E. Velázquez, "Another West Side Story: An Interview with Members of El Comité–MINP," in *The Puerto Rican Movement: Voices from the Diaspora*, ed. Andrés Torres and José E. Velázquez (Philadelphia: Temple University Press, 1998), 88–106; Sonia Marrero, "Lolita Lebrón desde la prisión," *Claridad bilingüe*, March 19, 1972; Borenstein, Chapter 13 in this volume; Glick, Chapter 14 in this volume; Mary Breasted, "30 in Puerto Rican Group Held in Liberty Island Protest," *New York Times*, October 26, 1977; Miguel Meléndez, *We Took the Streets: Fighting for Latino Rights with the Young Lords* (New York: St. Martin's Press, 2003), 199–212; Tony Schwartz, "Two Freed Nationalists Say They Can't Rule Out Violence," *New York Times*, September 12, 1979; reports of the PSP's CS, 1972–1980, PSP Archives; and Meg Starr, "'Hit Them Harder': Leadership, Solidarity, and the Puerto Rican Independence Movement," in *The Hidden 1970s: Histories of Radicalism*, ed. Dan Berger (New Brunswick, NJ: Rutgers University Press, 2010), 135–154.

100. *Informe, Comisión de Centralismo Democrático* (report on Seccional Committee meeting of March 24–25, 1979), 4.

101. *Informe de la Comisión de Centralismo Democrático Sobre la Última Reunión del Comité Seccional,* October 20–21, 1979, 1–2, PSP Archives.

102. Over the years, the author has become aware of some of his own contributions to the party's failings, especially in his role as a member of the central leadership. Arrogance and competitiveness were traits one often assumed necessary for effective leadership, but they were hurtful to compañeros and compañeras in the struggle. A projection of stoic discipline led others to feel disrespected or unessential to the common endeavor. Che Guevara said that the revolutionary must be guided by feelings of love. But often one's actions came from a bad place, not from love. It was poor politics as well to tolerate the misguided decisions or behaviors of others, whether out of deference to authority, a desire to be accepted by that authority, or continued benefits from the prestige of one's own leadership role. This was "liberalism" of the worst kind. These are lessons gained from one's experience in the struggle.

103. *Report on the Retreat of the* Comité Seccional *of November 9 & 10, 1980,* Commission on Democratic Centralism (published in February, 1981), PSP Archives.

104. Ibid., 1–2.

105. The objectives for 1980 were five-fold: (1) build patriotic unity, (2) push the Dellums Resolution ("Transfer of Powers"), (3) support the Vieques struggle, (4) organize the campaign against the Democratic National Convention, and (5) support the PSP's electoral campaign in Puerto Rico. Each of these objectives had subsidiary objectives and tasks.

106. *Report on the Retreat of the* Comité Seccional, 8.

107. Ibid., 11.

108. This delay may have been partially due to a decision to await an assessment of the results of Reagan's election in November 1979.

109. "PSP convoca Encuentro Nacional sobre el Socialismo en Puerto Rico," *Claridad,* January 29–February 4, 1981, 17; Wilfredo Mattos Cintrón, *Puerta Sin Casa: Crisis del PSP y encrucijada de la Izquierda* (San Juan: Ediciones La Sierra, 1984), xi–xxvi.

110. Juan Mari Brás column, *Claridad,* January 29–February 4, 1982. Mattos Cintrón, a member of the Political Commission, stated that the announcement was issued prematurely because the leadership had not yet agreed to this position; Mattos Cintrón, *Puerta Sin Casa,* lii. Shortly thereafter, he resigned from the PSP.

111. Ultimately, the internal struggle led to a deep fracture in the Extraordinary Congress of November 1982, held in San Juan. An opposition group published a dissenting document, *Afirmación Socialista,* signed by three dozen long-standing base militants and national leaders. This contingent was a minority, but it represented a cross-section of very experienced cadre. It was the worst ideological rupture in the history of the organization. Mattos Cintrón, *Puerta Sin Casa,* xxxix–li.

112. "Resolución del Comité Seccional—Aprobada, Abril 18, 1982," PSP Archives. The following discussion draws from this report.

113. Ibid., 1.

114. Ibid., 3.

115. Ibid., 8–9.

116. For a description of some of these campaigns, see José E. Velázquez, "Coming Full Circle: The Puerto Rican Socialist Party, U.S. Branch," in *The Puerto Rican Movement: Voices from the Diaspora,* ed. Andrés Torres and José E. Velázquez (Philadelphia: Temple University Press, 1998), 61–64. Velázquez aptly describes this period as one of

"Juggling Mass Work, Solidarity Campaigns, and Ideological Debate" (62). See also Chapter 14 by Ted Glick, Chapter 12 by Zoilo Torres, and Chapter 3 by José E. Velázquez Luyanda, América Sorrentini, and Pablo Medina Cruz in this volume.

117. The Congress took place at P.S. 171 on East 103rd Street.

118. Denis Berger, Emeterio Díaz, Carmen V. Rivera, and Andrés Torres. Rivera and Torres submitted a "Letter to the Members of the PSP, US Branch," December 1982, PSP Archives.

119. Partido Socialista Puertorriqueño, *Tercer Congreso Seccional: Suplemento de Tesis* (New York, 1983), PSP Archives. Elected at the Congress were the new CS and the new Political Commission, both smaller. The latter comprised Digna Sánchez (First Secretary), José Soler (President), José Alberto Álvarez Febles, Olga Sanabria, and María Vázquez.

120. For example, the sequencing of the 1983 Congress slogan ("unity" and "social justice" *before* "independence" [author emphasis]) in contrast to the slogan of the 1978 *Tesis*, which highlighted independence.

121. As in the process leading up to the Congress of 1978, members evaluated a series of pre-Congress documents collected in a Draft Thesis (*El Ante-Proyecto de Suplemento a la Tesis Seccional*), PSP Archives.

122. *Tercer Congreso Seccional: Suplemento de Tesis*, 5.

123. Ibid., 14.

124. "Planteamientos Generales," internal report summarizing feedback regarding *El Ante-Proyecto de Suplemento a la Tesis Seccional*, PSP Archives.

125. José Soler, "La Seccional: Un nuevo comienzo," *Claridad*, July 1–7, 1983. Note that the principal party campaign immediately following the congress was in support of the international work at the UN.

126. Carlos Gallisá, "La decisión del compañero Juan," *Claridad*, September 30–October 6, 1983, 9.

127. "Informe a la membresia," August 17, 1985, 1–2, PSP Archives.

128. "Declaracion Politica Sobre las Elecciones Presidenciales de los EEUU y Perspectivas de Lucha," August 29, 1984, PSP Archives.

129. "Carta Abierta a Los Puertorriqueños y La Comunidad Hispana en General Sobre los Sucesos en Nicaragua," undated but likely 1985, PSP Archives. "We oppose using Puerto Rico and Puerto Ricans being used by the U.S. for its plans of domination in that or any other region" (6).

130. "No to a False Plebiscite, Yes to Decolonization," undated but probably spring of 1990, 1. The proposal for an official plebiscite was canceled because of lack of agreement on the proper definition for each status alternative and because the U.S. Congress would not agree to a binding resolution to support the outcome. In December 1991, a "referendum" was held. The results: the PPD won 48.4 percent, the PNP won 46.2 percent; and the PIP won 4.4 percent. Ronald Fernandez, Serafín Fernandez, and Gail Cueto, *Puerto Rico Past and Present: An Encyclopedia* (Westport, CT: Greenwood Press, 1998), 260–261.

131. Leaflet announcing an event for August 10, at the locale of the Musicians Union (300 W. Forty-Second St.), with the Secretary General of the PSP, Gallisá. PSP Archives.

132. "Informe a la membresía," August 17, 1985, 1–2, PSP Archives.

133. "Informe de Trabajo," December 1, 1990, PSP Archives. This three-page report of activities and asks done during 1990 was likely compiled by the Coordinating Committee. By this time, the Coordinating Committee was headed by Mildred Colón, a

long-time activist with the PSP who had maintained positive relations with many former PSP members.

134. Julio Muriente, "A la asamblea con voluntad y optimismo," *Claridad*, March 12–18, 1999, 10. Speaking as a leader of the NMI Muriente (a former PSP leader), recounts the background to the founding of the NMI on October 5, 1993.

135. *Claridad* is still published, as is *En Rojo*, the cultural supplement. It is not directed by any political organization.

Milestones

Reflections on a Life-Journey of Activism
and the PSP in New York

José E. Velázquez

My journey began when I was born, José Emiliano Velázquez Luyanda, at the Ashford Presbyterian Hospital in El Condado. My mother, wanting to have at least one child born in Puerto Rico ("chosen one"), swore that was why I became an *independentista*. My birth certificate from the hospital in the "American zone" indicated "white" for race, although my father was black, and my mother was *trigueña* (light brown). That birth certificate would be the source of many accusations of falsehood whenever I presented it as proof of identity. I was raised in Harlem and did not make my first visit to Puerto Rico until the summer of 1973. Black consciousness was ever present in our household, since as a merchant marine, my father experienced segregation in the southern United States and in other parts of the world. He insisted that racism was alive and well in Puerto Rico, while the United States at least confronted the issue.

Like many Puerto Ricans, especially of African descent, my introduction to American (U.S.) culture was through the African American experience. I contended with black "consciousness" long before Puerto Rican "consciousness." Although my parents spoke Spanish at home, ate Puerto Rican food, and listened to Puerto Rican music and television, my consciousness was formed on the basketball court and in the streets through a syncretism of Puerto Rican and African American culture. I understood Spanish and knew that I was Puerto Rican, but Puerto Rico was a far-off paradise. Since basketball was a big part of my early years, my heroes were Oscar Robertson, Earl "The Pearl" Monroe, and local stars like Lew

Alcindor (Kareem Abdul-Jabbar), Herman "Helicopter" Knowings, and my older brother, Marcelino ("Moose"), who was more than equal to me on the basketball court. Our music was the piercing rhythm and blues of Frankie Lymon and the Teenagers, Little Anthony and the Imperials, Smokey Robinson, the Temptations, Patti LaBelle, and the Boogaloo fusion of Joe Cuba and Joe Bataan.

By seventh grade, I was sporting an Afro, a new style not yet fully incorporated into Puerto Rican culture. After several years in elementary school, riddled with delinquency as well as gifted academic performance, three African American students and I were placed at the lily-white, heavily Jewish, Wagner Junior High School on East Seventy-Sixth Street, where we experienced overt racism and class discrimination. Although my peers in El Barrio knew I attended this school for "gifted" kids, my prowess on the basketball court made me part of the street family.

In El Barrio, I met Fred Meely and Phil Hutchinson, organizers of the Student Nonviolent Coordinating Committee (SNCC), beginning my first political involvement in the SNCC Black Youth Congress. In September 1966, while attending the mostly white Lincoln Park Honors Academy at Louis D. Brandeis High School on West Eighty-Fourth Street, I became a founder of the Black and Puerto Rican High School Coalition (HSC), with chapters at Brandeis, Harren, DeWitt Clinton, Bronx Science, and various other high schools. At Brandeis High, we were fortunate to have H. Rap Brown (Jamil Abdullah Al-Amin) as our mentor. In 1967, the HSC merged with the Black Panther Party (BPP), leading major walkouts and student strikes for two years in protest of the war in Vietnam, for decentralization and community control in Ocean-Hill Brownsville, and for student empowerment.

My involvement in the BPP became a source of friction with Puerto Rican students at Brandeis, who criticized my membership in the Afro-American Club instead of ASPIRA. This view changed as many Puerto Rican students became radicalized, especially around the issue of Puerto Rican independence. Consequently, when the principal decided to purge my yearbook photos, ASPIRA students conspired to include me in their photo. So, there I am in the corner of the ASPIRA picture, sporting a big Afro and Black Panther attire among clean-cut students. Many students signed my yearbook in June 1969 with "Viva Puerto Rico Libre."

By late 1968, increasingly frustrated with internal struggles and the ideological direction of the New York chapter, I resigned from the BPP. Later, I attended a meeting in East Harlem with Enrique Vargas, a Colombian theater activist; Iris Morales; Felipe Luciano; and Víctor Hernández Cruz to explore forming a political street theater. Morales and Luciano would become leaders of the Young Lords Party, but this meeting led to the formation in early 1969 of the Third World Revelationists, a political street theater based in East Harlem. In September 1969, I also began my freshman year at the City College of New York (CCNY) School of Engineering. Known for my earlier involvement in the spring 1969 City College student takeover, I was elected president of Puerto Ricans Involved in Student Action (PRISA), the Puerto Rican organization on campus, in my freshman year. Along with meeting two of my lifelong friends, Willie Nieves and Eduardo "Pancho" Cruz, my involvement at CCNY led to a more profound development of Puerto Rican "consciousness." However, my youthful enthusiasm for the struggle led me to disregard my classes and drop out of college that year to become a full-time member of the Third World Revelationists.[1]

The Third World Revelationists was a collective of about twelve young African Americans and Puerto Ricans, led by Vargas, a Columbian émigré, who brought with him the conception of street theater as a political organizing tool, along with a Marxist ideology. Over a two-year span, the Revelationists developed a local and national following, opening a center in East Harlem to accompany our street theater efforts with "revolutionary nationalist institutions." However, time-consuming theatrical performances, limited membership, and the sacrifices of quasi-communal life made these goals unrealistic, eventually leading to the group's dissolution in early 1972.[2]

The Revelationists developed a working relationship with the *Movimiento Pro Independencia* (MPI) when it opened a storefront on East 121st Street, across from a building owned by the theater group. The MPI chapter, led by Marciano Santiago and Armengol Domenech, had "parachuted" into the black and Puerto Rican neighborhood without previous political work. One day, the African American brothers on the block approached us to discuss burning down the storefront, whereupon we quickly explained that they were actually part of the movement. Later, along with Pedro Pietri, we performed at Casa Puerto Rico, jointly showed revolutionary movies on East 121st Street, and collaborated in the making of a documentary, *Puerto Rico, Paraíso Invadido.*[3]

In early 1972, during the dissolution process of the Revelationists, I argued for supporting the Puerto Rican Socialist Party (PSP), as its increasing role in the Puerto Rican struggle in the United States and for independence for Puerto Rico, in my view, made it a vanguard organization. After evaluating various organizations in the movement, the Revelationists gave their substantial resources (vehicle, four-story building, and darkroom and photographic equipment) to the PSP. Those resources were immediately put to use for the photography, layout, distribution, and headquarters of the new party newspaper, *Claridad bilingüe.*[4]

Figure 2.1. MPI rally, Brooklyn, New York.

My first assignment as a PSP member was to serve as an administrator for the newspaper's bilingual supplement. Ramón Arbona, the president of the party in the United States and the editor of *Claridad bilingüe*, argued that given my past political experience, I should not go through the normal process of first being an *afiliado* before becoming a *militante de carnet rojo* (full-fledged card-carrying member). This fast-track was approved, and I would always be referred to as the *militante* who provided the resources for *Claridad*. Similar paths were instituted for other seasoned Puerto Rican activists joining the PSP, greatly enhancing the experience and standing of the U.S. Branch.

No Vietnamese Ever Called Me a Nigger

In 1970, I refused to register for the Armed Services, adhering to the SNCC slogan: "No Vietnamese Ever Called Me a Nigger." Likewise, the PSP was in complete opposition to the draft, having rallied youth in Puerto Rico to burn their draft cards. I was ordered to report to the Whitehall Induction Center to be drafted, where I was quickly arrested by the Federal Bureau of Investigation (FBI), while the party held a rally outside, arguing that my arrest was not just for draft refusal but for selective political repression.[5] After posting bail, the party's leadership began to discuss how to handle the case of its first U.S. member charged with two criminal counts of refusing the physical examination and induction, facing ten years in prison and

$20,000 in fines. The Young Lords Party leader, Pablo "Yoruba" Guzmán, had previously been sentenced to prison for refusing the draft. Although the PSP questioned the legitimacy of the U.S. courts, it chose to go to trial in a campaign against the draft. Two prominent constitutional attorneys, Michael Ratner and Richard Levy from the Center for Constitutional Rights in New York City, along with a distinguished attorney from Puerto Rico, Fermín Arraiza, took my case on a pro bono basis.

The defense attorneys presented fourteen pretrial motions to dismiss the case based on the colonial situation of Puerto Rico, the invalidity of federal courts, racism and discrimination within the military, and selective prosecution, among others. Making legal headlines in calling for the disqualification of the special U.S. attorney, the trial was presided by Lawrence Pierce, an African American judge. After reviewing pretrial motions, on April 24, 1973, Judge Pierce made a surprising decision, dismissing the entire indictment on a technical motion of inadequate notice to report, while indicating that the political motions might also have validity. What was seen as an early victory was quickly squashed when the U.S. attorney appealed Pierce's decision.[6]

On January 29, 1974, in a split decision, the U.S. District Court of Appeals reversed Judge Pierce's decision, remanding the case back to him for trial. The legal team now decided to appeal the decision to the U.S. Supreme Court, claiming double jeopardy. This appeal would allow me time to remain free, travel, and continue my work as a full-time organizer for the party.[7]

First Congress of the Puerto Rican Socialist Party U.S. Branch

As we battled my draft case, the U.S. Branch of the PSP celebrated its founding Congress on April 8, 1973. This event marked the conclusion of its ideological transformation, with a dramatic rise in working-class membership and a new leadership, half of whom were U.S.-born or -raised. The party was now a national organization with hundreds of members, and it reflected the dynamic reality of Puerto Ricans in the United States. Its social and demographic composition was quite diverse in age, region, language proficiency, culture, and class. I was elected to the *Comité Seccional* (the governing body in the U.S. Branch), along with other Puerto Ricans raised in the United States. That summer, I was also elected to the Central Committee in Puerto Rico. I was appointed secretary for student affairs, charged with organizing a nationwide Federation of Puerto Rican University Socialist Students (*Federación Universitaria Socialista Puertorriqueña* [FUSP]) as an affiliated student branch of the Seccional.[8]

On the way to my first meeting of the Central Committee in Puerto Rico, I was sent to Cuba to represent the PSP at a meeting with the People's Movement for the Liberation of Angola (MPLA), with whom the party had developed a strong relationship, along with the African National Congress (ANC) of South Africa. My prior involvement with the Black Power movement would lead to my representing the party in discussions with African American organizations, assignments I gladly welcomed.

Ironically, these visits to Cuba and Puerto Rico were my first trips outside the United States. Arriving in July 1973, the first time I set foot on Puerto Rican soil, I kissed the ground. I was impressed with the PSP's Central Committee, its large working-class composition, and its Afro–Puerto Rican president, Julio Víves Vázquez, who greatly increased my respect and admiration for the leadership in Puerto Rico. Secretary General Juan Mari Brás delivered an impressive political report, and Secretary Lolita Aulet took copious minutes. I said very little, as my Spanish was shaky, a skill that would improve in the following years.

When I returned to New York City, my enthusiasm and dedication to the party's growth was greatly enhanced, and I was often in the forefront of ideological debates around the "national question." People asked why, based on my background, I never became a member of the Young Lords Party, but I was genuinely representative of the transformation that was occurring in the PSP, including an influx of U.S.-raised Puerto Rican cadre in the leadership.

Year of the Massive Takeoff
(Año Del Despegue Masivo, 1974)

In 1974, much of the party's work focused on the celebration of the National Day of Solidarity with Puerto Rico (*Acto Nacional en Solidaridad con Puerto Rico*), a massive effort to mobilize twenty thousand supporters in Madison Square Garden on October 27.[9] The goal of mobilizing ten thousand Puerto Ricans, identified by name and address, was later used in an intense recruitment campaign resulting in the growth of the PSP in New York to seventeen chapters, eighteen community/labor study groups, and seven study groups in high schools.[10]

The National Day of Solidarity was a success, although I was not personally there. I had been assigned in June to attend a cadre school in Cuba for six months and to continue solidarity efforts with the struggle in Angola from the previous year. So, I celebrated the *Acto* over shortwave radio in Havana, while enjoying some ice cream at a *Copelia* venue.

When I returned to New York, I learned from my roommate that we had been evicted from the apartment we had shared in East Harlem, with all our possessions thrown in the street. Most of our things were gone, including my precious LP collection. I moved to the Lower East Side, where one night, unidentified men invaded the apartment, put a gun in my new roommate's mouth, and told him that if he wanted to live, he had to become an informant. For my roommate's sake, I asked him to find another place to live.

A change of residence was not the only move I encountered. I also found that the Comité Seccional and *Claridad bilingüe* had relocated to an office building on East Thirteenth Street, paying substantial rent, while Casa Puerto Rico on Fourteenth Street became the party's New York City headquarters. When I inquired about the building on 121st Street donated by the Revelationists, I could never get a straight answer, eventually discovering that the building had been retaken by the city. To me, this situation was unforgivable, as being in the middle of Harlem, it would have been the ideal location for *Claridad*, party headquarters, and an administrative center. Emotionally, I thought of resigning from the organization. The PSP I knew before going to Cuba had become a large, costly bureaucracy, draining many of the key local cadres to fill leadership positions and to meet the necessary demands of the Acto Nacional and the rapid growth of the party throughout the country.

Year of the Decisive Advance
(*Año Del Avance Decisivo*, 1975)

I was elected Secretary of the New York Zone in 1975, in the midst of the city's financial crisis, with the Emergency Financial Control Board (EFCB) proposing drastic cutbacks in social services. A report to party members in New York City stressed taking advantage of this crisis to immerse the Puerto Rican masses in class struggle. Anticipating harsh austerity measures by the EFCB, the party organized various campaigns under the slogan "Solution to the Crisis, Unity and Struggle!" Opposing increases in transit fares and demanding increased corporate taxes, we, called for people to jump the subway turnstiles with the slogan "Hell No, We Won't Pay! Let Big MAC Pay the Way!" The party also organized against hospital cutbacks, fielded candidates for local school boards, and organized support for the Local 1199 Hospital Workers strike.[11]

Calling for the creation of Puerto Rican mass organizations of *lideres honestos*, the Comité Seccional stated that the "vacuum of leadership in the Puerto Rican communities will not, nor can it be, filled by the already discredited poverty pimps." We organized *Acción Boricua* and called for a People's Congress, bringing together such prominent leaders as Evelina Antonetty, Frank Bonilla, Judge John Caro, Manny Diaz, Gilberto Gerena Valentín, Ramón J. Jiménez, Father John Luce (St. Ann's Episcopal Church),

Figure 2.2. Bronx nucleus members meet with *Seccional* leaders.

Willie Soto, and many others, including myself. This united front held marches and rallies against cutbacks in the Bronx and played a key role in the struggle to save Eugenio María de Hostos Community College, rallying more than five thousand in support on May 10, 1975.[12]

By the summer of 1975, the PSP had emerged as a major force in the Bronx, with five *núcleos* and four FUSP chapters. Informal meetings were held between an aide to the Bronx's Herman Badillo and me, unofficially representing the party, discussing how to challenge local powerbroker Ramón S. Vélez, labeled an "anti-poverty pimp." My relationship with the aide dated to the City College takeover of 1969. Badillo opposed Vélez but lacked a grassroots base and was dependent on the Democratic Party machine. Our discussions centered on ways the PSP could help upstage Vélez in exchange for Badillo's support for the release of the five Puerto Rican Nationalist prisoners and the promise to assume an anti-colonial stance in Congress. Badillo later called for the freedom of the Nationalists and even supported the release of *Los Tres de Santo Domingo*, PSP members who had been arrested and charged with transporting armed Dominican guerilla leaders to that island. The party kept up its attacks on Vélez, but our ambivalent position on electoral involvement inhibited us from building an independent electoral machine that could seriously influence Puerto Rican politics in the Bronx.[13]

The *United States v. Velázquez* Legal Battle Concludes

Meanwhile, my legal case was continuing. The earlier appeal to the U.S. Supreme Court concluded with a denial of a hearing and the case being remanded back to Judge Pierce for trial. Now, the legal team made the important decision to waive a jury trial, a rarely used right of a defendant. Pretrial experience showed that Pierce was sympathetic to our legal arguments and would probably rule for less prison time. In pretrial discovery, the government was forced to produce FBI files, indicating years of surveillance based on my "being engaged in activities leading to insurrection and seditious conspiracy." On May 13, 1976, Judge Pierce dismissed the refusing induction charge on a technicality, rendered a guilty verdict on my refusal to take the physical examination, and sentenced me to two years' probation. My record and conviction were to be sealed upon my completion of the sentence.[14]

The correctness of the strategy adopted by the party and my legal team allowed me to continue political activity outside a prison cell. The first time I reported to my parole officer, the woman, of Caribbean descent, looked up at me and said, "Hey, man, you're a political prisoner. I've got real criminals to take care of. Call me periodically to let me know how you're doing." She approved all my trips outside the prohibited hundred-mile radius. On January 21, 1977, President Jimmy Carter granted complete and unconditional pardon to all draft resisters between 1964 and 1973. On May 19, 1977, Judge Pierce ordered my unconditional discharge and the setting aside of my conviction. In the end, the party's strategy of making this political trial a showcase proved to be effective.[15]

Bicentenario Sin Colonias and the Elections in Puerto Rico

During the Acto Nacional rally, Mari Brás had called for a "Bicentennial Without Colonies," a mass counter-protest to the country's official July 4, 1976, celebrations. This campaign became the focus of the entire U.S. Branch. In addition, the Seccional was expected to rally around the PSP's participation in the 1976 elections in Puerto Rico.[16] I remember early voices of discontent in the base membership, saying that these massive campaigns distracted us from grassroots organizing and party building.

Much of this internal dissension was countered with the answer that the struggles for democratic rights and independence were dual priorities to be acted on simultaneously. Pedro Reyes, a leader of the PSP on the Lower East Side, recalls how some of the internal discord focused on the "separation between members at the local level and the Seccional leadership, especially those from Puerto Rico," who seemed to downplay the reality of the Puerto Ricans in the United States. Although Reyes alludes to some signs of factionalism, the organizational and ideological conflicts were basically kept in check.[17]

Faced with these disagreements, I recall that I was often tasked with putting out internal fires in local chapters (núcleos), although I too often disagreed with policies adopted by the leadership. Eduardo "Pancho" Cruz, one of my best friends, got to calling me "Robot" for the times I intervened, under the guise of democratic centralism, against criticisms raised in the Lower East Side chapter.

By early 1976, the PSP was heavily focused on the Bicentennial Without Colonies mobilization, in practice leading to a reduction in the focus on democratic rights by local chapters. The Comité Seccional's subsequent evaluation of this campaign emphasized its success. In a New York City assembly held after the campaign, my report attempted to refocus the work on the struggle for democratic rights. Now having thousands of sympathizers who were potential future members, I supported the call for a membership drive in addition to organizing initiatives in trade unions and workplaces. My report also called for the development of a program that would prioritize jobs and employment rights; expose the destruction of communities under the guise of urban renewal; and improve the quality of higher education, public schools, day care centers, and hospitals. The major goal was the creation of a citywide organization in defense of Puerto Rican democratic rights. The report also analyzed the strengths and weaknesses of *Acción Boricua*; *Coalición Comunal Para Salvar a Hostos*; and the *Comité Puertorriqueño Por Derechos Democráticos*, as examples of our best efforts in accomplishing this goal.[18]

Follow-up discussions in local chapters were held, at which criticisms of the New York and Seccional leadership were leveled as well as the lack of attention to organizing in workplaces and unions.[19] Additional criticisms were raised about the absence of political work among Puerto Rican women, machismo in the party, the weak representation of women in leadership positions, and the need for day care arrangements at all events. The Bronx nucleus called for an analysis of elections, including a position on the Badillo-Vélez conflict.

Despite these criticisms, by late 1976, the party's immediate priorities became participation in the elections in Puerto Rico, a mobilization to the United Nations, a Day of Solidarity Campaign with Puerto Rico, and attendance at the International Solidarity Conference with Puerto Rico, to be held in Cuba. The irony of our electoral participation in Puerto Rico was that the U.S. Branch was reluctant and ambivalent in participating in electoral politics in the United States in any form, despite opportunities to do so. With several mobilizations from August to December, we had no time to recover from the Bicentennial campaign. Although the Seccional leadership constantly stated that managing both *vertientes* (strategic goals) simultaneously was feasible, this proposition was far from realistic. We witnessed how a Puerto Rico–focused strategy undermined our participation in democratic rights struggles.[20]

Rectification Campaign and Crisis
in the New York Puerto Rican Socialist Party

The results of the 1976 elections in Puerto Rico brought a dose of reality to the PSP: the number of votes received by the party's candidates was much lower than anticipated. In response, the party initiated a Rectification Campaign that lasted for well over a year. This campaign had an anti-Stalinist bent, with an almost Maoist–Cultural Revolution intensity of individual evaluations and self-criticism. The discussion of the party's many deficiencies, also present in the U.S. Branch, meant that concerns over the role of the PSP in the United States would take a backseat to the process being led from Puerto Rico.

The membership's exhaustion from countless meetings about internal inadequacies led to resignations, stagnation of mass work, the increasing alienation of the leadership from the members, and internal rumblings about the emphasis on solidarity-type activities. A general sentiment emerged from the party's base in New York about the need to convene a Second Seccional Congress, one that would place democratic rights at the center of our work. I fully concurred with this push. Members called for the creation of commissions on labor, housing, health, and education; substantive discussions on abortion rights and homosexuality; and the formation of a Federation of Puerto Rican Women in the United States.[21]

A new Commission on Democratic Centralism was charged with making sure that information flowed within party structures in response to complaints that decisions of the Comité Seccional and their rationale were not being accurately reported to the base membership. The commission was also responsible for monitoring discipline and violations of party rules. Some members believed that these rules were not fairly applied. Freddie Rodríguez, raised in Bushwick, recalls the power of this commission when, having grown tired of being labeled a "dissident, reformist, or revisionist," he decided to leave the organization. He was called to a meeting at which the New York City leadership rejected his resignation, almost "crucifying" him, as he recalls. On another occasion, he recounts, two members of the commission unexpectedly came to his home: "They indicated that they were not going to allow me to be part of any other left-wing organization in the country. Lucky it wasn't time for hatchets; and I used to have little glasses too, you know, like Trotsky."[22]

The Rectification Campaign led to an Extraordinary Congress in Puerto Rico in the fall of 1978, resulting in the postponement of the much-needed Second Seccional Congress. In the meantime, the PSP's mass work remained stagnant as the organization focused on internal debates. After severe criticisms of my leadership, I tendered my resignation in late 1978. Physical exhaustion, lingering political differences, and the need to hold down a regular job and remake my personal life all contributed to my decision.

As an interim leadership group proved incapable of resolving the problems, the New York zone was temporarily put under the supervision of the Comité Seccional. By now, an open struggle was evident in the Seccional over the practice and theory of "dual priority." This struggle took hold in the leadership and was accompanied by growing dissension in local chapters.[23]

Another restructuring proposal, put forth by the Political Commission in early 1979, noted that the party had created a "grand super-structure . . . that had absorbed the most developed cadres for coordination and internal administration . . . [and concluded that] it is impossible that one person . . . given current conditions [could] pretend to lead a whole city organization." The assignment of several local cadres to the national leadership had weakened local organizational capacity, while prolonged absence of Seccional leadership added to a vacuum of political guidance for democratic rights campaigns. The new proposal called for New York chapters to be incorporated directly into the Seccional leadership structures. I supported this proposal but thought it came much too late. The membership rejected the proposal, fearing that it would threaten any autonomous functioning of the party in New York City.[24]

Moving away from the Puerto Rican Socialist Party: 1979–1983

In late 1976, many in the New York City leadership were assigned to work, particularly in the hotel, restaurant, and club industries (Local 6). I went to work as a custodian in the Racquet and Tennis Club, a rich private gentleman's club on Park Avenue. For years, full-time cadre lived on a pauper's salary; these jobs served to organize personal lives as well as contribute to the party's trade union work.

I remained a member of the Comité Seccional during the early 1980s but was often in open disagreement with the Political Commission. During a two-day retreat in November 1980, I strongly criticized its yearly report, which claimed modest successes in combating the annexationist conspiracy, reorganizing chapters, and successfully protesting at the Democratic National Convention in coordination with the People's Alliance. Stressing that the party's continued weakness was ideological, strategic, and tactical in nature, I noted that the political thesis adopted at a hastily organized Second Congress in 1978 had never been published. In my view, we were losing our links with the community as we moved away from our work on democratic rights, a separation resulting from focusing on the "patriotic struggle" as something different from the struggle for democratic rights. I argued that it was difficult to unite with other minorities, the North American working class, or the Left if we were not building strong roots in our own community.

A report from the November retreat circulated by the Commission on Democratic Centralism communicated the critique of a leading member of the Central Committee from Puerto Rico, claiming that my criticisms were really discontent with the Political Commission masked in ideological terms. It characterized viewing the struggle for democratic rights as being the center of party work as "economism and reformism," as compared to the strategic preeminence of the "patriotic struggle." In arguing against my supposed "negativism," the report stated, "We cannot have a mechanical and metaphysical mentality. . . . We must learn to think and act dialectically in analyzing the complexities of the events we confront." I do not recall the reaction of the membership, but based on past practices, it seemed to me that the Stalinist hammer had come down from the highest levels.[25]

On a personal level, in 1979, I married and relocated to Newark, New Jersey, concentrating my political efforts on electing a PSP member, Ivette Alfonso, to the Newark Board of Education. I returned full time to Columbia University's School of Engineering, ten years after dropping out of college, and began driving a yellow cab in New York City to support my new household. After two years, I switched to a Bachelor of Arts program in American history and sociology, receiving my degree in 1987. I became a full-time teacher in the Newark public schools, later completing a master's degree in education and also writing curricula for the school district during the summer.

With the pressure of school, work, family, and relocation, my involvement in the party was reduced to attending meetings of the Comité Seccional. In my last attempt to influence an upcoming 1983 party congress, I attempted to practice democratic centralism by asking to write an alternative to the official documents. The Seccional leadership flatly rejected my request. I could no longer in good conscience remain a member, so I simply walked away. By 1983, many members who had joined the party in the early 1970s had also left, either officially or informally. A long, drawn-out decline through the 1980s and into the 1990s followed. In 1993, the PSP officially dissolved, as did the U.S. Branch.[26]

Conclusion

The PSP built a revolutionary organization among Puerto Ricans in the United States, viewing the diaspora as a strategic pillar in the struggle for national liberation, as articulated in *Desde Las Entrañas*. In the mid-1970s, its growth reflected the ability to put this theory into practice. However, leaders in Puerto Rico and the United States accepted the mistaken notion of an imminent crisis of colonialism and believed that independence was "around the corner," as exemplified in the slogan "*Independencia Ya, Social-ismo Ahora Mismo!*" ("Independence Already, Socialism Now!"). Although *Desde* was a huge step forward in the PSP's view on Puerto Ricans in the United States, many party leaders still shared a tendency to see qualitative changes in the cultural and sociological character of the second generation as occurring only after Puerto Rico's (imminent) independence.[27] Conse-quently, they were reluctant to prioritize consistent work around struggles for democratic rights, often focusing instead on building solidarity for inde-pendence. By the mid-1980s, the U.S. Branch faced irreversible decline.

In 1983, I attempted unsuccessfully to argue that the PSP mistakenly saw the struggle for national liberation only from a Puerto Rico–centered per-spective. Party leaders failed to understand that Puerto Ricans in the United States, whether viewed as "part of the Puerto Rican nation" or a "national minority," were involved in a struggle that itself had national character-istics within the confines of the United States, similar to those of African Americans and Mexican Americans. The character of the democratic rights struggle was intimately connected to the colonial reality of Puerto Rico and its national liberation and was not simply a "reformist" struggle. Along with others, I joined the party because of the democratic rights struggle and its links to the colonial situation of Puerto Rico. However, the concept of "dual priority" (*dos vertientes*) often clashed in practice. The PSP's key contri-bution to the national liberation struggle should have been to develop the national democratic rights struggle within the diaspora, linking it to the national liberation of Puerto Rico and to its other objective—often forgotten—the development of a multinational socialist movement in the United States. The key to developing class solidarity and influence within the U.S. Left was to be in the leadership of the Puerto Rican community; ultimately, the party failed to do either.

As an integral part of an organization led from Puerto Rico, the ideolog-ical and leadership conflicts emanating from there ultimately determined the future of the organization. The U.S. Branch was unable to work out its strategic conceptions after *Desde* in 1973, despite several unsuccessful congresses. The internal conflicts and dissolution of the PSP in Puerto Rico put an end to this possibility. In my opinion, the dichotomy of "Worker's Party versus National Liberation Movement" being debated in Puerto Rico was unfounded. Undoubtedly, the first responsibility of a Marxist Party in a colonial situation should be to lead a movement for national liberation, but this task did not necessitate the dissolution of the party. On the contrary, other experiences have demonstrated the importance of a strong Marxist Party in leading a broader national liberation movement.

My time in the PSP was a determining factor in my ideological for-mation, which I define as critical Marxism. It was fundamental to my organizational and Spanish-language skills, to the expansion of my "Puerto Rican national consciousness," and to the deep relationship I maintain with Puerto Rico and family members who returned there.

I continue to remain active in attempts at national formations of the diaspora, joining efforts to revive the National Congress for Puerto Rican Rights and, more recently, the National Puerto Rican Agenda, a campaign whose success remains to be seen. Other efforts have included reaching a broad consensus in New Jersey for the successful campaign to free Oscar López Rivera and building progressive community institutions in New Jersey.

I believe that the PSP experience demonstrates the improbability of any organization from Puerto Rico organizing the diaspora, which today contains the majority of the Puerto Rican nation, and whom I believe will have a significant role in determining the future of Puerto Rico. Nevertheless, present conditions require a dialogue and coordination with forces in Puerto Rico, based on mutual acceptance, shared respect, and common goals. Recent acknowledgment from all political and cultural sectors in Puerto Rico of the importance of the diaspora echoes the view originally espoused by the PSP and the U.S. Branch and constitutes a main feature of the organization's legacy.

A negative aspect of the dissolution of the PSP was the dispersion of one of the most important organizations of the Puerto Rican Left and of the overall radical movement in the United States. Although some former PSP members have attempted to remain politically active, these efforts have not resulted in any organized formation. Nevertheless, Puerto Rican leftists maintain a presence in social justice movements, democratic rights issues, support for Puerto Rican sovereignty and independence, and post–Hurricane María recovery efforts. In this regard, the rearticulating of the Puerto Rican Left in the United States is key for the independence of Puerto Rico, the struggle of the Puerto Ricans in the United States, and the development of a cohesive socialist movement in this country.

NOTES

1. This meeting took place at what was called the Gut Theatre, a brownstone on East 104th Street in East Harlem.

2. Third World Revelationist documents, located in José E. Velázquez Papers—Third World Revelationists, at the Center for Puerto Rican Studies Library and Archives, Hunter College, CUNY, July 17, 18, 1971; October 1971; November 1971 (hereafter, Centro Archives).

3. *Puerto Rico, Paraíso Invadido* was one of the films produced by cinematographer José García.

4. Revelationists, December 28, 1971, Centro Archives.

5. *Claridad bilingüe*, June 25, 1972, "Urgent Memo to Acting Director," CENTRO FBI Files, July 6, 1972, Centro Archives.

6. PSP flyer, July 6, 1972; FBI files, July 1972; *United States of America v. José Emiliano Velázquez*, 72 cr. 851, Motion to Dismiss Indictment; Motion on Geneva Convention; *United States Court of Appeals*, Second Circuit no.170 – September Term, 1973 docket no. 73-1869, 1093-1104, CENTRO.

7. Supreme Court Case # 73-6493; *Velazquez v. USA*, April 29, 1975, CENTRO. Dissenting Chief Judge Irving Kaufman argued that double jeopardy did apply in this case, stating that "the danger with the majority's opinion is that balancing tests will be used to whittle away . . . the 'thicket' of double jeopardy protections until few branches remain to shelter the accused. . . . I cannot join in this process of attrition of one of the most basic constitutional protections."

8. *Claridad bilingüe*, April 15, 1973. PSP documents are located in the *¡Despierta Boricua!* Recovering History Project (hereafter, PSP Archives).

9. For a stretch of years, slogans were selected to foment the enthusiasm of members.

10. 1974 Ornigrama, handwritten document, December 1974, PSP Archives.

11. Informe del Comité de Zona de Nueva York, "Objetivos Políticos y Organizativos del Partido Para el Año 1975," José E. Velázquez, February 1975.

12. Ibid.; Ramón J. Jiménez, "Hostos Community College: Battle of the Seventies," *CENTRO Journal* 15, no. 1, (Spring 2003): 99–111. Chapter 12 in this volume.

13. These meetings are memorialized in the interviews of José E. Velázquez, stored in the Centro Archives. Also see *Carta Roja, Órgano del Comité Seccional*, 1975; *Claridad bilingüe*, 1975, PSP Archives; and "3 Puerto Rican Prisoners Say Dominicans Forced Confessions," *New York Times*, July 6, 1975.

14. FBI Memorandum, May 8, 1974; and Adex FBI File, July 22, 1974; Centro Archives.

15. *Proclamation 4483, United States White House, Granting Pardon for Violations of the Selective Service Act*, January 21, 1977, Centro Archives.

16. "Llamado a la militancia a cumplir nuestras metas para el bicentenario," *En Acción. Órgano de la Zona de Nueva York*, PSP, May 21, 1976, PSP Archives.

17. Pedro Reyes interview, PSP Archives.

18. "Llamado a la militancia"; "Abrir Camino Al Socialismo," *Informe del Comité de Zona. Asamblea de Zona de Nueva York*, August 8, 1976, José E. Velázquez, Secretario de Zona; "Informe del trabajo partidista para encauzar organizativamente la lucha de los puertorriqueños por sus derechos democráticos," *Comité de Zona de Nueva York*, January–July 1976; *Asamblea de Zona de Nueva York*; *Apendice al Informe del Comité de Zona. Asamblea de Zona*, August 8, 1976, presented by José E. Velazquez, Secretario de Zona, all in PSP Archives.

19. For a description of the Seccional's labor organizing, see Chapter 1 by Andrés Torres in this volume.

20. "Apéndice Al Informe del Comité de Zona A La Asamblea de Zona," August 8, 1976; "Notas de la Reunión Comité de Zona de Nueva York," August 1976, 36; *En Acción, Partido Socialista Puertorriqueño, Zona de Nueva York*, August 27, 1976; *En Acción*, August 15, 1976; "Numero Extraordinario—Ofensiva Socialista de Octubre," *Carta Roja*, September 1976; Órgano del Secretariado del Comité Secciona, n.d.; *En Acción*, October 15, 1976; *Partido Socialista Puertorriqueño, Zona de Nueva York, Tesorería*, July 1976; *Comité de Zona de Nueva York*, "Informe de Zona," January–December 1976, presentado por José E. Velázquez, January 1977; all in PSP Archives.

21. "Informe de Zona: enero-diciembre," Comité de Zona de Nueva York, José E. Velázquez, January 1977; "Informe de Zona: Enero-diciembre 1976," *Comité de Zona de Nueva York*, José E. Velazquez, January 1977; "Objetivos Políticos-Organizativos Para

El Año 1977, Informe Político Del Comité de Zona de Nueva York, Presentado para discusión en Asamblea de Zona," July 8–10, 1977, all in PSP Archives.

22. On Freddie Rodríguez, see his interview in the PSP Archives. Rodríguez would go on to live in Puerto Rico and become a prolific producer of independent films, living a life of commitment to the independence movement. The mention of Leon Trotsky refers to the fact that this coleader of the Russian Revolution had been expelled by Joseph Stalin and was later assassinated in Mexico, where he was living in exile.

23. "Memorándum a la membresía del Partido Socialista Puertorriqueño (MPI) en la zona de Nueva York," *Secretariado del Comité de Zona*, April 28, 1978; "Memorándum a la membresía en la Zona de Nueva York," July 12, 1978; *Comité de Zona Ampliado*, "Proceso de re-estructuración de la zona," 1978, PSP Archives.

24. "Memorándum sometido al Comité de Zona el 12 de febrero 1979 por Digna Sánchez," *Seccional de Estados Unidos, Zona de Nueva York*, PSP Archives.

25. "Informe del Retiro del Comité Seccional," PSP, *Comisión de Centralismo Democrático*, November 9–10, 1980, PSP Archives.

26. Velázquez interview, Centro Archives. Rivera and Torres, Carta de renuncia, November 20, 1982, PSP Archives.

27. *Desde Las Entrañas*, English paperback version, April 1, 1973. "This means that at least 10 more years are required before the so-called 'second generation' has sufficient impact to be able to change the objective characteristics of our community" (11); only after independence would "it be possible for the portion of our people that stay in the United States to develop its own characteristics . . . although they will still be struggling against North American cultural aggression . . . and make possible the development of a national minority of Puerto Ricans in the United States" (17).

The PSP in the Windy City

JOSÉ E. VELÁZQUEZ, AMÉRICA SORRENTINI,
AND PABLO MEDINA CRUZ

Introduction

After the post–World War II boom, Chicago (the "windy city") became a center of Puerto Rican nationalism and protests for social justice.[1] By the 1950s, the Commonwealth of Puerto Rico's migration efforts stretched from the Northeast to the Midwest, including contract labor in agricultural fields. By 1954, unofficial records estimated the Puerto Rican population in Chicago at twenty thousand. By the 1970s, it had reached more than 80,000, and 112,000 by the 1980s.[2]

As migration and poverty increased, city planners called for sending Puerto Ricans back to Puerto Rico. The Puerto Rican community in Chicago throughout its history has been affected by displacement and gentrification. By the late 1960s, the early Puerto Rican community of Lincoln Park had been dismantled by urban renewal, despite protests led by José "Cha Cha" Jiménez and the Young Lords Organization (YLO). A new concentration of Puerto Ricans in West Town and Humboldt Park (the Division Street area) became the center of the Puerto Rican community. This internal migration led to conflict with white ethnic groups, who often firebombed Puerto Rican homes and automobiles.

Although the Puerto Rico Migration Division tried to paint the community as a "model minority," these efforts collapsed after the Division Street uprising on June 12, 1966. Following the first Puerto Rican Week at Humboldt Park, a white police officer shot a young Puerto Rican, Arcelis Cruz, and then police dogs were released to disperse the crowds. A major watershed event in the history of Puerto Ricans in the United States, this uprising was a result of long-standing police brutality and economic frustrations in the Puerto Rican community.[3]

Early Pro-Independence Movement

During the 1950s, local Nationalist Party organizing efforts were exposed after the March 1, 1954, attack on Congress led by Lolita Lebrón Sotomayor, who had family members in Chicago. In the following weeks, a number of nationalists were arrested, with police claiming that they had supplied the weapons used during the attack.[4] Despite attempts by the Puerto Rican Migration Division to alleviate fears regarding the nationalist movement, the uprising painted a picture of protests linked to social and economic subjugation. Furthermore, support for the freedom of the five Nationalist prisoners reflected the construction of a Puerto Rican identity that linked the struggle against colonialism in Puerto Rico with social and economic justice in Chicago. A key organization formed after the uprising, the Spanish Action Committee of Chicago, faced constant surveillance and repression by the Chicago police intelligence unit. Labeled as infiltrated by Communists, the police sought to destroy its leadership and influence, including creating parallel organizations led by agent provocateurs.[5]

In the aftermath of increased repression, the independence movement had a diminished public presence in Chicago. However by the mid-1960s and early 1970s, such organizations as the Frente de Unidad Independentista (FUI), the Young Lords Organization (YLO), the Puerto Rican Socialist Party (PSP), and the Movimiento de Liberación Nacional (MLN) were developing roots in the community. On September 23, 1972, the PSP, the FUI, and the Union of Puerto Rican Students at Northeastern Illinois University (NIU) held a *Grito de Lares* rally that seemed to mark a "coming out" of the movement.[6]

Early Development of the Puerto Rican Socialist Party

The development of the *Movimiento Pro Independencia*–Puerto Rican Socialist Party (MPI-PSP) in Chicago began in the late 1960s with such members as Juan Méndez, Luis Pérez, Esther Noboa, Cana Noboa, Rosa María Álvarez, Antonio Hernández, and later David Santiago and Pablo Medina Cruz, most of whom were from working-class families with roots in Chicago. América (Meca) Sorrentini, Jim Blaut, Jorge Capote Orcasitas, and Mariecel Maldonado LaFontaine, among others, would join them in the formation of the PSP's Chicago-Midwest Region. Méndez, Álvarez, Hernández, Sorrentini, and Medina would preside over the PSP during the

Figure 3.1. Meca Sorrentini at immigration rally, PSP, Chicago.

following decades. Oral interviews of some of these members provide personal insights into their key roles in the party's development.

Meca Sorrentini, a key member, was born in Cabo Rojo, Puerto Rico. Her father was a founder of the 1930s Socialist Party in Puerto Rico, and her mother was a seamstress, making gloves, handkerchiefs, and straw hats. The family always talked about class and national struggles in their home. After completing high school at Escuela Superior Central in Santurce, along with distinguished student leaders Juan Angel Silén, Norman Pietri, and Emilio Huyke, Sorrentini enrolled at the University of Puerto Rico (UPR), majoring in anthropology and sociology and completing graduate studies in psychology. At the UPR, she met the love of her life, Jim Blaut, at an event in 1961 celebrating the independence of Chile. They later married, and as a result of Blaut's research and investigative assignments, they journeyed to Venezuela, the Dominican Republic, and the Virgin Islands before eventually moving to Worcester, Massachusetts.

In Massachusetts in the late 1960s, Sorrentini connected with members of the MPI and was highly influenced by the YLO, which linked the struggle for democratic rights with Puerto Rican independence. In 1971, Sorrentini and Blaut moved to Chicago, interacting with the YLO and members of the FUI that included Oscar López Rivera, Juan Méndez, Don Rosendo, and

Carlos Aulet. *Claridad*, the MPI newspaper, was already being distributed in Chicago.[7]

Another key member in the Chicago PSP would be Pablo Medina Cruz, whose family migrated to Chicago in 1968 when he was fifteen years old. His parents were devoted members of the Partido Popular Democrático (PPD), whose slogan was *"Pan, Tierra, y Libertad"* (Bread, Land, and Liberty). His mother decided to move to Chicago, four years after her husband's death, in search of employment opportunities. Nine members of his family settled on Division Street and Oakley, only to be displaced by the city's urban renewal program, beginning a process of constant displacement and resettlement. They rapidly learned the difference between their new home and Puerto Rico, as cold winters were also met with burning torches thrown at their building and constant harassment from Polish and Italian gangs on the way to school. After graduating from high school, Medina Cruz attended NIU, where he became a leader of the Federación Universitaria Socialista Puertorriqueña (FUSP) and later a leader of the PSP in the community.[8]

The early formation of the PSP in Chicago also benefitted from the arrival of Mariecel Maldonado LaFontaine and Jorge Capote Holcacitas. Maldonado LaFontaine grew up in Utuado, Puerto Rico, and studied at the UPR, interacting with FUPI leaders Sorrentini and Blaut. She later moved to complete her graduate studies in Chicago. Capote Holcacitas was born and raised in Cuba, where he was preparing for the priesthood at the advent of the Cuban Revolution. He was sent abroad, not as an exile but for religious studies, and was ordained in Michigan. In April 1968, in Washington, D.C., after the assassination of Dr. Martin Luther King Jr., he was almost killed in the heart of the black community as it went up in flames. Luckily, he was also a member of a largely black organization named Change, and a rioter yelled, "He's Latino!" and told him to "get the hell out of here." His priesthood days were short, as issues of racism and alcoholism within the Church led to his leaving the priesthood before meeting and marrying Maldonado LaFontaine. They eventually settled in Chicago, meeting up with Méndez, Rivera, Sorrentini, Blaut, and others in the movement.[9]

When a decision was reached to organize a chapter of the PSP in Chicago, some members of the FUI considered the move inappropriate, believing that a Marxist-Leninist party would negatively affect organizing in the Puerto Rican community. Others, like the YLO since its inception in late 1967, already united community struggles regarding displacement and fair housing with socialist views and independence for Puerto Rico. The People's Church takeover by the YLO in Chicago incorporated images of the five Nationalist prisoners hanging from the rafters. However, by the early 1970s, the YLO was suffering a decline as repression of its leadership and other internal problems took its toll; the PSP would fill that vacuum. Those who wanted to break with the FUI saw the PSP as a way to embrace nontraditional, unorthodox Marxism-Leninism, which viewed national liberation movements as a key aspect of socialist revolution.[10]

The new PSP chapter began to build momentum to attend the Founding Congress of the U.S. Branch, to be held in New York City on April 8, 1973. The party's dynamism and visibility were palpable and attracted support within the Puerto Rican community and growing solidarity from diverse sectors of the North American Left. I (Maldonado LaFontaine) remember how "sometimes we would get to the door, and they offered us food that they barely had for themselves. Many were unemployed, but they were very Puerto Rican, and never, never, did they not respond to us." I (Sorrentini) recall how "gang members watched over us, and that trust required serious and sustained work on our part with them. . . . They responded like soldiers of the Puerto Rican nation." The activities aimed at attending the Founding Congress cemented the development of the party in Chicago.[11]

After the 1973 Congress, the party set out to meet the goals established by the *Comité Seccional*, under the slogan "*Año Del Despegue Masivo*" (Year of the Massive Takeoff). Distributing more than one thousand issues of *Claridad bilingüe* on a weekly basis, we counted on a membership of more than eighty trained cadres. Developing several committees throughout the city—Juana Colón, Julia de Burgos, and South End—the party expanded to Milwaukee, Wisconsin; Waukegan, Illinois; Niles, Michigan; and the steel mills of Gary, Indiana. The chapter in Gary gave us new perspectives on the complexity of the diaspora, as we recruited workers who made $20 to $30 an hour but were often assigned the worst jobs, such as smelting in the ovens. David Santiago, a party leader, did exceptional work organizing these workers. In Waukegan, the party even gained support among religious groups and leaders. We were effective wherever we organized, as long as we exhibited flexibility with Marxist-Leninist dogma.

Our main headquarters became Casa Betances in the Wicker Park neighborhood, an area with many progressive organizations. The poorly kept building was in an area abandoned by white flight, although many owners had kept the titles to these houses, converting them to single-occupancy rooms. We visited community residents and told them about opening a storefront with the name "Betances," explaining its racial significance. By inauguration, we had an organized list of about five thousand people with addresses and skills that could help us in many ways. Other organizations in the area included the Association House, one of the first Settlement houses in the country; the Centro Segundo Ruiz Belvis; and the Latin American Defense Organization (LADO). The Ruiz Belvis Center, which many associated with the PSP, actually originated with the Association House, although the party played a leading role in its development.[12]

Heading to Madison Square Garden

In the summer of 1974, we hit the streets to raise funds for five buses to attend the National Day of Solidarity with Puerto Rico on October 27, 1974, at Madison Square Garden. The party organized tours of El Grupo Taone and Los Pleneros de la 23 Abajo as well as visits by leaders of the Seccional and Puerto Rico. The mobilization helped build the framework of a vibrant solidarity movement with Puerto Rico, coalescing in the Puerto Rican Solidarity Committee (PRSC). A conference on the status of Puerto Rico, organized by the PRSC, featured Ramón Arbona, the First Secretary of the PSP; Arthur Kinoy, a famed attorney and activist; George Beckford, from the University of the West Indies; and José López Rivera, a professor at NIU and leader of the MLN. Solidarity from the African American community, including Fannie Rushing, the President of the PRSC, was reflected in the statement, "Puerto Rico Is Our Fight Too." Other supporters included activist Cindy Zucker; the National Lawyers Guild; Jeff Haas, of the People's Law Office; and Earle Tockman, a professor of law at DePaul University, among others.[13]

However, the mobilization also heightened our differences with those associated with the Fuerzas Armadas de Liberacion Nacional (FALN) and the MLN. During the FALN bombings in New York City, we were on our way there and immediately decided not to make any statements to the press. When Juan Mari Brás, the Secretary General of the PSP, was interviewed about the bombings, he said, "We will continue with the event and reaffirm the right of the independence movement of Puerto Rico to utilize all methods of struggle." This statement reduced the stress, and our participation at the event provided comfort, energy, and catharsis. Hearing the resounding drums of Native Americans, the cries for freedom and solidarity by the twenty thousand gathered there, representing not only Puerto Ricans but also the best of the North American people, filled us with tremendous strength.

Our tense relationship with the MLN would continue, although we were early partners in the formation of Puerto Rican institutions in Chicago. The PSP supported armed struggle as a matter of principle, but tactical objections to the actions of the FALN heightened these differences. After the success of the Madison Square Garden event, many sectors of the North American Left began to revise their negative views of the PSP and increasingly sought to build alliances with the party. However, differences with the MLN led to conflicts even within the PRSC over its support of the PSP. Our history of common struggle and personal relationships with members of the MLN made this a difficult period that has only recently been healed by former leaders of both organizations.[14]

Organizing in the Community

As Chicago is a racially segregated city, many of our struggles centered around police brutality and fair housing in coordination with the Coalición Acción Latina and La Federación de Acción y Fe. Some critics on the Left viewed our alliance with a faith organization as contradictory, given our Marxist-Leninist principles, but Reverend José Morales and his church held progressive views, including having an anti-nuclear center in the middle of Humboldt Park.

In the mid-1970s, the PSP was part of a coalition against the Chicago Master Plan 21, a citywide gentrification plan that would displace many ethnic communities. Along with local community activists, such as Slim Coleman, who played a key role in investigating and denouncing these plans, we recognized that the future of the Puerto Rican, African American, Mexican, and poor white communities was at stake. Plan 21 had the support of the Roman Catholic Archdiocese, which paired with Mayor Richard J. Daley as two key power structures backing the plan. As early as 1970, the sirens of fire engines became a common scene in the Division Street area, endangering the stability of the Puerto Rican community. Puerto Ricans rallied against the fires and redlining policies, demanding to meet with Mayor Daley in July 1976 to establish a plan to end the arson. As a result of community pressure, the fires declined, but gentrification continued.

At a Chicago tribunal held on November 13, 1976, PSP leader Hernández recounted that more than 125,000 Puerto Ricans would be displaced and called for all working people to rise in opposition to this anti-people's plan. Progressive sectors in the African American community, such as the National Conference of Black Lawyers, the National Conference of Black Labor, and People United to Save Humanity (PUSH), joined Puerto Rican and Mexican communities, poor whites, and Native Americans to lead the fight. Along with the YLO in August 1976, we participated in the formation of the Committee for Puerto Rican Rights and called for a citywide referendum on Plan 21. The Centro Ruiz Belvis also played a leadership role in the struggle against the plan, and ultimately it was never implemented, although the wave of displacement continued and remains a key struggle today.[15]

Meanwhile, in the early 1970s, the right to celebrate for the first time a Puerto Rican parade in downtown Chicago became a battle with Mayor Daley, who opposed the idea, arguing that it would result in dirty streets and broken windows along the route. Furthermore, years earlier, parade organizers supporting the issue of fair housing had extended an invitation to Dr. Martin Luther King to one of their activities, infuriating the mayor. Some *independentistas* preferred to organize a Boricua Festival in Humboldt Park, the heart of the Puerto Rican community. While not opposing

Figure 3.2. Chicago nucleus fighting displacement and gentrification.

this festival, we chose to confront the power structures by inserting ourselves into the parade. In 1974, differences with parade organizers emerged around our proposal for a People's Contingent under the slogan "*Desfile Un Día, Pobreza Todos Los Días*" (Parade One Day, Poverty Every Day). Arguing that our contingent was not opposing the parade but rather making a statement about the daily reality of our people, we were allowed to march, receiving a mostly positive reaction along the parade route. Throughout the following years, we continued to organize the People's Contingent, denouncing colonialism in Puerto Rico, demanding the freedom of the five Nationalist prisoners, and drawing attention to the issues of police brutality, discrimination, unemployment, and Plan 21.[16]

From the Federación Universitaria Socialista Puertorriqueña to the Barrio

In the late 1960s, a struggle for increased Latino recruitment and curriculum emerged among Puerto Rican students at various local universities. One of those students, Pablo Medina Cruz, cofounder of the FUSP and later a leader of the PSP in Chicago, describes the history of this movement: "As a student at Northeastern Illinois University, I joined the militant Union of Puerto Rican Students that published an influential newspaper, *Que Ondee Sola*, which exists to this day. I attended classes with Professors Samuel

Betances and José López Rivera, who, along with PSP study groups, were important in expanding my world vision." NIU would become the birthplace of many future Puerto Rican community leaders, including Aída Sánchez, Miguel del Valle, Ines Bocanegra, and Luis Gutiérrez, among others.[17]

In Puerto Rico, the University Federation for Independence (FUPI) was in its prime, providing the PSP with some of its key leaders. Consequently, the Seccional decided to organize the FUSP based on the FUPI model. The keynote speaker at the FUSP's Founding Assembly was Papo Coss, the President of the FUPI, and its program for university reform was borrowed from this student organization. Together with Hernández, I (Medina) organized FUSP chapters at NIU and at the University of Illinois at Chicago Circle (UICC).

NIU was fertile ground for a student organization, such as the FUSP. Concerns about another student organization on campus were diminished as I "explained our intentions not to compete with the Union of Puerto Rican Students but rather [to] give political direction to a campaign of university reform. Although the FUSP functioned as a fraternal organization of the PSP, not all its members were in the party, though many did eventually join the PSP or the MLN." Its role in developing Puerto Rican leaders was exemplified when Gutiérrez, a member of the FUSP and a leader of the Union of Puerto Rican Students, later became a Chicago alderman and U.S. congressman.[18]

In the winter of 1974, the FUSP leadership, in consultation with the PSP, decided there was sufficient leadership among NIU students to relocate me to organize at UICC. There was a Union of Puerto Rican Students chapter at UICC, headed by members of La Colectiva Don Pedro Albízu Campos, who had experienced previous frictions with members of the party in the community. I met with leaders of the Union of Puerto Rican Students to explain the difference between the roles of the FUSP as compared to that of the student union. The meeting was surprisingly cordial, and UICC's Union of Puerto Rican Students agreed to work with the FUSP.

The first joint campaign with the Union of Puerto Rican Students was to insist on an earlier commitment by UICC to develop a Latino Cultural Center. In addition to Puerto Ricans, this struggle included Sociedad Estudiantil Latinoamericana (SELA), comprising primarily Mexican students. Claiming that there was no space on campus to build the facility or funding to pay personnel to run the center, the university resisted. After a yearlong struggle, a united student coalition forced the administration to comply. The trust developed through this campaign led the Union of Puerto Rican Students and FUSP leaders to respect each other and to develop important relationships beyond the student struggle. The new center was named in honor of Rafael Cintrón Ortiz, a beloved PSP mentor and educator who had been mysteriously killed in the midst of the struggle to establish the center. Cintrón, a key faculty member of UICC's Latin American Studies Department, conducted many of the FUSP and PSP study groups. He was found dead, Mafia-style, with a dagger through his heart. The Chicago police reported, without any evidence, that his death was a result of a conflict between two groups within the PSP over issues of armed struggle, a bogus manipulation of the evidence. The Chicago PSP was convinced that it was a political assassination.[19]

In 1975, students unleashed a new struggle when UICC announced higher ACT score requirements and admission policies, turning away from its "Urban Mission," a commitment made to the communities who had been displaced to build the campus. It took the best of UICC's progressive faculty and students to force the administration to withdraw the policy. The PSP assigned Blaut to organize professors, while I attended to the student body. Many individuals who joined that endeavor remain active in the struggle today. Among them was Jesús "Chuy" García, who became an alderman, state senator, and congressman; Eddie Cortez, who gave eighteen of his best years to *la patria*, incarcerated for activities related to the FALN; and Linda Coronado, a CASA activist. Providing support to students and faculty during this time were the PSP, the Latin American Studies Department, the Latin American Recruitment and Educational Services (LARES) program, CASA-Hermandad General de Trabajadores, and La Liga Don Pedro Albizu Campos.[20]

By the mid-1970s, the FUSP had chapters at NIU, UICC, YMCA Community College, Loyola University, and the University of Madison in Wisconsin. Despite its many successes, two factors led to the eventual dissolution of the FUSP. Political differences between the MLN and the PSP took its toll on the student movement, especially at NIU, where many students were pushed to divide their loyalty between the two organizations. The 1977 rectification process of the PSP also sounded the death knell, as the Seccional leadership dissolved the FUSP, a decision reached without consulting its members in Chicago, who were heavily involved in the campaign against the new UICC admissions policy. The decision to dissolve the FUSP was a brash, undemocratic decision, devastating for Chicago's FUSP leadership, who asked, "Why are we going to break up something that's functioning?" With about seventeen members in the FUSP, many who were new recruits, I decided not to announce the dissolution while leading the UICC struggle. In the end, the campaign was victorious; however, the FUSP chapter was dissolved, with some members joining the PSP or the MLN and the majority continuing as unaffiliated activists.[21]

Determined not to follow the path of many student leaders who never completed their degrees, I eventually graduated and years later received a master's degree in urban planning and policy from UICC. Meanwhile,

I returned to the heart of the barrio as a community organizer with the West Town Concerned Citizens Coalition (WCCC). The WCCC benefitted greatly from Sorrentini's and PSP input, but the training methods developed by Saul Alinsky were also a learning experience for us. After Ronald Reagan's administration's cutbacks affected its organizing component, the PSP helped negotiate the crisis while requesting that the WCCC develop a new housing entity to continue its commitment to the Puerto Rican community. Consequently, the Latin United Community Housing Agency (LUCHA) was born, which continues today as one of Chicago's leading housing agencies.[22]

Seeking Alliances in the Struggle

As the party developed its organization in the Puerto Rican barrios, it sought to build alliances with other sectors of the Left, Latino, African American, and poor white communities. We often celebrated traditional patriotic Puerto Rican holidays with the YLO, the Black Panther Party (BPP), the PRSC, casa, and the New World Resource Center as well as participating in solidarity activities with Nicaragua and El Salvador. Celebrating International Workers Day, a major historical event in Chicago, gave us a presence leading to greater dialogue and better understanding of our views on the Puerto Rican national question, including some in the U.S. Communist Party.[23]

Our alliances with the North American Left were strengthened by the theoretical contributions on the national question by Blaut, whose extensive academic credentials included having chaired a doctoral program at the UPR. The Left generally viewed Puerto Ricans as a "national minority" and opposed the organization in the United States of a party from Puerto Rico. Seeking to clarify the difference between a nationalism linked to an anti-colonial struggle, Blaut opposed the Left's view of Puerto Ricans in the United States as a simple "national minority." Years later, Mari Brás would pen the prologue to Blaut's book *On the National Question*. Blaut's contributions won unity and respect from the North American Left, even if its members disagreed with his analysis. Maldonado LaFontaine recalls how he interacted with many diverse people, including Sidney Mintz and Noam Chomsky, and describes Blaut as "among the major leaguers of progressive thinkers." Capote Holcacitas remembers how "he was very familiar and knowledgeable about the colonial relationship with the metropolis, for example, the Vietnamese and the French, and when he spoke on the priority of the national question in the colonial struggle, he was well respected."[24]

A significant effort at developing alliances was the National Hard Times Conference on January 30, 1976, bringing together an array of activists from

Michigan, Indiana, and Wisconsin to map out a strategy and program for a united struggle while also supporting the Bicentennial Without Colonies demonstration in Philadelphia. Among its leadership were Vernon Belle-court (American Indian Movement); Virginia Collins (Republic of New Africa); Evelina Antonetty (United Bronx Parents); Carlos Feliciano (Puerto Rican ex-political prisoner); Wilbur Haddock (United Black Workers); Jim Haughton (Fight Back); Jennifer Dohrn (Prairie Fire); and Florencio Merced Rosa, José La Luz, and David Santiago (PSP).[25]

Meanwhile the BPP was suffering brutal repression, making our relationship with the African American community even more important. Repression against the Left in Chicago included isolated assassinations, such as Rudy Lozano of CASA, Rafael Cintrón Ortiz of the PSP, and Fred Hampton of the BPP, among others. The party was a member of the Fred Hampton Committee while also developing ties with the Nation of Islam, the Uhuru Movement, and PUSH. A group was also associated with Ana Livia Cordero from Puerto Rico, who had a strong association with Malcolm X, and an anti-colonial consciousness already existed among sectors of the African American community. The significance of these alliances would become important later in our participation in the campaign to elect Harold Washington.[26]

On June 4, 1977, in the middle of Puerto Rican Week, two young Puerto Ricans, Rafael Cruz and Julio Osorio, were killed by the Chicago Police. A grand jury was formed to investigate this incident, which many in the Puerto Rican community recognized as a clear case of police brutality. The PSP and other sectors of the independence movement denounced the grand jury as a possible witch hunt against the independence movement. The party, which had previously filed a lawsuit against the Federal Bureau of Investigation (FBI) and the Chicago Red Squad, also denounced grand jury charges against the Centro Cultural Juan Antonio Corretjer in the investigation of the FALN. Our answer to increased repression was to not collaborate with the grand jury, build mass movements, expand solidarity with independence for Puerto Rico and the struggles in Latin America, demand the removal of the U.S. Navy from Vieques, and fight for freedom for the Nationalist prisoners.[27]

Electoral Participation

In the summer of 1981, the party endorsed the celebration of the First Boricua Festival sponsored by the Latino Action Coalition, which refused to support the electoral aims of Chicago Mayor Jane Byrne. When she attempted to undermine the festival, we countered with a call *"En Defensa de Nuestra Cultura, Por la Supervivencia Nacional, Una Patria Soberana"* (In

Defense of Our Culture, National Survival, and a Sovereign Puerto Rico). The festival was a great success and included the presence of Pedro Rivera Toledo and Lucecita Benítez. More important was the Latino Coalition's sponsorship of the First Puerto Rican Political Convention on November 21, 1982. We supported this effort to empower our people to seek political representation, foreshadowing the party's involvement in several electoral campaigns.[28]

Consequently, as the party prepared for the Seccional's Third Congress, events in Chicago would draw attention toward various elections that could change the political map of the city, beginning with the candidacy of Washington, an African American alderman who was leading a progressive coalition with a real chance of winning the Democratic mayoral primary. The Democratic Party machine, through gerrymandering and opposition to voter registration efforts, had thwarted earlier attempts at Puerto Rican political empowerment. In 1975, in its first electoral challenge, three Latino candidates, including "Cha Cha" Jiménez, had unsuccessfully challenged the Democratic machine for alderman seats. Despite their loss, they left the future open to increasing political participation.[29]

The Chicago PSP was aware of the ambivalence of the Seccional's participation in Democratic Party elections but believed that our participation was crucial. I remember calling Mari Brás and saying, "We are Marxist-Leninists, but the diaspora is a vanguard force in Chicago, with Latinos, poor whites, and African Americans forming the majority in Chicago. We don't see any contradiction with our participation via a front, but we want it to be the PSP openly fighting discrimination and defending principles." Mari Brás responded that the party in Chicago "should do what it believes, because so far everything you have done has produced good results, the party keeps growing, and you have maintained the integrity of our positions."[30]

So, the party marched forward, publishing "The PSP and the Elections," which showed pictures of Arturo Schomburg and Harold Washington and outlined our reasons for supporting his candidacy. The names of our headquarters, Centro Betances and the Segundo Ruiz Belvis Cultural Center, both with their abolitionist history, reinforced the relationship between Puerto Ricans and African Americans. If one of the party's axioms was racial solidarity and combating racism, then with a progressive African American candidate, the party should join with advanced sectors of the African American, Latino, and white communities. I met with Jiménez, who said, "I'm going to give him my full support and develop a committee to support Harold Washington." I agreed, responding that we were "on board."[31]

For the party, this tactical decision would advance the struggle. The PSP put its full support behind Puertorriqueños por Harold Washington, bringing along the Latino Action Coalition, the Centro Ruiz Belvis, and numerous community groups, while stating that Latinos faced the same economic and social prejudices as black people: "We may not know him, but Harold Washington knows us." Support for Washington led to the drive-by shooting of the Centro Ruiz Belvis and other attacks by right-wing forces angered by our unity with the African American community. After a victory in the Democratic primary, Washington was elected on April 12, 1983, with 51.2 percent of the vote, a great victory for progressive forces in the city and a defeat for the traditional Democratic Party machine. The slight margin of victory showed the importance of the PSP's participation, along with others, in garnering support for Washington, and party members felt proud to have been part of something so spectacular.[32]

Another electoral opportunity for the PSP arose in March 1984, when Gutiérrez decided to challenge the powerful congressman Dan Rostenkowski for committeeman, an elected position in Chicago. Gutiérrez won 24 percent of the vote despite having little money and low name recognition, a good sign for his political future and for the empowerment of the Latino community. This election further encouraged party members, novices in electoral politics, to be instrumental in later campaigns. The PSP continued its support for Gutiérrez by participating in the formation of the Independent Political Organization (IPO) in July 1985. The IPO brought together diverse political forces in the Latino, African American, and poor white communities in a movement independent of the Democratic Party machine. The PSP was heavily involved, developing strong fraternal and democratic working relationships within the organization and throughout the entire city.[33]

Meanwhile, in December 1985, the courts ordered a remapping of seven wards in Chicago and special elections to be held in May 1986. Gutiérrez and García, a CASA member, decided to run for alderman in separate wards. The MLN, opposing electoral politics, held back from supporting Gutiérrez, although this stance would change during his later congressional race. The party decided to participate fully in this campaign, assigning Pablo Medina Cruz, Antonio Hernández, and Emily Blais Alemany, among others, to run districts and protect the vote. Medina Cruz and ex-members of the FUSP became close advisers during this campaign, hitting the streets with the IPO on behalf of Gutiérrez. Gutiérrez received twenty more votes than the Democratic machine's candidate, Manny Torres, but with no candidate winning a majority, a runoff election became necessary. Gutiérrez won the runoff election with 53 percent of the vote. His victory provided the needed majority on the city council for Washington to continue his fight with the traditional Democratic machine.[34]

Electoral participation played an important role in the political development of PSP members. Having arrived from Milwaukee in December 1983,

Blais Alemany received her baptism in electoral politics during the campaigns for Gutiérrez and the reelection of Mayor Washington. Born in Massachusetts and growing up in Guayama, Blais Alemany studied at the UPR in Cayey, where she became an *independentista*, although she did not join any organizations. While visiting her mother in Milwaukee one summer, she decided to stay, graduating from the University of Wisconsin and later taking a job in Chicago and joining the PSP.

In Gutiérrez's 1986 campaign, I (Blais Alemany) was assigned to campaign in the Thirty-Fourth Precinct, a mixed neighborhood of ethnic Ukrainians and Puerto Ricans, with a small African American presence. Along with Puerto Rican activist Ada López, I led the efforts for Gutiérrez and the later reelection of Washington in this neighborhood, a victory highlighted in the local newspapers. "I recall the debate within the party; there were comrades for whom it was difficult participating in a Democratic Party election. But many [knew] the importance of the historical moment and of having a presence in electing Harold Washington, thereby solidifying the alliance between the Puerto Rican and African American community."[35]

In April 1987, Washington was reelected with 53.5 percent of the vote, although tragically on November 25, 1987, he suffered a fatal heart attack. After an interim African American mayor was chosen, a struggle broke out over Washington's replacement in a special election to be held in 1989 between the Democratic machine, headed by Richard M. Daley (son of former Mayor Daley) and a new formation called the Harold Washington Party, led by Alderman Timothy Evans. Viewing a third-party candidate as having no chance of winning, especially with many in the fractured African American leadership supporting the Democratic machine, Gutiérrez argued that the Latino community's best option was to negotiate with Daley. In a meeting of the IPO, Gutiérrez called for supporting Daley's candidacy, a move opposed by the PSP. Angered by Gutiérrez's decision and believing that it was made without consulting the forces that made up the IPO, party members left the meeting to avoid a serious confrontation. The IPO went on to endorse Daley, while the PSP privately continued to try to dissuade Gutiérrez from his decision. "In retrospect, this was the end of one of the most combative organizations in the Chicago electoral arena. The party helped develop the IPO but, because of our inexperience, allowed the real power to be in the hands of the committeeman, who in this case was Councilman Gutiérrez."[36]

In the aftermath, Daley won the 1989 special election, receiving huge margins in the white community, 25 percent of the fractured African American vote, and the majority of the Latino vote. Under Mayor Daley, Gutiérrez became president pro tempore, presiding over the council in the absence of the mayor, who would continually be reelected in the following years. Subsequently, in 1990, a federal district court ordered the creation of a new Fourteenth District with a Latino majority for the 1992 congressional elections. Gutiérrez received the support of Mayor Daley and broad support in the Latino district and won the Democratic primary for this seat with 60 percent of the vote. Despite its past differences with Gutiérrez, the party looked favorably upon his candidacy, a view then shared by other sectors of the independence movement in Chicago. He would go on to be continuously reelected with large margins until his resignation in 2018, at which time he gave his support to the election of Congressman García. Over the following years, the PSP in Chicago continued to work in the electoral arena, but not with the energy it had in earlier campaigns.[37]

Dealing with the Ideological Crisis in the PSP

Despite continued community building and party development in the Midwest throughout the 1980s and 1990s, the reality was that the Chicago chapter was part of a larger organization that had been in constant ideological crisis since the late 1970s, and despite its geographical distance, it could not escape the process leading to the eventual dissolution of the PSP in 1993. Capote Holcacitas and Maldonado LaFontaine had returned to Puerto Rico on the cusp of the party's participation in the 1976 elections, with Capote becoming the candidate for the legislature from Trujillo Alto. In his experience, "the electoral participation weakened the party structure and political education, leading to many cadres leaving the party. . . . In the 1978 Congress, I opposed participation in the elections of 1980, though I remained in the organization."[38]

Due to their geographical distance, Chicago PSP members felt a lack of knowledge of the dynamics occurring in New York and Puerto Rico. Many of these discussions, beginning with the rectification period of 1977, did not reflect the cardinal importance of the contributions of Puerto Ricans in the United States, given their experience of mass support, convening power, and ability to create alliances. Medina Cruz remembers reading the rectification analysis documents and feeling like I "belonged to one organization, and these documents were talking about another." The process was incomprehensible to me, and I greatly regretted moving away from the party. To me, the "problem of *gigantismo* was based on a belief of seizing power in ten years; that 'independence was around the corner.' Some got so attached to the revolution that they abandoned their families and other responsibilities." For me, rectification did not necessarily have to lead to the dissolution of the party: "It seemed that it didn't matter what we said in Chicago or New York—the decision had already been made." In analyzing the dissolution of the party, Sorrentini believes that the "empire triumphed by assuring that an anti-imperialist force with Marxist-Leninist principles in the belly of the beast ceased to exist as an organized force. By dissolving a vehicle for struggle, capable of bringing together forces both in Puerto Rico and the diaspora, the PSP committed an error."[39]

The Struggle Continues

Reflecting the complexity of the diaspora, many members of the PSP in Chicago returned to Puerto Rico, while others remained in the city. Those who returned point to the current precarious economic situation, unemployment, and mass migration as having an effect on the struggle. They reflect on how the lack of unity among the independence forces continues, albeit with a little more mutual respect, and they cite the positive and unifying efforts for the freedom of Oscar López Rivera, support for political prisoner Ana Belén, and the cleanup of Vieques. They see hopeful signs in the student movement in Puerto Rico, whose members understand that their struggle is part of the anti-colonial struggle.

After the dissolution of the party, Sorrentini joined others in Puerto Rico as a founding member of the Movimiento Independentista Nacional Hostosiano (MINH), which she views as a successor to the PSP and an instrument for social justice and national liberation. Since returning to Puerto Rico, she has dedicated many efforts to developing cultural spaces, such as the Fondo Puertorriqueño de Arte y Cultura, whose objectives include a center for *Diasporicans* and Puerto Rico's inclusion in the United Nations Educational, Scientific and Cultural Organization (UNESCO). She argues that the "U.S. ruling class wants to make Puerto Rico a fiscal paradise, an international tourist emporium, and begin the exploitation of the mines. . . . The movement must prioritize developing an alternative plan for a sovereign, independent country, deciding its own destiny."[40]

Other former members remain active in struggles in Chicago, battling many of the forces they faced for decades, joining with Puerto Rican organizations in efforts to empower the community. In 1995, Puerto Ricans celebrated the creation of Paseo Boricua on Division Street, with two fifty-nine-feet-high metal Puerto Rican flags marking a commercial and cultural area of Humboldt Park. Nevertheless, the gentrification of Humboldt Park and West Town, home of the Centro Cultural Ruiz Belvis, continues at a rapid pace, along with increased Puerto Rican migration to such suburbs as Cicero, Addison, Naperville, Schaumburg, and Waukegan.[41] Medina Cruz, who divides his time between Puerto Rico and Chicago, points out that "the same forces that displaced us from State and Grant, then Lincoln Park and Wicker Park, are the same forces we now battle in West Town. The only difference is that today, we have some political power and knowledge of how the system works to utilize in attempting to counter these forces."[42]

Independently or in joint initiatives, today ex-members of the PSP and the MLN continue to carry on the legacy of their movements by working on the consolidation and growth of LUCHA; the Humboldt Park Vocational Center; Centro Segundo Ruiz Belvis; the Corretjer Puerto Rican Cultural Center; the National Museum of Puerto Rican Arts and Culture (NMPRAC); and the Puerto Rican Agenda, among others. José López Rivera and Pablo Medina use the historical memory concept because they went through the difficult years of conflicts between the MLN and the PSP: "Learning from those mistakes, we now concentrate on what brings us together as we face the uncertainty of our common struggle ahead. Through the PSP and MLN, many dedicated a portion of their lives to the human right of Puerto Ricans to self-determination and independence, as well as the cause for social and political justice in Chicago. Though the list of names is too long to publish here, their commitment deserves the highest recognition."[43]

After spending decades in the struggle of the diaspora, Sorrentini stresses:

We are a Latin American nation, with five million of our nationals in the belly of a non–Latin American nation. This is a very difficult situation requiring great sensibility on our part. Our future will depend, in part, on how effectively we join these two realities. For me, the greatest influence in my life has been the diaspora, who has truly suffered uprooting, crossing the ocean and transforming that negative into a positive experience, providing an example for future generations. In dedicating my life to being a part of that—nothing compares to that, *compita*, absolutely nothing.[44]

NOTES

1. This chapter is based mostly on oral interviews of América (Meca) Sorrentini conducted by Carmen V. Rivera on December 4, 2015, and of Pablo Medina Cruz conducted by José E. Velázquez during the summer of 2017. Velázquez conducted further oral interviews in the summer of 2017 in two collective settings with PSP members Meca Sorrentini, Pablo Medina Cruz, Emily Blais Alemany, Dinorah Aulet, Mariecel Maldonado LaFontaine, and Jorge Capote Orcasitas. Additional interviews of Medina Cruz and Blais Alemany were conducted in February and March 2019. All of these interviews are available as part of the PSP-Interview file in the *¡Despierta Boricua!* Recovering History Project (hereafter, PSP Archives). This chapter is the final work of José E. Velázquez, but the analysis, descriptions, and narrative voice of the PSP in Chicago is that of Meca Sorrentini and Pablo Medina Cruz, unless otherwise noted in the text.

2. Merida M. Rúa, *A Grounded Identidad* (Oxford: Oxford University Press, 2012), 32–57; Lorrin Thomas and Aldo A. Lauria-Santiago, *Rethinking the Struggle for Puerto Rican Rights* (New York: Routledge, 2019), 125; and Lilia Fernández, *Brown in the Windy City: Mexicans and Puerto Ricans in Postwar Chicago* (Chicago: University of Chicago Press, 2012), 72–73.

3. Rúa, *A Grounded Identidad*, 57–63; Felix M. Padilla, *Puerto Rican Chicago* (Notre Dame, IN: University of Notre Dame Press, 1987), 78–98, 120–137, 144–179; Fernández, *Brown in the Windy City*, 72–76, 131–172; Thomas and Lauria-Santiago, *Rethinking the Struggle for Puerto Rican Rights*, 77–78, 110; Gina M. Pérez, *The Near Northwest Side Story: Migration, Displacement, and Puerto Rican Families* (Berkeley: University of California Press, 2004), 83–84; Felix M. Padilla, *Latino Ethnic Consciousness* (Notre Dame, IN: University of Notre Dame Press, 1985), 50–54; Wilfredo Cruz, *Puerto Rican Chicago* (Chicago: Arcadia Publishing, 2004); and Margaret Power, "Puerto Rican Nationalism in Chicago," CENTRO *Journal* 28, no. 2, (Fall 2016): 36–67.

4. Rúa, *A Grounded Identidad*, 47–50.

5. Ibid., 50; Padilla, *Latino Ethnic Consciousness*, 144–179; and Thomas and Lauria-Santiago, *Rethinking the Struggle for Puerto Rican Rights*, 77–78.

6. Sorrentini interview; "Que Ondee Sola," Union for Puerto Rican Students, Northeastern Illinois University, December 1, 1972, 10, PSP Archives.

7. Sorrentini interview.

8. Medina Cruz interview.

9. Maldonado LaFontaine interview; Capote Orcasitas interview.

10. Sorrentini interview.

11. Maldonado LaFontaine interview; Sorrentini interview.

12. Sorrentini interview; Medina Cruz interview.

13. Medina Cruz interview; flyer, "1er Concierto," Centro Ramón E. Betances; flyer, "The Status of Puerto Rico," Puerto Rican Solidarity Committee; "African Agenda," August–September 1974, vol. 3, no. 5; flyer, "National Lawyers Guild Invites You," October 5, 1974; all in PSP Archives.

14. Sorrentini interview; Medina Cruz interview.

15. "Speech delivered by Antonio Hernández Zone Secretary PSP Chicago at the Chicago 21 Tribunal," November 13, 1976; Organizing Committee for the Coalition to Stop the Chicago 21 Plan, June 23, 1977; flyer, "Por Nuestros Derechos En Unidad Y Resistencia," Comité Pro Derechos Del Puertorriqueño, PSP Archives; Sorrentini interview; Medina Cruz interview; and Padilla, *Puerto Rican Chicago*, 214–221.

16. Sorrentini interview; Medina Cruz interview; flyer, "Una Vez Más El Desfile," Partido Socialista Puertorriqueño, PSP Archives; flyer, "Marcha Por la Paz en el Desfile Puertorriqueño de Chicago," Partido Socialista Puertorriqueño, PSP Archives.

17. *El Boricua: Publicación Especial de Claridad en Saludos a Nuestros Hermanos Puertorriqueños en Chicago, Illinois* (Rio Piedras, Puerto Rico: Edición 2782, June 15–21, 2006), PSP Archives.

18. Medina Cruz interview.

19. Sorrentini interview; Medina Cruz interview.

20. Medina Cruz interview.

21. "In Celebration of Latino Week Activities," University of Illinois at Urbana, April 18–19, 1978, Union of Puerto Rican Students, PSP Archives; Medina Cruz interview.

22. Medina Cruz interview.

23. Ibid.

24. Sorrentini interview; James Blaut, "Are Puerto Ricans a National Minority?" *Monthly Review* 29, no. 1 (1977): 35–55; James Blaut, *The National Question: Decolonizing the Theory of Colonialism* (London: Zed Books, 1987); Maldonado LaFontaine interview; Capote Orcasitas interview.

25. Pamphlet, "Call for a National Hard Times Conference," Chicago, January 30–February 1, 1976, PSP Archives.

26. Sorrentini interview; Medina Cruz interview.

27. Medina Cruz interview; "Comunicado de Prensa del Partido Socialista Puertorriqueño," April 28, 1982, PSP Archives; "Defend the Right to Bail for Puerto Rican Political Prisoners & For All Working People," Chicago, 1985, PSP Archives.

28. Flyer, "El PSP y el Primer Festival Boricua de Chicago," PSP, Summer 1981, PSP Archives; "Amigos de la Justicia Social," PSP, November 1982, PSP Archives.

29. The three candidates were Miguel A. Velázquez, José "Cha Cha" Jiménez, and Frank Díaz. Jiménez and Velázquez won 27 percent of the vote in their wards; Díaz garnered 7 percent. Padilla, *Puerto Rican Chicago*, 194–200.

30. Sorrentini interview.

31. Ibid.; Medina Cruz interview.

32. Sorrentini interview; Fernández, *Brown in the Windy City*, 264–265; Luis Gutiérrez, *Still Dreaming: My Journey from the Barrio to Capitol Hill* (New York: Norton, 2013), 170–228.

33. Medina Cruz interview; flyer, "Que Somos? Nuestros Lazos Históricos Nos Unen. Vota Demócrata," PSP Archives; Gutiérrez, *Still Dreaming*, 247–262; and Thomas and Lauria-Santiago, *Rethinking the Struggle for Puerto Rican Rights*, 167.

34. Thomas and Lauria-Santiago, *Rethinking the Struggle for Puerto Rican Rights*, 129–134.

35. Blais Alemany interview.

36. Daley's machine won the election over the Harold Washington Party by 55.4 percent to 41.1 percent. The Republican candidate received only 3.5 percent, reflecting support for Daley from many Republicans. In the subsequent election of 1991, Daley easily won the Democratic Primary with 65.8 percent of the vote, facing a weakened Harold Washington Party that garnered 24.2 percent of the vote. Thomas and Lauria-Santiago, *Rethinking the Struggle for Puerto Rican Rights*, 167, 174; Padilla, *Puerto Rican Chicago*, 133, 228; Rúa, *A Grounded Identidad*, 99–100; Gutiérrez, *Still Dreaming*, 262–272; Sorrentini interview; Blais interview; and Medina Cruz interview.

37. Thomas and Lauria-Santiago, *Rethinking the Struggle for Puerto Rican Rights*, 167; Medina Cruz interview.

38. Capote interview; Maldonado LaFontaine interview.

39. Medina Cruz interview; Sorrentini interview.

40. Sorrentini interview.

41. Ibid.; Pérez, *The Near Northwest Side Story*, 13–35; Pérez, Gina, "Puerto Ricans" Entry in Electronic Encyclopedia of Chicago; *El Boricua: Publicación Especial* (Chicago: Chicago Historical Society, 2005), 3; *Puerto Ricans in Illinois, the United States, and Puerto Rico* (New York: Center for Puerto Rican Studies, Centro DS2016-9, April 2016).

42. Medina Cruz interview.

43. Ibid. See also Power, "Puerto Rican Nationalism in Chicago."

44. Sorrentini interview.

II
Testimonies

My Nation Is the Struggle

MARITZA ARRASTÍA

Writing and Resistance

I have come to realize that while I have had many objective obstacles to writing about my Puerto Rican Socialist Party (PSP) memories because of work deadlines and other life imperatives, I have also had a lot of resistance on unaware levels. It occurs to me that the resistance is actually at the heart of the story. My membership in the PSP was, other than leaving Cuba, the most formative experience of my life. My five years or so with the party prepared me for everything else I have done in my life. And at the same time, or maybe because it was so formative and generative and central, losing the party was a big hurt, a big loss, a multiple divorce. I do not think I have fully grieved it—maybe writing this account will be healing.

The party was all-consuming. When I joined, I made what I believed would be a lifelong commitment. I loved the people. I met my life partner in the party. My children were born into the party. Their *padrinos* (godparents) were party people. I did not expect those bonds to break. The bonds seemed at the time deeper than my blood-family ties because we shared a vision of the world we wanted, and together we were constructing the vehicle to make that world. But the bonds did break. I pretty much never saw or had much to do with any of the people again, and my sons never knew their padrinos.

As devastating as the loss of the party was for me, it was nothing compared to what it was for my partner, Alfredo López. I was female, and when I gave birth, it was quite easy for me to vanish into motherhood without any consequence. I also was not as high-ranking as Alfredo. I was the managing editor of the newspaper *Claridad bilingüe*; had been the Secretary of Information and Propaganda at one point; and had been a member of the *Comité Seccional* (CS), the leadership body of the U.S. Branch, but I had not been reelected in the Second Seccional Congress of 1978. Not being reelected had been my severance moment. I had cried all night but then had retreated to the numb inner place I had begun cultivating as a young person, the place that allowed me to survive childhood beatings, leaving Cuba at the age of fourteen, and any number of emotional and sexual traumas. It was different for Alfredo. He was a central leader, a key organizer who had been the editor of *Claridad bilingüe* and the lead of huge party projects, such as *El Acto Nacional* in Madison Square Garden, which brought together twenty thousand supporters of independence for Puerto Rico in 1974, and the Bicentennial Without Colonies massive demonstration in Philadelphia on July 4, 1976. When he became a father and therefore needed to generate income to support a family and wanted to work elsewhere, at *Seven Days* magazine, he was directly expelled from the PSP for refusing the order to go back to editing *Claridad*. (I have recently learned that he was not expelled but suspended, but neither he nor I knew that fact.) The PSP *reglamento* (bylaws) had a provision that stated that it was not possible to quit the party: quitting was merely grounds for expulsion. That was what we both believed had taken place—or what I believed that we both believed. I do not remember us talking very much about it. We had a newborn son, and we were busy enjoying him and surviving.

Living in the Future

I consider myself very lucky because I have gotten to live in the future several times in my life. Like many immigrants, I have gotten to travel in time and experience the different centuries and social systems of my countries of origin, Cuba and Puerto Rico, and the United States. In addition to traveling back in time as many immigrants do, I have gotten to travel to the future—once when I experienced the triumph of the Cuban Revolution in 1959 at the age of twelve and lived through the defeat of U.S. imperialism, and once when I got to be in the PSP for four or five years and experienced a prefiguration of an independent socialist Puerto Rico.

The first time I came to the United States was in 1952, when I was five going on six, and my father, who was a Presbyterian minister in Cuba, went to seminary in Chicago. We were living in Sancti Spiritus, one of the oldest cities in Cuba, in an old house with thick beams and a view of the Escambray Mountains from deep, high windows that opened onto an unpaved *callejón* (alley). At the time I left, I had only recently stopped believing that those purple mountains were heaven and stopped wishing that I could go there so I could get a look at Joseph's coat of many colors with my own eyes. We traveled by bus to Havana, a six-hour trip over the mountains, and then by freighter to Miami. There, my father bought a used white Plymouth, and we drove to Gettysburg, Pennsylvania, where he had a summer job being a pastor to migrant farmworkers before beginning his graduate courses at McCormick Seminary.

I had gone from my colonial city with cobblestones, narrow sidewalks, houses with doors flush to the sidewalk, houses built backward on hills, each room cascading down the slope, to my *abuela*'s house in La Habana, where bedrooms in rows accommodated twin aunts, my grandparents, a married aunt, her husband, and two cousins. Already La Habana was another century, with dense streets and lots of cars. The ferry landed us in Miami, tropical and foreign at the same time. Almost immediately, we set off driving to Gettysburg, where we lived in a decrepit, barren old farmhouse. I learned about skunks and was terrified that any chipmunk or squirrel might sprout a white streak of fur and make me smell. For an experiment, I ate dirt because if plants could, maybe I could as well. I did not like it. One night, bats swooped from the ceiling just as they used to do in Sancti Spiritus, but here I was allowed to crawl into bed with my parents.

I met a girl who was mixed American and Colombian and whose mother had named her Barbara while her husband was out of the country, unaware of how funny that name sounded combined with her surname Barriga. At their house, I was first served canned spinach and had to try very hard to swallow the green emulsion and not gag.

The greatest time warp was Chicago, where I lived in a multiple-dwelling building for the first time, the married students' dormitory, and had to learn English very fast. I went from knowing no words at all to painfully reading the words my second-grade teacher printed underneath drawings she made herself of a jug of milk, an iron. I remember noticing one day that iron was spelled *iron* but pronounced *iern*, and after that, next thing I recall, I was rattling off the English language with the other seminary children. Nevertheless, living in a future century and in English was difficult. In class, I was teased, and while I understood the spirit, I did not understand the content. One girl was saying that I would "Mary" a certain boy. I thought the tease was some mockery of my name, Maritza. Years later, I got it—they were saying I would *marry* the boy.

We went back to Cuba in 1959, this time to Havana, and my parents put us in a bilingual Episcopalian school in Havana so we would not forget English. Another time warp, another uprooting, another dislocation. My classmates were children of U.S. military families and consulate staff. We visited Sancti Spiritus, where a corner bodega was now called a "grocery." My various worlds converged and diverged. What was I? Which world did I belong in?

My father had gone to seminary in Puerto Rico in his very early twenties. There, he had met my mother in the church in Santurce where he had been a student pastor. They had married, and she had moved to Cuba, and I had been conceived soon after. As a Puerto Rican woman, my mother was quite foreign in Cuba. She did not belong, and neither did I. Despite many similarities, there were deep cultural differences between Puerto Rico and Cuba. My Cuban family had more consistency and lived close together, many in the same house. Not so for my Puerto Rican family, where my grandmother was forced to be the primary breadwinner by working in factories in New York. These differences showed up within my Cuban extended family and between them and my mother in the ways they interacted and socialized. I do not believe that my mother ever felt fully accepted, and she never was, in fact, fully accepted. Her sense of not belonging was passed on to me. In addition, because of being a Protestant minister's child, I was raised with restrictions that my Cuban relatives did not share, such as not being allowed to dance because, according to my father, that was people having sex standing up in front of other people. All that added up to a sense of neither of us fully belonging.

I grew up hearing stories of the *rebeldes* (rebels) in the mountains, the *torturados* (tortured). People suspected of, or caught at, "conspiring" against Fulgencio Batista's government were apprehended and tortured to extract information and to terrorize, as a deterrent. They might have their eyeballs gouged out; if female, they might be given vaginal douches with acid or have their breasts cut off. Many people did not survive these tortures, and their bodies might turn up by the side of a road or be tossed into the harbor for the sharks to dispose of. When we returned from Chicago, on a freighter, our luggage was searched, and my father's *caqui* (khaki) trousers were confiscated (perhaps because the inspectors believed that they could be used to impersonate a Batista army soldier). I was aware that the times were exciting and dangerous. Many Protestants were involved in *el clandestinaje* (underground activities). Faustino Perez, who was in charge of fundraising for the *26 de Julio* (a revolutionary organization that later became the political party led by Fidel Castro) underground, was a Presbyterian and my father's friend. We once hid him in our small apartment in El Vedado. My father told me not to mention to anyone in school that a man was sleeping on our couch. One day when I came home, I mentioned that my friend Anita's father was some kind of army officer and that she had been picked up from school by a uniformed *chofer* (chauffeur). My father got pale. I was not used to seeing fear on his face, and it shocked me. He asked me whether I had told Anita anything about our guest.

One of my father's jobs when we came back from Chicago was to be a chaplain for young Protestant students at the Universidad de La Habana. I would go with my father to a house near the university, where they boarded. Many of the young people were involved in the clandestinaje. They would come to my father with their moral dilemmas as they tried to reconcile their Christianity and their revolutionary work: What about killing? What were they to do if their revolutionary work put them in a situation where they had to kill?

Years later, I learned that in one of my father's customary evangelism trips, this one to Mexico, Faustino had enlisted him to deliver to Fidel ten thousand pesos that had been raised to buy the *Granma*, the boat used for the invasion of the insurrectionists. The young Protestants commissioned my father to ask Fidel whether he was a Communist, a Marxist-Leninist. My father later told me, when I was already an adult, that he had done this. He had met Fidel and Che Guevara, and their Spanish trainer, Alberto Bayo, a veteran of the Spanish Civil War who taught guerrilla skills to the insurrectionists-in-training. They had met in a house in the fancy Mexico City neighborhood El Pedregal. After a shared meal, they had sat at a marble-topped table, where Fidel had crumbled some bread and, as he spoke, spread it and mounded it and spread it on the marble top. My father had asked him the question, and Fidel had told him that he was anti-imperialist but that he was not and had never been a Marxist-Leninist. Fidel had explained to my father his vision for the insurrection: he expected that the revolution would be victorious in a year. He had told my father his vision of avoiding revenge bloodshed by holding summary trials of the *Batistatos* war criminals. He had invited my father to join the expedition as a chaplain. My father had told him that he had a family and could not. Fidel had given my father written messages to deliver upon his return, which my father had hidden among his sermons. If those messages had been found, he would have almost certainly been tortured or killed.

Fidel's tutelage supported my father through some of the vertigo he experienced at the high-speed revolutionary changes. He understood the summary trials. A serious stumbling block for my father was when the revolution, after relying on the Protestant church for technical assistance to design a literacy campaign, forbade the church from continuing its literacy campaign once the revolution launched its own. I was not allowed to go with my friends to be an *alfabetizadora* (literacy tutor). My father stopped my mother from becoming a *miliciana* (militia woman). After the Bay of Pigs invasion, I would hear my father and mother arguing about leaving Cuba. "Who have you been talking with who has changed you?" she would ask. My mother supported the revolution's initiatives. She loved that bathrooms and showers were built at El Salado, the beach close to where we lived. She liked the idea of a people's militia to defend the revolution. Her childhood had been uprooted. She had spent much of it in New York with her mother, who had worked in garment factories to support the family (my mother's grand-parents, aunt, and brother). For long periods, she had been left with her grandmother and aunt in Puerto Rico. After spending fifteen consecutive years in Cuba, she considered it her real home. She did not want to emigrate again, to be an exile. Her screams did not win that battle. I often wonder what my life might have been like if my mother had won those arguments instead of my father and we had remained in Cuba, integrated with the revolution. The irony was that we left because my father was offered a job in the Evangelism Division of the World Council of Churches in Geneva, but after we landed in Miami, when the church *burócratas* (bureaucrats) got wind that he no longer supported the revolution, the job offer was withdrawn. A very cautious man, my father would not have left Cuba without a job in hand. The church, whose anti-Communism stance had shaped my father's views (another time warp), had left those ideas behind and to embrace theology of liberation. My father was now loyal to an anachronistic master and had been left in the lurch by the master-de-jour. Had the job offer been withdrawn before we left, again, my family might have remained in Cuba.

I attended Cathedral, an Episcopalian bilingual school in El Vedado, from 1954 to 1958. All courses were in English except for a class called *Español*, which included history and language. The professor, Dr. Coronado, taught us that Communists canned children's flesh for food. Anti-Communism was thick. One day, when we were driving home (still in our old white Plymouth, which my father had brought back from Chicago on that freighter), we passed the rich neighborhood of Miramar on the way to our modest and distant *reparto* (neighborhood), Nuevo Santa Fe. I was staring at mansion after mansion with big curved driveways, and then I said, "I don't understand why they don't take the extra money those people have and give it to the people who don't have enough." My father looked at my mother and said, "*Nos salió comunista la niña*" (We got ourselves a Communist daughter). The thing was, I could hear a tone of pride and admiration in his voice. If Communism believed what I had just said, it must be good. I began to have fantasies of being in *una celula comunista* (a Communist cell), of being one of the conspirators against the Batistato I heard my parents, aunts, and uncles talking about whenever they got together.

The way I learned history in Cuba, I got the idea that the sole point of human activity was liberation. To be like José Marti, a revolutionary leader in Cuba's war for independence from Spain in 1898, was the purpose of human life.

But we did leave, and I arrived in the United States in 1961, in the midst of a revolution here. The Vietnam War, civil rights, and countercultural movements were on the rise, and I was swept up by them. The culture shock was overwhelming—several time warps colliding. In Cuba, my friends and I had long conversations contemplating whether it would be a positive thing for our prospective *novios* (boyfriends) to go to prostitutes so that they would not pressure us for sex. As a Protestant girl in Cuba, I was not allowed to dance, smoke, or drink. Even going to the movies on Sunday was a sin.

Because I had gone to a bilingual school, my English literacy was far beyond my cultural literacy. I landed by coincidence in a private New York City school. While apartment hunting in New York in mid-September, my parents asked the real estate agent at an apartment way above our budget whether she knew of any schools that had not started classes yet, and she mentioned New Lincoln. My parents only realized during the interview that this school was not a public school, but the school was looking to integrate racially, and its administrators tested my brother and me. We got placed— me as a junior, although I was fourteen, and my twelve-year-old brother as a freshman. My classmates could not tell from my English that I had just arrived here. They were sophisticated, well-to-do New Yorkers. Many were politically engaged participants of the counterculture who smoked, drank, and were sexually active.

I was so terrified to go to New Lincoln from my Puerto Rican grand-mother's tiny apartment on Eighteenth street in Chelsea that first thing just about every morning, I raced to the bathroom to throw up. This school was fairly small, and many students had been together since elementary school. For many weeks, I had no friends and would hide out in the library during lunch to avoid the lunchroom, especially the closed-off section at one end called the student lounge, where the cool kids gathered to smoke cigarettes (the very idea!) and play bridge. In the library, I wrote poems about death; one poem, which I called "Laberinto," about the constant human quest for what was only to be found within each of us, became my first published poem when my father included it in a small religious Spanish-language magazine called *Dialogo* that he published out of his office at the Inter-church Center on Riverside Drive.

Between classes one morning, three young women, sophomores and closer in age to me, who had begun to befriend me, called me into a class-room, sat me down, and announced that they had decided to be my friend even though I was a Cuban refugee. They were all supporters of the revolu-tion. In art class, a senior named Chris would sit next to me and talk to me about the revolution and why it was good and ask me what I thought about it. I told him that I certainly did not want the revolution to be overthrown because I did not want more bloodshed, but I could not bring myself to say that I supported it. The summer after my senior year, when I was visiting family in Puerto Rico, I wrote to Chris to tell him that I was rethinking my views on the revolution. When he wrote to ask me why I had sent him a letter in Spanish, I realized that I had mailed his letter to my parents and theirs to him, thus announcing to my parents my changing views. My parents never mentioned the letter.

It was not until close to two years later, when I was in Wisconsin University and saw a film about the Vietnam War, that I had recognized that what was happening in Vietnam was what had happened in Cuba. I realized that for me, it had been necessary to live in the belly of the beast to fully understand imperialism. I had a key existential question: what would have happened if my family had not gone into exile? I began to consider the possibilities. If I had stayed, I might not have understood imperialism well enough to grasp the historic and strategic significance of the Cuban Revolution. Had I stayed, without understanding the empire from within, the Cuban tradition of liberation might have resulted in my being a dissident. But in the United States, I was becoming a revolutionary.

After I graduated from college and moved back to New York, I had several friends who were trying to figure out how to be revolutionaries. One high school friend in particular took me under his wing. I believed at that time that of its own accord, capitalism would become more benign. He explained exploitation to me, surplus value, and the role of the reserve army of the unemployed. There could never be a form of capitalism in which everyone could have socially useful work. Unemployment was a pillar of capitalism. He destroyed my reformist dreams. There was no choice but to be a revolutionary, but where and how?

Perhaps it was he who told me about a rally at Dag Hammarskjöld Plaza about Puerto Rican independence because the United Nations Decolonization Committee was discussing the colonial case of Puerto Rico. I went to Dag Hammarskjöld Plaza in 1972 and stood at the far edge of the crowd gathered in the narrow rectangular space. From there, I could see the stage. A thin, mustachioed man in a long coat was speaking. I wondered, "Who are these people?" I had to know who they were because I knew I had found what I had been looking for—I had found my revolutionary organization. Thus began my second time in the future.

But before that, my first time in the future is important to tell because it has informed everything. My first time in the future was on the morning of January 1, 1959, when my brother came into my room in our small house in Nuevo Santa Fe outside Havana. He screamed, *"Batista se fue!"* (Batista left!). I thought he meant that Batista had gone away on a holiday trip, and I replied, *"¿Y que?"* (So what?). My brother came closer to my bed and stood over me, repeating, *"No, no, se fue, se fue."* And just like that, the thing you long for but deeply believe will never happen did happen: *La dictadura* was over. Batista was gone. We ran out into the street, where all the neighbors were gathered. We found red and black fabric to tie together for a 26 de

Julio flag. My father got all four of us, my mother, brother, and me, into our white Plymouth. We took pots to bang against the sides of the car. We joined the many other cars on the big avenue everyone called De los Dinosaurios because of the curved concrete streetlamps that looked like dinosaur necks. Everywhere, people drove cars with red and black fabric tied to the antennas or streaming from the windows, banging pots on the sides of the cars, screaming. At an intersection, we saw a small crowd uprooting hated parking meters. An entire nation was rejoicing, and I learned the most powerful lesson of my life: We can win. Victory is possible. History is not a succession of dictators. System change is possible.

Meeting the PSP

I am not sure of the sequence of events after my lightning-bolt encounter with the PSP at Dag Hammarsjöld Plaza. I do not remember whether I went there by myself or with my high school friend. I do not remember whether I met Jeff Perry there. Maybe we were standing close together, and we got to talking. He connected me at first with the Puerto Rican Solidarity Committee because he was part of that. I am not sure whether he helped me get a job at ASPIRA in Hoboken at the same time. I was living on Prince Street and commuting to Hoboken. Jeff hooked me up with a translation job at *Claridad*, and even though I lived in Manhattan, I began to actively participate in the Hoboken *núcleo* of the PSP. I identified as a writer, although before working at ASPIRA, I was employed at a day care center. At that time, I was trying to read my poems in open poetry readings like at Saint Mark's Poetry project. I had recently separated from a husband I had married at age twenty-three.

Claridad was a dream come true. It was writing with a purpose. The managing editor, Alfredo López, was the first person who took my intelligence seriously, listened to what I had to say, and respected my views. It was not long before I was asked to become a *redactora* (editor) and offered a job as a *funcionaria* (full-time cadre). I made $40 a week; my rent was $70 a month. The work was intense. We had a weekly deadline. Every Thursday was an overnight to lay out the paper manually on a light table, rolling waxed strips of typed text onto boards. We developed our own photographs and had to figure out mathematically the proportion of the photo to fit into the hole in the text. We proofread the text again and again and sometimes had to cannibalize old boards to find words or even individual letters and strip those in over typos with wax. We joked, we laughed, we cried. At dawn, some *compañeros* took the boards to the printer, and I walked home, watching the sunrise, from our office on Twentieth and Broadway, through Union Square Park, to my small Prince Street apartment. There is no joy like that of good work done to the very best of one's ability and the limit of one's strength.

Although we were doing our best, it was not good enough for some. In Puerto Rico, the joke among party people was that *Claridad bilingüe* was, in fact, *Claridad trilingüe*: Spanish, English, and Spanglish. We did not understand language oppression at that time and were not equipped to claim that language is a living organism and that what mattered was that we had figured out ways to keep our language, even if doing so required having it change. We laughed at the *trilingüe* joke, and yet we felt humiliated. This example was just one of the tensions in the party resulting from our *Una Sola Nación, Un Solo Partido* (One Nation, One Party) position. We were one, but there were cracks in the unity. One part of the party was "better."

The Committee to End Sterilization Abuse

I went to a National Lawyers Guild workshop of some sort held in a big, many-windowed room at New York University. A small group of women was meeting on the topic of sterilization abuse. Attending were Helen Rodríguez-Trías, Karen Stamm, and Carol McVicker. Also present was Nancy Stearns, a lawyer from the Center for Constitutional Rights, and Diane Lacey, a very experienced and well-known women's health activist working in the Health and Hospitals Corporation, who was already engaged in fighting for the approval and implementation of sterilization guidelines. The group was very excited about working on the issue, and I chose to join them. The PSP was also concerned about this issue and officially assigned me to work on this campaign. Puerto Rican women on the island had been manipulated over many years to have their tubes tied, and at that time, one-third of the women of child-bearing age had been sterilized. In New York, women of color were also being manipulated. The policy goal was "informed consent." We decided to continue meeting and soon gave ourselves a name, the Committee to End Sterilization Abuse (CESA). The acronym forms the word for *cease* or *desist* in Spanish.

While I was in Puerto Rico to work on the main *Claridad* as a kind of training, I got to interview the secretary of health, whose name I cannot remember. I think a visiting European journalist had lined up the interview for herself, and I somehow ended up being her interpreter. She let me conduct the whole interview and sat back and watched. The secretary admitted that all of it had happened. For decades, the United States had been entrapping women, sometimes bribing them, into get their tubes tied. If the women concluded that tied tubes could be untied, they were allowed to keep that impression and were not informed that the operation was essentially irreversible. It was empowering to get to write and publish a key story, a big scoop.

In New York City, the fight for informed consent was won. Being one of CESA's founders and leaders was joyous political work. Nevertheless, as it turned out, a culture clash was brewing that I was unaware of. My sole political experience had been with the democratic, centralist, Marxist-Leninist PSP. I showed up one day to what I thought was our regular meeting to find that all the other women—all white, as I recall—had decided to meet to address my *commissar* style of leadership. Nobody had forewarned me, and as I recall, only one person, I am not sure who, backed me. I remember walking out in a daze, gutted, numb. I think whoever the one kind woman was said something to me like, "They should have let you know they were going to do this."

El Acto en el Garden . . . Mi Nación Es la Lucha

In 1974, the party decided to organize an *Acto de Solidaridad con Puerto Rico*, a mass rally to express solidarity for Puerto Rican independence. The rally was to be held in Madison Square Garden on October 27. *Núcleos* mobilized in every city in which the party was organized. It was a massive effort. Alfredo López, my *Claridad* leader who later became my life partner, was the head organizer. *Claridad bilingüe* published many articles to mobilize and to denounce efforts to impede us. *El Acto En el Garden Va* (The Garden Rally Is On) read one headline. Famous people performed and spoke—Ray Barretto's orchestra that included a young Rubén Blades as vocalist, and Jane Fonda. Conservative TV personality Geraldo Rivera was booed. I was one of the *periodistas* (journalists) covering the event. While standing behind the front bank of seats and looking at the stage, watching Ray Barretto perform, I had an epiphany. Where do I belong, what is my country, had been an abiding existential question my whole life—in Cuba because I had been half Cuban and half Puerto Rican, Protestant in a Catholic country; in exile because I was not a North American; in the PSP because I was half Cuban. As I watched, I had this thought: "*Mi nación es la lucha*" (My nation is the struggle). I understood that no borders separated our liberation struggles. I had discovered my true nation—*la lucha* had been, was, would be my home.

Inscribed in Memory

Getting to work for *Claridad* gave me a direct connection to a means of production and creating a socially useful product every week. What a privilege! That Thursday all-nighter was exhausting, frustrating, challenging, and one of the most joyous experiences of my life. What a joy it was to solve difficult problems collectively. One week, to fill a hole in the board, we cannibalized a *New Yorker* magazine floating around the paste-up room and inserted a cartoon of a man skipping up a street. The caption read, "*Desfile un Día, Pobreza Todos los Días*" (Parade One Day, Poverty Every Day). That was the party's slogan for our contingents in the Puerto Rican Day Parade.

We had in-jokes that caused us to cry laughing. One of the compañeros, David Quiñones, once told a story about his grandmother in Puerto Rico screaming at him when he was in her *cilantrillo* patch, "*¡Fuera del cilantrillo!*" (Out of the cilantro patch!). Deep into the *amanecida* (early morning), around 2:00 A.M. or later, all it took was for one of us to call out, "*¡Fuera del cilantrillo!*" for us all to break into laughter. At those hours, with that level of exhaustion and frustration, laughter saved us, kept us going, embodied the depth of our connection, affirmed our joy. There is no greater human joy than that of doing good work, collectively, making the world better, the world we want, inch by inch, day by day, stripped correction by stripped correction.

I was in the second tier of party leaders, not in the *Comisión Política* (Political Commission) but *Jefa de Redacción* (the editor-in-chief) of *Claridad*. Later, I figured out that nobody else wanted to do it, but I was proud to be asked to represent the party at a forum on the Puerto Rican national question at the Methodist Church on West Fourth Street, near Washington Square Park. Representatives from *El Comité* and the Puerto Rican Revolutionary Workers Organization (PRRWO), formerly the Young Lords, were also speaking. I remember that the church was packed, and when it was my turn, I spoke on what I had studied, the party's line: Puerto Ricans in the United States and Puerto Ricans on the island are one nation. Independence in Puerto Rico constitutes the first democratic right for Puerto Ricans in the United States. The PRRWO had gone to China and been told by the Chinese that this view was incorrect: Puerto Ricans in the United States and on the island belonged to different nations. A friend who heard me speak later told me that I should have stuck to something I knew well. The truth was that I could not—my job was to present the party line. I survived the presentation and fielded some questions, and I felt elated as I filed out of the church with some of my PSP compañeros. As I reached the foyer between the meeting space and the front door, I heard a scream and felt from my left a woman lunge at me, arms swinging. Her comrades restrained her, so she did not land her punch. It was Gloria González Cruz, who had spoken for the PRRWO at the forum. Evidently my words had so deeply offended her that she needed to assault me. Sectarianism in the Puerto Rican movement was intense. The experience shook me to the core. I still shudder sometimes when I remember it.

I was not prepared for being *La Secretaria de Información y Propaganda* (the Secretary of Information and Propaganda). Working on *Claridad*, producing a weekly product, had kept us honest. I had never tasted party bureaucrazy yet, a rigid, top-down decision-making structure and practice. The meetings were endless and tedious, and they were ruled with an iron hand. Early on, I was excited because I had a lot of ideas after reading Paulo Freire's *Pedagogy of the Oppressed*. I imagined that I would have some leeway, and I came up with a detailed political education and propaganda plan. I do not remember a single element of it, only that I worked very hard on it and it was mine. It was quashed and crushed without a glance. There was no discussion of it. Nobody as far as I could tell even bothered to read it. My job, as it turned out, was to follow orders. I got my taste of alienation, and because I had been used to work that I was deeply engaged in shaping at the paper (while always obviously within the party line), the alienation was extreme.

At one point, I was directing information and propaganda, still working at *Claridad*, and very pregnant. I had done my all-nighter at the newspaper, twenty-four sleepless hours, and it was also my night to stand guard at the party offices (and *Claridad*'s) on East Thirteenth Street—we were under Federal Bureau of Investigation (FBI) surveillance and had decided someone had to be in the office twenty-four hours a day to prevent agents from coming in and rummaging through our files. That responsibility added another twenty-four straight hours of no sleep. As I walked out onto Thirteenth Street after my guard shift was done and made my way home to my apartment in Riis Houses on Avenue D, a thought that had been forming for a while bubbled up into my conscious mind: "There is something wrong with this picture." I began to wonder whether it made sense to be part of an organization that was so thoughtless that it could assign a woman in advanced pregnancy an all-night guard shift the day after her all-nighter putting the newspaper to bed. I began to realize that I had put my entire life in the hands of the party, and I began to rethink that decision. Maybe it was time I began to think about myself and my needs.

What We Know Matters

Many things converged: the wheel of history had turned, and the movements that had been on top of that wheel, that had made us believe that we were within sight of independence, were now being crushed underneath it. On that wheel, the party had taken on bigger and bigger projects: the Garden in '74, the Bicentennial Without Colonies mass rally in Philadelphia in '76, electoral participation on the island that same year. And Alfredo and I became parents. From where I sat, or lay breastfeeding, it looked like this: under the pressure of the turning historical wheel, the ideological, cultural, and class differences between U.S. Puerto Ricans and island Puerto Ricans that had always been present in the party began to crack the organization and erode its integrity. Alfredo was a U.S.-based Puerto Rican. The Political Commission was dominated by the Puerto Rico–based line. Under the guise of pressuring him to continue leading *Claridad* full time after he was a parent and needed a living wage, the party purged him. Leaving or being forced to leave the party almost broke Alfredo. My role in the party was smaller, and I was always somewhat marginal, seen as not a "real" Puerto Rican because I was half Cuban. But it seemed to me, from where I sat breastfeeding, that it was easy for me to disappear into motherhood. I do not remember anybody coming to talk to me about what role I might take. It might have happened, but I do not remember. I remember that I simply faded away from the party into motherhood.

I have been privileged to live in the future. Paradoxically, because we had the line "one nation, one party," and because we embodied that organizationally and waged campaigns that engaged both the island and the empire, we inserted the clarity and urgency that come from living where the system collapse is more advanced (the colony) into the reality of the metropolis in which the system collapse is more obscured. The benefits enjoyed in the metropolis of the empire, the fruit of imperialist exploitation, obscured the collapse of the system and softened it. But we inserted the colonial reality, operating from its urgency and clarity, into the belly of the beast.

And now that systemic collapse is within the metropolis. In a sense, the metropolis has cycled its way to a past it has avoided until now. For the first time, the United States has a visibly crazed ruler in power. The ruling class is falling apart and drawing its desperation cards: to fan a fascist movement and wage more wars. The ways we learned to think and strategize in the PSP—that we believed in victory and fought to win, that we knew it was important to take on not only the battles you were assured of winning but those that truly mattered to win—those are key lessons now, in the belly of the beast. We lived through an era of great struggles, key fights, and great political repression. What we know matters—even, or especially, what we know about how movements and organizations fall apart.

Writing this essay has allowed me to reflect on my painful multiple divorce from the party and to reclaim that lesson: *mi nación sigue siendo la lucha* (my nation continues to be the struggle).

5

The Personal Is Political

Children of the Puerto Rican
Socialist Party Speak

TERESA BASILIO GAZTAMBIDE
AND CARMEN V. RIVERA

Focus Groups with Children of the Puerto Rican Socialist Party: The Third Generation

F amilies create memories, and children growing up in homes with activist parents recall their upbringing in any number of ways. We are formed by memories; the way it feels to be who we are, our passions, expectations, and fears are all built upon what we have experienced before.

The home environment, their parent's or guardian's values and opinions, forms children's first impression of the world. As they grow, their engagement in community further fuels their outlook: the schools they attend, the friends they make, and the social and cultural exchanges they engage or identify with.

The writings in this book capture the history of the Puerto Rican Socialist Party (PSP). This chapter seeks to illuminate some of the experiences of home and family as recalled by children of the PSP. A handful of voices from these now young adults are included. They are third-generation Puerto Ricans, born in the late 1960s to early 1980s and raised in the United States. We wanted to know how the two influences of home and community affected and shaped these young adults: what their political and social beliefs were and whether they were involved in any political or social movements in the United States.

How did their upbringing influence their adult pursuits, identities, and relationship to Puerto Rico? What are their views on the political status of Puerto Rico and its relationship to the United States?

These voices add to the history of the past by demonstrating how that history is linked to the current moment. What can participants in current social movements and progressives learn from these voices? How can we forge productive intergenerational conversations that enlighten, inspire, and move us to create a world where justice and equality prevail?

We organized two focus groups involving seven participants.[1]

The focus group participants included four males and three females. Their selection was determined primarily by geographical proximity and convenience. During the time of their parents' involvement in the PSP, they all lived in New York City. They represent a mere fraction of the children of the PSP, but we believe that we can extract important lessons from the recollections of their parents' political involvement and how this activity influenced their own beliefs and values.

Camilo, thirty-seven years old, is a community health advocate; his brother Emil, thirty-nine years old, is a college counselor. Both their parents were *militantes* and base leaders in the Bronx from the 1970s through early 1990.

Jessica, forty-three years old, is a corporate health executive. Her mother was a base member in Brooklyn who led the party in New York during the final years of its existence, in the early 1990s.

Karim, thirty-nine years old, is a filmmaker. His parents were leaders of the U.S. Branch during the 1970s.

Lenina, forty-two years old, is a writer and media producer. Her parents were leaders based in Brooklyn. Her mother was also a member of the *Seccional* Committee in the late 1970s and early 1980s. Her father was also a cultural performer.

Orlando, thirty-five years old, is a human rights advocate; his stepsister Rachel, forty-eight years old, is a high school teacher. Both parents were leaders of the U.S. Branch throughout the 1970s and early 1980s.

Memories of Place and Time

Children of radical left parents can have dismal recollections of being dragged against their will to meetings, marches, and pickets. Making revolution and liberating a nation from its colonizer demanded a 24/7 commitment of *valor y sacrificio* (courage and sacrifice). PSP militants were convinced that independence and socialism was "right around the corner"—hence the 1975 slogan, "*¡Independencia Ya, Socialismo Ahora Mismo!*" (Independence! Socialism Now!). Party life was filled with meetings, study circles, weekly paper sales, mass mobilizations, pickets and demonstrations, and a host of fundraising events.

Steve Early's writing in *Monthly Review* online[2] speaks of leftist parents "who made their own politics a mandatory (rather than elective) subject, turning any related praxis into a grim family duty." In his book *The Children of the Movement*,[3] John Blake describes the emotional disconnect between many civil rights movement leaders and their children. Our focus group participants describe a less bleak picture of growing up with radical parents and the experience of being taken to political or social events.

For these third-generation participants, some recollections are joyful, but they also have questions and a desire to learn more about what their parents' radicalism was all about:

> To go to a demonstration, it would be so cultural and beautiful, and then there would be a lot of trust that anyone there would look out for your kid. [Lenina]

> I don't know about the rest of you all, but I just remember going to a lot of meetings. . . . They were constantly meeting. Quite a few [meetings] at Casa Las Americas on the weekends and even during the week. I can remember them always working. I don't know what they were working on, but they were always working. [Jessica]

Emil and Camilo also remember going to Casa Las Americas (Casa) on West Fourteenth Street in Manhattan, where the PSP held many *Viernes Socialista* (Socialist Friday) political and cultural forums open to the public. Casa was also a space for fundraising dances, organizing meetings, and membership assemblies. The members of Casa were Cuban supporters of the revolution and close allies of the PSP.

The annual summer outings, *Jiras de Verano*, were among many party fundraising efforts. Brothers Emil and Camilo recall these events fondly. In 1972, eight buses left from the Bronx, Manhattan, and Brooklyn, filled with members, sympathizers, and their families, all heading to Arrow Park in Monroe, New York. These outings served as a recreational outlet and moment of respite from the demands of political work for PSP members and their families:

> We would go to Arrow Park and Weiss Ecology Center . . . and went to cabins. . . . I always had in my mind this mix of . . . serious stuff going on, but there was always a party involved . . . some type of enjoyment. [Emil]

And there were always other kids around . . . and we'd just run around. [Camilo]

I always remember having that feeling . . . like people had a stereo-type of somebody who's an activist, like they didn't really have fun or, unless you were a hippie, then you had too much fun [*group laughter*]. [Emil]

Parental Influence on the Third Generation's Beliefs, Values, and Political Engagement

For most of this third generation, their parents' revolutionary beliefs and their long-term commitment to those values have been extremely influential in their understanding and analysis of current society. Some of that influence came from exposure to radical ideas, people, books, films, and events that directly led to their understanding of how power functions in society, but it also came from the ways they lived their lives:

The way he [father] put it to me . . . was that the people going through the situation have to be the ones to fix it and to lead it . . . be at the forefront of leading the change. And that's something that I took with me to the northwest Bronx. . . .

They [parents] showed me how to understand . . . power. . . . [I]t wasn't just about who gets elected as president . . . but that power relates to every single thing you're going to go through in life, start-ing from school, to when you move out, to when you are working, to when you have a family. . . . [T]here's individual power, and there's collective power, and capitalism in this country can lean towards individual power and the promotion of that, and we have a certain belief that says that collective power is the better, more just struc-ture. . . . [A]nd that's how I came into . . . being a progressive. So, they [parents] had a huge influence. [Orlando]

The PSP [asked,] "What is our goal?" The goal was independence, but not just any political independence, but also a combination of democratic values, and they implemented that in the way they would hold their meetings. It wasn't one person in the front, giv-ing orders to everyone; it was a collective. To me, any organization, whether they are Puerto Rican or from any other movement, it's to learn from that, to figure out what is your philosophy, what is your way of thinking, what is it that you are trying to do, your mission and your vision. [Camilo]

If their parents remained consistent in their engagement with social justice struggles, their children identify this influence as important to their ongoing engagement with and belief in social justice struggles:

> The fact that they never changed their minds about their commitment to a certain perspective about the world and certain values [has been key]. . . . Even though society changed, and their lives look different . . . but the core values and . . . the importance of having a radical thing that you are trying to do to change things profoundly . . . that they still continue to be active forty years on and still have these very strong beliefs and have not wavered or let any kind of confusions muck it all up in their minds—that's been a huge thing for me. [Karim]

Yet not all feel aligned with their parent's political ideology. Jessica feels distant from her family's political beliefs, having embraced a more spiritual practice in her life, but she still sees resonance in how her mother shaped who she is:

> I have very different beliefs and values than they do necessarily. But I think early on it helped me identify two things: one is, whatever I do, I have to make it better for whoever is coming behind me right, and that with the right folks together, you can make a difference.
>
> It may have come from at least observing the purpose of organizational structure happening in the meetings at people's houses; they would do stuff that I may not have understood what they were doing or why they were doing it . . . but recognizing that if you've got the right folks in the room, you can actually get a lot done. . . . [E]ven though I live a very different life . . . I still take that approach. . . . [W]e gotta make it better for the next go round, we learn from the mistakes that have been made, and we move forward, and we do this together as a group.

For Karim, the struggle to remain committed and hopeful in the midst of a very different historical moment from the one his parents experienced has been challenging:

> Even though I am from this very political family and I have the politics that I have . . . I have to reckon with the effect that growing

up in the U.S. has . . . being an American and kind of American-
ized . . . how it affects me and . . . [how I] live my life right now. I'm
close to forty years old, and I used to be much more active than I
am now. It's a real battle to figure out how to keep that central in my
life . . . hopefulness and really staying engaged. Trying to figure out
how to have a revolutionary life basically in this country and in this
time. It's different from when I was twenty or thirty years old. It's
a different world. How can I have a revolutionary life in every way
that I can? That's a personal thing that I am trying to figure out now.

For some, having parents who were engaged in political work meant that
they had a framework with which to evaluate and assess their own political
engagement. They acknowledge that they live in different times, but being
able to talk to their parents about current events and the experience of living in today's world has been invaluable. The ability to make sense of the
current reality, even if the children's opinions and values are unpopular, has
been important:

> With the political work that I have been involved with, I think that
> people are really trying to find . . . a political home. . . . I need a
> home . . . where you check in to see that you're in alignment, because
> we could be doing all this social justice work . . . but in the end,
> you don't know. We might have questions about, for example, heal-
> ing work. What of healing work is radical or revolutionary? What
> of it is problematic, or religion or something? You need places to
> check out and check back in. I don't know if the PSP served in that
> way, but I think in some ways it did because that's part of why our
> family . . . was so heartbroken when it ended, because they lost that
> space. But it's also a question of what are we doing to make that
> space for ourselves?
>
> I always feel that with my parents, I always have to check back
> in—they're this big influence in your life, and they're the one check-
> ing a lot of stuff. [Lenina]

Alongside providing their children with a progressive and radical lens
with which to understand the world, some of the parents were careful to not
dictate their children's beliefs. These parents encouraged critical thinking so
their children could discover and come to their own beliefs. Contrary to the
popular stereotype of radical parents as dogmatic and unwilling to dialogue
about their beliefs, many of these third-generation participants emphasize
their family's willingness to engage with their children's perspective and
analysis:

I know my parents talked a lot about . . . how they wanted me to understand their work and the relation of their work and their family. . . . [T]hey would never want me to be, like, a fanatic of anything. They would always want me to be critical of anything, even if it was their shit. I think that has also influenced me a lot as to how I approached [organizing]. [Orlando]

Culture and the African American Experience

The 1960s and 1970s marked a rise in civil rights activism and radical left formations in the United States as a response to Jim Crow laws and black disenfranchisement, the anti–Vietnam War movement, the persistence in poverty, and the height of urban destruction. This radicalism—propelled by a revived independence movement in Puerto Rico, the Cuban Revolution, and other anti-imperialist struggles—activated a new Puerto Rican movement in the United States. A new generation of Puerto Ricans born or raised in the 1940s or 1950s in the United States was incorporated into the struggle for the independence of Puerto Rico and revolutionary change in the United States.

To some degree, the third generation was influenced by similar conditions that contributed to their parents' radicalism—racism, inequality, economic oppression, and colonialism. For them, hip-hop culture, in which Puerto Rican New Yorkers played a significant although downplayed role, served as an expression of their *Puertorriqueñidad* (Puerto Rican–ness). Hip-hop culture can be described as a continuity of musical and spoken word forms indigenous to our African roots, demonstrating the interconnection between African Americans and Puerto Ricans who share a New York City history and who are both part of the African diaspora in the Americas.[4]

Emil assesses the influence that hip-hop had on his political consciousness:

I guess that rebellious streak was active in me because I got into hip-hop early on, and not just any hip-hop, but hip-hop with a message, like KRS-One and Public Enemy. . . . I made those connections early on . . . knowing that Albizu [Pedro Albizu Campos] was like a Malcolm X, and people on our side who were similar to Rosa Parks. . . . I remember . . . people who were trying to make things better for other people. . . . [G]rowing up where there was a strong mixture of African Americans and Puerto Ricans, we were just, like, together. . . . [I]t was seamless.

In 1973, the New York zone of the PSP proposed a fundraising dance called "Oldies but Goodies" featuring R&B and Motown sounds of the 1950s and 1960s. Some elder members were appalled, arguing that this theme was promoting the colonizer's culture. But the younger, second-generation PSP members had grown up listening and dancing to this music and made the case that this event was a way of welcoming that generation of Boricuas to the party.

This third generation is now making the argument to their elders about the significance of hip-hop culture to their political and social outlooks:

> The other thing I remember, because my parents made their politics vocal in the house, they didn't like that rap music cursed. I would try to explain the message, "No, no, but you don't understand, forget the curse words, listen to this song, the one about beef from KRS-One where he talks about how cows are fed poison and then [we] eat it. . . . [The song says,] 'Life brings life and death brings death. Keep on eating the death and what's left?'" She [Mom] was all about healthy eating and food, [and so] that song made a connection. [Emil]

Beyond the musical influences, race and the African American experience were major influences in the development of this third generation's political consciousness. Orlando, Lenina, and Karim speak of their gaining a political and social consciousness when introduced to the writings of Malcolm X and others:

> I started reading books on Malcolm X, and that really became one of the things that I gravitated toward in terms of my political learning, the difference between Malcolm X and Martin Luther King and connecting that to people that were closer to my experience. I could never get into the economic side of being a Socialist or a Communist. I tried to read Marx, and I couldn't get into it, even as a teenager, I could never quite connect . . . [but] I could to people who had been organizing around racial justice. . . . I would say, later on, economic justice was something I could connect to. [Orlando]

> About Malcolm X, I wonder if it is very common for it to be a pathway for young people to develop politically, because I had the exact same thing of being able to latch onto Black Nationalism in this country. I remember reading the autobiography of Malcolm X, and I remember reading *Roots*. That was graspable for me, and the militancy of it was very inspiring, but I couldn't yet get into what Marxism was until I had read *Marxism for Beginners*. [Karim]

I felt like when I hit high school, I just wanted to learn everything I possibly could about other revolutions and revolutionaries, and so I started reading a lot, and I remember Malcolm X. I remember [Noam] Chomsky, and I remember how he had a big influence on me. I remember listening to WBAI [a progressive radio station], and that had a big influence on me. . . . I was just trying to absorb as much as I could, the Sandinista Revolution, there were some things that I got into and wanted to learn more about. [Lenina]

The Puerto Rican identity with all its distinctions—Taino, African, and European roots—produces a spectrum of skin tones, hair textures, and physical features. U.S. society has historically framed who is black and who is white in ways that do not precisely conform to the Puerto Rican identity. The presumed superiority of whiteness as the socially constructed norm is perpetuated throughout society—politically, economically, socially, and culturally. As a consequence, Puerto Ricans have internalized and adopted this ideology of white supremacy within our own culture.

Lenina, who is light-skinned, describes the confusion and even hostility she experienced when growing up in forming her Puerto Rican identity and affirming her black identity:

I just remember being very little and feeling like I didn't know what I was, black or white, especially when we [moved] to Long Island . . . [reactions from people,] "Oh, your father's black." And when I was with African Americans, "Are you African American?" [My response was,] "I'm Puerto Rican." And my father being so vehement about my blackness, "No, you are black!" . . . They [my parents] wanted me to really feel that I was black and to embrace that . . . and feel really appreciative of that. But sometimes it was really confusing, because when I went to college, they were like, "You are not black! Who the hell do you think you are, thinking you can identify that way?"

Repression and Fear in the Family

Participants have memories of extended family members who were against their parents' involvement in the PSP. Some were opposed to independence and more so to Socialism as a political solution, while others feared that violence could lead to incarceration or even death for their families. The parents' participation in revolutionary work included the recognition of the very real surveillance, threats, and violence that their families faced from the Federal Bureau of Investigation (FBI), the New York Police Department (NYPD), and other repressive state agencies. Memories of family conversations and acts of repression stand out for some of the third generation:

> My *abuela* [grandmother] used to do tarot readings. . . . [S]he was doing a reading for my mother, and I was present, and she [*abuela*] said, "We have to pray for Andy because he's involved in dangerous activity." . . . [S]o now I'm hearing, *something's gonna happen to my father.* . . . [T]hat is my only memory of anyone ever talking in a disapproving way of my dad and his activism. [Rachel]

> I was home in Puerto Rico. . . . I might have been six or seven, and they had published in the newspaper in Puerto Rico a list of names, *las carpetas* . . . your FBI file. . . . I remember reading the names in the paper, and they were all names I recognized because they were pulling *carpetas* from people here [the U.S.] and from there [Puerto Rico], and a lot of folks from here [were] obviously family friends. I remember distinctly my mother's aunt, that I was staying with for the summer, speaking really negatively about it. . . . [M]y blood family was very, very upset because they knew who my mother was connected with, what she was doing.
>
> It was incongruous at that age because the names were of people that I knew, right, who were nice to me as a kid, nothing bad ever happened around them except that they were always in meetings, but my family's reaction was visceral. [Jessica]

> I have a lot of strong memories like that, of family members . . . comments that my grandmother would say, my mother's mother. . . . [S]he's a staunch Catholic, and she's a *Popular* [supporter of the Partido Popular Democrático]. [Emil]

> I do remember that when I was younger, things were just a little bit more chaotic because, my parents being *militantes*, this is a soldier-type thing, they were the ones driving around with the newspaper, distributing flyers. . . . I remember a couple of times the car got broken into and just flyers were taken or political materials were taken. And then, one time that happened in our house . . . it did feel a little bit like we ha[d] to be very careful, anything c[ould] happen, there was that type of energy when I was a little kid. [Lenina]

Intergenerational Relationships
and Difficult Conversations

Important reflections come from the question "What did you wish you had learned more about the PSP from your parents?" The majority wish they had known more about the intricacies of organizing work—the day-to-day dynamics of running a political organization within a revolutionary framework. They speak of wanting more communication, not just with their parents but also with others involved in the PSP who could share the specifics of their organizing activities and strategies and how they connected their local work to Puerto Rican independence. Some of these reflections underscore the various ways parents negotiated the demands of party membership with raising children. In some cases, parents openly shared stories of their involvement, but for others, a "curtain of silence" characterized their approach to their party's history. Some of this approach depended on the children's ages at the time of their parents' involvement with the PSP (and corresponding levels of government repression), and for some, it seemed related to the status of their parents within the leadership of the party:

> If I were to know more . . . it would probably just be about whether they felt the struggles were cultivating leadership constantly, and juggling what was happening here with what they wanted to achieve on the island. That whole divide of mainland and island struggles just seems, like, so central to everything that the Puerto Rican movement is. . . . I'd love to know more because I don't know a lot about the island necessarily . . . politically; why don't more people want, or are at least interested in, independence?
>
> They didn't do a lot of just the three of us talking about what went wrong in the PSP. I think they were worried about me [feeling] . . . that they didn't accomplish what they wanted to, and they were worried that that would scare me away . . . or even just not feeling like it wouldn't be worth it. [Orlando]

> I've read about different political organizations. . . . But when you start to learn, you realize that the Puerto Rican Socialist Party was one of the best-organized parties. . . . [T]he way they educated the cadres, their ability to organize, it was phenomenal. I think that's definitely something that can be pulled from by anybody that's trying to organize now. [Camilo]

> I would have appreciated understanding more about what they were fighting for. I think I knew it was about Puerto Rico, and I

knew—very vaguely—it was about justice, but I don't think I ever really understood what specific [really], it didn't become clearer to me until I was in college, because now I was politically involved, and I needed to learn how to run a meeting, how to create meetings about important issues; now I needed some advice, [and so] I turned to my parents to get some guidance. But, I guess, yeah, for me, I wish I had known that younger. [Rachel]

It seems that for some parents, the difficulty of negotiating their own mixed experiences or disappointments with the party kept them from sharing that history with their children:

I feel like my parents are this treasure-trove of history and knowledge that they didn't necessarily share with us. . . . [I] don't know why. . . . Sometimes it would come out here and there, but it wasn't like they tried to share with us about organizing skills, and I think a lot of it has to do with not even wanting to go there. I also knew that I had to figure out a lot of shit on my own. [Karim]

I'm just really interested in what it was like day-to-day . . . what were the day-to-day operations like? How did it function? What kind of work did [they] do, and how was it? Who did what? It was like a curtain of silence that we had in my house about the PSP. . . . I definitely get a sense that . . . it was hard for them to talk about it at times. [Lenina]

The focus group participants also sound a cautionary note about the toll that nonstop organizing and movement building can take on the family unit:

I would also say that you [have to] be careful that it doesn't become so much of your life—your social activism—that you forget your children, because then, we see the great leaders, how they were not there for their families, and those families have been destroyed. [Rachel]

Relationship to Puerto Rico and Living in the United States: Pre- and Post–Hurricane María

All the children express a deep sense of connection to and love for Puerto Rico. Each one has a different relationship to Puerto Rico as a physical and psychic place that to varying degrees they each yearn for and accept as part of their identity. For some, this relationship translates into a desire to be more connected to and engaged in the Puerto Rican freedom struggle. For others, it means creating and promoting a strong sense of Puerto Rican culture and pride wherever they are:

> To me, when I hear "Puerto Rico," I feel such pride, but it's just the cultural connection, it's not because I've lived there. I have visited, what, a handful of times. [Rachel]

> In terms of Puerto Rico, I don't see it limited to the island, I just feel it, like, it's anywhere we Puerto Ricans are, and every time we make a connection, we create Puerto Rico again. So, I worked a lot in El Maestro, a cultural center in the Bronx [where] we have activities. . . . [F]or me, that's also like a re-creation of Puerto Rico, and whenever we gather anywhere, I feel that connection. [Camilo]

> Whenever other Puerto Ricans are gathered, you feel that, that Puerto Rico has been re-created. . . . Where you find another Puerto Rican, wherever they're from, I think if you have a genuine connection or love or pride for your culture, it's natural to reconnect with them. I hope to visit and make the time there meaningful. [Rachel]

> It's very different now. It's not the Puerto Rico I remember when I grew up. I know [that was] the hardest part when I moved back, when I moved to live there and work. But you kind of get used to the fact that things are different, that they have evolved, and we've all matured, right? [Jessica]

Their parents' involvement with the Puerto Rican freedom struggle has had a lasting impact on their relationships to Puerto Rico and their understandings of the past and current sociopolitical reality. When we held these focus groups, Hurricane María had recently ravaged Puerto Rico. We spent some time in each group reflecting on the impact the devastation had on the participants and their relationship to the archipelago. Their reflections on what allowed this destruction to happen mirror their parent's critiques of U.S. colonialism and the need for a sustained movement toward decolonization. Similar to their parents' experience of organizing in the diaspora, they have different ideas and questions about what their roles can and should be while living in the United States:

As horrible and devastating as this hurricane has been to the island, I'm hopeful that a blessing is going to come out of it. It's just so horrible, I can't fathom that it could get worse, but I know that it can economically, because as we know the vultures [and] the corporations are going in there and attempting to take over. I'm hopeful that this will rise up in the people the ability to take back their island. I strongly believe in the power of independence, but I have such little faith in leadership that I'm worried about corruption. [Rachel]

I am still heartbroken, but I am hopeful. I go home [to Puerto Rico] every three weeks to check on my family, and what I see is a level of energy, particularly for the Boricuas that are mainland to help out on the island. . . . I'm hopeful that the commitment from the mainland Boricuas to the island continues, [because] then there is an opportunity for a real change. [Jessica]

I just feel that there's such a tremendous opportunity now to start fresh—nature has forced us, and obviously, I haven't even experienced what they have, but nature is forcing our people to start fresh. We have an opportunity to really build some stuff from the soil, and we have to take this opportunity. . . .
    One of the most important things that I learned about organizing and leadership development was . . . my father telling me, ". . . The PSP in the U.S. and all the groups in the U.S. made a huge mistake in thinking that they on the mainland could dictate to the island what was going to happen on the island and that we thought that we could be a huge force and influence in the movement for independence from the mainland." It has to be the people on the island moving that conversation and movement. We can help, we can be a mirror, or we can show what's going on, but there's no way that was ever going to happen. [Orlando]

Lessons Learned: Legacies of Movement Building

Overall, these third-generation participants see the need to connect the lessons from the past to prepare for the future. They are eager to make those connections and to forge a path forward for all Puerto Ricans rooted in the experiences, negative and positive, of their parents' PSP organizing:

I really want to spend a lot of time for the years to come on making the connections between the PSP era and the stuff that they were juggling to deal with then and what we're dealing with right now. Learning and not repeating mistakes and building leadership that is broad on the island and is young and that is there for the long haul but is also keeping an open mind and not repeating past mistakes. And mainland Puerto Ricans, I think, are uniquely positioned to help make that happen. So, that's where I see my role hopefully in the future. [Orlando]

This generation's understanding of movement building reflects evolving political frameworks and debates, including the role of healing justice work, how to identify and address internalized oppression, roads toward decolonization, and the impact of a politics of intersectionality on the path toward a free Puerto Rico. For example, the groups discussed the long-term impacts of physical illness exacerbated by the draconian austerity plan recently imposed upon an already dire colonial situation. These third-generation participants speak to a renewed call to address the weight of internalized oppression: the ways in which colonialism strips us of a belief in Puerto Ricans' ability to govern ourselves and to recognize our own collective power. Just as worrisome is the long-term emotional and psychological impact of trauma, grief, and depression on future generations of Puerto Ricans, particularly post-María. Recognition of the need to address healing justice in today's community organizing and advocacy goals is a strategy that has taken on increased visibility within the broader social justice, community-building movement. Many of today's organizers are reimagining and resurrecting ancestral cultural practices and healing modalities as critical strategies in addressing the harm of collective and historical trauma as well as supporting the resistance of colonized peoples:[5]

> My bigger concern . . . is the health care issue. . . . You've got a population that is malnourished. . . . What they have is not good food to eat. Why? Because they have no power in order to be able to have fresh food. And so it becomes this vicious cycle. . . . [F]ive years from now, what you're going to have is a bunch of very ill, hypertensive, metabolic syndrome Puerto Ricans who cannot get the care that they're going to need because there has been a brain drain. [Jessica]

> I think about a lot . . . emotional healing . . . also internalized oppression . . . that we have to figure out . . . has to do with feeling . . . really hopeless, feeling powerless. . . . I think that for our country, it's just a number that colonialism does to the mind. . . . I think it's just so intense . . . such a big battle that we all have to fight, internally even, to be able to hold on to, knowing and remembering that it's possible to fight and win. . . . I've thought a lot about being in the U.S. and being raised in the U.S., and in a different way the number that does

on us, on everyone that's raised in the U.S., no matter how political [you are] and if your people come from another country. [Karim]

I do think it's kind of important, again, for our generation to have an understanding that you *can* fight that much. You can decide you're going to fight that hard. You don't have to just be settling for little reformist battles. If you just go and uncover history, we see the greatness that we are, and I think we have something to contribute to the world, and I think we should join the rest of the world as an independent nation. But the future for Puerto Rico is Puerto Ricans relying on that connection, people to people and the building of that nation. [Camilo]

Conclusion

This group of seven children of the PSP retain many memories of their parents' years in the Puerto Rican Left. They share their parents' progressive values on issues of justice and a strong identity as Puerto Ricans, whether they have lived in Puerto Rico, visited frequently, or neither. All seven hold a deep anti-colonial outlook and concern for Puerto Rico. They see the recent devastation caused by Hurricane María as an opportunity to rebuild and achieve self-governance and prosperity.

They express a desire to have learned more from their parents on what it meant to be a member of the PSP, from the day-to-day workings to its strengths and weaknesses: What was the PSP? What were they fighting for? What was the day-to-day work like? How did they run a meeting? This conversation could instruct their work as organizers for Puerto Rican independence and as social justice activists, in addition to being history that they could share with other younger leaders. What are the lessons to be learned from that post-PSP era? What were the successes and failures? How can these elders serve as mentors to current social activists?

The two focus groups gave us a look at a rarely discussed aspect of revolutionary activism: the role of parenting and family on the beliefs, values, and work of generations of Puerto Rican activists. We are grateful for the generosity the participants displayed in sharing their personal stories. We believe that many such stories still need to be told and debated, and we encourage future researchers and writers invested in supporting stronger movements for justice to continue to unearth and uplift these histories. Other questions that we would encourage for further reflection include the following: What are the similarities and/or differences in the experience of children of PSP in Puerto Rico versus those in the diaspora? Do Puerto Rican organizers today view the reform versus revolutionary praxis debate differently than did previous generations? Do they see themselves playing a role in the Puerto Rican independence struggle? How can mentorship by these second- and even third-generation activists play a role in the generation of youth organizers coming up now?

Additionally, this historical moment asks that we delve deep into solutions to Puerto Rico's continued colonial situation. What worked in previous years may not work now, but then again, it may give us a guidepost from which to continue our organizing. The growth of decentralized organizing strategies by Puerto Ricans in the archipelago (such as the success and spread of *Centros de Apoyo Mutuo* [Mutual Aid Centers] after Hurricane María), the renewed connection among the diaspora and the archipelago forged after organizing needed supplies following the hurricane, and the large wave of Puerto Ricans forced to leave are three such new conditions that open possibilities for further study and strategy. Intergenerational conversations give us the unique perspective and understanding of how history is created, passed on, and struggled over. We hope this study is just the beginning of a larger conversation.

A further look into the experiences of the children of the PSP from the U.S. Branch and those from Puerto Rico would elevate our understanding of the role of radical, revolutionary parenting. The relationship that parents develop with their children has long-term lasting effects on their lives. The ways in which we apply the values of love, justice, and equality at home are the ways in which we will "show up" in our political practice—the personal is political.

NOTES

1. Focus Group 1 met on October 29, 2017. Focus Group 2 met on May 6, 2018.

2. Steve Early, "From the Old Left to the New: Perils of Progressive Parenting," *Monthly Review*, October 22, 2017, available at https://mronline.org/2017/10/22/from-the-old-left-to-the-new-perils-of-progressive-parenting.

3. John Blake, *Children of the Movement: The Sons and Daughters of Martin Luther King, Jr., Malcolm X, Elijah Muhammad, George Wallace, Andrew Young, Julian Bond, Stokely Carmichael, Bob Moses, James Chaney, Elaine Brown, and Others Reveal How the Civil Rights Movement Tested and Transformed Their Families* (Chicago: Lawrence Hill Books, 2004).

4. Raquel Z. Rivera, *New York Ricans from the Hip Hop Zone* (New York: Palgrave MacMillan, 2003), 1–4.

5. Autumn Brown and Maryse Mitchell-Brody, *Healing Justice Practice Spaces: A How-To Guide*. Just Healing Resource Site, December 18, 2014. Available at https://just healing.files.wordpress.com/2012/04/healing-justice-practice-spaces-a-how-to-guide-with-links.pdf.

6

Hostos Community College

Battle of the Seventies

RAMÓN J. JIMÉNEZ

From Harvard to the South Bronx

In 1974, I taught at Hostos Community College, at that time the only bilingual college in the United States.[1] Its main building was an old tire factory, the size of a storage warehouse at my alma mater Harvard University. The college was located on 149th Street and the Grand Concourse, the Champs Elysées of the Bronx.[2]

Over two thousand students, mainly Puerto Ricans, attended the college. There were single mothers, students from every Latin American community, and the Afro-American and Caribbean population comprised 20 percent of the school. For many of the older students, Hostos was the last stop, the final hope, *la última parada* for transfer students who had failed at other institutions, neighborhood folks attempting to get off the welfare lines, brothers and sisters and ex-cons participating in their last opportunity to make it.

I was 25 years old—an underpaid, overworked adjunct professor teaching two courses in the C.U.N.Y. system. Upon graduation from Harvard Law School, I received a John Whitney Fellowship to conduct a first amendment prison project during the day. The South Bronx was now my working base.

The South Bronx: Myths, Values, and Culture

The South Bronx community was known as the poorest neighborhood in the United States. From the late seventies into the eighties each presidential election usually involved a candidate's pilgrimage to Charlotte Street, the worst block in the United States. Inevitably, the candidate would promise to rebuild the area, a vow soon forgotten after the elections. Even John Paul II gave the neighborhood his papal blessings.

I had heard many stereotypes describing the South Bronx. Wild gangs such as the Savage Skulls were roaming the streets at all times ready to rob, steal, and hurt you. I was told to watch out for junkies, who supposedly surrounded every corner. They were searching for weaknesses, which would give them the courage to rip you off. They further told me that the community was flooded with welfare recipients who spent all their time buying Cadillacs, playing the numbers, drinking, producing children and deceiving the system.

I found the South Bronx nothing like it had been described to me. The neighborhood quickly adopted me, treating me like a son . . . a hero. . . . I was that rare specimen, a Puerto Rican graduate of Harvard Law School.

My oral Spanish was awful, but my understanding was fluent. I had heard Spanish all my life from my mother Alicia, but I was always hesitant to speak it, even though in many ways my upbringing was Latino. My father Ramón played the music of Tito Rodríguez, Orquesta Aragón, Pérez Prado, and Lucho Gatica, and I loved my rice and beans, *pasteles*, and other dishes of Puerto Rican cuisine. But until the age of twenty, I had always identified myself with my Afro-American friends and community. I was black and only black.

At Hostos, I suddenly received a crash course about my entire "Rainbow culture," and about my language. I was initiated into the Puerto Rican rank and file. At Harvard, I had become an experienced organizer/activist in the anti-war movement. I gave numerous speeches in Washington, D.C., Boston Commons, and New York City. I was a student/organizer for the Puerto Rican group *La Organización*.

At Hostos, while teaching courses such as "Law and Social Change," I witnessed the evolution of students who began to learn about the history of social movements (civil rights, labor, women, etc.). They were receptive to the new politics and began to interpret the laws that challenged their past experiences.

Save Hostos Community College Committee

Early in the 1975–76 school year rumors began to circulate that Hostos Community College was on a list of institutions to be closed. A small group of professors, counselors, and students began to meet in order to plan a response. Only five years old, Hostos had nonetheless produced success stories. Born out of community struggle, its existence had always been tenuous.

Enemies of bilingualism had attempted to abort it even before its birth. Mayor Abraham D. Beame and other powerful elected and appointed officials decided that Hostos had to be sacrificed to satisfy the ravenous appetite of this monster that had invaded New York City, called the fiscal crisis. At that time, the budget at Hostos Community College was only four million dollars, but there was a fiscal crisis; it was a time for budget balancing . . . a time for cutbacks.

Hostos Community College organizers included professors Gerald Meyer, María Barbosa, and Leopoldo Rivera; counselors Félix Ruiz, Carlos Gonzáles, and Wally Edgecombe; students Efraín Quintana (president of the ex-prisoners organization), Nilsa Saniel (a single mother of three challenging the welfare system), and ex-Vietnam veterans Victor Vásquez and Amos Torres. The group circulated a simple petition demanding that Hostos Community College be kept open. As experienced organizers we understood that for many staff and students this was their first act of resistance.

We collected over five thousand signatures and organized a letter writing campaign. The Save Hostos Committee included community organizations such as United Bronx Parents and St. Ann's Church. We informed South Bronx elected officials of our concerns. But many of us felt it was absolutely necessary to wage a creative, disruptive, civil disobedience campaign to force Mayor Beame to change his decision. Powerful political forces had little compassion and respect for the Puerto Rican/Latino community. They expected little or no resistance to the closing of the old tire factory. We understood that our potential army, consisting of students, staff, and community, had little experience and were fearful in confronting the enforcers of the political order.

The battle had its David vs. Goliath dimensions: a few people from a community that was from the poorest per capita income area in the nation were engaged in a struggle against Mayor Beame, a mostly hostile City Council, the City University of New York, and the Emergency Financial Control Board. No one believed that Hostos would survive the blow. Other institutions facing closing or significant budget reductions were public elementary schools, libraries, hospitals, fire and other essential services.

The official rhetoric consisted of the following: Everyone had to sacrifice, or the city would go into bankruptcy. Everyone had to join in the effort to save the city. But the powerful, the upper- and middle-class strata, faced no such reductions. Mayor Beame was offering Yankee Stadium over sixty million dollars for renovations, a figure more than fifteen times the yearly budget of the only bilingual college in the United States.

Coalition to Save Hostos Community College

Around December 1976, there were strong rumors that Hostos would be merged with Bronx Community College, a bigger campus with numerous buildings. As a bilingual college, Hostos would be eliminated. The first demonstration, worked out by the Save Hostos Community College Committee, was held in December 1975.

Over one thousand protesters marched through the streets distributing flyers, asking people to join our campaign. The march ended at the Chase Manhattan Bank on 149th Street. Thousands listened to speakers condemning Mayor Beame and all the powerful political interests orchestrating the cutbacks. As MC/speaker, I gazed at the crowds from the platforms and felt the stirrings of a new force being born in New York City politics.

The first march created great enthusiasm, for it was an action unlike any ever seen in the South Bronx. Shortly after, the Community Coalition to Save Hostos was born as an expansion of the original committee. It had no relations to the Hostos administration, included community participation, and was more militant. I was selected as Coordinator. The Save Hostos Committee had members of the administration who reported all decisions to President Candido de León, who was negotiating behind the scenes for the Presidency of Bronx Community College merger. We distrusted him. When the time came to become more militant, it was impossible to plan with the administration represented. Thus, the Coalition was born. Despite the split, many members of the Save Hostos Committee supported us. They continued pursuing more traditional efforts, such as lobbying and letter writing.

My tasks were many, but perhaps the most difficult was keeping all the groups together and united. In the South Bronx there were so many divisions among Puerto Ricans, Dominicans, South Americans, blacks, and Latinos, Afro-Americans and those from the Caribbean, men and women, younger students and older students, minority and white professors. Only by working together would we be successful in keeping Hostos alive.

One of the worst effects of oppression is that the oppressed, humiliated by the power structure, often turns around and does the same. The Puerto Ricans criticize the Dominicans and vice versa. Psychologically there is always someone less human who receives the blame. The oppressed Latino or black male looks down on the female, justifying his domination by using irrational theories of inferiority. The Afro-Americans make fun of Latinos unable to speak English, or ridicule Caribbean blacks for having an accent. The phenomenon of one group attacking another is both so devastating and so entrenched that it enables the powerful to maintain the status quo. All through the campaign, this issue emerged. It was our job as leaders to help overcome these problems.

Consensus Building

Consensus building was not an easy task. The original Save Hostos Committee had been dominated primarily by white professors and staff. The division between the Community Coalition to Save Hostos, coordinated by myself, and the Committee to Save Hostos, led by Professor Gerald Meyer of the Communist Party, continued throughout the entire campaign. Jerry Meyer had been the resident radical professor/advisor to young black and Latino students before a group of young Latino professors came to Hostos and took his place. He was used to having everyone agree with him. He felt very threatened by young Puerto Rican radical professors such as Leopoldo Rivera and myself. The coalition that broke away from the Save Hostos Committee, composed of professors and staff (mostly black and Latino), student groups, community groups, and individuals, was more democratic.

The Coalition was an umbrella-type organization that included many different groups espousing a myriad of ideologies, attitudes, and tactics. An important group within the Coalition was the Puerto Rican Socialist Party (PSP). There was constant friction between groups such as *Puente Unidad Latina* and *Federación Universitaria Socialista Puertorriqueña* (FUSP). The *Puente Unidad Latina* students (ex-prisoners) viewed FUSP as young, idealistic, and more prone to rhetoric than action. The Vietnam Veterans often sided with *Puente Unidad Latina*. There was an intense schism between independent women (who were evolving into feminists) and the super macho males, who often led subcommittees within the Coalition. At one time during the first takeover, the women actually walked out, demanding equal representation and the opportunity to be involved in all levels of leadership. The women's walkout ended with "the sisters" having more representation and less of the dirty work. Nilsa Saniel, a student in my Introduction to Sociology class, was one of the leaders of the women's movement. She was a long-time tenant organizer in East Harlem. I still tease her about how reluctant she was to speak in front of the college. She froze, and only after much coaxing did she finally make her first political speech.

The Coalition also included the People's Park, a street gang in a small public park located on 141st Street near St. Ann's Church. Its members consisted of ex-gang members, ex-cons, and active addicts, some of whom were involved in crime and practically living in the park. They were all Puerto Rican nationalists and, when sober and straight, good soldiers in the war to save Hostos. They supported us in full force but were extremely difficult to control. During one march, they took over the front lines drinking liquor and smoking marijuana at the same time. We forced them back. Some time later they attacked me with a lead pipe, fracturing two of my fingers. Despite this we forgave them, and they continued to support us and accept our directions. Thanks to the members of *Puente Unidad Latina* and the Vietnam veterans, we were often successful in bringing out a good aura.

Meetings were often very tense. Group after group attempted to promote its philosophical and political point of views. The meetings at first were hot

Figure 6.1. Save Hostos Community College, PSP nucleus.

and heated, often full of rhetoric and therefore very long. In the nine-month period of our struggle, I participated in and chaired more meetings than perhaps I would do for the rest of my life. We had PSP meetings, Committee to Save Hostos and Community Coalition to Save Hostos meetings, steering committee meetings, and assemblies of students, local, civic, and citywide organizations. There was always tension and conflict.

In recalling some of the adventures that took place during these meetings, I remember the rhetoric of some of the Dominican leaders who had faced the 1965 U.S. Marine invasion of Santo Domingo. When they gave speeches to the students, their slogan, *educación o la muerte*, tended to scare the older students, who were just becoming involved in protest politics. Leaders such as Juan Valdez (Dominican Students Organization) and Nelson Pérez were often extremely radical but nonetheless very important to our campaign.

Many community groups participated, but none were as important as United Bronx Parents. This multiservice community and citywide agency supported us with community experience, contacts, foot soldiers, and last but not least, food. Rosa Escobar and Evelina López Antonetty were among my first elder political mentors. It was their spirit and strength that inspired us in times of despair. Evelina and Rosa had begun their activism during the Marcantonio days. Their struggle for free breakfast and lunch programs and other issues were nationally acclaimed.

Our PSP nucleus was made up of professors, former leaders of student movements both in Puerto Rico and in New York, Vietnam veterans, single mothers, gays, ex-pimps, and community and civic leaders. The nucleus was anti-dogmatic and in conflict with what we felt was the upper-class arrogance and air of superiority showed by some of the PSP leadership. There were many socialist leaders/participants, many of them members of the PSP. I was the leader of the PSP Hostos nucleus, which grew from four to at least twenty-two members. Many of the strategies discussed and developed by these individuals later became the strategies of the entire movement. But I was always in conflict with the PSP National Committee, led by José Alberto Álvarez Febles, who often wanted to inject the issue of Puerto Rican independence into discussion as a primary concern. We believed first teach/organize people about basic issues, such as education. It is in the process of fighting for education that the people would develop and struggle for greater things. Individuals such as PSP New York leader José Che Velázquez made peace between our rebellious nucleus and the PSP National Committee.[3] Despite our differences, somehow the common greater goal, saving Hostos, won out. As we struggled and socialized together, we found less conflict and tension.

Closing of 149th Street and the Grand Concourse

The Coalition joined a citywide movement protesting proposed cutbacks. Often we were the largest contingency. A small leadership cadre believed it was time to go beyond petitions, letter writing campaigns, and demonstrations. We had received only sporadic media coverage.

Nothing had changed the decision to close the school. We believed that our initial group was now prepared to participate in more militant tactics. A decision was made to stage a massive civil disobedience action.

We pondered many issues. Would the students follow the organizers? If the actions failed, would the leaders be arrested? We did not fear detention, but we understood that to achieve a goal in a campaign of civil disobedience, an arrest should push a movement further, create support and sympathy, and win public opinion. Arrests for the sake of arrests have no place in a serious movement for social change. We made decisions as to who would be arrested if we failed to mobilize faculty and students.

It was early March; the temperature was comfortable. We had picked a perfect day, and our adrenaline made it appear warmer. Classes began. We split into two groups. One group began dragging chairs to the Grand Concourse. Another group went from classroom to classroom with or without the professor's permission. We began announcing our intentions, exhorting people to join us.

Outside, hundreds of passersby were shocked! What were these crazy students and staff doing? The Grand Concourse invaded! We proceeded quickly to overwhelm our adversaries! Older women were dragging and pushing chairs!

Desks were blocking all traffic . . . in all four directions. . . . [W]e began shouting *consignas* and chants . . . united in our demonstration. The circle completed, we began street classes with one thousand students and staff.

The traffic, confused, screeched to a complete halt. Bystanders and drivers were surprised, even amazed as well as being angry and upset because of the intrusion in their lives. "You are closing our school! We are continuing our classes, our education. Where? Right here in the streets of the Bronx." Standing in the middle of the crowds, I slowly stepped back in amazement and began my class, Introduction to Psychology.

The police arrived in chaos and confusion. We declared to the officers that we indeed intended to disrupt business as usual. Television cameras, newspaper and radio reporters arrived at the scene. We had alerted them. This was the kind of story they enjoyed; headlines might read: "civil disobedience by hundreds" . . . "possible violence" . . . "mass arrests!" More police. More officials. We continued class. More people joined the classes, even those who had no relationship to the school. Firemen with water hoses, intending to dispatch the crowds and protected by the police, slowly began approaching the demonstrators. We did not budge. The crowd of onlookers grew larger and more supportive.

The confrontation was looming. Participants would be hosed. Arrests would take place. There was a traffic backup, as far as six blocks long. Tension continued to mount. As I spoke, from the corner of my eyes I saw police officials involved in heated discussions among themselves and with Fire Department officials. The confrontation was seconds away.

We prepared for the worst. Suddenly, for reasons I have never been able to determine, the firemen began retreating slowly. . . . The entire crowd burst into applause. In the eyes of many participants, this was the beginning realization of the power they possessed when united . . . when determined . . . when resolute.

We continued classes for thirty more minutes. The Coalition's goals and objectives were achieved; there was citywide and nationwide coverage. The media became more sympathetic to our cause. The little South Bronx nation had begun to roar! Most important of all, participants in this action began to realize the potential to educate, motivate, and if necessary, disrupt the establishment.

Takeover of C.U.N.Y. Chancellor's Office

In the second week of March 1975, we learned that Hostos was closing down. Nothing we had done had changed that decision. The Coalition planned another major action, at the C.U.N.Y. Board of Higher Education, located on 80th Street, on the Upper East Side of Manhattan. Chancellor Robert Kibbee was an architect of Hostos' closing. Previously, more than two thousand people had picketed his house and burned his figure in effigy. This time we targeted his office to achieve maximum publicity and citywide support.

We were ready to seize the Board of Higher Education. We believed that the building could be taken over by a small group, while hundreds of demonstrators would protect the invaders. Our purpose was to gain publicity, force the media to tell our story, and avoid violence and arrests. It was to be a peaceful action that involved militant tactics. Ex-Vietnam war veterans were involved in the takeover. The night before, a small group slept in apartments near 80th Street. We never told anyone the destination of our buses. We believed that the students and staff had confidence in us. They had been part of our cause for several months. Their fear and passivity had begun to disappear. Their trust created a great responsibility. We would never accept leading people into massive senseless arrests, violence or injury. We walked a very fine tightrope.

At 9:30 the next morning, thirty members, in groups of four to six, approached the five-story building from different locations. We easily overcame the security guards in an active but nonviolent manner. Each group was assigned a floor. We brought chains, and a large supply of crazy glue. We politely ordered all employees and visitors to leave the building. We quickly sealed off all entrances and applied crazy glue on the locks. One side entrance was kept intact as an exit for the employees. All cooperated with little resistance, behaving as if a fire drill was taking place. A small group of organizers arrived at the Chancellor's office. He was the first and only individual who resisted leaving. Nilsa Saniel, one of our organizers, sought to convince Kibbee to leave on his own. She then joined a group rolling Kibbee, as he sat on his chair, out of his office. Kibbee soon realized the futility of his protest and walked out the building. The Board of Higher Education was now ours!

Busloads of about 1500 hundred students and supporters arrived. Massive pickets were quickly formed. On the fifth floor we unfolded massive banners that said "Save Hostos Community College" and "Cutbacks on the Banks."

The police did not arrive immediately. We had informed them we were planning a demonstration at City Hall. Our attorney Andrew Vachss was ready to negotiate.

Finally, ten to fifteen police cars and at least two groups of tactical force police arrived, apparently prepared to force the building open and arrest the invaders. But they were confused and unsure. They were afraid their actions might result in a riot in such an upscale neighborhood.

Shortly after, the main television stations, newspaper and radio reporters were at the scene. Wide-eyed neighborhood residents, the protestors, our attorney, and the media were scrutinizing the police. The street was in complete chaos. The picket lines grew louder. The police waited for their orders. The organizers shouted slogans and chants from the fifth-floor windows.

Confrontation appeared imminent. Vachss and the police were involved in heated discussions. Minutes later we received a call from our attorney. He had arranged with the police that if we "leave the premises there will be no arrests or criminal charges filed." Everyone would be "allowed to leave peacefully." We had avoided being charged with the crimes of trespassing, menacing, disorderly conduct, destruction of property, and other criminal acts! New York City once again heard the story of the planned execution of the first and only bilingual college in the United States.

We decided to accept the proposal. We would leave the building to a standing ovation no less than the one Roberto Clemente received when he played in New York. The media rushed to speak with the escaping invaders, whose interviews began to tell New York the Hostos story.

Takeover of Hostos Community College

The Hostos administration continued to play both sides of the fence. Strong rumors persisted that President de León was more interested in becoming President of Bronx Community College than he was motivated to keep Hostos alive.

The moment called for some drastic measures. Soon after the Board of Higher Education takeover, we decided to occupy the actual college. Our plan was to hold regular classes, but completely lock out the administration. As organizers, we hoped that seizing the institution would enable us to utilize phones, copy machines, and other resources to further our campaign, seek maximum support, and command daily media coverage. It was our expectation to pressure Mayor Beame and the Board of Higher Education.

The takeover was initiated early in the morning on March 24, 1976. Among the key leaders were students Efraín Quintana, Félix Vega Peña and Mario Serrano (all ex-prisoners), Nilsa Saniel, Amos Torres and Victor Vázquez (both Vietnam veterans), and community leaders such as Vicente "Panama" Alba, Evelina López Antonetty, head of United Bronx Parents, and Father John Luce (from St. Ann's Church) and many others. Once again we used long chains and locks to limit entrance only to the front doors of the school. Security was placed in front of these doors. The President's office was immediately occupied, and later became a daycare center for students with children.

Many of the student organizations participated, including the FUSP, the Black Student Union, some members of the student government, the Organization of Dominican Students (led by now president of the Dominican Parade, Nelson Peña), the Organization of Latin American Students, and, later, a group formed during the takeover—Women United for Struggle.

The most active student group was *Puente Unidad Latina*, the ex-prisoners group. All these groups were represented in the Coordinating Committee, along with community and political groups such as United Bronx Parents, ASPIRA, the Puerto Rican Socialist Party, and the People's Park. Among the individuals very supportive of the protest was Assembly member from the Bronx Seymour Posner, who as a young man had fathered a child with a Puerto Rican woman. He was deeply sympathetic to all progressive Puerto Rican causes. Along with Posner, many elected politicians visited us. We treated them with caution. We knew it was their tendency to seek publicity while doing very little for our cause.

It was Posner who broke this barrier for politicians. He volunteered to help in any way, including cooking and cleaning. Posner was a public relations assistant for the 1964 march on Washington led by Martin Luther King, Jr. He had important ties to the media and used them to connect us to many sympathetic ears. Posner was the equivalent of a socialist Buddy Hackett. He always kept you laughing, but his humanistic progressive side always steered him in the direction of important social causes.

The first few days were focused on maintaining control of the college. President de León set up headquarters elsewhere. He was hesitant to order arrests, fearing community backlash. During the first week, we received citywide support from many organizations, politicians, and a large cohort of community activists. Hostos became the symbol for rebellion on a citywide basis.

Movie producers, entertainers, and artists came by frequently to support our cause. Each night we held rallies, teachings, and film and cultural presentations. This helped to educate all new visitors, while keeping our troops motivated and inspired. I, and numerous other activists, slept in the college for the entire twenty days. We slept on the floor with our regular clothes, perhaps using a jacket for a pillow. I still remember Alexis Colón, then militant leader of the FUSP and now a big time real estate salesman. He slept every night in the room next to me wearing a new pair of silk pajamas.

The school issue remained on the front page of Latino papers. Each week we gained more media allies and expanded coverage. We organized events outside the school. One of the most successful events included more than five hundred children of all ages and colors who shouted: "Save Hostos—We too want to go to college." They encircled the school. They held a protest with their own speakers, the youngest being three years old, and the oldest sixteen. To this day, almost twenty-five years later, I still meet these activists, now grown up, who remember their participation in the struggle to save Hostos. These types of creative actions were key to keeping support growing for our campaign.

The police maintained communication with us, but kept a distance. The Coalition always made sure that the police understood they were not our enemies. Our only goal: the salvation of Hostos Community College. Some police officers were very supportive, while others anxiously waited for the orders to take back the school.

After about nine days, an injunction was issued naming myself and other leaders, along with numerous individuals named John and Jane Doe. The preliminary injunction ordered us to leave the premises and refrain from any actions preventing the administration from operating the school. The occupants received the court order, but decided to ignore it, while recognizing the possible consequences.

President de León was in a quandary. He was afraid of ordering the arrests of so many staff, students, and community residents, especially since these people had become heroes and heroines in the eyes of many concerned New Yorkers. De León expected the takeover to ease out; then he would be able to oust the few remaining resisters. Instead, the takeover took on a life of its own, grew larger every day, and became a symbol of defiance for all New Yorkers fighting the status quo.

As the days passed, we received more and more positive publicity, support grew, and classes continued as normally as possible under the circumstances. Finally, on April 11th, de León ordered the arrests of the protestors. The police met with us to explain their orders and inform us that we had twenty-four hours to leave the building. We informed them that we would vacate all those who were not going to be arrested. We made them understand that some of us would stay and face the consequences. Both parties agreed that the arrests should take place after 9 P.M., for the sake of innocent students who were simply attending class. As organizers, we made our only request: namely, that, when arrested, we all be chained together, or at least in small groups. The police agreed.

On April 12th we vacated the building, with the exception of forty people, including myself, who decided to face arrest. About 9 P.M. over one thousand protestors picketed the school, including students, staff, religious leaders of the Episcopal Church such as Bishop Paul Moore, community leaders, and groups and activists from all over the city. President de León arrived for the first time in weeks. The crowd booed him, a few spit at him, and others threw objects. The police immediately protected him, but the anger he encountered would harm his educational career.

The police cut the chains off the entrance doors and immediately began to arrest us. There was no resistance.

The March to the Courthouse

We were marched out of the building in chains. The crowd erupted in support and in protest. Hundreds of police kept the crowd at bay. We were placed in police vans to be taken to the old Gothic Courthouse building on 161st Street and Third Avenue.

It was now 11 P.M. As we drove away, hundreds of protestors took to the streets and began an energetic, explosive march to the Courthouse. The South Bronx had never seen a protest of this magnitude. The noise level could only be compared to a Yankee Stadium World Series victory.

Forty of us were booked, processed, fingerprinted. At 2 A.M. we were released on our own recognizance and given the same return date. The crowd gave the exhausted organizers of this twenty-day occupation a hero's welcome. The takeover became the longest in the history of the city university system, perhaps the longest in the history of New York politics. The Community Coalition to Save Hostos took over the school on March 24, 1976, and held it until April 13, 1976. It was one of the most incredible experiences I have ever had as an organizer. I remember returning to my apartment excited, sleepy, and tired because there had been no time to rest. I fell asleep with a chuckle, recalling what is now my fondest memory, Evelina López Antonetty complaining after my arrest that the emergency notice had her quickly adjusting her girdle to prepare for the demonstration battlefields.

I spent the next day with my parents, nervously hoping that they would not buy the *New York Post*. On the front page of the paper, there was a picture of Vicente "Panama" Alba and myself, in chains, being escorted to the police van. My mother understood most everything, but seeing her Harvard Law School son arrested would perhaps have been too much for her. Shortly after the takeover, on March 30th, a bill to save Hostos Community College (Bill 11855 A) was introduced in the New York State Assembly by Louis Nine, José Serrano, Armando Montano, and Angelo del Toro, and in the Senate by senators Robert Garcia, and Efraín González. The Act was "to amend the education law, mandating that the Board of Higher Education in the city of New York—maintain a bilingual college providing career programs and courses in health studies and technology."

Rally at the Emergency Financial Control Board

The semester was almost over. We needed more action. We joined thousands of students, community residents, and Hostos staff in a march from

116th Street and Lexington Avenue, the heart of El Barrio (East Harlem), to 56th Street and 6th Avenue, the central offices of the Emergency Financial Control Board (EFCB). Close to ten thousand people, the majority of them Puerto Ricans, participated in this historic march, carrying pictures of the members of the EFCB with their corporate affiliations. The march, which included within its ranks people protesting all the cutbacks, was a resounding success; it was one of the largest Puerto Rican–led marches in the history of New York City politics. More than fifty people carried a city-block-long Puerto Rican flag.

The Second Hostos Occupation

The pressure on Beame, Kibbee, and the EFCB became overwhelming. One week after the march, we occupied the college a second time, an action that lasted three days. Through sheer creativity, combined with *un poquito de suerte*, we were able to avoid arrests, despite the pending charges and the existing permanent injunction.

About 9 P.M. on the third night, Amos Torres, one of the original organizers, looked out the window. Two hundred tactical police, all wearing helmets, brandishing nightsticks, apparently were ready to invade the building. This time we had received no warnings or communications from the police. It was only quick, creative thinking that prevented disaster. As the police began cutting the chains, we quickly dispersed into three classrooms and chose volunteer professors to initiate lectures. The occupants sat in chairs at full attention. The police entered each classroom to face no resistance, violence, or protest taking place. Instead of arresting us, the police ordered us "out of the building." Once again, we had escaped arrests and confrontation with the law.

Towards the end of April, there was one final takeover, but it lasted only one day. By this time many of the organizers were exhausted, having sacrificed their families, jobs, and grades to keep their school open. It was in late April or early May when the news finally arrived, after all the protests, lobbying, petitions, demonstrations, takeovers, and publicity: the decision "to close Hostos Community College has been reversed." The New York State legislature approved Bill 11855 A. The college would be kept open. Suddenly, additional state monies were appropriated.

We had won! We experienced explosive moods and feelings! The South Bronx had finally won a major battle! Mothers who had never won . . . [s]tudents who had never won finally joining together! *Una victoria* was theirs! As an organizer I compared it to the popular Puerto Rican story about *Urayoán*, a Taino cacique who lived during the initial Spanish invasion. The Taino in Puerto Rico initially believed the Spaniards were immortal gods. It was *Urayoán* who ordered a Spaniard drowned. It was *Urayoán* who discovered the Spaniards were not gods and could be defeated. It was the Community Coalition to Save Hostos, with much help and assistance from members of the Save Hostos Committee, that along with the community was successful in reversing the decision to close Hostos and discovering that the powerful Mayor . . . City Council . . . and the EFCB were not gods and could be defeated.

This was one of the many lessons learned from the successful campaign. Organizers also understood the importance of working with people through a slow process of learning, realizing that it takes time for people to understand that they can beat City Hall. Organizers displayed maturity and wisdom in dealing with the police and avoiding arrests. The campaign in fact produced leaders who for the last twenty-five years have been organizing in the poor neighborhoods of New York City.

The price for all organizers was costly. Although the criminal charges against the forty arrested were later dismissed, President de León eliminated my entire department (Behavioral Sciences), resulting in the layoff of many of the young professors, including myself, who had been instrumental in the campaign. My Whitney Fellowship had ended, and it took me a long time to find employment. Some of the students suffered bad grades and mounting financial problems. Yet everyone agrees the battle was worth the wounds.

Two years after this incredible community/student battle to preserve Hostos I remember walking down 149th Street and Third Avenue and seeing plastered all over the lampposts, deserted buildings, and telephone poles a political poster bearing a picture of Abraham Beame, with the legend "He made the tough decisions." He sure made one tough one in the South Bronx. We made it tough, and WE WON with the people's collective wisdom, experience, leadership, and support!

NOTES

1. This chapter is reprinted from CENTRO *Journal* 15, no. 1 (Spring 2003): 99–111. The editors of the present volume thank Javier Totti and *CENTRO* Journal for permission to reprint this article. The original editor included this note: "CENTRO *Journal* respects the way individuals write their names. We have checked the spelling of the names for all those mentioned in this essay. Their names are spelled accordingly." Ramón J. Jiménez passed away in 2016.

2. Original dedication from the author: "There are many names not mentioned in the text of this story that played important roles in saving Hostos, too many to mention. This piece is dedicated to you."

3. *Editors' note:* This was actually the *Seccional* Committee (*Comité Seccional*), based in the United States.

Journalism, Organizing, and Revolution

ALFREDO LÓPEZ

It was probably the most formative four minutes of my life.

I looked up at the big clock over the playing floor of Madison Square Garden, and it said 3:56.

That meant that, under contract, we had to get more than seventy people onto the flat stage over Madison Square Garden's ice—the New York Rangers were playing hockey that night—and if we did not finish the final performance of the afternoon during those four minutes, we would have to pay a huge fine.

We did not have the extra money, but we had a full house waiting for an encore of the seventy people who had performed or spoken to walk onto that stage. I took a breath, and then something happened that has never happened before or since. I shifted my gaze to the crowd: faces of all colors, many cultures and languages, different backgrounds and histories. And they were all looking at the Garden stage. I took a deep breath and told myself that, at this moment, we were making history, and a few minutes more did not matter.

I gave the signal to bring everyone on for the finale.

They started to flow through the tunnel of the Garden onto the stage: a huge contingent of Puerto Ricans, more than fifteen people from the American Indian Movement, leaders of just about every movement in this country . . . people as diverse as the crowd, who had traveled all distances to support Puerto Rican independence. And they stood on the stage and danced as *Grupo Taoné* played their final song, and the thousands upon thousands screamed, clapped, and danced. At that moment, nothing else, not even the four minutes, mattered.

On October 27, 1974, we filled Madison Square Garden for the largest event supporting Puerto Rican independence in U.S. history. The Puerto Rican Socialist Party (PSP) led that event. I was the principal organizer. I have never lived another moment like that one, and I have had a long time to match it—after all, I am seventy years old now, and that afternoon, I was twenty-five.

But more on that later. For now, the moment . . . because what I am about to share either leads up to it or recedes from it. October 27, 1974, the Day of Solidarity with the Independence of Puerto Rico—the day the PSP took center stage.

The *Claridad* Days

"I want you to edit the paper."

Ramón Arbona smiled when he said that to me, but he was not joking.

This was late 1971, and we were at Casa Puerto Rico, the PSP's offices on Fourteenth Street in Manhattan. Arbona had recently taken over the leadership of the PSP's U.S. zone, and one of his first initiatives was to create a U.S. edition of the PSP's venerable newspaper, *Claridad*.

It was the first time I had laid eyes on Arbona, a man I would work under for several years on many projects, buoyed by his encouragement and battered by his withering criticism. He was one of the most difficult people I have ever worked with: thin as a chopstick and with a heavy mustache covering his upper lip, he was a diminutive cloud of unpredictable energy. He was supersensitive to the point of being neurotic, easily distracted, highly disorganized, disturbingly attracted to superstar intellectuals; and he was politically brilliant, completely fearless, charming and warm, committed, and absolutely confident that people around him, no matter how young or inexperienced, could do what was needed, given the space and support to do it.

He was the first true leader I ever worked with and my first real mentor: a genius at recognizing people's abilities and nurturing them, the first person who actually believed in me . . . much more than I believed in myself. His influence is still stamped on my consciousness, molding who I am and how I think. He was among the most important people in my life.

But, at that early point, I had just met him.

A small group of us had been called together to talk about the newspaper. I did not know any of them. For the most part, these were people who were coming into the PSP from the old *Movimiento Pro Independencia* (MPI, its predecessor). My path had been different.

I had entered Puerto Rican revolutionary politics through Manhattan College, where I had met my *compadre* Andy Torres, and we had formed the Latino student organization League of Unified Cooperative Hispanic Americans (LUCHA). This was a time of remarkable turbulence and struggle at colleges throughout the country. In New York City, students were closing campuses all over. At City College and its sister public colleges, the struggle focused on a simple concept: if you are a public university, you need to open your admissions to let everyone who wants to study have a chance to.

That concept might seem obvious today, but in the late 1960s, it was an issue people were being beaten and jailed for. Puerto Rican students were on the front lines of that struggle, bringing a heretofore absent sense of community into the university setting, and a lot of people, including some other students, did not like that idea at all. So, it was a confrontational and empowering time for many of us. We who knew little about our own homeland were now exposed to it as a banner we were holding and protecting with our lives. We were learning in the process. I myself was still working on my first book, *The Puerto Rican Papers*, and so the time was a combination of study, reading, and militancy.

I was finishing college, and while many of my fellow students agonized over what they would do with their lives, I was pretty sure what I wanted to do with mine—my calling, I believed, was as a revolutionary.

At the time Arbona approached me with the *Claridad* challenge, I was working with the Carlos Feliciano Defense Committee at the invitation of Ruth Reynolds. I was visiting Reynolds to interview her for my book, knowing little about her or her background. All I saw when we met was a matronly lady with a calm, nurturing demeanor and a Midwestern accent. It was only during that interview and a couple that followed that I learned that she, in fact, had been arrested during the 1950 Nationalist uprising in Jayuya. A Quaker pacifist living in Puerto Rico since the early 1940s, she had ended up serving nineteen months in prison. It was a jarringly contradictory picture: a woman who my biases told me probably spent her days knitting, associated with the militant Pedro Albizu Campos, who had withstood the arrest and torture the Puerto Rican police visited on those Nationalist heroes.

Toward the end of that first encounter, she showed me a leaflet about Feliciano and suggested that I come down and start working with the committee, then being led by Reverend David Garcia at St. Mark's Church in the Bowery. We won most of that case, and Feliciano always believed that this victory was attributable to the committee's work. I can only say with certainty that the committee made his case a cause célèbre for the Puerto Rican movement and that as a leader of the committee, I played a role in that success.

Arbona had become familiar with the committee's work and publications and inquired about who wrote the materials. That was, undoubtedly, the first he had heard of me.

I remember that first meeting well. A group of us sat around the table to talk about building *Claridad* in the United States: Digna Sánchez, a Lower East Side activist whose diminutive body bristled with energy and power; José "Che" Velázquez, an actor, poet, and high school activist whose background was probably closest to mine and with whom I would develop a deep and formative relationship; Carmen Ortíz Baerga, originally from Puerto Rico and a stalwart of the MPI; and Arbona himself.

Time has taught me that you do not make history in a two-hour meeting—but this meeting came close. We were talking about launching a bilingual edition of *Claridad*, and the proceedings had an undercurrent that would prove historic beyond the publication of a newspaper.

There are two things to understand about that.

For a revolutionary party, a newspaper is not just a newspaper. In fact, it is not only the "voice" of the organization, although that is a major role it plays. It is the conscience of that organization and the link it has with the people it is trying to organize. *Claridad*'s major source of information was the membership of the party itself, the people who were working in communities throughout Puerto Rico and, as of that meeting, in the United States. Not only did the members feed us the stories and news; they "circulated" the newspaper. Every Saturday, members would each take a stack of newspapers and bring it to an ever-expanding "periphery" (*periféria* in Spanish) at their homes or workplaces. These were people who bought the paper every week, giving the member the opportunity to speak with them about events in the paper, the political analysis of those events, and any activities the party was planning for the coming week . . . to which the buyers would be invited.

Claridad was an opportunity to have one-on-one conversations, otherwise difficult to make happen, with people whose support we needed and wanted. The *venta* (sale), as we called it, was our main form of organization, mobilization, and, we hoped, recruitment.

Recruitment is the second point because, with the establishment of *Claridad bilingüe*, the PSP was committing itself to organizing not only Spanish language–dominant Puerto Ricans who were born on the island but also those who had grown up in the United States and spoke English as their first language, people called "second-generation" Puerto Ricans.

Today, this distinction may seem of little import, but in 1970, the debate about how to politically and socially place Puerto Ricans who had grown up and were living in the United States was raging. It raged within the MPI with a fire stoked by the suspicion of and animosity toward anything that emanated from this complex U.S. society that swallows people's history, lives, and culture like a crazed shark, spitting out the results with the disdain of cultural supremacy and racism. For a Puerto Rican militant whose life was formed on the island, to hear Puerto Ricans speaking English was a reminder of the potential cultural genocide that is the ideological nutrient of imperialism and colonialism. Needless to say, not everyone in the PSP was all that comfortable with what we were about to do. The existence of a bilingual version of *Claridad* would influence the perspective of the PSP, and the Puerto Rican movement in general, in dramatic and ground-shifting ways.

At the time, we did not know that. We were starting a radical newspaper that would fill a gaping hole in our communities with little idea of how difficult that task would be and how important it would prove.

I myself was in another dimension. I had never worked on a newspaper like this one and had never experienced this kind of commitment to seriousness among Puerto Ricans like me. My first dose of that was, ironically, about a key.

Our edition was to be a four-page supplement wrapped around the newspaper coming from Puerto Rico, a Spanish-language publication already sold in this country's Puerto Rican communities. To make it happen, we rented a one-room office on Twentieth Street in Manhattan, a few blocks from Casa Puerto Rico. We acquired a couple of desks and a drafting table (to do layout and pasteup) and installed me as a kind of managing editor and Velázquez as an administrator.

As I sat in that office on that very first day, I was blown away by Che. I had never encountered a Puerto Rican with a background like mine who was so able to do things so confidently and negotiate with the outside world. He quickly arranged for the installation of a telephone (which would go on my desk), and then he said, "I'm going to get the keys made." When he returned, he gave me the first office key I ever had.

Che's energy and confidence stunned me, and I remember expressing surprise that we would have our own keys and a phone so quickly. He turned to me and, waving his arms for effect, said, "Yeah! This has got to be a great paper. If we believe in doing it, it's got to be great." I nodded blankly and let that sink in for a few minutes. And then the rocket in me launched, and I never looked back.

Trilingüe

It is always tempting to see the past as a fairy tale. Because most things "work out" in the end, we tend to remember them as divinely directed, painless processes driven by an infused and natural optimism. In reality, life only "works out" because, in hindsight, we have lowered our expectation of the past to jibe with what actually happened. Getting there is painful and anarchic: a portrait of achievement painted against a background of ever-shifting, goal-altering reality.

To be real: *Claridad bilingüe* started out as a mess, written by amateur journalists, edited by Arbona when he would stop by a couple of times a week, and, most of all, organized by a person (myself) who had almost no idea what he was doing. As a result, the paper we first produced mixed Spanish and English articles in a layout hodgepodge that only the most committed person would read.

But we did it. While many people (including some from our own organization) made fun of the newspaper and its often fractured Spanish translations (calling it *Claridad trilingüe*), the party militants born in this country increasingly took it seriously, criticizing its flaws and claiming it as their own. Slowly, at first, they began contributing stories to the paper, and after some months, it began to take on a more journalistic form. Each issue had more stories coming from our community-based chapters (*núcleos*), more responses from officials we were covering, more reactions (encouraging and critical) from our militants, better photos, particularly from Bomexí, our quirky, inscrutable, and relentlessly committed photographer. We also were doing larger features, including roving interviews at demonstrations and visits to migrant labor camps (including one amazing feature from volunteer journalist and long-time PSP militant Sonia Marrero).

We worked all week, and on Thursdays, our staff pasted up the edition in an all-night session (ending after daybreak) that became a tradition. We never missed a week. It began to feel like a real newspaper.

The great moment of transition was when we moved to larger offices on Thirteenth Street, affording us a larger editorial room, a small darkroom for photo development, and a separate space for layout and pasteup. There, I proposed to the PSP's leadership that we take the paper to eight pages, allowing us to publish four in each language, carefully mirroring the same coverage bilingually. Now there were two front pages and identical inside material with an opinion column, an editorial, and a lot more art.

And our staff was growing. We brought on Dagmaris Cabezas, a Cuban-born writer with the ability to interview just about anyone. She became our most prominent street reporter. Bomexí's photos, shot when he was not in our darkroom developing film, appeared all over our pages. And we hired a Cuban Puerto Rican, born in Cuba, named Maritza Arrastía.

Can I be allowed a personal note? I will keep it short. Those of us who pretend to sophistication insist that "love at first sight" is a myth. As I remember it, when I first met Maritza—her incredible energy, immediately obvious intelligence, beautifully expressive face, and remarkable eyes—I was a goner; and so I know that you *can* fall in love at first sight. While it took a few years for us to become a couple, after forty-two years of being together, I fall in love with her more deeply every day. So much for the "myth," and so ends my personal note.

The PSP was growing. In fewer than three years after the launch of *Claridad bilingüe*, our organization was the largest Puerto Rican revolutionary organization in this country and among the tightest, best organized, and most community-rooted in the U.S. Left. Its militants carried on relentless political work in dozens of towns and cities of this country. Its newspaper had the largest circulation of any in our movement. It held rallies and meetings and events of all types every week of the year. And its reach into the organized Left of the United States (the source of solidarity it would rely on) was deep, energized, and based on genuine respect.

Larger organizations existed in this country's Left, and several other organizations were dedicated to Puerto Rican causes, but none was as organized, disciplined, and deeply embedded in their communities. Using the tentacles of contact and political work, we extended into the complex and wide-reaching Puerto Rican community on a weekly basis (through our newspaper circulation); we had a base of more than ten thousand people.

This reach was no small feat. The Puerto Rican community of that period was a motley combination of generations and subcultures. People who had recently arrived from Puerto Rico shared our communities with people who had come here many years before and a whole generation of younger people who identified strongly as Puerto Ricans but whose relationship with the island was built on sporadic visits and communications with family. We organized them all, driven by a unique formulation of our reality that captured this diversity perfectly: Puerto Ricans in the United States were not some displaced minority or just a natural source of solidarity with the independence struggle. Rather, we were part of a nation comprising Puerto Ricans no matter where we were found—and we still are.

In 1973, we held our First Congress of the PSP's U.S. Branch, at which we released our main document, *Desde Las Entrañas*, a cry of resistance against imperialism's ceaseless tendency to displace people and divide them. This publication sprung from intense internal analysis and discussion throughout the entire party based on the experiences we lived day to day. *Desde* explained our main theory: for all of imperialism's attempts to batter our people and to obfuscate our history, Puerto Ricans in this country continued to identify as Puerto Ricans. The fact that our homeland was a colony, permitting constant back-and-forth travel, rejuvenated, perpetuated, and deepened that identity and drove it into people's political consciousness.

If we needed any proof of the truth of that, as if the growth of our organization was not enough, we had the Day of Solidarity with the Independence of Puerto Rico at Madison Square Garden.

Going to the Garden

We were sitting around a table at Casa Puerto Rico in a *Comisión Política* (Political Commission) meeting, discussing how to stage a major event to strengthen solidarity with Puerto Rico's independence. Arbona came up with an idea: why not do a major demonstration around Puerto Rican independence, a convergence of our membership, periphery, and the entire solidarity movement that supported our work? Whether the proposal originated in his head or in the PSP's national leadership (of which he was a member), I do not recall. In any event, without Juan Mari Brás's full conviction, the idea would not have materialized in action.

As we discussed the idea, it grew like an expanding stain. "What," Arbona asked, "was the largest venue for convergences in New York?" "Madison Square Garden," I answered. I saw his eyes light up, and his head started to bob.

"This has to be the biggest demonstration ever," he said, his body starting to bounce, hands flailing. "Everybody has to be there. *Everybody.*" Names were thrown around—Jane Fonda, Angela Davis, a major Latin music band, major artists from Puerto Rico, speakers from every organization. As I sat there, as the idea began taking shape, I should have been scared. Arbona was looking at me to coordinate the logistics and the construction of the committee that would support and sponsor this action—something never before done, almost incomprehensible in its sweep and audacity—and I was a twenty-four-year-old kid. I had never even been to the new Madison Square Garden, and here I was, going to play a role in filling it up and covering its stage with leaders and celebrities. I could not conceive of what to do.

Sunk into my head, though, was a truth that Arbona articulated for me later. We were sitting in his office, when he leaned forward and smiled: "We have to come up with the boldest actions we can think of, even if nobody else is thinking of them. If we're right and our analysis is good, people will respond. They want to do big things. They're just waiting for someone to propose them." He laughed. "That's leadership."

"Don't worry," he added. "The entire party is doing this. We can do this."

I was pulled from *Claridad* and thrown into what seemed, a year before it would take place, an impossible task. Madison Square Garden cost a small fortune to rent: $40,000 for an afternoon rental and another $40,000 for services, including a special sound system and the support of the Garden's unionized staff. It had never been used for an action like this before. My job was to rent the thing, set up the staff who would make this event happen, and organize committees in cities across the country to mobilize solidarity activists to the action. The party would handle mobilizing the Puerto Rican community.

Every leader of the PSP in the country was pulled in to support that work, but I was the point person (my official title was Executive Director of the Puerto Rican Solidarity Day Committee), and I traveled constantly to meet with people, set up committees, and oversee their preparatory work, all the while voicing the argument about how vital this struggle over the status of the most important U.S. colony was to the entire movement in this country.

At the same time, I worked with a completely volunteer staff of more than a dozen activists in a small office in lower Manhattan, donated by the War Resisters League. The ace in our deck was my principal assistant, Rosa Borenstein, a remarkable administrator and organizer who handled so many of the nuts and bolts of the action. Not only did she arrange trips and speaking engagements; she invited dozens of the speakers and performers who would join us that day.

People look back on that moment and often ask me, "How in the world did you people do that?" It was intense, complex, and often daunting, but the truth is that it was not hard. Arbona was right: you come up with the most audacious idea you can think of, one that will truly move a struggle forward, and if you have done the necessary work, people will respond. Not once in my many travels, phones calls, special meetings, and scores of events I spoke at all over the country—not once did anyone question whether this event was a good idea. Not once did anyone ever approach me and say anything other than, "We're definitely going to be there."

We had touched some nerve, sculpted some kind of dream for the movement's activists in this country—the idea that you could take over an arena associated with the highest echelons of power and make it a venue for revolutionary fervor. We were sure, four or five months out from the event, that we would fill that place.

Not to say that there were not challenges. Only a couple of months away from the event, the Garden actually canceled it. The backdrop to this decision was the controversial history surrounding the Puerto Rican independence movement and the increasing reluctance by the U.S. government to allow a platform for it. It took a major meeting, with about ten people from our Solidarity Committee (including Arbona and legendary attorney Arthur Kinoy, who was integral to the support of the effort) to meet with the Garden's general manager, Michael Burke, and convince him to let us proceed. It helped, of course, when I informed him of something he did not know: we had already taken delivery on the thousands of tickets for entrance to the event and had distributed most of them. "There are gonna be a lot of people at your door that afternoon, Mike," I said, shrugging. "I think it makes sense to let them in. Don't you?"

The show went on.

Challenges also came from inside the Puerto Rican movement. *El Comité*, a highly active revolutionary organization based primarily on the mid–West Side of Manhattan, gave only grudging support to the event. The Young Lords, which by that time had morphed into the Puerto Rican Revolutionary Organization, did not support it at all. People from both organizations showed up, but they did nothing to build it. The most wounding experience for me personally was when Feliciano, the freed political prisoner whose defense committee I had led, refused to support the event. I am still not sure why he did such a destructive thing, but I remember how heartbreaking it was. That defense committee basically kept him from going to jail for the rest of his life, and his repayment was to take a stand against this historic action.

You cannot describe a political action like the Day of Solidarity with words. Actions that change realities and make history ride the wave of people's emotions and the invisible connections people feel at certain moments. For me, the most emotional moment was when I entered the arena two hours before show time and looked at the seats. Hung on each seat was a program developed by artist Liz Mestres with a cover designed by the Puerto Rican grandmaster Lorenzo Homar. I realized that my hands were shaking. This was our afternoon!

Under the pictures of the Puerto Rican political prisoners that hung from the Garden's rafters—freed Nationalist prisoner Rafael Cancel Miranda once told an audience that he cried when he saw photos of these pictures as he sat in his cell—participant after participant took that stage, following a script carefully timed and arranged by PSP organizer Gina Cestero. The sense of solidarity and pride bounced off the Garden's walls—the cheers and chants deafening, the splash of clothing colors covering those seats. A population that had always been viewed with derision by the powers in the country, the expression of its pride relegated to a yearly, corporate sponsored parade, had filled this country's best-known gathering place.

More than that, we had unified all kinds of people from all walks of life and pursuits. Artists, leaders, musicians, actors, and poets from Puerto Rico and the United States came to New York for that action. Jane Fonda flew in from Europe (where she was attending conferences) to speak. Ray Barretto brought his band to perform (an early performance by the great singer Rubén Blades). Lucecíta Benítez, Puerto Rico's premiere vocalist, took the stage for a three-song set. Angela Davis spoke movingly. Medicine Man Leonard Crow Dog spoke and introduced the American Indian Movement's song and dance troop, which brought the entire Garden to its feet, stomping and clapping in unison with the drums. PSP leader Mari Brás delivered a rousing, climactic speech. On and on . . . everyone was there.

Figure 7.1. Opening ceremony with Medicine Man Leonard Crow Dog and Russell Means of AIM.

One final story about what it all meant. A couple of staff members and I shared a cab with Fonda to attend the after-action reception, and the young, long-haired cabbie quickly recognized her. "You're Jane Fonda!" he said with a huge smile. Fonda, friendly and extremely humble in person, nodded and told him we had just been at the Garden action. "I know," he said. "I've been listening to it on the radio all afternoon." WBAI had broadcast the entire event live. It was then that I realized how broad its impact had been.

At that moment, on that day, we had reached our pinnacle. We had done something no one else had ever done. We had fulfilled our historical mission, and, no matter what followed, nobody can take that away from the PSP.

End Game

One of the outcomes of the Garden event was that it positioned our party as a major force in the U.S. Left. That ranking was a nutritious poison. On the one hand, we were invited to be involved in almost everything going on in the movement in this country, which allowed us to insert the independence issue in just about everyone's program. At the same time, most of the PSP was involved in the work we had always done—our primary political responsibility of organizing in Puerto Rican communities. As that work

Figure 7.2. Jane Fonda at National Day of Solidarity with Puerto Rico, Madison Square Garden, New York City, October 27, 1974.

achieved unprecedented success, we were also being pulled by our responsibilities to the U.S. Left. We were, we stated, a party of the Puerto Rican
people but also a part of this country's left-wing movement.

It made a lot of sense at the time, and as our leaders traveled to conferences nationwide, took part in so many coalitions, and handled work on so
many diverse issues, we gladly dove into the conflicts and divisive tensions
from which the Left in this country has long suffered. The amount of work
we did between 1974 and 1977 could fill a book, and I am not writing it. Suf-
fice to say that our immaturity as leaders was nurtured by the acclaim and
respect our organization had won.

It is not as though we were not warned. At a Comisión Política meeting
one afternoon, our visiting leader Mari Brás clearly stated, "Our role in this
country is to represent the Puerto Rican people and movement and not try
to lead the U.S. revolution." But it is difficult to dismount from a vehicle
that is moving at such speed, and the near veneration that we received from
so many quarters lured our young, inexperienced minds deeper into what
would prove to be a destructive mess.

In hindsight, I can see it all coming, as our leadership meetings concentrated more on the issues of the U.S. Left and less on the community
work our organization was still successfully doing, as the membership
meetings often degenerated into increasingly harsh criticisms of our leadership, and as we demanded more and more of our militants at the community level, responding to the challenges of the broader movement work
we were doing. This car was heading toward a wall, and it crashed into the
wall on July 4, 1976.

On that day, we had planned a major demonstration of the entire Left.
It had started with the slogan "Bicentennial Without Colonies," but as we
recruited the leftist movement and its political virtual civil war into the
action, things broadened. In that demonstration, we ended up with a series
of more than forty demands covering the major issues raised by each of the
scores of movements that composed the Left. We pushed and insisted that
the movement had to sponsor an anti-imperialist demonstration to counter
the blind patriotism of the official celebration of the Bicentennial, and the
Left responded by mobilizing tens of thousands of people to march through
the streets of Philadelphia on July 4, ending at a rally with a long list of
speakers who served to dramatize how divided the Left had become.

On its face, the demonstration was successful. In reality, it only showed
the impossibility of the task of unity we had taken on and the arrogance of
a Puerto Rican organization, representing a small fraction of the population
of this country, trying to lead the entire U.S. movement. It broke us. We continued our work after that demonstration, but things were never the same.
Slowly but surely, the rank and file of the PSP began to rebel, battered by the

rain of tasks we ordered it to perform, unsure of its role in the struggle, restless under the yoke of the democratic centralism that, in crisis, had become a repressive nightmare.

After decades spent thinking about that situation—because I was among the most active leaders in the work with the U.S. movement—I really do not think we could have done any differently. We lost our balance, between organizing the Left around Puerto Rican solidarity, or for unity among the Left in general, and organizing in our Puerto Rican communities around day-to-day issues; I am still not clear how we could have achieved it. I do know that the failure to achieve that balance destroyed us.

It certainly affected me. In working toward the Garden action, I had developed a style that can only be described as "arrogant bullying." Anyone who disagreed with us fundamentally or who expressed any reservation about what we were proposing to the Left was subjected to a portentous, often mocking, speech that battered rather than convinced. In fact, that same style found its way into my work inside the party. Not that I became a monster; I was a thoughtful and effective leader. But I was insensitive, hurtful, and convinced that I knew everything . . . and that others did not know all that much.

Several of our leaders suffered from the same baseless arrogance, and this style managed to glue together coalitions that had no business existing and accept analyses that were, as often as not, just plain wrong. While I was in the party's leadership, I told myself that these means were justified by the end. Since that time, I have come to realize that when the means are sullied by undemocratic practice, the end is never a desirable one.

The demise of the PSP in this country is as much my responsibility as anyone's.

Some have looked back on that period as proof that the U.S. Left is incapable of mounting a successful revolutionary struggle, but I heartily disagree. It is a misunderstanding of what actually happened and a blindness about how changes in the country's objective reality had made the Left's premises outmoded. Married to the traditional concept that a working class would lead this revolution, the Left debated that premise in often venomous ways. And one can never overlook the role of repressive forces stoking these differences. In the end, the incessant debates split that movement badly. Historically, when debates like that raged, reality would prove someone right. A rise in working-class struggle would prove that people who viewed its centrality were right.

The problem, though, was that this proletariat we all looked to (or rejected) as our leadership was rapidly disappearing with the onset of factory technology. As an example, one automobile plant in Detroit employed more than twenty thousand people in the 1960s. Today, it employs two hundred, making even more product than it did then. Overall, the number of people who used to work in manufacturing has fallen from a third to about 10 percent of all workers. In the end, it was a change in the conditions that would demand a change in that thinking—a change that only now is starting to take hold.

Like a house whose walls start to crack when its foundation is removed, the U.S. Left's movement was falling apart, and we had inserted our party into that crisis.

To be clear, serious problems had developed in the main PSP as well. The party in Puerto Rico was falling apart under the pressures of failed strategies and tactics and the inability of our leadership to see that. The situation in the U.S. Branch (*Seccional*) was a reflection of the crisis in the entire PSP.

The PSP reached its de facto end sometime in the 1980s. I cannot be sure of exactly when because, by then, I had been expelled.

The Final Days

I handled many different responsibilities aside from those already described during my years in the party. I worked in the information and propaganda department, led a Secretariat called *Acción Comunal* (Community Action), worked in the Secretariat of Organization, and returned to run *Claridad bilingüe* for a year or so.

In 1977, Maritza and I had our first child (our son Karim), and I went to work at *Seven Days Magazine*, a left-wing publication led by the legendary David Dellinger. At the same time, the *Claridad* bilingual edition was in trouble, and the PSP leadership believed that I should return as editor. This request was a problem for me in many ways, but the most important was that, as leaders, we lived in poverty. When it could pay us, the party would be able to pay only a few dollars—less than subsistence. I knew that I could not raise a kid under those conditions, and I asked the party's leadership to choose someone else.

They refused, insisting that I take the position. I refused, explaining that doing so would be the summit of irresponsibility. Democratic centralism demanded that I obey the leadership's majority, but flexibility would have been possible had the conditions inside that organization been different. But that was not going to happen.

The PSP's battering, recent fractures throughout the organization, several campaigns that had failed (although the July 4 campaign was initially perceived as a success, we later saw the price we had paid), and the festering acrimony that it all produced ripped the leadership apart, showing the gap in the several tendencies that were part of it. Our leadership and organization had always had fundamental differences. Some of us were, in fact, schooled Marxists. Others were community activists of radical orientation who were not grounded in any ideology. Each of the members of the Political Commission during the majority of the 1970s had a different perspective that, behind the drive of our community and independence work, never really came up in the early years. But eventually, given our place in the Left and the complex challenges we were now facing, they surfaced with the bite of a shark. We were venturing into the future without a map, and it had become clear that some of the very top leaders did not want me on the trip.

At a meeting of the Political Commission, I was expelled. Later, the Branch Committee (*Comité Seccional*) met and lowered that to a yearlong suspension—an important distinction because you could return to active duty after a suspension, but if you were expelled, you were gone. That difference meant little to me. As I walked out of the meeting in someone's apartment, I walked away from the organization I had served for eight of the most important years of my young life, dazed, with tears in my eyes and absolutely no idea of what I would do from then on. After all these years, the feeling singes me still, and I never want to feel that way again. The PSP had been my life, occupying virtually every minute of it, and now it was gone.

This story is not a tragedy. I had Maritza and our family, which grew with the addition of our second son, Lucas. They are still the center of my life, but it is a life of revolution. Today, I still do full-time revolutionary work, having just celebrated my fiftieth year in this movement. I still lead and make speeches and organize events and conferences, and it is a funny thing: whatever I do, whatever decisions I make, whatever thinking I put forward, there is always a part of it I learned in the PSP. And I learned the most important lesson of all: etched in the memory of the clock at Madison Square Garden and the many thousands of faces staring at that stage, in the countless activities we did, in the pride we could take at facing down the most powerful imperialism in human history with an organization that was genuinely born of a people who refuse to disappear, in those precious moments, it was clear to us that we were what our people needed and had created. Do the most audacious things you can imagine, and if you see things clearly, the world will follow.

A *Pamper Rojo* Boricua Baby
of the Puerto Rican Socialist Party

Lenina Nadal

He intimidated me—Vladimir Lenin, that is. My mom opened a book once and said to me, "This is the man that has your name." The man with my name was bald, stern, with a goatee, and he always looked like he was ten steps ahead. He led a revolution of millions of workers and peasants to fight against a royal family who was hoarding wealth as people starved in a big, cold country. And he killed off all that royalty, the czar's family, because he knew that lineage matters; if he had not taken these measures, the less than 1 percent of that period would have come back to stake their claim. Imagine workers reigning over the world. This history and the mythology of Lenin, the photos of the Russian Revolution, have been a backbone religion for me since I was very young. I knew this Lenin guy was a badass and, at the same time, seemed to have very different life circumstances than a female Boricua kid born in Brooklyn. I mean, what did Lenin know about growing up near beaches and lush tropics, *bacalaítos* (cod cakes), salsa, hip-hop, and the Ponce massacre? However, very early on, I carried this responsibility to be like this man, to assess political dynamics, to fight for justice, to do what seemed impossible. I still feel cursed with the need to best represent my contribution to revolutionary practice in my lifetime.

Being Raised by *Militantes*

Born in 1975, at the height of the Puerto Rican Socialist Party's (PSP's) success and climactic influence, I entered a flurry of movement. Just the year before, 1974, Madison Square Garden had been flooded with twenty thousand people converging to support the Puerto Rican independence struggle. And when I was one year old, in 1976, the bombing of the newspaper offices of *Claridad* took place, and the Federal Bureau of Investigation (FBI) searched my parents' car as counterintelligence programs (COINTELPRO) stepped up their attacks and investigations.

My parents gave their full lives to the party. My mom entered the party at about twenty-one years old after organizing with a City University of New York (CUNY) chapter of the Congress of Racial Equality (CORE), a campus-based organization called the Puerto Rican Alliance, and the *Movimiento Pro Independencia* (MPI), which later became the PSP. She did anti-war work motivated by the fact that both of my uncles had been drafted and were serving in the U.S. military against their will. My mom was no stranger to politics. My grandmother had organized in the Brooklyn community and was active in her union, 1199, before she died at age forty-two from asthma and cancer after suffering for years with the poor air quality at the laundry she worked in. My *abuelo* (grandfather) had been a nationalist on the island.

However, even with her background, she noticed that a level of privilege existed within the PSP leadership. Often activists from more middle-class families from the island tended to have more say and influence. The leadership of the party often assessed who had cultural capital and seemed to exclude working-class members like my mom from the higher ranks. She proved herself to be a respected *militante*. First, she had to manage a full-time job to support herself, and she was a mother. But, when she was not working, she was at *Claridad*, the PSP's international newspaper. She dragged me to the offices with her, to finalize her articles, see that the paper was printed, and plan for circulation and delivery in the community.

My father was just starting his career as a professor in the Puerto Rican Studies Department at Brooklyn College, a victory that was hard-won while I was still in the womb. He became interested in politics through my mother and was an integral part of the struggle to establish the Puerto Rican Studies Department there. He had been a Spanish teacher, and as a Nuyorican, his skills in Spanish were more advanced than those of some of his comrades. He was called on to translate Juan Mari Brás's *comentario político* (communiqués for *Claridad bilingüe*) and was the lead singer for Conjunto Taiborí and later Conjunto Bembé, the salsa band that was often expected to play at fundraisers and events at Casa de Las Americas. My father was also the president of the Brooklyn College *núcleo* and later coordinated the work of all the university nuclei. In addition, he wrote feature articles for the intellectual publication *En Rojo*.

When he was not working on his career as a professor, or taking care of me, he was preparing political education workshops for the PSP and writing songs and rehearsing with the band. Early on, my father was performing a lot, often coming home in the middle of the night, which sometimes led to tensions at home.

I often stayed on Bergen Street (where my mother grew up) with my grandparents during these years, watching Spanish television, going to church with my step-grandmother, learning to do chores, and helping my *abuelo* tend his garden.

When I was with my parents, it felt like we were always at a party. The fundraisers were dance parties, and, as they say, after the party was the after-party. The after-party consisted of blasting salsa in a van full of comrades and laughter and kids running around being only mildly monitored. We played and danced until we collapsed into sleep on folding chairs, in laps, with someone's coat thrown over us. We recited such chants as "*¡Rifle, cañon y escopeta este pueblo se respeta y si no maceta, y si no, maceta!*" In English, that means "Rifle, canon, and shotgun, our people will be respected, and if not, we rumble!" Not the most nonviolent of chants. We learned to sing "La Borinqueña," "Que Bonita Bandera," and "Preciosa." We drew pictures of our lives and had drawing pals who were the same age in Puerto Rico, Vietnam, and other countries.

I remember the childcare room of the *Claridad* newspaper. It held a bunch of kids in what felt like a closet, and often we tried to entertain ourselves but looked forward to escaping for food and water requests from our parents. When a bunch of us tried to sneak out of this claustrophobic room, they packed us back in. I do not remember many toys or child comforts to keep us entertained. We had to work with paper and pencil, tape and scissors (if we were lucky), and each other. It was not fun. And looking back, I would say it was even a little disrespectful to the needs of children.

On the positive side, at an early age, we learned what a print shop looked like and what a mimeograph machine sounded like when it ran at full blast. Often, we had to wait while our families printed flyers, newspapers, and other propaganda. As children, we were taken to rallies weekly and learned to make placards and protest signs early on. Perhaps my interest in media and design came from these early memories of seeing how newspapers and organizations created community, identity, joy, and belonging.

I remember one time floating in a sea of hundreds of people at a rally against the Vietnam War. I was about three or four at the time, and although I had no idea where my parents were, I simply went up to strangers and opened my arms for them to carry me. I felt loved and protected in rallies, as though I could trust anyone. Being raised red and Boricua inspired this faith in people.

The Reagan Years and Dark Times in the Suburbs

In the early 1980s, things shifted drastically. As the momentum of the party was slowing down, there was less talk about the party and more about the work at Brooklyn College. As my parents always say, "We didn't leave the party—the party left us." My cousin Ritchie had been living with us in a two-bedroom apartment in Brooklyn, and when my aunt moved back to Puerto Rico from her home in Long Beach, Long Island, we decided to go there.

The love and nurturing of the party and the relationships we had all seemed to fade. My world became one of learning to accommodate the white majority in the suburbs of Long Beach. Now, the rich history of being Puerto Rican just meant that I was a random "spic." Here, I was not just Puerto Rican but mixed race, because my mother was light-skinned, and my father was black—and therefore I was black too. People believed in this town that Ronald Reagan was a good president and had to be respected. Coming into Whitelandia at eight years old meant that I had to unlearn love. I had to find my place in the hierarchy of American patriotism, the quality of our possessions, and the ability to know whom to socialize with and whom to ignore. The values I learned from the comrades, of respecting difference and diversity, of embracing nonconformists and madness, of fighting for the poor, of listening to music loud, and of dancing and singing, were all challenged here.

My name became a wound. The name that lit up people's eyes with joy in the movement, the name that signified workers' love, had now become something I would lie about. I tried to tell people whom I was named after, but as soon as I would say "Communist" and "Russia," it was as good as saying I was named after a serial murderer. So, I quickly learned to cope and would say things like, "Yes, my name means 'little girl,' *la niña*, sure, that is where it is from."

Call me a sellout, but that was where I was at the time, and yes, I was dying inside every time I became a traitor to myself.

I did not doubt that my parents had the best intentions, nor did this new community make me doubt that Lenin was a badass. However, I knew that a lot of this political ideology and influence would have to be tucked away for a while if I was to survive.

While the years in the suburbs tamed my spirit and dampened my wings, if I had not faced the racism there, the segregation in schools, the class divisions, I may have never become the activist I became later in life. As I headed toward becoming a teenager, I was clear that boys, marriage, or even a stable career meant nothing to me; I wanted to know how I could change the world. I wanted to honor my namesake. I read American history voraciously, I asked more questions at home about the history of Puerto

Rico, and my father would take the time to explain colonialism and the status issue to me. I was part of the local Latino organization *Círculo de la Hispanidad*, and there I met the children of the caretakers, restaurant workers, and nurse's aides. Many immigrants from South America became my friends. While with them, I listened to Spanish music, performed in Spanish plays, and danced in our free time to Mary J. Blige. However, in school, I passed them in the halls and entered spaces like band and honors classes that were mostly for white kids.

I remember how easy it was to be seen/not seen in the white spaces. I will never forget when the most popular football player threw gum in my hair and dared his friend to throw too; "Her hair is like Brillo, it's great for gum," they said. A close friend joked that my hair was like Jesse Jackson's and that I should do cornrows. I felt humiliated and, like many a Boricua with black blood, developed "hair issues."

Another "friend" broke down the three parts of Long Beach to me like this: "The poor white people live in the west, the middle class and poor people of color live in the middle, and the rich people live in the east." While I did not live behind the railroad, I did live in the middle with the brown crew. A popular street called Riverside was dubbed "Niggerside." Riverside was where many of the black students would get on and off the school bus.

Living with too much knowledge of oppression and racism made me resent my family. I wanted them to "like white people" instead of joke about our differences. At the same time, I knew that resisting society's racism and classism was the only way to get through.

At ages fifteen and sixteen, I attended meetings of eighty-year-old Communists at the Long Beach Public Library. I canvassed my neighborhood when an environmentalist group had informed our high school that a cancer-inducing incinerator was infecting the local population just walking distance from my home. I wrote lots and lots of poems.

One time, as I did not see any Puerto Ricans represented in our advanced literature classes, I asked my father whether we had any writers of significance. He gave me a book by Jesús Papoleto Meléndez and told me that he was also political; then came Pedro Pietri, and Miguel Piñero, and Sandra María Esteves, and Julia de Burgos. He explained the relationship between poetry, politics, and declamation. I learned that reciting poetry was indeed resistance in our culture and practice.

After a big race riot in Long Beach High School, meaning one hundred kids brawling in a segregated cafeteria that had reached its limit in tolerance, the school was looking for "constructive ways" to address the problem. Since I had learned of our spoken-word traditions, I organized our high school's first spoken-word poetry reading because I wanted to be like the Nuyorican poets—I wanted to create space for students in my high school to express their fears, hopes, and frustrations. I also helped create an underground zine that visually and in content challenged the official literary magazine of the school.

I spent hours after school talking to a Spanish teacher I had who would make statements like, "Slavery is alive and well. Slavery never ended." He challenged me to dig deep and not accept conventional narratives. I gravitated toward the eccentric, those who wore black and listened to alternative music. Alternatives seduced me with their message of a reality that was more honest than the one I was living. I gravitated toward anyone who would question the tyranny of yellow ribbons to honor soldiers during the first Iraq War, pacifying the rage of brown and black people, and bake sales.

When I read the biographies of Mahatma Gandhi and Pedro Albizu Campos, I felt a kinship. I too was a locally celebrated token who had to be clandestine with my understanding of colonialism. I was a gem of a writer for my English teachers, a history teacher's pet, an actress in school plays, in the band, on the soccer team, and my civic engagement was acknowledged. Inside, I hated the society I was in; I felt nauseated when the United States was celebrated in any way because I understood that this country was rich due to its extracting the resources of native peoples worldwide and seizing the economic leadership and power of various countries' sovereignties. I just wanted to find the revolutionaries of my generation; I wanted to see where they were hiding because I knew that I needed to honor my life's calling.

Meanwhile, my parents were now fully a part of the Brooklyn College leadership and dealing with daily microaggressions to defend the ethnic studies departments they had fought to build.

Growing My *Cojones*: The Student Liberation Action Movement and a Chance to be a Revolutionary on My Terms

In the 1990s, I started attending Hunter on the cusp of citywide riots. The CUNY board of trustees threatened to cut services and end the policy of open admissions and remedial programs, such as *Search for Education, Elevation and Knowledge* (SEEK). The board also proposed extensive hikes in tuition. These changes in the university would mean a massive number of students of color, particularly black and Latino students, would have to go through many more hoops to gain entry. The city was laying the bricks for the gentrification of public education.

The students from the Black Student Union, amazing people like acclaimed writer Asha Bandele and Tk'ala, were organizing takeovers across CUNY and locking up the campuses. These student strikes inspired the city, and as the leaders of those movements graduated, they passed the torch down to us.

In comparison to the slow and quiet conservative town I had spent years in, Hunter was electric. Hunter was like stepping into a bit of every corner of the world. The bubble burst. Hunter was a place where a study group could have a woman in a hijab, a seventy-year-old *abuelita* coming back to school, a Christian stepper from Nashville, an Iranian transfer student, a Puerto Rican from the Bronx, and a recently arrived Chinese student all figuring things out together. It was like trans-Benetton, intersectionality without the code words. It was the international in a global city.

Hunter felt like a train station—people whizzed by with their agendas, professors never sat down, students moved from class to work to student clubs. Everybody studied and worked and partied hard. It is just how it was.

Within days of learning of Albany's plan to cut services at CUNY, students were calling for a collegewide meeting. Networks formed across campuses. At Hunter alone, for weeks on end, hundreds of students came together to figure out what needed to be done.

As in any student movement, some people had more experience organizing and had been in political parties like Love and Rage and the Revolutionary Communist Party as well as in political parties in Latin America and the Caribbean. Some of us were the sons and daughters of the Communist Party, Puerto Rican socialist groups, and the Black Panthers and had parents who were cadre. Some had families who were involved with the Free Palestine movement. We had the sons and daughters of leftists and activists everywhere who willingly took the lead in the new and growing movement. I became part of the core group of organizers of mostly "red diaper babies." We wanted to use the outrage against the cuts to CUNY as a jump-off to organize students in CUNY around local, national, and international issues, including police brutality, racism, workers' rights, political imprisonment, solidarity movements with the Zapatista uprising in Mexico, and support for a free Palestine. We formed the CUNY Coalition Against the Cuts and a year later named ourselves the Student Liberation Action Movement (SLAM).

In 1995, SLAM took over student governments on such campuses as Hunter, City, and Hostos and had bases of students in Brooklyn, Queens College, and Baruch. Like the Lords and the PSP, we became the known leftist entity in the city in the 1990s. We were not a hierarchical group; we had a rotating steering committee, and much of your status depended on how much time you could put in. We also shared ideology; although I would say that many of us were socialists, people joked that SLAM stood for "Socialists, Liberals, Anarchists, and Maoists," because all of those ideologies had been at play, often combating and learning from each other.

We did have to run a student government, which meant accountability for student fees. I became the coordinator of student clubs, and as we educated the student clubs around our politics and intentions, we were able to recruit them to be part of the movement.

In the first five years, not only did we create a radical student campus and lead several successful actions; we also created space for many organizations that are now recognized social justice nonprofits, such as Desis Rising Up and Moving (DRUM), FIERCE, the Taxi Workers Alliance, and a flurry of groups that are now part of the base of such coalitions as Communities United for Police Reform. At the time, people organizing homeless and queer folks, immigrants, and taxi workers did not have the space or resources to do their work. We created space for them on campus and used student resources to help these groups remain able to do the political work they were doing in the city. We also had a high school organizing program tied to the student government that was a pipeline for future cadre. Many poets and artists grew followings from speaking and reciting at SLAM rallies, including folks like Mariposa, the Welfare Poets, Tato Laviera, Yerba Buena, and poet Suheir Hammad.

In 1996, Puerto Rican groups in New York City, such as the National Congress for Puerto Rican Rights and El Puente in Williamsburg, started growing and doing relevant political actions. The *Muévete* (Move) conference brought together hundreds of young Latinxs to talk about the issues of the day. The release of Iris Morales's film *¡Palante Siempre Palante!* (Forward, Always Forward!) in 1996 became a central resource in educating our generation about the history of the Puerto Rican radical socialist movements in New York. The Young Lords, in particular, became incredible folk heroes, and we could not stop comparing our movements and struggles to theirs. It was around that time that I connected many dots and realized that my parents were part of a previous generation that had tried to make the revolution. But I did not rely on them or their history, for I was committed to forging the path that my generation needed to claim.

Shifts in Nueva York and the Demise of the Student Liberation Action Movement

When I graduated in 1997, I left SLAM and Hunter to do community work in Sunset Park and then pursue a dream to make documentary films and study at George Washington University. SLAM continued with a new generation of organizers and became engaged in the anti-globalization movement. I returned to work for the student government in 2002 and created an organizing curriculum.

At this time, organizing in the city was receiving more funding support. Several people of color's organizations that did not need to before had to begin caucusing due to the scarcity of brown and black political leftists in the leadership and the membership. As the city was changing demographically, so was the access of people of color to the university and the ability to have thousands of brown and black students, particularly those from New York City, involved in political work. To maintain balance, we instituted quotas and actively recruited students of color into SLAM. The quotas became complicated because sometimes we fought about who was authentically a person of color and who had class privilege and light-skinned privilege. Vicious attacks on each other and defensive posturing wasted a lot of energy and time and took away from the work.

While the funding of social movement work began to provide some forms of sustainability, it was also a way to depoliticize the work and disconnect reform and bread-and-butter fights from the broader fights against capitalism, imperialism, and white supremacy. As funded groups, we could not openly train young people in radical politics because the ideology was to stick to the reform fight, not to address systemic issues. It shifted the focus to what funders wanted and pleasing them and their diverse set of ideologies and agendas rather than focusing on what the key needs of students and the community were. It also created rivalries between organizations that received more or less funding. Sometimes organizations that did less work but branded better received more funding, which grew resentment. *Note:* Many philanthropic organizations are sensitive to this concern, but the development of "star" groups by funders continues to be a hard issue.

Eventually, after eight years of popular uprising and radical politics, the administration was able to malign SLAM and say that we were a radical fringe group. The first year that Hunter instituted digital voting machines was also the first year that SLAM lost the student election. Some claimed foul play, but the exhaustion of trying to fight the negative campaign against us led to the end.

SLAM taught me a lot, and I feel blessed to have been given a chance at such a young age to have worked with amazing comrades who have become my close friends and political allies for life—we call ourselves "SLAM fam."

Movements Today: Many Ways to Move and More Necessary Than Ever

Movements in the 2000s are produced by nonprofit professionals and staff and are also spontaneous and organic. Professionally driven campaigns, led by usually progressive liberal institutions, are the ones that people like Steve Bannon attack. These campaigns are often led by heavily or not so heavily funded leftist organizations. In these organizations, a core group of paid career organizers often lift relevant political issues without challenging the state's structure or offering members an organized and deeper understanding of how capitalism works to oppress them. Some paid activists and organizers in social work and social justice groups, despite government and foundation funding, do fearlessly address the structural problems of capitalism with their members. However, even with the best intentions, staffing leads to hierarchy and structures that do not lend themselves to mass leadership and an organic growth of resources to build a movement.

Organic movements, such as Occupy Wall Street, Black Lives Matter, and the presidential campaigns for Bernie Sanders, are also now under attack by the alt-right and neo-Nazi factions growing in America. The funding generated for these movements to grow predominantly comes from the individuals they engage. These movements are more sporadic and viral, building on media momentum and then structuring themselves around long-term initiatives and campaigns. They are generally more accountable to people's ideological tendencies and political analyses. They tend to have more roles for volunteers and the ability to fight for more radical demands.

One of the chief differences between movements now and those forged by groups like the PSP is that now assembling or coming together happens in a diversity of ways—webinars, social media groups, websites, online petitions, online event sign-ups, DIY online toolkits to help you build your campaign. This variety means that a lot of organizing is happening remotely and virtually. The advantage of this reach, for example, is that within seconds, any person can record gross violations of injustice and share them with the world. A cop beats a kid in Harlem, and the Black Lives Matter movement in Colombia is tweeting about it and sharing to people in Nigeria within an hour. The youth are global citizens developing an international consciousness and sensitivities to race, class, and gender at a very young age. They can teach themselves anything through Googling.

However, the discipline of work, commitment to a long-term struggle, and key leaders who have a particular guiding wisdom and leadership style based on study and shaping a broader analysis are harder to hold accountable to specific movements. Our leaders are like helium balloons that we have to reach for when we are in the struggle as opposed to being in the trenches, learning alongside us. Many people are eager to work locally so that they can see their impact beyond a list of followers or friends who are in cyberspace. People are going back to hand-drawing flyers, old-school canvassing, and meeting in person to create real communities and accountability.

All of this activity is happening in the most repressive era of our time for Americans and people around the world. The failure of Democrats and neoliberal policies globally, including the cutting of welfare, the inability to enact real health care reform, the massive surveillance of global citizens, and the targeted drone attacks on vulnerable communities, has led to massive distrust in the established Left, such as the Democratic Party. Global right-wing and fascist regimes spew rhetoric about empowering working people but in truth only grow the elite and expand an unstable and alienated workforce divided by race. In this gig economy, it is hard to know or care about your neighbor because your neighbor has little to do with what you need to survive in your immediate life. Any social safety net we fought for in the 1960s is being dismantled, and the environmental justice movement, the labor movement, the women's movement, and the fight for racial justice are all under attack.

Where Is the Love? Right Here, Baby.

Yet dare I say that as the repression is growing, so is the love. National networks like the Right to the City Alliance that have worked to connect local groups across the country in fighting gentrification and displacement and affordability in cities are linking with groups like Grassroots Global Justice and the Climate Justice Alliance that focus on environmental justice. The day after Donald Trump was inaugurated saw the largest demonstrations in recorded history and a call for the global respect of women. The coalition of immigrant rights groups that have been stopping deportations one family at a time, #Not1More, is growing into a national Latinx network called *Mijente* (My People). Mijente is also working on and recognizing the issues of Puerto Rican austerity and, as Latinx immigrants, showing solidarity with the colonial issues faced by Puerto Ricans despite their so-called privileged access to citizenship. The movement to elect Sanders made the word *socialism* attractive, and according to organizers of the Democratic Socialists of America, they have seen a spike in participation from sixty or so people to six hundred people in a meeting.

Long-time political prisoner Oscar López Rivera was finally released in 2016. And in Puerto Rico, an occupation took place in the capital, and a younger generation has ushered in a surge in coops and small businesses and farms as they try to reignite a suffering economy on their terms.

The questions that organizers face now: How do we open and invite people into our *casa*? How do we create a political home that is worthy of stability, consistency, and a disciplined membership that will commit to fighting for a new American Revolution?

What Is to Be Done?

The lessons from the PSP—clear leadership, political study, and defined roles for members—are important to incorporate into politics today. Political parties will be essential in this Trump era, to win the narrative of socialism on a local level and to centralize the ability to study and work together cohesively. It is essential for intergenerational global and local networks to examine what it means to organize under fascist conditions in this political moment. The Puerto Rican community has been radically dispersed in New York except for the Bronx and parts of Brooklyn, but we need to notice and support new colonies in Florida and other states. It will be critical for *Diasporicans* to invest in businesses and land on the island and to continue to promote culture and art on a large scale so that it is not completely lost to new investors who consider our culture a ghost or something cute to put in a museum. As Puerto Ricans here, we need to continue to link our struggle to the broader Latinx diaspora and the African diaspora, and we need to seek support and help in solidarity efforts with empowering the resistance groups on the island while educating them on the issues we face here.

And we need to be openly and unapologetically fabulous socialists. Because the more we project our vision, the more we will feel the impulse not just to participate but to lead.

Conclusion

Writing this piece, I put a post on Facebook for people to share their stories about being red diaper babies, to discuss what it meant to grow up in a party. I got responses from my friends who are the sons and daughters of Jewish Communists who were members of the Communist Party. But the sons and daughters of the Panthers and the Lords and other parties with a majority of people of color did not respond. While the Broadway show *Party People* has become a success, we have a long way to go concerning documenting the lives and stories of the children who grew up in these movements. Some of us ran away, and some of us moved toward the work. But we all know the experience had an impact, and we have a distinct way of looking at the world. Whatever we end up doing as *pamper rojos*, we do with great empathy, a need to heal, and a fighting spirit.

¡Puerto Rico Libre y Socialista!

A Philarican in the Struggle

José-Manuel Navarro

Abuela's Chickens

My *abuela* (grandmother) provided me an early lesson on the typical Puerto Rican mind one day in the summer of 1968. Twelve years before, my parents had already moved us to Philadelphia. In the summer of 1968, I had finished my junior year in college and had the good fortune of taking classes as a visiting student at the University of Puerto Rico in Río Piedras. After classes ended, I spent a month with my grandparents in San Lorenzo.

Abuelo y Abuela had a small farm that included laying hens. I asked my grandmother one day to tell me about the different kinds of chickens and hens she owned. Among others, she mentioned the Manila (named for its origin in the Philippines but long-established in Puerto Rico) and the American.

"Which is the best one?" I asked.

"The American one," she answered, black dress framing her thin body.

"Why?"

"Because she comes from the United States," she emphasized.

"Is that the only reason, Abuela?"

"That's all that matters, son."

Her open hands waved above her shoulders, indicating her words as a matter of fact.

My grandmother never left the island of Puerto Rico. She completed only four years of schooling and had been immersed in the colonial ideology rampant in Puerto Rican schools and life that exalted all things American and deprecated all things Puerto Rican. Thus, her comments about the superiority of American chickens over Puerto Rican chickens were simply her repetition of the colonial toxicity in which she lived. For me, Abuela's comments about her chickens were a confirmation of the colonial mentality of accepting anything made or coming from the United States as superior to anything produced or made in Puerto Rico.

Abuela confirmed for me the analyses that Albert Memmi and Frantz Fanon make in their works; I had read both authors before going to Puerto Rico. In Abuela's comments, I found a personal example of how the colonized completely defend the worldview of the colonizer because that is what they are taught. Fanon's concept of the "colonial mentality" argues that the colonized adopt as normal the views imposed upon them by the colonizer. Those views ensure that the colonized depreciates himself or herself exactly as the colonizer wishes. The result of those views is that they relegate the colonized to an inferior status in the colonizer-colonized relationship. The colonized people laud, esteem, and value all things of the colonizer and discount, devalue, condemn, depreciate, and despise themselves and all their cultural and spiritual beliefs. Later, in retrospect, I could see that these were the ideas that Abuela expressed.

Beginnings of an Awakening

I had been exposed to anti-colonial writers such as Memmi and Fanon during undergraduate studies in Philadelphia but was still a novice on the real history of Puerto Rico. However, this blind spot changed rapidly during my summer classes at the University of Puerto Rico, where I enrolled in courses on Puerto Rican history and literature. I had gone there to search for my cultural and ethnic roots.

Román Medina, my professor for the literature class, was enlightening, inspiring, and passionate about his subject. He took me on flights of pleasure and wonderment as I read and came to understand Puerto Rican literature. Although I had read some Puerto Rican literature on my own before I took the course, Professor Medina opened my mind and eyes to such poets as José Gautier Benítez, José P. H. Hernández, Juan Antonio Corretjer, Francisco Matos Paoli, and others. These wordsmiths took me deeper into myself as I learned to cherish the literary heritage that is mine and that had been denied to me as a Spanish major at my home university in Philadelphia.

Short-story writers René Marqués, Tomás Blanco, Emilio S. Belaval, José Luis González, and others spoke to me of a Puerto Rico whose social and economic problems were unknown to me and that had been excluded from my Spanish literature courses. Eugenio María de Hostos, the nineteenth-century Puerto Rican polymath who wrote in such diverse fields as sociology, literary criticism, essays, fiction, and ethics, was particularly provocative. My daily readings of these authors in the college library and my dorm room were a source of emotional fulfillment, individual cultural affirmation, and self-discovery. To this day, I remain grateful to that professor for guiding me into and through my literary cultural heritage.

However, Julio Domani, the professor of history, was a different academic animal. A Puerto Rican expatriate who lived and taught in what he considered "civilized" Paris, France, he was teaching at the University of Puerto Rico for that summer semester only.

Domani covered the history of Puerto Rico from 1898 to 1952 in a one-hour class lecture during the last day of the course. "What the United States did in 1898 was an invasion of Puerto Rican soil. That's what Harvard historian Arthur Schlesinger Sr. says," he told the class. A few minutes later, he said, "Senator Joseph Foraker sponsored the bill that became the Foraker Act, the first Organic Act of Puerto Rico, establishing a Puerto Rican citizenship but allowing Puerto Rico no more rights than it had under Spain with the 1897 Autonomic Charter." He did not explain what those rights were.

A few minutes after that, Domani informed the class that the "United States Congress approved the Jones Act in 1917. As of March 2, 1917, anyone born in Puerto Rico is a citizen of the United States." Continuing his quick run through fifty-four years of Puerto Rican history, Domani informed us, "In 1947, the United States Congress approved the Elective Governor Act, allowing Puerto Ricans to vote for their own governor for the first time in history. That's how Luis Muñoz Marín became the first Puerto Rican to be elected governor in a free election." In what seemed another historical blur, Domani brought the class up to date.

Domani continued his lecture: "In 1950, the United States Congress approved Law 600, allowing Puerto Ricans to write their own constitution and the establishment of the Commonwealth of Puerto Rico in 1952. And that's where we find ourselves today, ladies and gentlemen." There was no way to find out anything else because the professor used no textbook for his class. Information to the students came only from his lectures. Domani, I suspected, timed his lecture to coincide with the bell ending the class, because barely two minutes after he finished telling the class about the developments of 1952, the bell ending the course rang.

More significant than what Domani said was what he left out. He did not mention the glorious struggles of the Puerto Rican Nationalist Party during the 1930s and 1940s for the cause of Puerto Rican workers and independence. He ignored completely the martyrdom and persecution suffered by

Don Pedro Albizu Campos, Puerto Rico's leading twentieth-century apostle for independence, who turned down possibilities of becoming a financially successful attorney by working for U.S. corporations and chose, instead, to defend the rights of Puerto Rican workers and the poor. To my regret, he covered nothing of the Puerto Rican diaspora to the United States from 1948 to 1964, the historical process that frames my life.

In addition, Domani said nothing about the enormous heroic struggles of college and high school students, parents, and educators to keep Spanish as the language of instruction in the public schools and universities of Puerto Rico. He did not inform students of the numerous plans to exterminate the population of Puerto Rico through birth-control programs and the forced sterilization of women, programs launched under U.S. governmental sponsorship. And he said nothing about the debates reigning in the United Nations (UN) about the colonial relationship of Puerto Rico with the United States, a debate that continues to this very day. In sum, he presented a completely placid view, devoid of conflict or struggle, of Puerto Rico's destiny under the control of the United States.

In spite of the fact that I had an A average going into the final, I received a final grade of B for the Puerto Rican history course. I compared my grade with that of other students who had witnessed my avid class participation. Two students who earned grades in the high 80s on the final earned an A for the course; I scored 93 out of a possible 100 points on the final and received a B for the course. When I asked my professor to explain how an A average could turn into a final B, he merely said, "This is your final grade." He then walked away. I could not appeal the grade he gave me. After all, he was returning to France at the end of the course, and I was returning to Philadelphia. I was stuck with the grade.

It dawned on me later why I had received the unfair final grade. I recalled the conversation I had had with Domani after the second day of class.

"So, you're from the United States. What part of New York are you from? Brooklyn, Manhattan, the Bronx?" Professor Domani asked.

"None of them, professor, I'm from Philadelphia," I answered, my eyes avoiding looking directly at his eyes as a sign of respect.

"Ah! Philadelphia." He seemed ecstatic, eyes glazing over, voice dropping to an almost prayerful whisper. "That's the Cradle of American Liberty, home to Independence Hall, Carpenters' Hall, and the Liberty Bell. You don't know how fortunate you are. You'll be able to learn English fluently and become a full-fledged American citizen, unlike your classmates here."

"Well, yes, I speak and write English fluently. I've lived and studied in Philadelphia since the fourth grade. I'm now majoring in Spanish in college to keep my fluency in both languages flowing." My answer seemed to please him, if his nodding was an indication.

"I understand that most Puerto Ricans in the United States want Puerto Rico to become the fifty-first state of the federal union, just as I do." This time his voice was firm, emphatic.

"Well, professor, I believe in an independent Republic of Puerto Rico," I said.

"Really? That's very interesting," he said.

And that was the end of it. Or, so I thought. Little did I know that my political belief would negatively affect my final grade.

By 1968, I had spoken with many Puerto Rican intellectuals in Philadelphia who had nurtured my belief in seeing a Puerto Rican republic. Moreover, my numerous discussions with students from Latin American and African nations who were studying at my university made me think that a Puerto Rican republic was possible. By the time I enrolled at the University of Puerto Rico, I understood that Puerto Rico and Puerto Rican culture could survive only in an independent Puerto Rican nation.

This was 1968. Freedom of speech is enshrined in the constitution of the Commonwealth of Puerto Rico. It is also a right of all Puerto Ricans under Article II of the Constitution of the United States of America. However, daily living in Puerto Rico took another turn.

Anyone who declared himself an adherent or proponent of the independence of Puerto Rico suffered social exclusion, potential alienation from friends and family, possible expulsion from university studies, and firing from employment as well as threats of physical violence. These practices were enshrined as proper daily practice. Years after leaving the University of Puerto Rico, I met students in Puerto Rico and New York who had been expelled from the University of Puerto Rico for their steadfast support of and actions for Puerto Rico's independence.

The expulsion from employment hit closer to home. A few months after I left Puerto Rico, I found out that an uncle, who still lived in Puerto Rico, had been demoted in his job. My uncle, an electrical engineer at the Electrical Authority of Puerto Rico, was a firm advocate for the independence of Puerto Rico. The Electrical Authority of Puerto Rico needed my uncle's skills. Thus, the company could not fire him. However, his supervisors made his life miserable.

For years, my uncle trained new hires who worked under him. They would rise to supervisory positions throughout the Electrical Authority, while my uncle was kept in the same position with no advancement. About fifteen years after my coursework in Puerto Rico, I learned that my uncle secured an attorney willing to argue the case that he had suffered discrimination for his political views. My uncle won his suit and was promoted to the level he deserved. As part of the judgment, he obtained a substantial cash settlement for the pay owed him for decades, representing increases in the salary he would have earned if he had been treated fairly and professionally during the previous decades of his life.

Professor Domani punished me for my political beliefs, just as my uncle suffered for similar political beliefs.

From *Movimiento Pro Independencia* to Partido Socialista Puertorriqueño

In the summer of 1969, a few months after I graduated from college in Philadelphia, I met Sor María Martorelli, a Puerto Rican nun who was a member of the Sisters of the Most Blessed Sacrament. She was a proponent of Puerto Rican independence.

Sor María gave me two documents that she said "[would] educate [me] about the Puerto Rican struggle for Independence and teach [me] entirely new lessons on the History of Puerto Rico." One was the booklet *Presente y Futuro de Puerto Rico: La Doctrina de la Nueva Lucha de Independencia* (Present and Future of Puerto Rico: The Doctrine of the New Struggle for Independence). The other document was a copy of a newspaper, *Claridad.*

The pamphlet was the political thesis of the *Movimiento Pro Independencia* de Puerto Rico (Puerto Rican Pro Independence Movement), known by its initials as MPI. The MPI was founded in 1959 by proponents of Puerto Rican independence. The pamphlet taught me numerous lessons about the history of the United States and the history of Puerto Rico, a history I had never seen before.

In a musical Spanish, the work sketched the socioeconomic and political reality of Puerto Rico as a colony of the United States. I learned that, as a result of the December 1898 Treaty of Paris, ending the War of 1898, Spain had ceded Puerto Rico to the United States. Spain had already granted Puerto Rico autonomy through the Autonomous Charter of 1897. One of the provisions of the charter was that Puerto Rico would be consulted about any changes in its future political relationship with Spain. Yet Spain did not consult Puerto Rico about its future political relationship with the United States.

I found out another significant aspect of U.S. history previously denied to me and obscured in the lectures of Professor Domani: through the Treaty of 1898, Cuba, Samoa, Guam, the Marianas, and the Philippines had also become property of the United States. Collectively, the new Caribbean and Pacific island acquisitions had become known as the "island possessions of the United States."

By ratifying the treaty, the U.S. Congress made the United States a colonial imperialist power in the Caribbean Sea and the Pacific Ocean. This situation had never happened before in the history of the United States.

Presente y Futuro de Puerto Rico did not merely educate me about U.S. and Puerto Rican history. It enlightened me about the specific economic reasons why I found myself growing up in Philadelphia and not my hometown of San Lorenzo. It told me about the U.S. destruction of the sugarcane industry in Puerto Rico. My father had been a sugarcane worker. The destruction of the sugarcane industry is what had forced us to leave rural San Lorenzo and move to Philadelphia.

The *Tesis*, as it was known, concluded its analysis of Puerto Rico under U.S. rule by presenting a plan for the development of Puerto Rico as an independent nation. This remarkable document became my political guide on Puerto Rico, land of my birth and paradise of my imagination.

Starting that fall and continuing to the next summer, I pursued and completed a master's degree in Latin American studies at a California university. Thereafter, my life turned increasingly to applying intellectual beliefs to political practice.

In August 1970, my wife, Mariana, and I moved to New York City, where I took a position with ASPIRA of New York as an academic counselor to Puerto Rican and Dominican college students. I had been granted conscientious objector status to the Vietnam War; I could not condone war as a way to solve differences between civilized nations. Moreover, I had no conflict with the people of Vietnam; they had never hurt me in any way. But the war was raging, and all male citizens of the United States between the ages of eighteen and thirty-five were required to register and risk serving in the U.S. armed forces. If a man did not choose to serve in the military, he had only one option: become a conscientious objector to war. But that came with a price. The Selective Service System required that I work for two years on a job that "served the national interest of the United States." The job with ASPIRA of New York fulfilled the requirements. For Mariana and me, that first year was consumed with setting up our household and getting acclimated to my new job and to the cultural and political scene among the largest concentration of Puerto Ricans in the United States.

Maryann Christine Briscoe is an African American woman who joined the movement for Puerto Rico's independence because she believed it was a "necessary struggle for people who support anti-imperialist policy. In my trips to Puerto Rico before we met, I encountered a lovely people enslaved to U.S. colonialism. I saw parallels between the struggle for Puerto Rican independence and the struggle for African American self-determination."

Mariana and I had met during my student activist days at Temple University. We were both studying Italian. Our teacher gave everybody Italian names; she was "Marianna," and I was "Giuseppe." Because I liked the sound of her name in Italian, I started referring to her as "Mariana." I found out that her name in Italian would become the Spanish name, if I dropped one "n." So, I did. All members of my family still refer to her as "Mariana." My nephews and nieces, wanting her blessing today, ask for it according to proper Puerto Rican cultural norms: "*Bendición, Titi* Mariana," they say. Anyone who met her during our PSP days liked her name. It reminded them of Mariana Bracetti, the woman who sewed the Puerto Rican flag used by the revolutionaries in Puerto Rico's major revolt for independence from Spain, the Grito ("Cry") de Lares, on September 23, 1868.

While at ASPIRA, I met my fellow counselor Digna Sánchez, who was a member of the MPI. She and I engaged in numerous conversations about Puerto Rican history and culture and Puerto Rico's colonial relationship with the United States. At the agency, I also met Andrés (Andy) Torres, who was pursuing a doctorate in economics. Andy invited me to join his weekly study group on Marxist economic theory. For the next year, Andy and I met weekly with Arthur Felderbaum for discussions on a variety of economic and political issues that opened my eyes and world view. These discussions have been fundamental to my political and scholarly development. Also among the staff of the educational agency were others who were sympathetic to the ideas of Puerto Rican liberation.

I joined the MPI in the summer of 1971. When the MPI became the PSP, I continued my activism in the new organization.

Claridad

By the time I joined MPI, its weekly newspaper, *Claridad*, based in San Juan, was the most widely read *independentista* publication in the United States and Puerto Rico. Along with the decision to expand organizing efforts in the United States and to transition into the PSP, the leadership of the MPI decided to increase the paper's U.S. circulation and to publish a bilingual version. This publication would be a supplement to the San Juan–based edition and add reporting and analyses about issues dealing with the Puerto Rican communities in the United States. I started working with the New York–based weekly as a correspondent and moved up through the ranks. Eventually, I was promoted to the position of editor of *Claridad bilingüe*.

My responsibilities included writing a weekly editorial on political and community events and contextualizing the surrounding issues. Local issues and struggles in Puerto Rican communities in the United States received editorial support.

One of my editorials identified Puerto Ricans as "the Palestinians of America," paralleling the Palestinian diaspora throughout the world, a result of Israeli settler colonialism, with the Puerto Rican diaspora to the United States, a result of U.S. colonialism. Juan Mari Brás, the Secretary General of the PSP, adopted this terminology and gave it greater audience in a column he wrote. His weekly column for *Claridad* circulated widely in Puerto Rico and the United States.

Even in the English version, *Claridad bilingüe* referred to Puerto Ricans as *boricuas*. This term derives from *Boriquén*, the Hispanicized term for the name the indigenous Arawak-Taínos gave the island before it was conquered by Christopher Columbus. In the original language, Boriquén means "Land of the Proud Lord."

Other editorials I wrote expressed support for the contemporary ongoing Angolan, Mozambican, and South African struggles for sovereignty and independence and the struggles for human rights of African Americans, women's rights, and Native Americans in the United States. Other editorials espoused the causes of all working men and women in the United States. Whenever I wrote an editorial, I was not merely engaging in a writing exercise to determine how successfully I could pull words together. The goal of my editorials was to denounce an abusive moment or condition and to tell readers, "This is wrong. We don't have to stand for this abuse. Here are some reasons why and how we can make the change. Let's not waste any more time harping or crying. Let's organize. Let's change this. And this organization—the PSP—will support you in any way you deem necessary."

During my role as editor, I supervised four full-time reporters, a managing editor, and several other staff, including a photographer, a layout artist, a typesetter, a business administrator, and the head of circulation. The majority of the *Claridad bilingüe* team were women, of whom two were Cuban American. This crew was abnegated and supremely competent.

Our full-time reporters were supplemented by correspondents in all areas where the PSP existed. Correspondents would call in the details of a story or event in their town or nearby community from anywhere in the country, and the Manhattan staff would turn the facts into a news article. As a result, *Claridad bilingüe* featured wide coverage of events affecting Puerto Rican communities all over the United States.

We worked in a seventh-floor loft on East Thirteenth Street in Manhattan from 9:00 A.M. to 7:00 P.M. Monday through Wednesday and from 9:00 A.M. Thursday to 3:00 A.M. Friday (that's right: 3:00 A.M.!). Late fall and winter were especially demanding, because we operated out of a cold seventh-floor loft.

"The homeland demands courage and sacrifice," Albizu Campos affirmed. The reporters and workers at *Claridad bilingüe* honored Don Pedro's words by living them daily. Staff members made great sacrifices for the cause. Our salaries were, at best, stipends. In my case, upon assuming the position of editor, I gave up a well-paid full-time job at Queens College of the City University of New York (CUNY) as an academic counselor to first-generation African American, Puerto Rican, Dominican, and Euro

American college students. I was able to find a part-time job, so I did not take a stipend. My wife gave up a full-time job as an assistant in a college president's office. Sure, some of our members at the newspaper collective complained when a check was late and a dinner or two had to be skipped. But we helped out one another as well as we could.

The newspaper was printed on Friday afternoon. By Friday evening, many party members in the New York City boroughs and northern New Jersey towns had the current issue in their hands. The Circulation Department shipped the newspaper to PSP *núcleos* outside New York City. In the beginning, these were in Hartford, Connecticut; Chicago and Waukegan, Illinois; Boston, Massachusetts; Philadelphia, Pennsylvania; Camden, New Jersey; and San Francisco and Los Angeles, California.

The PSP did not merely mouth or write about supporting workers' or people's democratic rights; it supported those rights with concrete actions. These actions included picketing with striking workers and student leaders, organizing and leading community struggles for cultural affirmation and accessible housing, organizing for the release of Puerto Rican political prisoners, and calling for rigorous public education through forums and pamphlets. *Claridad* was an enormously important instrument for supporting these campaigns.

One of the unanticipated benefits of working at the newspaper was that I did not need a watch or a clock. One particular day early in my new position, I lost track of the time and was worried that I would be late for a meeting I had to attend uptown. I ran out of my office into the newsroom, looking for someone with a watch.

"What time is it? I can't be late for this meeting."

"We don't use watches or clocks around here," Isidro, one of the reporters, told me.

"Why not?"

"Pick up the phone, wait for a minute, and you'll see."

I did as he suggested. As I looked at him with questioning face and hand gestures, I heard a news report coming from the phone. After the report ended, I heard the voice of a male speaker say, "This is WCBS news radio in New York City. We give you all news, twenty-four hours a day. The time now is eleven thirty-two in the morning."

"Clearly, we're important enough to be monitored by the New York City Police Department and the Federal Bureau of Investigation," I chuckled at Isidro.

From whatever office was being used by whatever surveillance agency came the sound of a radio that was left on all the time. Was this incompetence or perhaps intentional? After all, we worked under the belief that our phones were tapped.

Through the illegal activities of the New York City Police Department (NYPD) or the Federal Bureau of Investigation (FBI), I accessed a cost-free, reliable clock that facilitated my daily and weekly schedule. I guess I can say that I obtained some benefits from a politically repressive system.

Dealing with surveillance was not always a light-hearted matter. Always present at our rallies and public events were the undercover agents. They usually wore suits or army fatigues. They stood out because they appeared to be reporters, except they never asked the speaker any questions—but they did write down everything the speaker said. When I spoke at a rally or ceremony or when I myself reported on an activity or event, these interlopers were always present.

Once I was sent to Philadelphia as a party representative in the local Puerto Rican Day Parade. Our float, with a contingent of some forty to forty-five people, marched down the parkway from Twenty-Fourth Street to the review stand in Liberty Square at Sixth and Market Streets. This is the area housing Carpenter's Hall, the Liberty Bell, and the National Constitution Center.

From the float, I spoke to the crowds we passed on our march, denouncing people we viewed as co-opted community leaders and city hall bureaucrats; their actions were "treachery to our Puerto Rican people," I said. Whenever I got off the stage with the microphone and walked out into the crowd to shake hands with parade watchers who knew me, I was accompanied by men in suits, one on my right side, and the other on my left. They walked on either side of me, as apparent escorts.

However, these men—they were always men—were neither Puerto Ricans nor uniformed Philadelphia police personnel; they were clearly FBI. When I arrived at the review stand at Sixth Street, I denounced the surveillance we had been under for the previous twenty blocks. Immediately, about fifteen to eighteen men left our contingent, scampering every which way. They looked like cockroaches fleeing insecticide.

Language, Culture, and Identity

My upbringing in two worlds of language and culture prepared me for the role of editor and writer. *Claridad* as well as life in the PSP provided me with continuous enrichment in Spanish vocabulary and use of the Spanish language. It was another unanticipated benefit, if you will, of being engaged in revolutionary struggle. Mari Brás, the Secretary General of the PSP, in his writings and speeches used a sonorous Puerto Rican Spanish whose harmony enthralled me. Hearing and reading him reaffirmed the rhythms, phrasings, and melodies of the language I spoke and wrote exclusively for the first eight years of my life.

Language has been a defining point in my life. I spoke and wrote exclusively in Spanish until the age of eight, when I arrived in the City of Brotherly Love. In Philadelphia, everything was in English: the church services, class discussions, radio, and television. I heard Spanish only from my parents and their neighbors, because we children learned in school that we "had to abandon the ways and culture of the old country." That meant to us Catholic elementary school students that we had to abandon Spanish, the language of our heritage.

Thus, we learned to view Spanish as a "hick language," the language that ignorant country bumpkins spoke. We youngsters did not want to be confused with our parents. We believed that we were advanced, civilized, not ignoramuses like they were. We learned from our teachers that English was the language of culture and civilization, the vehicle we needed to master. Spanish was the language we must abandon. We all knew, by unanimous silent consent, that we could not speak Spanish if we wanted the respect of our teachers—all of them Sisters of St. Joseph—and the diocesan priests of the parish.

For the fourth and fifth grades, I was in a classroom with a nun who spoke some Spanish. In that room, I could speak to her in Spanish and be understood. The unstated consensus of all of us elementary school students of Puerto Rican background about the use of the Spanish language still prevailed. It was the policy at our Catholic grammar school that students would get a detention if they spoke Spanish within a two-block radius of the school. We called it "being left in jail" (*quedarse preso*). I lived a mass of confusion. In my home, I had to speak in Spanish to my parents and their friends. But I had to speak in English to my brothers and sisters, all of our friends, and my Irish American and Polish American classmates. This confusion lasted only until the eighth grade. By the end of the eighth grade, I knew exactly which language I should speak depending on the specific situation. This requirement became my first insight into appreciating my own multilinguistic abilities.

My high school experience further attacked my cultural heritage. When it came time to choose a foreign language of study in my junior year, I enrolled in Spanish class. After all, I wanted to preserve my cultural heritage. There was much futility in following the teacher's pronunciation when he said, "¿Cómo está *you*sted" when I knew the correct form was "¿Cómo está *u*sted?" But this futility paled in comparison to other moments of insult, as when my teacher, Father Wrigley, whose last name reminded me of the chewing-gum brand, gratuitously mocked me two weeks into the school year. I give the encounter as I can best recall it.

"*Señor* Navarro," Father Wrigley asked. "What do Puerto Ricans say for 'car'"?

"We say '*carro*,' Father," I answered.

"Please stand, Señor Navarro." It was the norm at our school for all boys to be addressed as "Mister" by the teachers. Another one of the rules was that students had to stand anytime they were called upon for an answer or were to be disciplined. I thought that maybe he was mocking me by calling me "Señor" instead of "Mister."

Father Wrigley then turned to the other twenty-nine boys in the room.

"Gentlemen," he said, this time using the English title of respect, "Mr. Navarro has just used a word that is common to Puerto Ricans but that is not the Castilian Spanish of Cervantes. The correct word is '*coche*' or '*automóvil*.' Puerto Rican is a bastardized dialect of the Spanish language. In this room, you will, under my guidance, learn the proper Spanish language."

With my ears afire from embarrassment, I quietly sat down at my desk.

Yet although he had me pegged as speaking "a bastardized dialect of the Spanish language," Father Wrigley called upon me that whole year for clarification of pronunciation, grammar use, and vocabulary. I had not studied Spanish grammar or in Spanish since the third grade. Nonetheless, I was the thesaurus, dictionary, grammarian, and phonetics teacher to the entire classroom.

Undaunted by the linguistic stupidities of teachers, in ninth grade I began reading books in Spanish from our local public library. Literary classics of Spain and Latin America took me on flights of intellectual and linguistic delight. Father Wrigley embarrassed me in the classroom a few more times that year, but my readings told me that everything I did and read gave me a higher grasp of the "language of Cervantes," as he called it, than his heavily accented spoken Spanish, pitiful vocabulary, and poor grammatical use of the Spanish language.

Meanwhile, in all my readings I encountered Spanish vocabulary that I did not understand or had ever seen, much less imagined. Wanting to understand the meaning of the strange words I encountered led me to purchase my first dictionary in Spanish. I was unstoppable from then on.

Now, I could not only read in Spanish but also find out what the words that I did not know meant. My vocabulary and fluency in Spanish increased markedly. I knew words that even my parents did not know. To me, this knowledge was a sign of definitive Spanish-language growth and development.

When I went to college, I majored in Spanish. However, I continued reading the great English-language writers from England and the United States. This steady practice of reading intensively in both languages on my own is what gave me the deep knowledge of both languages. My *compañeros* and *compañeras* in the PSP would note positively my full fluency in Spanish and English.

My study of the similarities and differences between the Spanish and English languages continues today. I still read as much literature as I can get in Spanish. In addition, over the past few years, I have written poetry in English and Spanish. Cultivating my Spanish-language cultural and personal side is a fundamental practice I must continue in order to nurture that young boy who was born into the Spanish language and was made literate in it by the age of five-and-a-half by his mother.

Cultivating and deepening my knowledge of the Spanish language, more than any economic benefit I may derive from it, allows me to nurture the very intellectual, emotional, psychological, and cultural bases of my being. Moreover, enriching that heritage is for me a political and moral obligation. With Puerto Rican Spanish and culture under exterminating attack by U.S. government and corporate policies and practices, in Puerto Rico as well as in the United States, I deem it essential to speak Puerto Rican Spanish. It is my own strictly personal way of screaming to the world, "This Puerto Rican will not let Puerto Rican culture and language die!"

Many PSP colleagues in Puerto Rico believed that members whose dominant language was English were not as Puerto Rican as those who grew up in Puerto Rico and speaking Spanish. I witnessed many debates among members in New York and other U.S. cities as to who was more "Puerto Rican" than another. I found the whole debate superficial; what mattered to me was that we were exploited equally as a people and oppressed as colonials whether we lived in San Lorenzo or Jersey City, Barranquitas or the Bronx, Ponce or Philadelphia.

The concepts of *Nuyorican* and *Rican* gained new strength in those days. The terms had been around for a while, but the population boom of stateside-reared Puerto Ricans in the decades of the 1960s through the 1980s made them even more significant. *Nuyorican*, still used today in an offensive manner, is what some people in Puerto Rico call the children or grandchildren of Puerto Ricans in New York City. Many of my colleagues turned this term on its head, using it positively to refer to themselves.

Rican was the term that many of us who grew up in the United States, regardless of geographical location, often used. I followed the party's theory that all of us were members of the Puerto Rican nation. Through that theory, we understood that Puerto Rico is a divided nation. This nation had one half of its population living on the Caribbean archipelago carrying that name and the other half living in the United Sates.

Consequently, I referred to everyone as "Puerto Rican." I believed that if we were going to seek the freedom and democratic rights of people of Puerto Rican descent in the United States as part of the struggle for an independent Puerto Rican republic, we needed to make manifest at all times that we were one people, both in the Caribbean archipelago of Puerto Rico and here, in the "belly of the beast," to quote José Martí, the apostle of Cuban independence from Spain.

My Spanish- and English-language skills provided me with another role in the structure of the U.S. Branch of the PSP; modesty aside, I was the individual who came up with "U.S. Branch" when we needed a name for the PSP organization in the United States. I became the de facto simultaneous interpreter for visiting party leaders from Puerto Rico. At the congress establishing the U.S. Branch, I made full use of my bilingual skills as chair of the deliberations.

In addition, I served as the voice of Spanish-dominant party leaders in public forums before non-Spanish-speaking political allies and persons wanting education about the Puerto Rican struggle. Other assignments included supervising the printing and distribution of the *Tesis*, the political platform of the U.S. Branch, in Spanish and supervising its translation into English. In addition, I translated some of the first documents that the Cuban Embassy submitted to the Decolonization Committee to reopen the Colonial Case of Puerto Rico at the UN.

To Puerto Rico . . . and Back

In September 1974, Mariana and I moved to Puerto Rico. The polluted Manhattan air had wreaked havoc on my health. During every seasonal change, I spent a week to ten days in bed with allergenic colds.

The demanding working hours at the newspaper in a drafty and cold loft further weakened my immune system. Doctors assured me that my continued presence in New York would bring about a severe case of bronchial asthma. They told me I had to leave New York City. The only option we had for a change of climate was Puerto Rico, where I had family with whom we could live until we settled.

A few months before our son was born, I met with Ramón Arbona, the editor of *Claridad diario*, the PSP's daily newspaper. Arbona, who had served as the First Secretary of the PSP U.S. Branch and editor of *Claridad bilingüe*, had himself returned to Puerto Rico previously. Arbona offered me the position of assistant editor of the International Department and editor of the U.S. News Department at the daily. I accepted and started working at *Claridad diario* in October 1975. Mariana was recruited to work as a typesetter. The weekly salary we received was so small that we qualified for food stamps. Like many other *Claridad* employees, I received my monthly allotment of this vital supplemental income that became critical for our survival in Puerto Rico. Eventually though, the financial strains of a low-income position, the impossibility of securing better-paid employment, and the sheer difficulty of trying to survive in Puerto Rico with my family forced a new relocation. We remained with *Claridad* until November 30, 1977, when we returned to Philadelphia.

On December 1, 1977, our son, Mariana, and I landed in Philadelphia. In the following years, we juggled our pursuit of professional and family goals with our continued activism. This journey took us to several cities where the PSP happened to be organized. In Philadelphia, I served as the Secretary of Political Education in the PSP nucleus. A year later, I was awarded a fellowship in policy making in Washington, D.C. By September 1979, I was in Chicago, engaged in doctoral studies in U.S. and Latin American history. Chicago, a city with the second-largest concentration of Puerto Ricans, was also home to a PSP organization, so I found myself participating in activities and collaborating whenever I could squeeze it in between classes, study, research, and part-time jobs.

We left Chicago in June 1983 and returned to Philadelphia. In June 1983, I started my first full-time college teaching position at Gallaudet University in Washington, D.C., the international university for the deaf. I became the director of the International Studies Program and assistant professor of romance languages and history. Three of us made up the nucleus of the PSP in Washington, D.C., then. We worked in building solidarity with the struggle for Puerto Rican independence with fraternal organizations and some members of Congress.

Space limitations obligate me to dwell primarily on my experience with *Claridad*. However, it was not unusual for cadre to be assigned different roles over the course of their years in the organization. Individual skills and circumstances, and organizational needs, could land a *militante* in a variety of assignments. In the course of more than a decade and half of PSP activism, I ended up playing a variety of roles: overseeing the area of political education, teaching classes in Puerto Rican history and Marxism, translating speeches of PSP leaders in public events to English-language audiences, participating in community meetings, and giving speeches.

Censurable Practices

The PSP was not without censurable practices. My biggest disenchantment with it lay in its sexism, homophobia, and racism. Few women were in top leadership roles. When I lived in New York City, we did have one female member in the Political Commission (PC). Until the late 1970s, no women participated in the PC in Puerto Rico, headquarters of the whole party. Also, while the romantic dalliances of any male leader were overlooked, any woman who was seen as violating norms of male sexism was frowned upon.

Homophobia was a serious problem. Gay men were viewed with benign contempt. They were seen as "disordered, easily bribable." I never understood where the idea of gay men as "more bribable" than anyone else came from. Still, the common way to describe a gay man was to say, usually below breath, that "he has problems." While no one would specify what the "problem" was, it was understood to mean that the man in question was homosexual. I state outright that, at the time, I had little understanding of gay and lesbian oppression and the struggle for their liberation. That understanding came later. However, I did not have the virulent attitude against gay men that I saw in many of my male colleagues.

Still, I had to contend with this partywide stupidity against gay men. Lesbian women were not seen as a "problem." I suspect this attitude was part and parcel of male sexist views. At *Claridad bilingüe*, we had a gay man, a dancer, who worked in layout and photography. He posed for some artistic photographs with another gay man. The PC decided, over my objection, that the pictures were "homoerotic" and, therefore, "damaging to the image of the party." Over my objection again, the PC decided that I had to censure the *compañero* and apply whatever sanctions I, as a member of the PC, editor of the newspaper, and head of the newspaper collective, deemed necessary. I resisted the order as unfair to me and the artist. As a result of my position, the Secretary of Organization, the second in command, for the U.S. Branch met with me privately about this issue. Here is how I best recall the conversation:

HIM. You must set the tone on this issue. We can't have the party's image damaged with homoerotic pictures and art that borders on pornography. As head of that collective, you must discipline this *compañero*. It's your responsibility.

ME. What he has done is art. An artist has the right to critique society any way he or she chooses. All Marxist theory agrees with that. Besides, "homoerotic" is in the eye of the beholder. I see those pictures as extoling the beauty of the human form, not something to be condemned or censored.

HIM. They border on pornography. We can't have the party linked to pornography.

ME. That's an exaggeration. They're art.

HIM. Look, I don't want you getting into trouble. The PC has spoken. You must obey. Warn this compañero that we can overlook this incident this time, but he must tread carefully from now on. His membership in the party could be at stake. *¿Comprendes, camarada?*

ME. *Sí, comprendo.*

I met with the artist later that week, when he came in to work at the newspaper collective. Here is how I best recall that conversation:

ME. Eugenio [not his real name], I must talk with you about those pictures that everyone is talking about. The PC has asked me to talk to you in my capacity as editor of the newspaper and head of the collective here.

EUGENIO. Okay. *¿Qué pasa?*

ME. The PC has asked me to tell you that they view these pictures as "homoerotic" and damaging to the image of the party. They also want me to tell you that you should be warned not to engage in this kind of behavior in the future or you may put your membership in jeopardy. And they want me to apply disciplinary sanctions against you.

EUGENIO. So, you don't think of this as art, and because you don't, I run the risk of being ejected from the party. Is that what you're saying?

ME. I'm saying that this is the position of the PC. It's not mine. I was instructed to talk to you, and that's what I'm doing. So, consider yourself warned and sanctioned.

EUGENIO. But you haven't imposed any sanctions. And what do I do about my art?

ME. I just told you that you're sanctioned. And you are. As to your art, continue being a creative artist in whatever way you deem proper. Do we understand one another?

EUGENIO. *¡Claro que sí!*

We shook hands, hugged, and parted. Eugenio returned to his job in the paper's photography room, and I returned to my desk.

The following week, at the weekly meeting of the PC, I reported back about the "issue of the erotic pictures." I told them the truth: I had "spoke[n] with Eugenio as instructed and told him that he was sanctioned."

The racism issue touched me much more personally. My wife, Mariana, was the PSP representative to a defense committee for Puerto Rican political prisoner Eduardo "Pancho" Cruz. She faithfully attended the weekly meetings of the committee for more than a year and reported to a member of the PC about her work. After a successful campaign to get him out on bail, the committee held a welcome home ceremony for him.

The PC decided that it would be "more politically proper" to have a member of the PC welcome him "in the name of the whole party." My wife, a mere rank-and-file member, and the only African American on the defense committee, was completely bypassed as the welcoming person. I concluded that, in the opinion of the PC, my wife was good enough to do the grueling work demanded of the members of the defense committee and to set type for hours on end, without a salary, at the newspaper. She also set type for the few journals and magazines that used her services, the funds for her services going to the newspaper's fund, never to her. However, Mariana was not born Puerto Rican. Thus, in the eyes of the U.S. Branch PC, she could not, therefore, "welcome our political prisoner home." That memory still stings.

Another issue related to racism occurred when the PC met in my absence. When I returned, I was informed by the Secretary of Organization that I had been named the "party liaison with African American organizations." Here is how I recall that conversation:

> HIM. While you were away, the Political Commission named you our party liaison with African American organizations.
> ME. Why me? There are other members of the Political Commission who have as much knowledge of the black movement as I do. In fact, some members have more.
> HIM. We thought you would be the best candidate.
> ME. I don't agree.

This happened a few months before Mariana and I left for Puerto Rico in 1974. I did not schedule any meetings with any African American organization, with the newspaper and my plans for relocating to Puerto Rico taking up all my time. More importantly, I did not want to schedule any meeting. The only reason I "would be the best candidate" was that my wife is African American. I found the PC's attitude patronizing, racist, and insulting. I never did represent the PSP in any meeting with an African American organization.

In my view, the party never addressed racism in Puerto Rico directly. Many of us in the United States constantly referenced this issue. The comments given to someone who raised concerns about racism in Puerto Rico were that "Puerto Rico is not the United States" and "you're letting your experience of racism in the United States cloud your judgment about racism in Puerto Rico." It was a pitiful state of affairs for an organization that sought social, political, and revolutionary change in the Caribbean archipelago.

What I Still Carry with Me

In 1993, to my eternal regret, the PSP officially disbanded. Party leaders argued that it had achieved its goal of putting socialism on Puerto Rico's electoral agenda. They also argued that Marxism-Leninism had been "discredited" in the modern world. From those beliefs, the central leadership concluded that the ideological basis of the PSP should be diluted. This, at least, is my recollection. [*Editors' note:* The PSP then, with others, transitioned to a new organization: El Nuevo Movimiento Independendista (The New Independentista Movement [NMI]).]

I disagreed then, and I still disagree. The democratic rights of the part of the Puerto Rican nation making up the Puerto Rican diaspora to the United States still go unfulfilled. In fact, the diaspora is increasing daily. This time, it is not industrial or agricultural workers emigrating from Puerto Rico. The majority, in fact, are white-collar professionals. The Puerto Rican population in the United States is now larger than the population in the Caribbean archipelago. Moreover, Puerto Rico is still a colony of the United States.

Let me emphasize that my activism with the PSP left me with several tenets that I still cherish. As a citizen of the United States, a "colonial citizen" at that, I do not want my country besmirched throughout the world. We the people of the United States must take up the case of its colony and demand that the U.S. Congress allow Puerto Rico to exist as an independent republic. Why the U.S. Congress? Because in all of its decisions regarding Puerto Rico, the U.S. Supreme Court has ruled that Puerto Rico "belongs to, but is not a part of the United States"[1] and that "Puerto Rico's sovereignty is in the hands of the Congress of the United States."[2] One hundred twenty years of U.S. colonialism is a crass example to the world. It is time to end the colonial oppression of the Caribbean nation.

Also, I believe that Marxism-Leninism is still relevant in the world today. Karl Marx and Friedrich Engels formulated a theoretical construct that is applicable to all nations within their cultural and historical processes and is a valid heuristic tool for social, cultural, and historic analysis. Practitioners of Marxist theory admit readily that Marxism is effective only when its practitioners adapt it to each nation's social, economic, and political realities and respect the cultural and linguistic heritage of the nation's peoples. No absolute formula applies in the same way to every struggle. Therefore, a Puerto Rican republic can easily adapt the theories and democratic practices of Marxism to its political reality.

Finally, I believe in a free, independent, egalitarian, nonracist, socialist, and democratic Republic of Puerto Rico. I do so because I want Puerto Rican music, literature, and ways of being to continue existing in a geographical territory that honors its ecology and environment. In addition, I want that geographical entity respected, honored, and accepted as a nation by the rest of the independent nations of the world.

I espouse this belief even though I know and accept that I will never live in Puerto Rico permanently but only visit it when I visit family members. I cling to this belief accepting fully as well that my children and grandchildren will never have Puerto Rican Spanish, with its magnificent blend of African, Taino, and European elements, as their first language. They will live and die in the United States and will share with their Spanish-speaking island-residing cousins only at family gatherings.

In addition, I believe that all men and women should treat one another with fairness, integrity, and respect. I extend that principle to the way nations of the world must interact with one another. As the metropolitan colonial power, the United States should treat Puerto Rico with the integrity, fairness, and respect it expects from other nations. Therefore, I insist that the United States should honor its democratic heritage and grant Puerto Rico its self-determination and political independence.

Whenever we marched against an abuse or affront during my years with the MPI-PSP—from 1971 through 1983—we did so under the slogan of *"Despierta Boricua, defiende lo tuyo."* That translates into English as "Awake Puerto Ricans, defend what is yours." We accompanied that slogan with another equally potent slogan: "Free Puerto Rico Right Now!"

I believe it is time that we Americans honor that last slogan completely. Puerto Ricans can defend what is theirs only if the United States negotiates the political independence of the Caribbean nation immediately, paying reparations to Puerto Rico for its century-and-a-quarter of economic exploitation, biological and cultural genocide, and forced population displacement.

When that time comes, I believe Puerto Ricans living outside the Caribbean archipelago, in the United States or elsewhere, should be allowed to carry Puerto Rican citizenship, along with U.S citizenship or the citizenship of the nation in which they live, if they choose to do so. Many countries of the world allow dual citizenship, and I cannot see any reason why the Republic of Puerto Rico should be any different.

NOTES

1. *Downes v. Bidwell*, 182 U.S. 1 (1901); César J. Ayala and Rafael Bernabe, *Puerto Rico in the American Century: A History since 1898* (Chapel Hill: University of North Carolina Press, 2007), 33. Also see José Trías Monge, *Puerto Rico: The Trials of the Oldest Colony in the World* (New Haven: Yale University Press, 1997), 44–51.

2. *Commonwealth of Puerto Rico v. Sanchez Valle et al.*, 579 U.S. (2016).

From El Barrio to the United Nations

Olga Iris Sanabria Dávila

The history of the Puerto Rican progressive movement of the 1960s through the 1980s is made up of many persons, each one with an individual story as well as a history and perception of how the movement influenced them individually. There is also a history as to where we all went individually and what we bring into each scenario we are in as a result of that experience. All the stories converge into a process that shaped and continues to shape our individual and collective present.

The conditions under which I grew up were not atypical of the 1950s' and 1960s' Puerto Rican family experience in New York City: migration from Puerto Rico, adjustment problems, family separation, language and identity issues, discrimination, unemployment, instability, and other social problems. These experiences made me and many of my contemporaries receptive to the social movements of the 1960s and 1970s.

The emphasis on Puerto Rican identity during my upbringing, and the movements of the 1960s, made me become interested in the island's history and its colonial status. My involvement in the politics of the Puerto Rican independence movement, in particular the Movement for Independence (MPI) and the Puerto Rican Socialist Party (PSP), has resulted in myriad experiences that I would never have imagined for myself.

I was a young girl from a Puerto Rican migrant family, searching for an identity, and ended up working at the international level as a representative of the decolonization and independence movement of my country. It is a journey that took me far from the ghetto tenements of the Lower East Side and East Harlem public housing projects to four continents and some forty countries and to work with and meet remarkable people.

Starting Out

My mother, Nérida Dávila Morales, and my father, Saúl Sanabria Cintrón, left Puerto Rico in the early 1950s, as part of the massive migration that brought hundreds of thousands of Puerto Ricans to New York City during that decade. Before my parents migrated, my father owned a small restaurant in Old San Juan. A local midwife brought me into the world at home, on Calle San Sebastián in Old San Juan on February 25, 1952. Now Calle San Sebastián is world known for the amazing Old San Juan Festival (*Fiestas de la Calle San Sebastián*), which originated there as a small block party.

Once we had migrated from Puerto Rico to New York City, the Williamsburg section of Brooklyn was the first place where we lived. Once in New York City, my mother worked in the garment district, and my father worked in grocery stores. Often when he was out of work, he would stay at home and take care of my older brother, Carlos, and me. He was much older than my mother, and soon after our arrival in New York, they separated. Carlos and I, of course, remained with our mother. We have an older brother, Félix, from my father's first marriage. He was close to us but lived with his mother and stepfather and their growing family. Before moving to Manhattan, my mother, my brother Carlos, and I lived on State Street in Brooklyn, in a furnished room.

The period prior to my teenage years was marked by much instability. Each time we moved to a new neighborhood, Carlos and I would go to a new school, so during our elementary school years, he and I went from neighborhood to neighborhood, from school to school. We were constantly separated from friends and teachers—a lot of fear, sadness, and insecurity—my mind has erased a lot of it from my memory, including, I'm sure, many happy moments.

We lived at quite a few addresses on the Lower East Side of Manhattan—Clinton Street, Rivington, East Thirteenth Street, and East Second Street—including at first several other addresses of relatives in the neighborhood now often referred to by Puerto Ricans as "Loisaida" (a clever play on the words Lower East Side, but also on the name of a famous town in Puerto Rico, *Loíza* [formerly *Loíza Aldea*]). We enjoyed the most stability on East Thirteenth Street. From there we moved, around 1969, to the East Harlem Taft Houses, a public housing project on Madison Avenue between 112th and 116th Streets. Much of our instability had to do with my stepfather, whom my mother adored but did not marry. I visited him frequently after my mother and he finally broke up after many separations. We would go bicycle riding, and in my teenage innocence, I would try to convince him how he could improve his life.

I blossomed socially during our years at 545 East Thirteenth Street. In junior high school, I enjoyed myself. I was happy and did well in school. Before that, I had been shy, partially explained by language issues. My mother would say, "You are not Americans, you are Puerto Ricans, and you'll speak Spanish in this house." And, thus, speaking English in the house was practically forbidden. My brother and I were not to speak English in the house even between us, much less to Mom. But in elementary school, I remember being forbidden to speak Spanish, even in the play yard during recess. That was all very confusing, and I think that is partially why I was shy, and I didn't talk much in school until I got to junior high school.

We had a little blackboard that Mom bought when Carlos and I were learning to write English in school. She used the board to impart all she had learned during her limited years of schooling regarding the basic rules of writing in Spanish.

To me, being Puerto Rican mainly meant eating rice and beans. Yet I have those vivid memories of my mother's sense of "Puerto Rican-ness." Years later, when I learned about the crucial role the Nationalist Party played in saving the Puerto Rican national identity and Spanish as our vernacular, it dawned on me that my mother's concern with passing on the Spanish language probably came from the Nationalist influence during her early years. As if that was not enough, it turns out that the building housing the small restaurant my father had owned in Old San Juan on Calle Cruz also lodged Pedro Albizu Campos and the headquarters of the Nationalist Party on the top floors.

My mother would proudly tell us the Nationalists left the keys to the offices in the restaurant. And I would imagine that the Nationalist Party congregated in my father's restaurant. I remember her telling me how Albizu Campos himself had held my brother in his arms. During the 1970s, the same locale housed the famous café La Taona, a bohemian hangout where independence advocates Roy Brown, Antonio Cabán Vale (*El Topo*), Flora Santiago, and other outstanding Puerto Rican poets, songwriters, and singers often performed.

"Puerto-Rican-ness" and National Pride

In the tenth grade, I joined ASPIRA of New York, a Puerto Rican organization founded in 1961 by Dr. Antonia Pantoja to promote Puerto Rican pride, leadership, and our progress through higher education. At the time I joined, even though I appeared very Puerto Rican, with *pelo vivo* (lively hair), as the poet Mariposa would say, my knowledge of Puerto Rico was weak.

My knowledge of ASPIRA was also limited. All I knew was that it was an after-school club for Puerto Ricans in my school, Seward Park High School. At Seward Park, I was influenced by the Black Student Society. Mark, the leader of the society, was a mature, dynamic, and extremely active student. I remember overhearing a conversation of his with someone about the Black Panthers and some arrests that had taken place. I was in awe of his seriousness and dynamism. Those years coincided with President Lyndon B. Johnson's Real Great Society and the war on poverty, the Martin Luther King dream, the flower children's and hippies' counterculture, and the civil rights and black power movements.

Seward Park generated activity against the war in Vietnam, following the lead, I believe, of the National Peace Action Coalition (NPAC), the National Coalition for Peace and Justice (NCPJ), and the Student Nonviolent Coordinating Committee (SNCC). I recall demonstrations against the war by teachers and students in front of the school. They also supported decentralization and community control of the New York City school system.

Rosita Perea, an enthusiastic Puerto Rican teacher of Spanish, was adviser to the Juan Morel Campos ASPIRA Club at Seward Park. I think she was the one who got me involved. She was very supportive of the students in general and of me when I became president of the club. The club held discussions on Puerto Rican identity, something I had never been exposed to or even felt the need to participate in. I also remember the ASPIRA Manhattan Center, then located on Sixty-Sixth Street and Broadway. At the time, the Puerto Rican community in that area was being displaced due to the construction of Lincoln Center.

A Crash Course

The organization sponsored programs in leadership development and cultural awareness. From the moment I heard about a course on Puerto Rican history and culture, to be given on Saturday mornings, I jumped at the opportunity. I worried I would not get there in time to sign up. Before then, as with most Puerto Rican youth in New York, I knew little about my cultural origins or Puerto Rico's outstanding historical figures. I later learned that this lack of knowledge was true for most young people in Puerto Rico too. The course was offered by a young man, Roberto Ortiz, a draft resister in Puerto Rico and a fervent opponent of the Vietnam War who had a grave air about him. He dressed rather thinly for New York City's cold in September and October. He impressed me deeply, and I have often wondered what became of him over the years. I never ran into him again.

The classes opened an entire world for me, a whole new context that combined the personal, social, historical, and political. To learn about

Puerto Rico was to learn about myself. Our text was a brief pamphlet called "Puerto Rico: Island Paradise of U.S. Imperialism," written by someone named Patricia Bell. I never learned who Patricia Bell was, much less get the opportunity to meet her; little can she know the enormous influence that short pamphlet had on me. It was like a primer, the ABCs of the colonial status of Puerto Rico. I think Ortiz had purchased a stack of them, maybe at Casa Puerto Rico on East Fourteenth Street or Liberation Bookstore on West Twenty-Third. I remember after reading it, a classmate, Mildred Zeno, said emphatically, "I was so angry when I found out all those things." I stayed in touch with Mildred over the years because she was a cousin of a fellow PSP member and friend, Shelley Karliner.

The second thing that stands out in my mind from those days is attending a performance of the *Nuevo Teatro Pobre de América* (America's New Poor Theater) company. During one scene, a *piragüero* (a vender of *piraguas*, the Puerto Rican refreshment consisting of crushed ice covered in fruit syrup) screamed, "Get me a job, if you don't want me selling *piraguas* on the street!" He was yelling this as he was being harassed and arrested in the street by a policeman. That really hit home. Maybe that sparked my social consciousness. I think I related the scene to my stepfather's frequent joblessness. I remember his coming home one day after a day of fruitless job-hunting and lying down on the small couch in our overcrowded living room, his shoes on and his eyes staring at the ceiling, saying that he had found nothing.

After seeing the *Nuevo Teatro Pobre de América*, that night I went to Casa Puerto Rico, then located on the upper west side. There, I met Vanessa Pascual, now a retired University of Puerto Rico professor, another *independentista*. She was living in New York at the time, and I believe that she had just returned from Cuba, volunteering with the Venceremos Brigade. It was the first time I went to the now historic Casa Puerto Rico, later located at 106 E. Fourteenth St. in lower Manhattan. I did not know it at the time, but that was the main office of the Misión Central Vito Marcantonio of the MPI in New York. An activity was being held that night for the brigade. Sonia Marrero, a young reporter for *Claridad*, was present. Sonia was probably the first journalist to interview Lolita Lebrón, who had been jailed since 1954 for her participation in the Nationalist attack on the U.S. Congress. It was the first time in almost two decades that the public saw a picture of Lolita and received news about her—thanks to Sonia. (Sonia passed away from cancer before she was forty.)

The Young Lords

Then came the winter of 1969 in East Harlem, El Barrio, and my first direct political experience. The Young Lords Organization (YLO) had established its national headquarters on Madison Avenue between 110th and 111th Streets in East Harlem, down the block from where we lived in the Taft Houses. In retrospect, I say I did not go to the YLO—the YLO came to me. The now historic First Methodist Spanish Church was, and still is, located on 111th Street and Lexington Avenue. I would pass it on my way to the IRT train station while going to or returning from high school.

Members of the militant YLO, demanding the independence of Puerto Rico and better living conditions for Puerto Ricans in the United States, were determined to use the church's basement for a free breakfast program and day care center. The church declined, and the YLO organized constant community pressure in favor of its demands.

Carlos and I were swept up by this militant struggle and got involved in supporting the organization's demands. Finally, the YLO took over the church by force and set up the two programs as well as ongoing political and cultural activities. All the while, dozens of police officers, sometimes accompanied by special weapons and tactics (SWAT) teams, nervously stood watch outside. Inside, I joined many other volunteers, members of the YLO, and nonmembers, using our numbers to make a political statement. To keep the activities going, close to a hundred volunteers at a time worked throughout the church and in the kitchen. My mother was ill at the time and was hospitalized on and off. She worried about our involvement.

I remember poet Pedro Pietri, during the cultural activities, reciting the now classic "Puerto Rican Obituary," and the presentation of such documentaries as *The Battle of Algiers*, about Algeria's struggle for independence from France. Many of us slept inside, and many were out in the community getting food and other donations from merchants and residents of the area.

The YLO was political, militant, and *angry*! Its members demanded justice and respect for Puerto Ricans in the United States, and I totally identified with them, although I did have my doubts as to how soon their demands could be achieved. Press coverage was extensive, and it was amazing to me that something was happening in our community and getting attention from the outside world. Usually, the newspapers only reported crimes and other depressing news coming out of the ghetto.

I was totally engaged by the YLO's message on the colonial oppression of the Puerto Rican people by the United States and the abysmal living conditions Puerto Ricans faced in this country. The poor housing, discriminatory education, and lack of health and social support services were what I had seen all my life. The kaleidoscope of disadvantage in ghetto life now came into rudimentary focus. This was what I had gone through. This was my life—up close.

My social and cultural contexts were now being explained to me with a bang (!), as the poet Víctor Hernández Cruz might put it—something I had yet to comprehend, despite my involvement with ASPIRA. I was quickly, and at a very basic level, making all kinds of connections, and I was elated. It was uplifting to know the context of my reality, to know there was dignity in my community and my life experiences, and to know that our problems did not come from deficiencies of ours but mainly from Puerto Rico's colonial status and the deficiencies of the society we lived in.

All this activity was going on during my last year in high school. A tremendous transformation began for me and for many thousands of young Puerto Ricans who had grown up in New York City and other urban areas. We were gaining a sense of who we were and our place in the big picture of the Puerto Rican and U.S. reality, understanding that we were a part of broader social and historical processes. Directly or indirectly, the YLO's action triggered a loud burst of Puerto Rican identity, pride, and radically channeled anger, especially in the massive second generation of Puerto Ricans. These were the youths who, like me, had grown up in New York City and were coming of age at the time.

Throughout this period, I was a follower of the YLO. Then Carlos and I became involved in the Columbia University chapter of the equally militant Puerto Rican Student Union (PRSU), which was closely connected to the YLO. We became involved in many issues as other groups, such as the MPI, *El Comité*, and the Puerto Rican Independence Party (PIP), were growing in influence along with the YLO. This time of great movement activity lasted for several years, bringing militant politics to the struggles in the workplace, in unions, in health care, education, and housing—cultural, educational, and racial justice and other struggles. In our community, these times, especially until the mid-1970s, were hot, boiling over with energy and enthusiasm.

Mom's Was a Short Life

My mother died in early 1970. She was thirty-eight years young. Carlos and I had been taking care of her over several years during her battle with Hodgkin's disease. Her difficult childhood, her angst over our living situation, her oppression as an assembly-line worker in the New York City garment district, and the cold were probably all factors in the illness that killed her. Perea, my teacher at Seward Park and the sponsor of our ASPIRA Club, was a tremendous source of consolation. She said this loss was something one never gets over. Mom was one of those described in Pietri's "Puerto Rican Obituary": "Juan, Miguel, Milagros . . . all died today and will die again tomorrow." Carlos and I shipped her body to Puerto Rico. We had to identify her body at the airport before bringing her to her final resting place in Manatí. To this day, I miss Mom's wonderful cooking of *comida criolla*, (Puerto Rican food), and I *mean* "criolla."

The trip was important to me, as I was then eighteen years old and had an entirely new view of my homeland as compared to the last time I had been there, at age ten. In June, as soon as I finished my schoolwork, I immediately went back. I did not bother with my graduation ceremony and with the prom, which I thought were silly affairs anyway. That summer, I spent three months at my aunt Rosa's home near Caguas, the most time I had ever spent in Puerto Rico since migrating to New York.

Breaking into Higher Education

When I returned to New York, I entered Fordham University at the Lincoln Center Campus. Fordham was tough on me, and I was tough on Fordham. I just could not identify with the college. I could not fit in. I found it all so sterile when, in my way of thinking at the time, things in my neighborhood were so fertile and dynamic. The impact of the movement created confusion in me as to how I could best contribute to change. My mother had just died. I was on my own and almost paralyzed as to what to do with my life.

At Fordham, I took courses in the Puerto Rican Studies Department, which was set up and headed by Professor J. A. González-González, *El Profe*. I have met many selfless people in the movement for Puerto Rico's independence, but few with the dedication of this man. I could write chapters on this cultured, deeply honest, comical, ethical, and selfless Puerto Rican who, until his last breath, devoted his life to advancing the cause of Puerto Rico at the United Nations (UN). He was little understood by many of his students at Fordham. He did not seem to understand the evolution that Puerto Rican culture was going through as a result of migration and the Puerto Rican experience in the United States, the Nuyorican experience and culture. Much less was he understood by the university administration, who ultimately dismissed him. He was a mentor and a model to me as he helped me see the importance of work at the UN and international solidarity for Puerto Rico, a cause that I ultimately became involved in. I took practically all the courses in the Puerto Rican Studies Department and several in the African American Studies Department.

In Puerto Rico and other Latin American countries, *Profe* is an affectionate way of addressing and referring to a professor. That is how González-González came to be called by all his comrades. I feel proud that he was really my Profe in quite a number of courses I took at Fordham. Was he a father figure to me? I am not sure, but he was a mentor and important to me, even now as I frequently remember him while walking the halls of the UN. Even though I did not complete my bachelor's degree there, I left Fordham with a course major in Puerto Rican studies.

During my time at Fordham, something in the back of my mind kept me from formally joining the YLO. I could not adhere to the organization's absolute radicalism. I wished that its members had more depth in their political analysis and a more realistic strategy for achieving their goals, even though you could not deny the vast community support they enjoyed and the broad media coverage they generated. It also seemed to me that their talk of armed struggle projected more of a youthful energy than a viable plan. Although I could identify with their analysis of the problems affecting the Puerto Rican community, it was difficult to see them as agents for long-term social change. Yet ultimately, along with other organizations, they were, despite my misgivings.

It needs to be said that I believe that the work of the YLO and the PRSU laid the groundwork for Puerto Ricans born and raised in the United States to become involved in the MPI-PSP. Before that, almost all the people involved were Puerto Ricans who had grown up in Puerto Rico. Thus, the MPI and the PSP were different when comparing their impact on second-generation Puerto Ricans.

Choosing the *Movimiento Pro Independencia*

In 1971, I traveled to Cuba with the Fourth Venceremos Brigade, another intense experience that had a great impact on my political transformation. In Cuba, I came into contact with several people from the MPI with whom I conversed extensively, including Angelo Alicea, whom I have remained in touch with over the years. When I returned to New York, I remained close to the MPI and Casa Puerto Rico. I eventually joined the organization several months before it became the PSP. The MPI struck me as having a well-thought-out analysis on Puerto Rico's situation and a coherent strategy. I was also impressed with its weekly newspaper, *Claridad*, which has been published uninterruptedly in Puerto Rico since 1959. (I later came to be one of the directors of the bilingual edition of this paper, which was published in the United States by the U.S. Branch of the PSP.)

In my early involvement in the MPI, I was an activist in the Misión Bolívar Márquez, which at the time was established in East Harlem on 121st Street near the building that had belonged to the Third World Revelationists before they donated it to the MPI. Bolívar Márquez Telechea was a Nationalist who during the Ponce massacre wrote on a wall at the scene with his blood, "¡Arriba la república, abajo los asesinos!" (Long live the republic, down with the assassins!). I have often seen the very famous photograph of that scene. The office was run by Armengol Domenech. Another key leader was Marciano Santiago ("Marcianito" to everyone), who was a great example to all of us. About Marcianito, I could write pages and pages for his dedication,

Figure 10.1. Olga Iris Sanabria Dávila at MPI rally in El Barrio, New York City.

warmth, and understanding of us Nuyoricans and his capacity to grow with the new times and new organizations, despite being a 1940s Nationalist.

We did real grassroots work, distributing *Claridad* door to door and selling it on the streets. We sold books on topics related to the struggle in Puerto Rico and in the United States and Puerto Rican flags and symbols. We visited people in their homes to talk about MPI campaigns, and we set up political study groups. Along with other MPI missions in the city, we coordinated many activities. We carried out a campaign against the harassment of street vendors. A simple thing, like allowing people to carve out a subsistence living as mini-entrepreneurs as they sold *piraguas* and trinkets, was too much for the police. By then, we had relocated our office to 116th Street, which was teeming with street vendors who were receptive to our message conveyed in our community bulletin, ¡Agúzate! (Get wise!). We organized welfare mothers whose benefits were under attack, as usual. Although these efforts were not complete successes, they served to educate our community and let people know that we would stand up for their rights and support them.

In 1971 and 1972, by which time the MPI had become the PSP and the missions had become *núcleos*, we were heavily involved in the campaign to convince the UN Decolonization Committee to examine the colonial case of Puerto Rico. We set up tables with letters addressed to the ambassadors of the twenty-four member-countries of the UN Decolonization Committee. I remember many of the names seemed strange to me. As people walked by, we asked them to sign letters to be sent to these respective UN ambassadors. This approach gave us the opportunity to talk about the colonial issue as well as problems in the community. After my acquaintance with *El Profe*, this work also gave me an early taste of the international aspect of Puerto Rican independence.

My experience in the MPI, and later the PSP, was very rich in terms of learning and personal growth. The exceptional people with whom I had the opportunity to work and the chance to do many different tasks offered me such experiences as coordinating, organizing, articulating, and writing politically. My work at *Claridad* was particularly challenging, as I was holding a full-time job. Most of us held full-time jobs and went to evening meetings during the week. I would work at *Claridad* several nights, including one night until about 10:00 or 11:00 P.M. and way past midnight on the day we put the paper to bed. I remember so many remarkable things we accomplished, such as our national organizing and assemblies, the large events, our newspaper, and its national distribution to Puerto Rican communities throughout the United States. We created a stimulating environment of political debate and decision making; these fast-paced learning experiences built our resistance and resilience.

We carried out intense organizational efforts that bore fruit in the form of massive mobilizations, such as the October 27, 1974, event at Madison Square Garden, and massive grassroots campaigns. Along with other organizations, we were important in the founding of many enduring institutions of the Puerto Rican community in the United States that now play a role or have been a model for Latinos(as) in the United States in general. Something about the *Seccional* that was very important to this development was the quasi-autonomy it enjoyed in the United States.

Our movement generally reached its peak in the late 1970s and early 1980s, but we have been very active since, and most of us continue to work for independence and social change. The PSP in the United States, like other radical and independence organizations, went into decline by the mid-1980s.

In the case of the PSP in Puerto Rico, many factors led to its decline. Intelligence work and repression against it and the invasion of U.S. government subsidies—food stamps, student financial aid, housing assistance, and others—served to neutralize the PSP's social demands, besides errors committed. Further, the pace of the PSP's work was unsustainable. Cadres who had put their lives on hold were forced by life circumstances to focus on personal and professional needs as they realized that independence was *not* around the corner. Changes on the international front also affected the PSP, particularly developments in the socialist camp. These factors also affected the U.S. Branch. In addition to the quelling of the 1960s' effervescence and the broad shift to the right in the United States, problems in the organization in Puerto Rico, where much leadership came from, also affected the U.S. Branch.

But young people are constantly joining the struggle. Although membership in pro-independence organizations in Puerto Rico has been at an ebb for some time, base work of different sectors is very dynamic around such issues as the environment, culture, women's rights, civil rights, and sustainable development. In the United States, Puerto Ricans have continued to work for social justice and decolonization, and we are involved with international solidarity and the causes of other racial/ethnic sectors that are so similar to ours.

The International Front: With Nicaragua and in Cuba

In the early 1980s, while active in the PSP's U.S. Branch, I came to work in the Permanent Mission of Nicaragua to the UN. Its administrators were looking for an interpreter/translator. PSP leader Rafael Anglada López recommended me to Ambassador Javier Chamorro Mora, and I happily took the position. Ambassador Chamorro Mora was an amazing person, a leader of the Sandinista movement that took power in 1979 and expelled dictator Anastasio Somoza Debayle, who had ruled the country for decades. The ambassador and his mission staff had a busy pace of work, to the tune of probably seventy hours or more per week. I was glad to be a part of that team. Even with the long hours and complexity of assignments, on my "free" Sundays, I could not wait to go back to work on Monday.

To the extent that I was able to perform my tasks competently, it was thanks to all those years of learning how to go from one language to the other during meetings and in writing. Other sources of my skills: Mom, the Nationalist Party, and speaking Spanish in the PSP. As a reporter for *Claridad*, I had also written (in Spanish and English) about the case for Puerto Rico's independence at the UN. I was a journalist long before I eventually got my journalism degree (1998), an example of learning by doing.

I was the interpreter for President Daniel Ortega Saavedra during his historic 1985 trip to the UN and afterward as he traveled throughout the United States. At the time, travel in the United States by Nicaraguan officials was limited because of U.S. hostility to the Sandinistas and the covert and not so covert war of the "contras." The travel demands during President Ortega's trip were intense and constant; during his U.S. tour, the press described me as "the very tired interpreter." For a Puerto Rican independentista and socialist such as I, doing this work for a revolutionary government was an honor.

In 1986, the PSP asked me to assume the important role of being a delegate in Havana, working at the PSP Mission there. At this time, I was a member of the national Central Committee of the PSP and had been in the leadership of the U.S. Branch since 1973. I was told that my job working at the permanent Nicaragua Mission would be solid preparation for an official role as a representative of the PSP in international forums. I would be replacing veteran leader Doris Pizarro as the delegate to Cuba, since she was to take over the role of Deputy Secretary General of the PSP. The PSP's national leader, *compañero* Néstor Nazario, approached me about the idea, saying this work was extremely important. He did not need to press the point, as I was ready for the change. When I said yes right away, he could not believe that it had been so easy to persuade me. I lived in Cuba for three memorable years.

With Havana as my base, I participated in many international activities and initiatives. I traveled with delegations and sometimes by myself to conferences of governments, nongovernmental social movements, nongovernmental organizations, and Conferences of Heads of States of the Movement of Non-Aligned Countries and their foreign ministers. I worked with other PSP cadre who were equally committed and who encouraged and supported me. I was one of a stream of compañeros and compañeras who, over the years, had taken on temporary assignments in the international arena.

From the 1980s onward, this international work (with Nicaragua and in Cuba) took a young Boricua woman from New York City to places and situations she would never have imagined. Some of these situations were funny, some not so funny.

At one time, stressful to say the least, I had to fly to the West Coast to be available for translation duties. I was accompanying President Ortega's entourage, including his press secretary, a short man, comical and easygoing. Arriving at Los Angeles, we all had to deplane quickly, as per Secret Service instructions, and in the commotion, the press secretary and I became separated from the main group. We were stranded at the airport.

It was a while before we finally figured out where to go and rushed in a cab to where we had to be, a press conference where I was supposed to interpret. When we got there, the hosts and President Ortega were on a stage in front of about three hundred people, including the press. First Lady of Nicaragua, Rosario Murillo, was nervously poised at a microphone. She was a fluent English speaker, but translating was not why she was there. As I rushed to the stage, she spotted me and signaled, with a relieved look on her face. I stepped up, she stepped back, President Ortega began to speak, and I began to interpret. Close call!

Sometimes my status as a U.S. citizen working against U.S. colonialism could be confusing to those not well-informed about the case of Puerto Rico. I was later issued a credential that identified me as a "Delegate of the United States"—another mess to clear up and correct. At international meetings and events sponsored by countries hostile to the United States, people would naturally be concerned with the presence of U.S.-identified individuals. In one case, I traveled to a country (that was not exactly friendly to the United States) that was holding a conference. Upon my arrival, immigration officials asked me whether I was sure I was supposed to be at this event. Why would a U.S. citizen want to be there? I then explained the unusual situation of Puerto Rico, my work at international events, and why I carry a U.S. passport. "Puerto Rico is a colony of the United States, and we Puerto Ricans do not have our own passports," I assured the official.

During my stint as the PSP representative in Cuba, I occasionally traveled to Nicaragua. On one such trip, I decided to travel to Puerto Rico, and to get there, I had to stopover in another Central American country not friendly to Nicaragua. The local security officials singled me out as I stepped off the plane and escorted me to a small dingy office, where two sloppy-looking men received me. They had two-day beards, greasy hair and complexions, and intimidating gazes. One sat behind a desk; the other, who seemed to be an assistant, stood by while I was instructed to sit in front of the desk. The man behind the desk took my handbag and briefcase. He went through my handbag and removed my passport, handed it to his assistant, and ordered him to "call the consulate [obviously, the U.S. Consulate]—this is of interest." The assistant walked away with my passport. I knew that normally the job of the U.S. Consulate is to help travelers from home, but this situation was different—the United States frowned on citizens who visited Nicaragua. The official behind the desk proceeded to meticulously go through my wallet, whereupon he came across my Cuban driver's license. I explained that I was a journalist for *Claridad* and that "there are so many international events in Havana."

Next, he moved on to the tiny address book in my wallet. Of course, these people have a sort of code: if your address book has words like "coalition," "solidarity," "trade union," "workers," "international," and so forth, they suspect that you are an activist. Again, I explained that "so many events [occur] in Havana that I cover where I meet people from different groups." He proceeded to ask other questions. Was this an interview or an interrogation? What I was mostly worried about was being alone, without my passport, and no one even knowing where I was. Eventually, the questioning was over, my passport and belongings were returned, and I was allowed out into the terminal to resume my trip to Puerto Rico, where I wanted to attend the funeral of beloved *compañero* Pedro Baigés Chapel and report on some meetings I had while in Nicaragua. Out in the terminal, as I had used the money I had to leave Managua, I had to wait for my ticket for the leg of the trip to San Juan to be sent to the airline by telex. That was a tense wait. This and other similar ordeals were typical in situations involving travel between countries where official relations were either antagonistic or nonexistent. You learned how to keep up a front the whole time.

My international work later led me to Panama City in December 1989. I was attending an event organized by Panamanian political studies centers to update U.S. media about tensions in that country. Manuel Antonio Noriega Moreno, a former ally turned enemy of the United States, was president. It turned out that the people involved with the think tanks knew that an invasion was imminent and wanted to disseminate information to the international community about the situation. You could feel the tension at the event, as there was a sense that the United States was poised to send in its military. Ten days later, the invasion was launched. My departure had been several days prior. I still have letters that I received shortly afterward from two people who lived in the community of El Chacao, which was bombed during the invasion that killed at least four thousand people.

I recall serving as President Ortega's interpreter during a meeting with the president of Burkina Faso (formerly a French colony known as Upper

Volka), Thomas Sankara. He was often described by third-world revolutionaries as the "Che Guevara of Africa." Translation in this meeting was a three-stage process: Sankara spoke in French; his translator spoke to me in English; and I translated into Spanish for Ortega. It was not the only time this process happened. Sankara was killed a few years later, in 1987, in a situation that was similar to the assassination of Maurice Bishop in Grenada, supposedly due to struggles with his close collaborators. Later investigations have suggested that other African leaders who were close to U.S. interests were involved in his assassination.

I cannot neglect mentioning the struggle of the people of the Western Sahara. My trip there in 2001 touched me deeply, as people in the refugee camps faced among the harshest climate conditions in the world while awaiting a solution to Morocco's occupation there and compliance with international community mandates, especially those of the UN. I often think of the people there, the efforts of the Polisario movement, the desert horizon, and the night sky, a dome of a million stars.

These are a sampling of memories and anecdotes of the international experience. I have about two hundred anecdotes and memories for at least one book.

Living in Puerto Rico

After completing my "tour of duty" in Cuba in 1989, I returned to New York for a short while. Then I made the big decision to establish myself in Puerto Rico. I wanted to have that experience. Through most of the 1990s, I lived in my homeland, continuing work with the PSP and later extensions of that organization. I wrote for *Claridad* and stayed involved with international work. I lived in the countryside (*Humacao*) for a while, employed by a regional newspaper, *El Oriental*. There, I was constantly traveling through rural towns, covering politics and local controversies. It was a leap back, you might say, from the global to the local.

I gave talks in many towns and rural communities on the international issues I had experienced firsthand and that I had written about. I was also asked to speak quite a bit about the communities and struggles of Puerto Ricans in the United States. Then, as now, I liked living in Puerto Rico, not because I believe that you must live here to be Puerto Rican but simply because of the experience of living and being involved here. Along with other Puerto Ricans whose lives involve going back and forth between the island and the diaspora, I returned to New York for interim periods: once during 1995–1998 to complete the bachelor's degree at Empire State College that I had long postponed, and once during the 2000s as an adjunct lecturer in the City University of New York (CUNY), among other roles. I call them "interim periods" even though each lasted a considerable length of time. The idea of returning to Puerto Rico permanently was always present in my mind.

During my adult years in Puerto Rico, I took advantage of the opportunity to pursue legal study. I also had the opportunity to work closely with one of the most inspiring persons I have had the privilege to know. I first met Juan Mari Brás years before, after a talk he gave at an ASPIRA Center in New York. At the time, he was the Secretary General of the MPI, and I was so absorbed by his words that they became an important reason for my joining the organization. After my years of PSP activism, I pursued legal studies with him at the Eugenio María de Hostos Law School in Mayagüez and worked closely with him on several of his projects. He had a visionary perspective on the crucial importance of internationalizing the question of U.S. colonialism in Puerto Rico. In 1995, Perla Franco and I interviewed him for about twenty hours for a documentary on his life that was being produced by Freddie Rodríguez. I also worked as his assistant during my law studies. He was an extraordinary human being, leader, and jurist. The United States owes Puerto Ricans for targeting Mari Brás throughout a career of struggle for a people's liberation. (He passed away on September 10, 2010.)

Nicaragua's Challenge

The 1979 Sandinista Revolution was the international experience that most influenced me. The leaders were so young when they came to power and—lo and behold—had in their hands the management of a state that was a work in progress and under attack. The Sandinistas were voted out of power in 1989 and then returned as part of a coalition government in 2007, with Ortega once again serving as president. I worked for the Nicaragua Permanent Mission at the UN once again from 2007–2009.

The coalition government did not hold the same revolutionary positions of the original Sandinista government, but even a modified version of Sandinista policies was intolerable to some internal and external interests. At present (as I write from San Juan in December 2018), the ideals of justice, progress, and national sovereignty have been threatened. A country that a few years ago could take pride in relative social peace, a low crime rate, almost zero drug trafficking, growing tourism, and a generally growing economy had changed, it seems almost in a blink, to the opposite and is only now getting back to normal.

Given the adverse conditions under which the Sandinistas returned to power in 2007, it was a matter of time before imperialism determined to neutralize the present expression of the Sandinista revolution. The

Organization of American States (OAS) has played an active role in attempts to isolate Nicaragua diplomatically and is poised to play an even more active role should a "regime change" be successful, which is the objective of the United States and the still powerful reactionary forces in Nicaragua.

The path of the Sandinista process must not be dictated from the outside. The Nicaraguan people and government should be left to their own devices to resolve the present situation through a peaceful process.

Progress Does Not Follow a Linear Path

International work has allowed me to witness important historical moments. The transition from the Apartheid system in South Africa; the independence of Namibia and Timor-Leste; the inclusion of Palestine as an Observer Member State of the UN (I was present in the General Assembly Hall when this resolution was adopted, to a festive atmosphere)—these are emotional examples.

A more recent high point was the successful effort for the release of Puerto Rican political prisoner Oscar López Rivera. The international work complemented the many forms of support work for a humanitarian cause that became a rallying point of Puerto Ricans everywhere, including all ideological sectors.

But progress toward liberation, justice, and social transformation is not a straight road; *la derecha no duerme* (the Right doesn't sleep). We have seen this situation in Nicaragua and elsewhere among Latin American countries with center-left governments.

Now more than ever, we need to emphasize the need to apply international law to our process of decolonization. Thus far, we have ensured that the UN Decolonization Committee and the Movement of Non-Aligned Countries express their concern over the U.S.-appointed Fiscal Control Board that now controls Puerto Rico's public budget and finances and thus all Puerto Rican affairs, besides reaffirming the applicability of international law to our case. I continue this work from Puerto Rico, where I reside presently, through my activism with the Committee for Puerto Rico at the United Nations (COPRONU, by its Spanish acronym), which coordinates many aspects of the presentation of the colonial case of Puerto Rico.

To devote ourselves to bringing our country to freedom is totally worthy of an entire life—not, as someone once said to me, that this is *all* I have done with my life. It is what I have done with much of my life, and I am proud of that. It is a great honor to be engaged in a struggle for liberation. For me, the personal and the political are indivisible, and as Juan Antonio Corretjer, Puerto Rico's great national poet, once stated when asked whether he thought he would ever see Puerto Rico's freedom, "That for me the independence of Puerto Rico is a truth, it is real, and I have lived it because I am free."[1]

Vestiges of the PSP

To me, the greatest triumph of the PSP, along with other organizations, was to have given continuity to our struggle for independence and our struggles in Puerto Rico and the United States at an important historical moment. It is because of this kind of historical continuity that we have maintained our nationhood and the option of independence in the face of cultural, economic, environmental, and other forms of aggression since 1898. In the present moment, as U.S. colonial power in Puerto Rico intensifies, I have no doubt of the possibility of yet another upsurge of our movement in Puerto Rico and in the United States in a different form. I witnessed the now historic protests of the summer of 2019.

Perhaps the most important thing I can say about the impact of the PSP on me, and on many others who were members, is the sense of empowerment that we achieved. This feeling is different from gaining a greater Puerto Rican identity. The PSP operated on so many levels and encouraged so many facets of transformation. Collective work, individual responsibility, camaraderie, international solidarity, theoretical development—we were involved in all these things simultaneously over a long time. This work involved a lot of sacrifice; in many ways, we sacrificed everything during one stage of our lives, but we also gained in many ways.

We learned to emulate rather than to envy, resent, or gossip about those who stood out, as promoted in the overall capitalist media. We shared an uncontainable esprit de corps and assertiveness. Through our camaraderie, *compañerismo,* and our work and its results, we overcame a lot of the low esteem we bore as a result of our colonial oppression and exploitation and the racism and discrimination we face in the United States and in the ghetto. We learned the value of evaluation and criticism. Through international solidarity, we learned to love the peoples of other struggles and their movements. They became a part of us.

We understood new meanings of participation and democracy. None of what we did was perfect—no human endeavor can be—but we also learned how to deal collectively with a situation of vastly unequal power. We learned the value of sacrifice and that with responsible leadership, dedication, and focus, a group of people can achieve the unthinkable, which in our case has been to sustain a centuries-long movement for sovereignty and dignity. As I have said on occasion, *"El pueblo puertorriqueño ha sido tan guerrillero, tan luchador, tan solidario y tan soñador como cualquiera otro*" (The Puerto Rican people have been fighters like any other people, we have struggled, expressed solidarity, and dreamed like any other). And we, too, shall succeed in the process of decolonization, independence, and social transformation.

NOTE

1. From the inside title page of Juan Antonio Corretjer, *La patria radical* (The Radical Homeland), 5th ed. (Ciales, Puerto Rico: 2000).

Mi Camino

Digna Sánchez

Early Years

L ife is a winding road, bearing many twists and turns. As you go about traveling that road, you are often unaware of the significance of certain events. It is only years later that you begin to connect the dots and understand how one event was related to another.

I arrived in New York from Puerto Rico in late 1950, at the tail end of my third year of life. My father had come that spring, a migrant worker in the fields of Vineland, New Jersey, saving money to send for *Mami* (Idalíz Jiménez); my brother, Edwin; and me. I learned later, in 1985, when my daughter, Belisa, interviewed my father, Serafin Sánchez, for a fourth-grade project that he had to get a *carta de buena conducta* to get the job as a migrant farm laborer. This *carta* was a letter issued by the Puerto Rican police saying that he was a person of good repute. This letter was an instrument of the police and the powers that be in Puerto Rico to embed fear in the general populace and to repress the Nationalist Party. Such was the fear instilled by that period of colonial repression in Puerto Rico that my father kept the letter, as a sort of guaranty should he need it later.

Both sides of my family were from Barrio Esperanza de Arecibo; they were *jíbaros* (country folk) who worked the land. I was born in the city of Arecibo, where my parents settled after marrying and following my father's return from World War II (having been stationed in Hawaii). In 1950, we joined the flow of the Great Migration from Puerto Rico primarily to the northeastern United States. We first settled in Williamsburg, Brooklyn, and in late 1951 crossed the Williamsburg Bridge into the Lower East Side (LES) of Manhattan.

That bridge looms large in my memory, growing up in the LES. My family would gather to cross the bridge during the summer months as a form of free recreational activity. The Hassidic Jews, a growing community alongside Puerto Ricans, would cross from the Williamsburg side of the bridge during their holy days to attend the LES synagogues or to shop along Orchard Street. In the early 1950s, pushcarts still sold a variety of goods cheaply on Orchard Street.

My family first settled at 69 Norfolk St., one block south of Delancey Street on the corner of Broome Street. It was apartment number 1 at the top of the stairs in an old tenement built in 1879. We had one bedroom and shared the toilet facility in the hallway with three other families on the floor. Our bathtub was in our kitchen, and a porcelain slab covered it when the tub was not in use. That little apartment was the "reception center" for various family members who started to arrive from Puerto Rico in the early 1950s. I marvel today at how my mother managed to keep that space clean and looking nice. In 1958, we moved north of Delancey Street to 115 Norfolk St., where happily the toilet was inside the apartment—a definite step up. The fire escape became our balcony, and the roof was our summer retreat. Now I visit the Tenement Museum on Orchard Street to see once again what it was like when, from ages four to fourteen, I lived in an apartment with the bathtub in the kitchen.

We lived in what had been the Jewish neighborhood of the late nineteenth and early twentieth centuries in New York City. As Puerto Ricans moved in, many of the Jewish residents left, but I do remember being paid a nickel to turn lights and stoves on and off for my Jewish neighbors during their holy days. I was a *Shabbos goy*.

The LES was a very diverse neighborhood. During the 1950s, as Puerto Ricans moved in, the Jews moved to areas around Grand Street. As the Chinese moved in, the Italians moved out, and what was once Little Italy would become an expanded Chinatown.

However, the neighborhood's diversity did not reflect peaceful transitions. Ethnic tensions marked New York City throughout the 1950s and 1960s. The youth gangs represented the many ethnic and racial groups living in the LES. Word would spread throughout the neighborhood if a rumble were to take place in Forsyth Park or under the Williamsburg Bridge or the Manhattan Bridge. Forewarned meant "stay away." Some of the gang members were known neighborhood and school friends, so my parents made it clear that we were not to be involved with them.

Mami was a stay-at-home mother during my elementary and junior high school years, and my father was a strict disciplinarian. Papi worked for several years at the La Rosa spaghetti factory, so, as you can imagine, we ate loads of spaghetti. Later, he worked in the hotel industry, as did many Puerto Ricans. He retired as a Local 6 member (Hotel Trades Union) after thirty-eight years at the Essex House. To make extra money, which was always needed, he held part-time jobs in the evenings, cleaning offices. My mother took in piecework at home, which I helped with. I remember one of the projects involved attaching feathers to small magnets for children's toys. The house was always filled with feathers, despite the constant cleaning.

In 1961, the Sánchez family moved out of the tenements and into the Lillian Wald Projects on Houston Street and the FDR Drive. Again, the ethnic transition pattern repeated itself; as we moved in, several Irish neighbors moved out. We were so happy and excited that our nice two-bedroom apartment had a separate bathroom with a bathtub; no longer would we have a bathroom in the kitchen. Nevertheless, with only two bedrooms, my brother was relegated to the living room, while I was given the smaller bedroom.

Education—Learning and Doing

My father's strictness was mainly projected onto me and not my brother. The traditional role for males and females was the order of the day for my *jíbaro* family. Because I was not allowed to go out with friends, I channeled my energies into school, becoming a bookworm and an honor student. I was class representative and part of the school patrol. I made my parents proud when, along with my good friend John Clarke, I received the Mayor's Scholastic Achievement award from Mayor Robert Wagner at city hall in May 1961.

As a reward for my good grades and my junior high school graduation, my parents treated me to a two-month trip to Puerto Rico. This trip was my first time back since we had arrived in New York, and sending me was a big expense for the family, so I was honored and grateful for the opportunity.

That trip was momentous for me. The year 1961 was also the year of *West Side Story*, and at fourteen, I was very aware of the discrimination that existed in the United States. The verse of a song from *West Side Story*, "'Cause every Puerto Rican's / A lousy chicken!" was often heard in the hallways of my junior high school.

What a reaffirming experience to arrive in Puerto Rico, where even the bus drivers were Puerto Rican. As the daughter of a beloved son and daughter of El Barrio Esperanza, I was given a huge welcoming party, where they roasted a pig and music filled the air. Family members told me stories about my father the prankster and acknowledged my mother's beauty. I was raised to speak Spanish, so this ability facilitated the communication and bonding with my cousins, aunts, and uncles. The next time I visited Puerto Rico was in July 1964, when I graduated from Seward Park High School.

The 1960s were a volatile time of struggle for civil and human rights, led initially by African Americans and others who were less visible. Like many, I was outraged at the racism, discrimination, and violence inflicted upon black people. Always the activist, I was involved in school government and the Catholic youth movement. When the 1963 Alabama church bombings killed four young black girls, I went to the priest who supervised the youth group and asked that something be said about this during Mass. When told that the Catholic Church is about love not "politics," I decided to leave the Church. This decision caused a major uproar in the family, but with time, they accepted it.

The most important thing that happened to me during high school years was my introduction to ASPIRA. My father read about the organization in an article published in *El Diario* and said we should visit it. We met with Antonia Pantoja, the executive director and founder of ASPIRA, who told him that the program was free but then described how I would "pay" by organizing an ASPIRA Club at my high school. She explained that ASPIRA would work with me to make it happen. I accepted the challenge and began my journey with ASPIRA.

As an Aspirante, I had the opportunity in 1964 to go on its first leadership trip to Puerto Rico. The trip included a panel presentation by representatives of each of the island's political parties. The independence speaker particularly impressed me, as I already identified as an *independentista*, in part because of a Puerto Rican history course given by ASPIRA the previous year. Politically, I had been parting ways with my family, who were all *Populares* (supporters of the Popular Democratic Party).

While at Seward Park, I developed a love of languages, so I had taken courses in Russian and Chinese and dreamed of a career as an interpreter at the United Nations (UN). But the ASPIRA trip heavily influenced my views on Puerto Rico and the plight of Puerto Ricans in New York, causing me to shift my education plans.

In September 1964, I enrolled at the City University of New York's (CUNY's) Hunter College, where I majored in sociology. During my college years, I participated in a community-based organization called the Real Great Society (RGS), comprising former gang members. Upon release from prison, several of them had founded the RGS to "fight poverty instead of each other." Chino Garcia, a previous head of the Dragons gang, was a charismatic and innovative leader.

During the summer of 1966, I attended the Encampment for Citizenship in Puerto Rico, sponsored by the Ethical Culture Society of the United States. More than sixty young people ages nineteen to twenty-five from North and South America, the Caribbean, and Europe attended. We lived in the Henry Barracks in Cayey, today the site of the University of Puerto Rico Cayey Campus. When differences between the director of the program and the participants came to a head, the youth took over the encampment and had the director removed.

I learned two important lessons from these experiences: one was the need for creativity and flexibility in community-based organizing, and the second was the role and power of exercising citizenship rights to depose those who work against the best interests of the people.

Into the Seventies

Our family life was upended while I was studying at Hunter College. My brother became addicted to drugs, and my parents blamed each other. Edwin was a loving, humble, and respectful young man and always held a job. He struggled to quit "cold turkey" on his own. I would go to see him during these attempts, and when he relapsed, I went into the drug dens to get him out. After several stints in the Bernstein detoxification unit at Beth Israel Hospital, he finally got clean in 1969. By then, he had a two-year-old son and a baby daughter who were his key motivators. In late July 1970, he decided to relocate to Florida, where he had a job contact. Once settled, he would send for his family. Before leaving, he asked me to always look after my nephew and niece, whom he named after me. His dream was cut short; Edwin died on August 1, 1970, in a car accident as he traveled to Florida.

My brother's death marked a pivotal point in my life, as I began to question the reality that surrounded us. Key among them was the level of injustice that Puerto Ricans were subjected to. By then, I understood that the colonial reality of Puerto Rico was the root cause of the discrimination and exploitation of Puerto Ricans, combined with the inherent racism of the United States. I decided that I needed to become more actively involved in the struggles of the Puerto Rican people.

In October 1970, three months after my brother died, I joined the *Movimiento Pro Independencia* (MPI). Dixie Bayó and Rafín Baerga convinced me to join. I had been a sympathizer since 1968; bought its newspaper, *Claridad*; and attended Friday night events at Casa Puerto Rico on East Fourteenth Street.

My choice to join the MPI instead of the Young Lords Organization (YLO) was questioned by some. I remember a conversation with Gloria Cruz, a LES YLO activist and someone I had known since junior high, during which she questioned the validity of MPI, which she considered a "foreign organization of Puerto Ricans from the island." My response was that the people of Puerto Rico are one, no matter where we live or grow up; after all, it is because of the colonial situation that we were forced to come to New York. I believed strongly that the movement to end colonialism in Puerto Rico required an intergenerational membership. Building a nation means having all ages and sectors united, and, in my view, that goal was best manifested in the MPI and not the YLO.

By 1970, the MPI was intensely engaged in discussions about the need to transform the movement for independence within the context of class struggle. Study groups were formed to discuss Marxist theory and its applicability to Puerto Rico and to Puerto Ricans in the United States. The discussions were animated, and I loved that they included younger twenty-somethings such as I along with the middle-aged folks who never went to college or even high school. Over the course of several years, we covered such works as Karl Marx's *The Communist Manifesto*, Vladimir Lenin's *What Is to Be Done?*, Georges Politzer's *Principios Fundamentales de Filosofía*, David McLellan's *Karl Marx: His Life and Thought*, and James Blaut's "Are Puerto Ricans a National Minority?" These writings and many others formed the basis of intense discussions around Marxist theory.

In the spring of 1971, Ramón Arbona, the MPI leader and a journalist and writer, approached me to join the team he was setting up to develop a bilingual edition wraparound to *Claridad* from Puerto Rico. I was excited at the prospect but told Arbona that I had never worked on a newspaper. He allayed my concerns, telling me that he would conduct workshops to prepare for the launch of *Claridad bilingüe*. Arbona became the Director of *Claridad bilingüe*, and I was named the Deputy Director (*Sub-Directora*).

By late December 1971, we had begun to discuss when we would launch the supplement. Sonia Marrero, our key reporter, and I suggested launching for International Women's Day on March 8, 1972. We thought that if we could get an interview with Lolita Lebrón—imprisoned in Alderson, West Virginia—it would be a tremendous push for the freedom campaign for the Nationalist prisoners. Arbona agreed, and we were on a fever pitch to get ready to launch in March. I remember the night that we closed the first edition of *Claridad bilingüe*. We eagerly awaited Sonia's return from West Virginia with her photo of Lolita. We worked very late into the night, and when the paper hit the streets, it was an instant success. Even *El Diario La Prensa*, the largest Spanish-language newspaper in the Northeast, had to acknowledge our scoop.

Figure 11.1. Lolita Lebrón and Sonia Marrero, *¡Viva Puerto Rico Libre!*

La Seccional

Three thousand attended the April 8, 1973, congress at the Manhattan Center in New York City. The excitement was palpable, and so was our collective pride at having brought together Puerto Ricans from as far away as Illinois, Massachusetts, Connecticut, Pennsylvania, and California. The political thesis *Desde las Entrañas* (From the Belly of the Beast) was approved, Arbona was elected First Secretary, and I along with five other *compañeros* were elected to serve in the Political Commission. A *Comité Seccional* was elected, comprising thirty members. I was appointed Secretary for Press and Propaganda and continued as the Deputy Director of *Claridad bilingüe*.

From the very moment that the MPI transitioned to the PSP, we began a series of discussions about the independence struggle and the role of the diaspora. We zeroed in on the "Curtain of Silence" hiding the colonial conditions of Puerto Rico from the U.S. progressive forces that would be our allies. To break through that silence, we elaborated a plan that had been launched in 1972 with the formation of the Puerto Rican Solidarity Committee (PRSC). Alfredo López, a member of the Political Commission, was assigned to be the National Coordinator, and Rosa Borenstein, a North American ally, became the Director of the New York PRSC. Chapters of the

PRSC organized throughout the United States and in some Latin American and European countries. The decision was made to hold an event at the world-famous Madison Square Garden in New York City on October 27, 1974, the closest date to the 1950 *Jayuya* uprising of the Nationalist Party in Puerto Rico.

Puerto Rican art master Lorenzo Homar designed the poster for the event, which was also used as the cover of the program. A crew of PSP members worked prior to the event to place twenty thousand programs on the back of each seat in Madison Square Garden. When Homar saw the programs with his inspired creation on the seats, he was emotionally moved. His rendering of the flags of Puerto Rico and the Lares flag superimposed on the words of the creation story of the Kiche people of Guatemala told in the Popul Vuh language tied us to our indigenous Taino roots.

We wanted members of the American Indian Movement to open the event in a traditional ceremony, with the drums and voices representing the original peoples of North America. This decision highlighted our recognition and support for the native peoples of the United States and for the American Indian Movement. It was an incredibly stirring opening that still moves me when I recall that day. The native peoples of the Americas welcomed us to the lands that had been stolen from them with a vibrant showing of their culture and their solidarity.

The day before the Garden event marked an action of the Fuerzas Armada de Liberación Nacional (FALN). Their action heightened tensions, causing the Garden's management to attempt to renege on our contract and deny us access to the facility. However, they were unsuccessful, and twenty thousand people filled the Garden, decorated with the pictures of the five Nationalist prisoners hanging from the rafters.

As 1974 ended, so did my first marriage. I remarried in 1975, to José Alberto Álvarez, the First Secretary of the Seccional at the time.

With *El Acto Nacional* completed, we were already working on the second major piece of our plan to tear down the "Curtain of Silence." Alfredo became the National Coordinator of the July 4th Coalition (J4C), established to organize a massive demonstration on July 4, 1976, the country's Bicentennial. The J4C, in conjunction with the PRSC, Arthur Kinoy's Mass Party, and the U.S. Branch of the PSP, called for a massive march to be held in Philadelphia. We had already projected this slogan at El Acto Nacional in 1974. Once again, we undertook a gigantic mobilizing effort across the United States. On July 4, more than sixty-five thousand people marched through the streets of Philadelphia, San Francisco, Los Angeles, and other cities.

Throughout the 1970s, the Seccional always understood the importance of working with movements representing other so-called minorities.

It was a demonstration of mutual support for each other's issues, a two-way solidarity. This work made it possible for us to spearhead such important mass campaigns as the Day of Solidarity with Puerto Rico and the Bicentennial march.

The success of the massive gathering for the Bicentennial was not something we could dwell on for long. We were immediately thrust into playing our part in the 1976 elections of Puerto Rico, in which the PSP had decided to run candidates. The U.S. Branch undertook the task of raising one hundred thousand dollars as our contribution to the electoral campaign. We did everything from selling raffle tickets to hosting fundraisers, and after much effort, we reached our goal. Many *compañeros* and *compañeras* from the U.S. Branch went to Puerto Rico to assist with the elections; all this activity took place in a year when we were also mobilizing for the July 4 counterdemonstration.

The Woman's Role

Throughout the history of the organization, the issue of women's equality was present, sometimes in prominent ways and sometimes below the surface. The buildup to the First Congress of the U.S. Branch (1973) included discussions on various subjects. One topic was a controversial proposal for the creation of a Women's Commission. Folks weighed in on both sides, and Juan Mari Brás, who was present, spoke up when it appeared that this debate was causing a potential schism in the group. He said this issue could be taken up subsequently after the PSP Congress. Sonia Marrero, other women, and I challenged this position. We swayed most participants, including some women who had initially supported the "let's wait" stance.

Once established, a year or two later, the Women's Commission had an active program of raising awareness of women's roles in the party and the movement at large. We undertook political education discussions that reaffirmed feminist principles in support of reproductive rights and challenged the patriarchal underpinnings of our culture. We pointed out how machismo permeated our language and our values, which not only men but also many women promoted.

In the years to come, the commission got involved in such work as volunteering with the Committee to End Sterilization Abuse (CESA), speaking at International Women's Day events, and participating in feminist forums. In 1975, I attended the Socialist Feminist Conference in Yellow Springs, Ohio, with Helen Rodríguez-Trías, at which the Third World Women's Alliance (TWWA) perspective clashed with that of (predominantly) white radical feminists. I saw a difference in two perspectives put forth: TWWA women placing feminist theory in the context of our oppression, and white radical feminists posing women's issues as the central and often primary focus of struggle. We also sent out compañeras as part of Voices of the Third World, a business project that was sponsored by the PSP and administered by Denis Berger, a long-time PSP member.

Rodríguez-Trías was a mentor to many women in the PSP and beyond. She was a warrior on behalf of all women, but especially women of color. The greatest lesson I learned from her was to listen to women regarding their needs in reproductive health. I was in my twenties and outraged that 35 percent of Puerto Rican women of childbearing age had been sterilized, many under the misconception that the procedure was reversible. I wanted the procedure to be outlawed. Helen said, "Digna, we can't do that! What needs to happen is to inform the women about what it is, and then they can decide. It's their choice."

Harassment and Repression

Anyone involved in the independence movement understood they were a target for personal harassment and repression. Not that long after I had increased my involvement in the MPI and the PSP, an anonymous letter was sent to my then-husband, who was not a PSP member, saying that I was having an affair with someone in the organization. This tried and true method of harassment by government agents was the first of many to be visited upon me.

The Federal Bureau of Investigation (FBI) harassed me and my family throughout my PSP activism. They visited the apartment where I lived with my second husband, José Alberto, then the First Secretary of the U.S. Branch, and our daughter, Belisa. They spoke to the co-op administrators and told them we were terrorists. Soon after my daughter was born, they would call me or knock on our door and say they were investigating me. At the time, we got legal support from the Center for Constitutional Rights. Through a Freedom of Information Act (FOIA) request, I received my FBI file in 1978.

In 1981, the FBI went to my workplace at the Puerto Rican Legal Defense and Education Fund (PRLDEF) and met with Cesar Perales, the President and General Counsel. They told him that I was suspected of having ties to Assata Shakur, a black activist living in Cuba after escaping from U.S. incarceration on trumped-up charges. It was no coincidence that they visited the office during a week I was in Cuba, attending a conference on minorities in the United States. Perales told the FBI agents that he was satisfied with my work at the fund, had no problem with my activism, and defended my right to be in Cuba.

In 1983, coinciding with my being elected as First Secretary of the PSP, I received threats from Cuban right-wing terrorist groups. At the time, I was also on the board of MADRE, a U.S.-based woman's organization working in solidarity with women in Central America. Once I received a postcard produced by MADRE to highlight the delivery of an ambulance equipped for maternity delivery for the people of El Salvador. The card showed my face circled with a bull's-eye graphic and the word *pronto*.

For decades, the Puerto Rico police had illegally monitored individuals active in the independence movement. In 1988, *las carpetas* (police surveillance files) were made accessible to those who had been *carpetiado* via court order. Although I had not lived in Puerto Rico since 1950, I had a carpeta. In 1992, I requested and received a copy of my carpeta, filed as number 7990 by the Negociado Investigaciones Criminales—División Inteligencia (Intelligence Division of the Criminal Investigations Department). The file included clippings from *Claridad bilingüe* covering the U.S. Branch congress held in 1973 in which I was mentioned and copies of some of the *Desde Las Entrañas* opinion articles that I had written. It also included lists of the meetings of the PSP Central Committee that I attended during the 1970s and 1980s. This cloud of repression remained with my compañeras and compañeros and me, but it did not deter us from continuing to struggle for the independence of Puerto Rico.

As common as these incidents were, few independentistas of the modern era had to suffer the tragedy visited upon the Secretary General of the PSP. On March 24, 1976, Santiago Mari Pesquera (Chagui), the eldest son (age twenty-three) of Mari Brás, was kidnapped and assassinated. At the time, Mari Brás was in New York on a fundraising tour for the elections in Puerto Rico. I was designated along with Rafael Anglada to accompany him and his wife, Paquita, to Puerto Rico. The reception at the airport was intense, and the days that followed are etched in my memory. I was a new mother, I had experienced the death of my brother when he was twenty-two years old, and I had lived through the pain this loss had caused my parents. I was overwhelmed with compassion for Juan and Paquita and felt angry at the political injustice and repression that this act signified. To pay the price of one's life for an ideal is a choice you make, but to have your child singled out is barbaric. Such was the climate of repression at that time.

The murder of Chagui occurred a few months before the march on Philadelphia. Nevertheless, it did not affect the turnout or Mari Brás's determination to persist. He was the closing speaker at the Philadelphia mobilization. Over the next months, he continued the electoral campaign as a socialist candidate, the first in the postwar period, for the governorship of Puerto Rico.

Struggles for Democratic and Civil Rights
and the Struggle for National Liberation

While organizing for the Madison Square Garden event and the Bicentennial, our local chapters were also involved in many struggles for the democratic and civil rights of Puerto Ricans across the Northeast and the Midwest. We were very much a part of this highly politicized era and influenced by the African American civil rights movement. We understood that in the United States, we needed to struggle against the discrimination and abuse that our communities of color were subjected to.

In New York City, we were instrumental in the fight to save Hostos Community College in the Bronx as a bilingual institution. Some of the leaders of that movement were also PSP members. We participated in the *Por Los Niños* struggle on the Lower East Side. We were part of a New York City coalition that sought to establish the Center for Puerto Rican Studies at Hunter College, a goal we achieved.

In other cities, PSP chapters played an important role in local struggles. Key among these was the establishment of low-income housing in Boston's Villa Victoria. In Chicago, we worked to establish the Ruiz Belvis Cultural Center; in Philadelphia, we were part of the group that established Taller Puertorriqueño. All these institutions continue to thrive today.

We were essential to the development of the People's Contingent in the annual Puerto Rican Day Parade (*el Desfile*) in New York City. In 1981, when Gilberto Gerena Valentín, then a city councilman, spearheaded the development of a Committee to Rescue the Parade from the hands of Ramón S. Vélez, a local powerbroker, I was recruited to join Gerena Valentín's alternate *Desfile* board.

The capacity to link these local struggles with the struggle for Puerto Rican independence was always a conflict-ridden one. This strain would build over time, especially as the struggle for independence came to the point of major fragmentation.

In the first U.S. Branch congress, we issued our political thesis, *Desde Las Entrañas*, and established the dual nature of our work in the United States: we were to struggle for national liberation and fight for justice and our rights in the United States. But throughout the 1970s, the tension between focusing on the independence of or class struggle in Puerto Rico and the fight for the democratic rights of Puerto Ricans in the United States was constant in the U.S. Branch.

Thinking back, we were so busy with our local work in addition to working for the independence of Puerto Rico that the divisions developing on the primacy of the class struggle versus the national struggle—or, in the case of the U.S. Branch, the struggles for democratic and civil rights versus that of independence for Puerto Rico—took me somewhat by surprise. I was especially surprised by the intensity of the party's debate in Puerto Rico. This tension then erupted into a crisis following the 1976 elections in Puerto Rico that led to what a decade later would cause the last major crisis of the PSP. We had really thought that independence was around the corner, and when that did not happen, many people felt disillusioned and abandoned the organized movement for independence.

We were young and inexperienced, and as a result, we made mistakes. The mistakes, which I greatly regret, are those that unjustly denied the rights of fellow PSP members, which included some cruel measures. The practices of criticism and self-criticism were sometimes carried to an extreme that negatively affected decent, hard-working members. As a leader of the organization, I should have been more aware of the damage being done by myself and other leaders. That I did not exercise the needed awareness and that I did not seek to stop this damage are things that I truly regret and am sorry about.

Throughout the 1970s and 1980s, I held several leadership positions in the national PSP and the U.S. Branch, and in 1983, I was elected First Secretary of the U.S. Branch. The Ronald Reagan presidency was a time of a badly weakened PSP in Puerto Rico and the United States, yet there was much to do. During the 1980s, we focused on mutual solidarity with Central Americans involved in revolutionary struggles in Nicaragua and El Salvador. We continued our promotion and financial support of the struggle for Puerto Rico's national liberation. And for the first time, we delved into electoral politics by supporting individual progressive candidates while making it clear that ours was not a blanket support for the Democratic Party. As such we supported Jesse Jackson in the Democratic presidential primaries; Harold Washington, who became the first black mayor of Chicago; and Mel King when he ran for mayor of Boston. Faced with growing family responsibilities and an inability to balance a full-time job with the demands of party work, I resigned from the PSP in 1988. My resignation, however, was not a reflection of a change in my core beliefs of the absolute need to carry on the struggle for national liberation while also struggling for social and human rights.

Mi Retorno a Puerto Rico

The twenty-first century started out as a difficult one for my family and me. On a personal front, I battled cancer, which was diagnosed on my fifty-fourth birthday, in 2001. In addition, my father went blind and subsequently was diagnosed with Alzheimer's in 2003. The years of my father's battle with Alzheimer's were very painful for our family. My mother became the key caregiver. For the longest time, she refused to have a home attendant for my father; old entrenched values are not easily changed. My father passed away in 2005. Five years later, I lost my mother, and the sense of being left alone was immense. Nonetheless, I am blessed with my daughter, Belisa; so many wonderful cousins; my one surviving aunt; and a group of friends who support and inspire me.

In December 2013, I returned to Puerto Rico after sixty-three years as part of the diaspora in New York City. I was nervous about the transition and sad that I had not been able to have my mother with me as we had planned. The fact that my daughter had chosen to live in Puerto Rico, staying after completing her studies at the University of Puerto Rico in Rio Piedras, added a joyful element to my return.

Another change in more recent years was my return to the Catholic Church. As a young teenager, I was greatly disillusioned by my priest's attitude regarding what to do about the Alabama church bombings in 1963. It took many years and the influence of liberation theology for me to participate, albeit sporadically, in church services. There are still many things I do not agree with, but I find that progressives within the Church and the influence of Pope Francis serve as beacons of hope and camaraderie. The greatest connection I have to the Church is that I believe that it links me to my childhood and family.

Upon my return to Puerto Rico, I connected with others who had come back, and in 2014, we organized a group called the DiaspoRicans/DiaspoRiqueños. We see ourselves as a link between efforts in Puerto Rico for progressive change and the support that the diaspora can lend to these efforts. The island is now experiencing a new level of crisis: the economic crisis of a huge debt, much of it "odious" and illegal, and the imposition of a fiscal control board by the U.S. government. We are seeing efforts of a major "garage sale" of Puerto Rico itself, which the control board and the pro-statehood government of Puerto Rico intend to carry out, thereby robbing the people of Puerto Rico of our assets, our land, and our very existence as a people.

This phenomenon is not totally new. Over the decades, the colonial reality of Puerto Rico has been the root cause of these imposed economic models, which led to the Great Migration of Puerto Ricans following World War II. Now, once again, we are witnessing the migration of hundreds of thousands due to the worsening economic situation, especially since Hurricanes Irma and María in September 2017.

Before the catastrophic passage of Irma and María, I had never been in Puerto Rico in the middle of a hurricane. It was very scary, as the sound of the winds during María made you feel as though you were inside a jet propulsion engine. To observe the wreckage to structures and a landscape with leafless trees was heart wrenching. Of course, the lives lost directly or indirectly to the storms were painful. Amid this devastation, my daughter's father, my former husband and comrade of the PSP Seccional, José Alberto Álvarez Febles, suffered a stroke and eventually passed away.

In 2014, I joined the Movimiento Independentista Nacional Hostosiano (MINH), and a year later I was elected to the national leadership group. Although I was new to the MINH, I was known to many given my years in the PSP and the Seccional. I firmly believed that if I were to uphold my political principles, I needed to work within a collective to maximize my efforts. The MINH to a great extent has inherited much from the PSP experience. Its political program *"Otro Puerto Rico es Posible"* (Another Puerto Rico Is Possible) resonates with me.

The tension between Puerto Ricans from the diaspora and those from Puerto Rico is one that I was aware of upon my return. It should not surprise us because it is a very difficult reality to confront. Those who stay in Puerto Rico often believe that those who left in effect abandoned Puerto Rico and everything Puerto Rican, while those who are part of the diaspora believe that they are not valued for the sacrifices they have made because Puerto Rico could not provide for them and they had to leave. Further, people on the island lack understanding and acknowledgment of the daily struggle in the diaspora to maintain Puerto Rican identity and culture.

Yet today there is a growing consciousness of the contributions made by Boricuas in the diaspora to Puerto Rican culture, sports, and the arts and to the sacrifices made in the battles for the decolonization of Puerto Rico.

While the identity tension is still a dynamic, people on the island have shown greater understanding and recognition of the positive role of the diaspora. This truth has been greatly manifested in the response of the diaspora to the devastation caused by Hurricanes Irma and María. This immediate and massive response influenced the consciousness of the people of Puerto Rico. Over and over, everyone now refers to the Puerto Ricans in the diaspora as "brothers and sisters." We are truly one people, *"la gran familia Boricua."* Of course, we have also witnessed the massive numbers of people leaving Puerto Rico due to the hurricanes, adding to those who had left with the worsening economic situation over the past decade. Today, more Puerto Ricans live in the diaspora than in Puerto Rico itself. This situation will determine our very existence as a people, in Puerto Rico and in the United States. Our national land base is being undermined, and we must stop the depopulation of Puerto Ricans and their replacement by others so as not to become another Hawaii. The political implications of this issue are numerous and will continue to be explored.

Despite the tension between the national struggle for independence and the struggles for human and civil rights, I firmly believe that we must wage our struggle on these dual tracks. My experience has been that our reality demanded it in 1970, when I first joined the MPI, and it still does today, whether in the diaspora or in Puerto Rico.

I firmly believe that for progressive Puerto Ricans in the United States, the dual nature of the struggle remains and will continue until Puerto Rico is a sovereign nation. The struggle for national liberation cannot be set aside while the struggle for democratic rights is waged—we must do both! The balance of how much effort is given to one versus the other will, of course, depend on the conditions that exist at a given time.

A political commentary about *Desde las Entañas* that I wrote for *Claridad bilingüe* (October 6–12, 1978) is still true today: "The 'myth of the return' is too often not realized because the promises have not been kept. We must, however, struggle so that those who can and would return will have a country to return to."

What the Puerto Rican Socialist Party Nurtured in Me

Zoilo Torres

A Young Boricua Goes West

In the fall of 1974, Jerry Mendez and I were leaving New York on a cross-country trip, heading for Los Angeles, California. It was about two months after Richard Nixon had resigned the U.S. presidency and six months after Patty Hearst, the daughter of millionaire newspaper publisher Randolph Hearst, had been photographed robbing a bank with a .30-caliber carbine in her hands. Previously she was thought to have been kidnapped for ransom. Now she claimed to have joined her abductors, the Los Angeles–based Symbionese Liberation Army.

These are things you do not forget, and they were scandalous moments accompanying an unforgettable time in my teenage years. Also unforgettable was the fact that just as Mendez and I crossed the New York–New Jersey state line, we heard a one-minute radio broadcast about a gathering of thousands of people at Madison Square Garden in what was billed as a National Day of Solidarity with Puerto Rico. The three-thousand-mile cross-country trip and the radio broadcast inaugurated a new period of my life.

Political activism was not alien to me when I decided to venture to Los Angeles. In the mid-1960s, my parents, fearing the drugs and violence prevalent in the Gowanus neighborhood of Brooklyn, New York, decided to move our family of seven kids (an eighth sibling had gotten married by this time) to the suburban town of Bellport, Long Island. More than a year of tormenting boredom had passed before I began to gravitate toward a local community gathering spot called the Bellport Community Center.

The Bellport Community Center was funded by the Office of Economic Opportunity, an anti-poverty program of President Lyndon B. Johnson's Great Society. After some months of hanging around the center, I was offered a part-time job as a youth organizer. I was fifteen and about to enter my sophomore year at Bellport High School. At the community center, I met a black woman, Elaine Frazier, who had been hired as a summer intern from the State University at Old Westbury. She was also a black power activist. That summer, we formed what amounted to a small study group of five youths recruited from the center's Summer Youth Employment Program. We spent long hours studying and discussing what was then a waning civil rights movement. We also studied black history, the Student Nonviolent Coordinating Committee (SNCC), the Black Panther Party (BPP), and the Young Lords Organization (YLO). By the fall, we had organized a black and Puerto Rican student union at the high school.

Bellport, about sixty-five miles east of New York City, was like many suburban communities of the day. It was divided into two sections—North and South Bellport, separated by the proverbial railroad track, in this case the Long Island Rail Road. In South Bellport, the residents lived in a segregated white neighborhood of middle- and upper-middle-class households with a sprinkling of very rich families. In North Bellport lay a predominately black neighborhood with a subdivision of newly arrived Puerto Ricans.

This North Bellport neighborhood had supplanted a working-class white community frightened into flight by a real estate industry that warned of incoming black and brown people who were bound to lower property values. The local real estate industry bought cheap, performed low-cost renovations, and resold to people of color at artificially high prices. Because of the physical, economic, and racial divides, the residents of North and South Bellport rarely interacted, except for when the children were in school. One school district served all black, white, and Latino students, and it was there where all the perennial social and economic inequities were exposed for all to see.

Whites predominated numerically and culturally. They ruled the hallways and the classrooms. They dominated the teaching and nonteaching staff, the cafeteria choices, and the academic curriculum. It would not have been difficult for a politically astute activist to articulate a class- and race-based narrative with which even some liberal-minded whites would have agreed. But we were too young and inexperienced to have that kind of insight. From the very evident circumstances, we were able to lift a list of demands for more black and Puerto Rican teachers, a history course relevant to people of color, and more ethnic diversity among guidance counselors. The administration's response was the issuance of a harsh student disciplinary code, which provoked a student strike and a police/student confrontation that closed the school for a couple of weeks. The crisis was recorded in the *New York Times* and *Newsday*, among other publications.[1]

What started as a unified student movement broke down into sporadic, racially polarizing fistfights all over the school. We were too naïve to comprehend what was happening. Nevertheless, these developments pressured the Bellport School Board into mandating that the new principal hire black and Puerto Rican/Latino personnel and implement a black and Puerto Rican history course. The board also fired the sitting school superintendent and hired a private security company that stationed scores of security guards in the halls of the high school building. This repressive measure impeded student mobility and school organizing, which over time quashed student activism.

All this activity played out in the span of over a year. By my junior year, my parents could no longer afford to live in the suburbs. They decided to take another chance at living in Gowanus and moved the family back to our old residence. There, I received a high school diploma from John Jay High School, eventually followed, many years later, by a hurried college degree in political science.

The student struggle at Bellport High School had a huge emotional effect on me, and it also induced a compelling desire to learn more about a reality that roared for social justice. After teaching black and Puerto Rican history as a para-professional teacher at an alternative high school for two years, I decided to travel cross-country. For Mendez, my fellow traveler, the trip was an opportunity to have fun in the excitement of a new happening. For me, it was a chance to see firsthand the continent I had learned so much about and wanted to learn so much more.

For the next six days, we navigated through the states of New Jersey, Pennsylvania, Ohio, Indiana, Illinois, Missouri, Kansas, Colorado, Utah, Arizona, the southern tip of Nevada, and onto Los Angeles, California. The trip was an awesome sight of scenic landscapes. We saw expansive farm fields, barren deserts, and pitch-dark nights illuminated by the headlights of our car. And the dangerous meanderings of two-lane highways seemed endless.

Boricuas Organizing in the City of Angels

On our arrival in Los Angeles, we joined friends I had known in New York City who also had decided to start a new life on the West Coast. After a couple of months of living in a rented apartment in Long Beach, California, Mendez decided to fly back to New York. I moved in with my New York friends, who owned a small house in Bell Gardens, a fifteen-minute car ride from downtown Los Angeles.

With a driver's license and a job with Model Cities in East Los Angeles, the search was on for a social life. Before long, our small group connected with some Puerto Rican graduate students at the University of California, Los Angeles (UCLA). They were all Spanish-dominant and young social scientists. Placido, an older Puerto Rican worker who had migrated from New York City in 1957, also in search of a new life, joined us.[2] Felípe, a Dominican brother who had fled political persecution in the Dominican Republic (Trujillo) and later in Chile (Pinochet), rounded out our group, which included live-in partners, spouses, and local acquaintances. The graduate students had related to the Puerto Rican Socialist Party (PSP) when they were students at the University of Puerto Rico. In social gatherings, we intermingled with members of the Centro de Acción Social Autonoma: Hermandad General de Trabajadores, or CASA: Brotherhood of Workers. This neo-socialist Mexican and Mexican American organization was very helpful in publicizing the Puerto Rican independence movement in Los Angeles.

Our group of nine Puerto Ricans and one Dominican agreed to petition the national PSP headquarters in Puerto Rico for official recognition as a local chapter. National headquarters forwarded our request to the U.S. Branch in New York City, and after a brief exchange of information, the Los Angeles chapter of the PSP was founded. Our first undertaking was to set up weekly study group meetings. For me, the study group opened a world of investigation and intellectual inquiry.

We studied Marxist theory of social change and applied it to Puerto Rican history and current events. Felipe, a former medical student who had scientific training, led discussions on dialectical and historical materialism that were fascinating. The writings of Karl Marx, Friedrich Engels, and Antonio Gramsci influenced me tremendously. Serious political education provided me with a world view through which I could filter the flood of historical and contemporary events. The PSP study group was perhaps the most revelatory experience I had on the way to becoming a lifelong political organizer. Without the tools to grasp and understand the world, the alternative was to surrender to a state of ideological confusion and eventually drop out from any kind of social involvement or activism. I realized this alternative had been the case for so many friends and family, all good people, who had lived and survived as politically oblivious victims of capitalist oppression. I arrived at the realization, as Marx said, that the real aim of life was not merely to understand the world but to change it.

There we were in Los Angeles, more than five hundred miles away from the closest Puerto Rican community, which at that time was in San Francisco's Mission District. Our research found that in 1975, the Puerto Rican population in Los Angeles was about eighty thousand. But because of the sprawl of Los Angeles County, no definable Puerto Rican community could be found. We were aware that without a realistic organizing strategy, the LA PSP chapter would perish, stillborn. We did not exclude anyone from joining, as long as socialism and an independent Puerto Rico were their political priorities. But our organizing targets were Puerto Rican workers.

We decided that our outreach approach would be to conduct activities that lured Puerto Ricans to the organization rather than to look for Puerto Rican households among the sprawl. We conducted public activities that emphasized Puerto Rican culture, attracting Boricuas who were likely isolated and spread out. Soon, we contacted folks who frequented MacArthur Park on weekends to play congas and meet other Puerto Ricans. We made media contacts through the only salsa radio station in Los Angeles and the plentiful Spanish-language newspapers. But the numbers we encountered were still insufficient to build a thriving PSP chapter of working-class families. Then we found friends who could connect us to Mexican American neighborhoods, where we might find embedded Puerto Rican households. Those friends turned out to be members of CASA.

CASA

CASA was an organization of Mexicans born in the United States and Mexico who, prior to the formation of the PSP chapter, had independently established bilateral relations with the PSP in Puerto Rico. CASA was launched as an organization of laborers who became radicalized around issues of immigration and Mexican nationalism. Its theory was similar to the PSP's stance on the so-called National Question, as elaborated in the 1973 PSP political thesis, *Desde Las Entrañas.*

Similar to the PSP, CASA's perspective was that national liberation is the main contribution a colonized people can make to the cause of worldwide working-class socialism. CASA was unequivocal in its assertion that the expropriation of land north of the contemporary Mexican border was an act of U.S. colonial aggression akin to the U.S. invasion and colonial domination of Puerto Rico in 1898. CASA believed that the U.S.–Mexican border was an artificial barrier to what would otherwise be a natural migratory flow between Mexico and North America.

CASA was very helpful in building the LA PSP chapter. It provided channels for contact and communication with the Mexican community, which informed the chapter of where Puerto Rican families were known to live. We held well-advertised fundraisers where new Puerto Rican faces would appear alongside CASA members, who also attended our events to assist with financing the chapter. PSP chapter members joined CASA's rank and file in many protest demonstrations where members and affiliates would unfurl the Puerto Rican flag that accompanied a PSP banner and thus project a Puerto Rican presence in the Los Angeles area.

One important event the chapter participated in was the memorialization of the 1970 killing of Mexican American journalist Ruben Salazar by a Los Angeles sheriff's deputy. The deputy had fired a tear-gas projectile into a restaurant where Salazar was calling in a report to the *Los Angeles Times* about the massive Chicano moratorium demonstration against the Vietnam War. More than two hundred LA police had attacked the moratorium's rally, sparking a major riot in East Los Angeles.

The PSP chapter marched with thousands of Mexicans and Mexican Americans along the route of the moratorium to the same rallying point, now renamed Ruben Salazar Park. This event was significant not only for the massive publicity the chapter received on the evening news but because CASA had also invited Florencio Merced, a member of the PSP's Central Committee, to be a keynote speaker.

Mentoring from San Juan and New York

Merced's visit occasioned a learning opportunity for the chapter in the practice of party building and the professionalization of political organizing. Merced met with the chapter and assured us that we would begin to receive regular bundles of *Claridad*, the party's national newspaper, which in the United States included an English-language supplement. *Claridad* was to be our main news source covering the Puerto Rican revolutionary struggle in Puerto Rico and in the United States. It was to be the primary instructor of the party's internal and external policies and a medium for engaging and recruiting new members.

Merced brought copies of the party's bylaws, which, to our surprise, required a monthly sliding-scale payment of dues. He also suggested, because of our "reversed outreach" organizing strategy, which he endorsed, that we rent a low-cost public center of operation as soon as financially possible. The center would serve as a meeting space for internal gatherings, public forums, and one of the most effective organizing tools—public cultural activities, including salsa-dancing parties.

He impressed on us that party building required strategic planning and an annual work plan to be reviewed every three months. He said that the plan should contain annual goals and objectives, a budget, and a timeline of specific activities with specific assignments for every member. He suggested an agenda structure for all internal meetings that included constructive-criticism sessions and group political education. He advised that we should research the county's institutions of power and their political leaders, including the local media. This information would be useful when mobilizing public opinion and support for political actions in Puerto Rico and the United States.

Merced's advice was instrumental in our building organizational capacity and constructing the LA PSP chapter. His visit was followed by check-ins from other leaders of the PSP, included Alfredo López, the coordinator of the Puerto Rico Solidarity Committee; José Alberto Álvarez Febles, the First Secretary of the U.S. Branch; José La Luz, the U.S. Branch Secretary of Organization; and Denis Berger, the head of U.S. Branch finances. Two of the top U.S. Branch women leaders who helped mentor the chapter included Digna Sánchez and Carmen V. Rivera. National leaders besides Merced included Juan Irizarry, the president of the Association of Agricultural Workers; Jenaro Rentas, the Secretary of Organization of the PSP; and Juan Mari Brás, the Secretary General of the PSP. The chapter even hosted major cultural events and presentations by Roy Brown and Andrés Jiménez, two well-known Puerto Rican protest singers and songwriters, and Teatro Cuatro, a New York–based theater group.

The chapter took Merced's advice to heart. CASA members and leadership were impressed with our heightened commitment and organizing style. We opened a storefront on Whittier Boulevard in East Los Angeles. Reading the pages of *Claridad* helped us understand the function and importance of what today is called "branding." We labeled our space a Puerto Rican cultural center by incorporating the name the U.S. Branch had assigned to one of its offices in New York City: Casa Puerto Rico.

Having set up operations in the mid-1970s, the chapter could not ignore that it was organizing in the context of a social economic crisis. Ten years after the Watts riots against police abuse in the African American community, Los Angeles's communities of color were central objects of numerous police killings. Police could be seen regularly wielding drawn guns while conducting traffic stops of cars filled with black and brown faces. Having myself been a target more than once of such traffic stops, I understood the intimidation practices of law enforcement. These practices would become the cause of massive civic rebellions after I returned to New York City.

Combined with the perilous police-community relations and the fall of Saigon capping the worst military defeat in U.S. history was the mid-1970s economic recession. The recession was characterized by economic stagnation and high inflation, which pundits and economists dubbed "stagflation." Puerto Ricans migrating from other parts of the country, including the Northeast, and Puerto Rico represented a new round of economic refugees. The chapter found itself needing an organizing project that merged the demand for social and economic justice for Puerto Ricans in the United States with the broader, longer-term objective of Puerto Rico independence. We found that project in the party's campaign for a "Bicentennial Without Colonies."

Bicentennial Without Colonies: Before and After

We were excited when the leadership of the U.S. Branch proposed a campaign for two major demonstrations: one in Philadelphia and one in Los Angeles, to be held on July 4, 1976. San Francisco and Seattle were subsequently added as West Cost demonstration sites at the request of area organizations that wanted to mount their own regional events.

For us, the campaign captured the contradiction of the U.S. government's celebrating the country's day of independence while possessing Puerto Rico as its colony in the Caribbean. We framed our message by defining colonization as an act of violent domination and human exploitation, with the goal of achieving control over people and land. We explained that an imperial power that held others captive cannot possibly guarantee its own people social-economic justice and true democracy. So, we framed "Bicentennial Without Colonies" as a domestic goal that sought to take down barriers to democracy and justice and replace them with genuine channels for political participation and representation. "Bicentennial Without Colonies" further meant placing all U.S. inhabitants in a position conducive to achieving a more equitable distribution of the social wealth generated by the population's physical and intellectual labor. Rejecting the economic and moral values of colonialism would lend itself to the demand for more jobs, higher educational opportunities, better and more housing, quality health care, and equal justice under the law. So "Bicentennial Without Colonies" was not only relevant to people under direct colonial domination but germane to the rights of all people living within the borders of the colonizing power.

But the organizing project was not without controversy. Some members of the chapter were reluctant to align the island's liberatory goal with the perceived-as-secondary demands for economic and democratic rights in the United States. The demand for Puerto Rico's independence, they said, must be the overarching goal that should be adopted by all the participating organizations.

Some of us argued that the main objective of our organizing project was to present the rationale for our demand for national liberation to broader sectors of the North American public. We also wanted our organizing efforts to build and strengthen our LA PSP chapter. Attaining these objectives was the responsibility of PSP members and affiliates in Los Angeles, not the responsibility of other organizations in a future coalition for a Bicentennial Without Colonies. A majority maintained that we should invite potential coalition members to adopt the same approach to their own organizations and issues. We did not want to dominate or be dominated. Fortunately, the proponents of limiting the political spectrum of the July 4 marches to

Puerto Rico's independence were in the minority and were overruled. However, the controversy did not wither away—it persisted during and after the July 4 activities.

We learned with this internal debate that members had differences in organizing priorities. Some wanted to focus solely on the independence of Puerto Rico as the dominant demand. Others wanted to have a more flexible approach, understanding that while organizing in support for Puerto Rico independence, at times our reality in the United States would make it necessary for us to address the immediate needs of the Puerto Rican working-class community in the diaspora. I shared this point of view. We later discovered that a similar debate was raging in the entire U.S. Branch of the PSP.

We eventually talked with the leaders of CASA, who in turn consulted with the leaders of the U.S. Branch. CASA agreed to convene the Los Angeles Coalition for a Bicentennial Without Colonies (the coalition). Some fifty representatives of local and statewide left and left-leaning organizations met at the Haymarket, a center of left-wing activism that also housed the People's College of Law in Downtown Los Angeles.

The first coalition meeting went well until a representative of the Los Angeles Committee against Police Abuse demanded that the issue of police violence be designated the coalition's primary issue. He became very loud and belligerent toward Antonio Rodríguez, CASA's general secretary, who was chairing the meeting. The individual became so disruptive that the group voted to remove him from the premises. This individual did not return to subsequent coalition meetings. It was later rumored that he was seen in a police uniform, patrolling in South Central Los Angeles.

From the fall of 1975 onward, the coalition dedicated itself to mobilizing for the July 4 demonstration. The organizing process demanded that PSP members hone their resources and learn new skills. As the LA PSP chapter, we had to construct messages to pitch to specific members of the Latino media, with whom we had to cultivate relationships. Developing concepts in the graphic arts was necessary for the design and production of bilingual flyers, posters, pin-ups, T-shirts, and brochures. Many items, such as press releases and talking points, required that we sharpen our writing skills. Among our targets were African American and Latino students, which took us into the college and university circuit, where we scheduled numerous speaking engagements. All of this work meant developing fundraising techniques.

We could not do any of these activities in a vacuum. The LA PSP chapter was part of a coalition that had to structure the human and material resources of its multiethnic/multiracial components into one democratic organizing operation. The coalition formed a representative Steering

Committee, which in turn oversaw the formation of a Publication and Media Committee, an Outreach Committee, and a Fundraising Committee. The constituents of member organizations with the appropriate skills were channeled into the respective committees. As the day of the demonstration approached, brigades of coalition volunteers were dispatched into various neighborhoods and Downtown Los Angeles to engage the public and saturate the areas with publicity.

One of the many lessons learned during this period was taught by right-wing Cubans and the religious right we faced on the streets from time to time. That lesson was and still is that left-wing political organizing in certain parts of this country can be downright dangerous. On the positive side, the process rendered profound lessons in organizing and capacity building. Years later, many of us would revisit these skills in our professional lives.

The Bicentennial Without Colonies event was a political success. In Philadelphia, it mobilized upwards of fifty thousand people. In Los Angeles, six thousand made their presence felt. In San Francisco, five thousand attended, and in Seattle, where I was assigned to speak, another four thousand participated. Some members of the LA chapter, however, believed that the Bicentennial Without Colonies event was not such a success. Their opinion in summary was that the extended expenditure of human energy and financial resources weakened rather than strengthened the chapter. They maintained that the stress and tensions had frayed internal relationships. A contradiction emerged within the chapter that may have had its origins in the members' varying class inclinations. Those most critical of the chapter's Bicentennial campaign were the graduate students who aspired to careers among the sociopolitical elite back on the island. For them, their stay in Los Angeles was a passing affair, and the chapter a brief pastime.

On the other hand were those of us who were struggling to keep jobs and survive in relative comfort. For us, the chapter was an empowering union designed to achieve a sort of social equity and fair play, whose members would come to each other's aid when needed.

The conflict was one of diverging interests that eroded the chapter's unity, leading to its eventual breakup. Be that as it may, for many of us, the establishment of the LA PSP chapter was a seminal experience. It taught us the importance of developing clear messages, using *Claridad* as our main source of information on Puerto Rico. We were speaking to a Puerto Rican population who was in constant migration to and from the island and U.S. states.

From 1974 to 1978, the chapter kept organizing and educating, talking about the economic situation on the island and how conditions there and in other Puerto Rican communities in the United States fed a continuous migration to places like California. Some of these encounters forced us into discussions that could be illuminating but also quite challenging. We had to explain in plain language the facts and consequences of a forced economic dependency on the people of Puerto Rico and the role played by U.S. corporations and federal legislation restricting all merchant marine transport to U.S. vessels. It was not easy for our listeners to hear or for us to describe that Puerto Rico imported what it did not produce and exported what it did not consume. Even the commonwealth government's attempt, as reported in *Claridad*, to invest in a limited fleet of merchant ships (*Las Navieras de Puerto Rico*) failed miserably because it could not compete with the better-equipped and more potent U.S. private merchant marines.

We had to buffer the party from the reverberations of the bombing of Fraunces Tavern in 1975, for which the *independentista* group Fuerzas Armadas de Liberación Nacional (FALN) took responsibility. The action killed four innocent people and injured many more, and the PSP's national leadership condemned it. In Los Angeles, political opponents and supporters put us on the defensive for a tense period of time. Well-informed college students opposed to the FALN bombings confronted me on a number of occasions. There were also condemnations of the bombing by some Puerto Rican professionals who had family in New York City and Chicago. That Downtown Los Angeles experienced a well-publicized bombing of an office building, attributed to an unknown group, during that same period did not help the situation.

We were seriously concerned when statehooder Carlos Romero Barceló was elected governor of Puerto Rico in 1976. The success of the New Progressive Party, the pro-statehood party, ignited a grueling debate in the PSP's leadership in Puerto Rico and in the U.S. Branch, each with a somewhat different emphasis. The LA chapter could only decipher what was going on from a distance. It appeared that some members questioned the party's electoral participation from the beginning. They believed that we did not have a social base sufficient to take on such an ambitious endeavor. Rather effectively broadening and strengthening the party, the campaign narrowed and drained the organization.

In the U.S. Branch, from what we in Los Angeles could tell, the debate was about the need to set our local organizational priorities as opposed to following the priorities set by national headquarters in Puerto Rico. Some believed that the national organization relied on the U.S. Branch primarily for fundraising and providing organizers for campaigns in Puerto Rico. More than a few members of the LA chapter believed that formulating our own distinctive organizational policies was beyond our authority. By 1977, the LA chapter's members had gotten the sense that a volatile debate was afoot at all levels of the PSP.

In early 1977, I was asked to represent the LA chapter at a U.S. Branch assembly to evaluate the work of the previous year. It was a nail-biting three-day assembly. Many controversial issues were raised, a number of them stemming from the aftermath of the Bicentennial Without Colonies event and the 1976 islandwide elections. None of the issues was resolved by the assembly's closure. I returned to California, knowing that I had to report on an internal organizational crisis. Our LA chapter, itself weighed down by internal and political differences, was unable to survive the conflicts that affected the overall organization. In the fall of 1977, I decided to travel straight through eleven states in a used Fiat on my way back to New York City.

Back in New York: The Puerto Rican Socialist Party, Vieques Support, and the National Congress for Puerto Rican Rights

I ended up in Brooklyn, in a Sunset Park apartment. By now, the PSP's internal debates ranged deep, long, and wide. They went beyond erroneous organizing strategies and misplaced priorities; they now plunged into ideological questions about the class character of the PSP and its leadership in the United States and in Puerto Rico and into issues of gender and sexual orientation as well.

In New York City, while debates raged in local chapters in the Bronx, Brooklyn, Manhattan, and at branch-level headquarters on the Lower East Side, members locally continued to do the political work of engaging community residents, selling *Claridad* on major commercial strips, fundraising, conducting home visits, and attending neighborhood forums about issues of civil and democratic rights. But in the confines of community-based PSP chapters, the content of the conversations very much mirrored that of the higher-level leadership—at least, this was the case with respect to the local chapter in Sunset Park to which I was assigned.

Members acknowledged that as a Puerto Rican socialist organization, we may have been the largest in the United States, but nonetheless, we were still a very young and small group. I was asking myself what some may consider very elementary political questions amid an intense internal party debate.

Many issues were on the table; many of them in the final analysis remained unresolved. Some spoke to the question of whether we were a party that really reflected the Puerto Rican working class. Were we a party of the Puerto Rican petit bourgeoisie? Could we really be "One Nation, One Party" with 40 percent of our population living and working for generations outside the island? In this context, what should be our political and organizational priorities? Should we focus on coalition building? To what degree were we all under the thought and cultural control of the U.S. ruling class? The issue of sexual preference was also raised, revealingly provoking the exit of many active gay members. These issues and questions evoked many more. They accounted for many punishing hours of meetings that engendered complicated discourse and sometimes convoluted arguments. Over time, the daylong deliberations began to exhaust the leadership and rank-and-file members. I observed that diverse political stances found supporters who congealed into groupings that were followed by frustration, despair, and numerous resignations.

During this time, the Vieques question, a long-running controversy since World War II, arose again. Carlos Zenón, the president of the Vieques Fishermen's Association, approached New York City council member Gilberto Gerena Valentín for help. I was assigned to represent the PSP on the newly formed New York Committee in Support of Vieques chaired by the councilman.

Politically, the PSP did battle against making the issue the sole property of the independentista movement. We, along with other Left, faith-based, civic, and labor organizations, maintained that what was taking place on Vieques was a human rights violation that the entire Puerto Rican society should denounce. Some of our independentista friends were not very happy with us. It was clear to us, however, that we could educate people that the Vieques issue was tied to colonialism. So, we held our ground and conducted weekly meetings at which a variety of representatives from the island would come to speak.

The committee sponsored scores of pickets and educational forums; marched in the National Puerto Rican Day Parade; and partook in numerous demonstrations against U.S. intervention in Central America; in support of cuts in the nation's military budget, demanding the transference of these funds to human needs; and in support of ending the nuclear arms race. We maintained that all these issues were linked to U.S. militarism on Vieques in violation of the human rights of the Puerto Rican people.

The main activities started in New York City, but the Vieques support movement soon became national in scope, organizing chapters in Washington, D.C., Philadelphia, Boston, Chicago, and elsewhere. PSP leader Carmen V. Rivera represented the party in a corresponding National Steering Committee. A major mobilization to Washington, D.C., brought more than four thousand supporters to Lafayette Park in front of the White House on May 1, 1980. The entire PSP organization took a hiatus from lingering party debates to ensure the success of this historic event, the first national demonstration in the United States in support of the people of Vieques.

As the country crossed into the Ronald Reagan era, the PSP remained locked in a draining debate that precipitated the departure of more leading members. From my standpoint, many issues in the PSP on the island as well as in the United States continued unresolved. The socialist cause for Puerto Rico's independence became quiescent, while the socioeconomic concerns of the Puerto Rican people in the United States became ever more pressing.

April 1981 saw a new development in Puerto Rican activism: the founding convention of the National Congress for Puerto Rican Rights (NCPRR), a national group created to address these pressing socioeconomic concerns. Attending the convention were representatives of an array of Puerto Rican–led community, student, faith-based, and labor organizations. Many of the original NCPRR leaders were former members of the YLP. The NCPRR also included current and former members of the PSP and El Comité–MINP (Movimiento de Izquierda Nacional Puertorriqueño), along with anticolonial activists, including nonaffiliated folks who were activists in the Vieques Support Network. The NCPRR was ostensibly a politically center-left coalition with a civil rights orientation and officially nonpartisan.

Beside approving the name, the convention also approved bylaws and a leadership structure requiring regional representation on a national board, which was to select an Executive Committee. It mandated that at least 50 percent of its national board be female, a novel requirement for a Puerto Rican coalition at the time. It also approved a multi-issue political platform and elected its first national president, Juan González, a former leader of the YLP turned journalist.

Arising from the many impassioned PSP debates was a cogent dedication to democratic rights struggles in the United States. Not having the wherewithal to launch a PSP-led Puerto Rican–based democratic rights movement, joining the NCPRR became a focal point for engaging the U.S. Puerto Rican community. But in doing so, the PSP did not want to give the appearance it was setting aside its principled and historical demand for Puerto Rican independence. Cognizant of what a mistake it would be to impose this potentially divisive debate on such a young and politically liberal-centrist NCPRR, the PSP leadership opted to submit a resolution in support of a process for the decolonization of Puerto Rico rather than a straightforward demand for independence. Support for the decolonization process took the form of proposing the endorsement of the so-called Dellums Resolution. House Joint Resolution 215, also known as the Puerto Rico Transfer of Power Resolution, was submitted to the U.S. Congress by Congressman Ronald Dellums of Oakland, California.

Lobbying the NCPRR for support of the Dellums Resolution was a confidence-building effort and an educational endeavor. A good number of the members—even some independentistas—were leery of the PSP. In certain quarters, the PSP had gained the reputation of packing meetings and steamrolling agendas. Moreover, many had not heard of the Transfer of Power resolution, much less imagined what it might contain. The majority of NCPRR members knew, however, that the status question had divided the Puerto Rican people for generations. So, they came around to the notion that the Dellums Resolution could be a unifying alternative by speaking to a decolonizing process rather than a particular political status outcome. This bill aroused the curiosity of many NCPRR members. Explaining the relatively complex Dellums Resolution (which had been drafted with substantial input from the PSP's General Secretary Juan Mari Brás and the prominent constitutional lawyer and PSP ally Arthur Kinoy) was at every turn a challenge for me, who at best had some low-level paralegal training. Unfortunately, not enough pressure could be put on other members of Congress to move it forward, and the bill died in committee. On the positive side, the resolution did leave a decolonization structure that could be revisited and revived in later years.

Thus HJ Res. 215 allowed NCPRR members to address the right of the people of Puerto Rico to self-determination in the context of supporting a sovereign transitional process of decolonization without necessitating an immediate debate on political status options. The process of solving the problem became as important as the solution itself. This approach was strategic to the unity of this democratic civil rights coalition. It was comparable to the human rights approach to ending U.S. Naval activities on Vieques versus immediately demanding Puerto Rico's independence. The struggle for the removal of the U.S. Navy—ultimately attained in 2003—became strategic to the understanding of the colonial underpinnings of its presence in Puerto Rico and thus the nonexistence of Puerto Rican national sovereignty.

The NCPRR eventually incorporated support for the Dellums Resolution into its platform, which provided independentistas, especially current and former members of the PSP, the political space to work, if they preferred, on resolving the political status of Puerto Rico within the NCPRR structure or to focus on the civil/democratic rights of the Puerto Rican community in the United States.

It was upsetting to observe that the more the NCPRR grew as a coalition, the more the PSP shrank as a political party. The interminable debates in the PSP went from cordial oratories to acrimonious verbal altercations. In Puerto Rico, some members accused the leadership of bourgeoisie elitism, intellectual dishonesty, and, in one open forum I attended, overt political thuggery. The debates in the United States, which mainly occurred in New York City, were not as caustic but biting, nevertheless. At one meeting of the U.S. Branch, visiting party leader Carlos Gallisá, reporting on the debates in

Puerto Rico, said that some members had criticized the island-based leadership of using party resources to feed an organization that operated like an inverted pyramid, having a large paid staff and bureaucracy that engaged a minute portion of Puerto Rican society.

It even seemed to me that the debates in the U.S. Branch were questioning whether Puerto Ricans here and on the island were truly "One Nation." Was this proposition being perceived as dubious? We PSP members were essentially not only reexamining ourselves for past errors but also trying to figure out where we wanted to go as an organization. The whole affair became an immobilizing ordeal that lapsed into organizational atrophy. I inevitably turned to concentrating my organizing efforts on the NCPRR without officially resigning from the PSP. I took with me fifteen years of political organizing experience, ten years of which were obtained in the PSP.

Despite the success of getting the Dellums Transfer of Power Resolution adopted within the group, many NCPRR members continued to hold PSP members and former members suspect. The underlying notion was that whenever the PSP got involved in a coalition, it was with the intent of taking it over. I was the only recognized PSP representative in the NCPRR. I never talked with anyone about my PSP status or its internal crisis. Many thought the PSP was as vibrant and aggressive as it had been in the preceding ten years and that I continued to be an active PSP member.

The positions of controlling influence over NCPRR policy, especially in the New York City chapter, were held by former members of the YLP. The Justice Committee was one of the most active committees of the New York City chapter, with a focus on police brutality and abuse, a cardinal issue of the defunct YLP. It was mentored by the late Richie Perez, an ex-YLP leader. Other NCPRR committees in which YLP perspectives held sway were in Education, Language Rights, and, for a brief period, Housing, Health, and Women's Committees. Many were concerned that the PSP would bog down the NCPRR's meetings in an everlasting debate around what its members considered alien political agendas. Having made many contacts in organized labor when working on the Vieques issue, I decided to concentrate on forming a Labor Committee (LC) of the NCPPR city chapter.

The LC brought together labor organizers and activists from the hospital workers Local 1199; the Teamsters; the American Clothing and Textiles Workers Union; the American Federation of State, County, and Municipal Employees; and the United Federation of Teachers, among others. The LC mobilized a campaign that denounced the board of directors of the Puerto Rican Day Parade for conducting its annual gala in an anti-union hotel. It picketed Coors Beer for helping finance the anti-Sandinista contras in Nicaragua. It helped get resolutions passed in scores of union locals, demanding the cessation of U.S. Naval operations on the island of Vieques. It sought to unify Latino labor and civil rights activists in the first Latino Labor/ Civil Rights Conference of the East Coast. When the issue of Puerto Rico's political status was raised, the LC informed people that the NCPRR was on record as supporting the Dellums Transfer of Powers Resolution and encouraged members to organize support for its passage. All these activities, along with the publication of member news and commentaries on the pages of a monthly paper called *The Puerto Rican Worker*, were examples of the LC's broad range of undertakings.

The first chapterwide work plan was drafted in the LC, intended to give the chapter's work coherence and accountability. NCPRR leaders appreciated the plan for its configuration and specificity. The other working committees used the chapter's work plan as a model for drafting their own. No one knew that the idea of a comprehensive work plan was taken from the PSP's organizational best practices learned in Los Angeles.

By the mid-1980s, the NCPRR's national leadership had resolved to march on Washington, D.C., in protest of the dismal socioeconomic conditions in Puerto Rican communities throughout the United States. Studies showed that Puerto Ricans had the highest poverty and unemployment rates in the country. Single-parent households were among the highest and also had the lowest rates of educational achievement. Health outcomes in Puerto Rican communities were also among the worst. We attributed these conditions to socioeconomic institutions that denied Puerto Ricans equal opportunity for advancement, practices that were framed by historical institutional racism. Denunciation of these illegal but unspoken systems had to be taken to a national public square.

For the second time in fewer than five years, more than four thousand Puerto Ricans marched on Washington, D.C., this time in support of Puerto Rican civil rights. People traveled to Washington whichever way they could. In New York City, the LC took charge of transportation operations with the financial support of Local 1199. The chapter moved thirty-five busloads of people to the front of the White House. There, Jesse Jackson, the founder of the Rainbow Coalition and a candidate for the Democratic Party's presidential nomination, was among the keynote speakers at the NCPRR's concluding rally.

Three years later, in Hartford, Connecticut, in my capacity as chair of the New York City LC, and now regarded as an ideological moderate, I was elected national president of the NCPRR at its Fourth Biannual National Convention in 1987. I soon left my regular job with United Auto Workers District 65 (as an associate editor of its newspaper) to work full time for the NCPRR. I went on a speaking and organizing tour in cities with high concentrations of Puerto Ricans in Massachusetts, Connecticut, New Jersey, Pennsylvania, Ohio, and Illinois. Many PSP members mobilized in support of the NCPRR in their respective cities, which proved to be very effective in establishing new NCPRR chapters nationally. Much time was expended explaining the politically center-left nature of a civil rights coalition and why this approach was correct given the conditions facing our communities. This stance notwithstanding, the NCPRR became a magnet for leftist groups that wanted a mass base from which to recruit new members.

Many on the Left failed to realize that organizing beyond the Left meant discarding left-wing jargon and styles of work, which may have dazzled left-wing cohorts but was a stretch from the vernacular of the Puerto Rican mainstream, whether professional or laborer. Cringes abounded when a young man or woman would stand up at a meeting and begin to harangue those present about solving our problems by overthrowing the capitalist bourgeoisie ruling class and replacing it with a revolutionary socialist government. Such words, however true, rang hollow to an audience wanting the government to protect their rights in the short term. Some on the Left repudiated the idea of uniting behind issues built on the most common denominator and dogmatically persisted in forcing votes that they could not win. More mainstream members on various sides of an issue just stopped attending meetings after long, frustrating hours of debate.

Despite the occasional setback, the majority of NCPRR members, particularly in New York City—the biggest and most robust chapter—arrived at a consensus that spoke to the need for institutionalizing the NCPRR. Most agreed with the idea of establishing separate Political Action Committees (PACs) to encourage legislative activities and voter registration. The New York City chapter agreed to work on establishing a separate 501(c)3 entity that could raise funds to pay staff. It resolved to emphasize building local committees. It most importantly decided to encourage the notion that fundraising, budgeting, and planning were just as important as political organizing.

Indeed, following through on these tasks was essential to long-term growth and survival. The chapter could not thrive only on monthly membership dues, even if they were consistently paid, which they were not. Unfortunately, this level of development through incorporation and full-time staffing was never attained—on a chapter level or nationally. In the spring of 1989, I decided not to run for a second term as president of the NCPRR. Instead, I prepared for a major political organizing opportunity in New York City.

The Electoral Arena

By the summer of 1989, a historic event was percolating in New York City. For the first time in the city's history, an African American, Manhattan

Borough president David Dinkins, was lining up to run for mayor. This campaign was unfolding amid deep-seated racial tensions fueled by the incumbent mayor Edward Koch, who presided over a city wallowing in official corruption.

Concurrently, the city charter was on the ballot for voters to approve significant revisions. It was likely that among other things, the revisions would raise the number of city council seats from thirty-five to fifty-one. The possibility of a citywide community empowerment campaign via a historic mayoral race and the opportunity of filling sixteen open city council seats with more black, brown, and Asian representation was irresistible.

This opportunity had the potential to go beyond electing the first black mayor and more people of color to positions of political power. It was about taking advantage of a historic opening to mount a citywide network of informal, community-based PACS in Puerto Rican/Latino communities, not unlike what the NCPRR and the PSP's U.S. Branch at some point had contemplated in the form of chapters. This network of committees would continue political organizing in the electoral and multi-issue arenas well after the 1989 Democratic Party mayoral campaign. These informal PACs would later run and elect Puerto Rican/Latino representatives to the city council, state assembly, and state senate. Judgeships were also in the mix.

The Puerto Rican/Latino PACs would run candidates in the heavily Latino-populated community districts of Williamsburg, Sunset Park, and Bushwick in Brooklyn; the Lower East Side, East Harlem, and Washington Heights in Manhattan; and about twelve community districts in the Bronx. The informal PACs would be instrumental in holding elected officials accountable to the voters and would function as schools for politics, centers for voter education and registration, mobilizers of voter participation, and centers for political empowerment by supporting progressive Latino candidacies. These districts also had many activists drilled in the organizing traditions of the PSP and the NCPRR.

Many Puerto Rican/Latino activists participated in the mayoral campaign. They came from the ranks of the Dominican community, NCPRR activists, former PSP members, the YLP, and members of El Comité–MINP as well as more conservative civic, labor, and faith-based organizations. Dinkins won the 1989 Democratic Party primary with 70 percent of the Puerto Rican/Latino vote. He went on to squeak a win in the November general election and in January 1990 was sworn in as the first African American mayor in New York City's history. This event was enhanced by a historic increase in the representation of communities of color in the city council. Dinkins went on to change the direction of city policies.

These policies included limiting tax increases for low-income workers, which affected the majority of black, Puerto Rican/Latino, and Asian city dwellers. He implemented a community policing program to combat crime and increase public safety through better police/community relations. He began the process of cleaning out the illegal drugs prevalent in Manhattan's Forty-Second Street "red-light" district. He expanded a network of community-based health clinics and established evening Beacon Schools for youths and their families. And he began the process of child welfare reform to reduce child abuse and neglect and relieve pressure on the city's foster care system.

Of greatest significance is what developed politically in the Puerto Rican/Latino communities. Riding on the political organizing activities during the Dinkins campaign and broad voter registration efforts, Richard Rivera was elected as the first Puerto Rican civil court judge of the Williamsburg/Bushwick district in Brooklyn. This win was important because the Puerto Rican/Latino community was locked in a housing distribution dispute with the city that could only be decided in Brooklyn's civil court. Although Rivera's election did not guarantee a decision favorable to the Puerto Rican/Latino community, it did enhance the probability of an even-handed resolution.

There was also the election of Javier Nieves to the state assembly from Sunset Park, Brooklyn. In Washington Heights, Guillermo Linares was elected the first Dominican city council member in the city's history. Adam Clayton Powell III was elected to the city council, crowning the beginning of the dissolution of corrupt political leadership in East Harlem's El Barrio. These campaigns galvanized many former PSP members and members of El Comité–MINP as well as other left-wing activists.

I believe the experience and the legacy of the PSP are here to be passed on to future generations as stages of political change. The PSP's U.S. Branch comprised an interesting blend of the Puerto Rican political experience. The Puerto Rico–born worker who migrated to escape the cruel insecurities of colonial domination converged with the sons and daughters of the emerging Puerto Rican diaspora in the metropolis. More than forty years after the great Puerto Rican migration of the 1940s and 1950s, the younger and elder generations of Puerto Ricans had to find appropriate organizational forms for protecting our sense of community and ensuring our collective survival. We looked for ways to "make the road by walking," to borrow from Paulo Freire.

Some of us wanted to return to a good job on an island free of colonialism. Others longed for the same but realized that this dream was not coming about any time soon. So, we hunkered down to live on and raise a family here in the United States, the best realistic option. Despite occasional visits to the island, for many second-generation Puerto Ricans, the United States has become our permanent home.

But the desire for community and self-preservation prevailed, despite the incessant battering of our dignity and self-respect by the dominant culture. That desire took many organizational forms over the decades. Some activists stayed in the radical political Left, and others moved toward liberal political spaces. The PSP helped me understand the importance of coalitions like the NCPRR. Both projects were enriched by a political mission that sought to find the appropriate organizational design for its expression. The PSP and the NCPRR were not failures in this respect. They were historical and experiential stepping-stones in the direction of progress.

Many of us former PSP members never stopped using the methodologies and organizing tools we learned in that group. I first encountered them in Los Angeles, carried them to Brooklyn, and used them as co-coordinator of the New York Committee in Support of Vieques, as chair of the New York City NCPPR LC, and eventually as the NCPRR national president. They were instrumental when codirecting field operations in the Dinkins primary campaign and in every position I have held in organized labor, in the nonprofit world, and in government.

The PSP taught us how to look at the bigger picture, break it down into its component parts, and get a handle on understanding events and proposing solutions large and small. It taught us to look critically at social, political, and economic phenomena and to analyze them in their dialectical interplay. It instilled an empowering self-confidence. My hope is that my children and the young people of today will experience similar life-changing events born from participation in a mission-driven organization like the PSP.

NOTES

1. Some articles published at the time include "The Trouble at Our High Schools— Why?" *Long Island Press*, November 2, 1969; "Bellport High Remains Closed," *Newsday*, January 1970; "L. I. School Still Closed as Racial Factions Confer," *New York Times*, January 20, 1970; "Bellport [High] Reopening Possible Tomorrow," *Newsday*, January 20, 1970; and "Suspended Bellport Students Return," *Newsday*, January 30, 1970.

2. Names of group members have been changed.

III
Coalitions and Alliances

Building Solidarity for Puerto Rican Independence

Rosa Borenstein

Introduction

I started working with the solidarity movement for Puerto Rico's independence in late 1973.[1] My interest in Latin American political struggles was sparked during a trip to Cuba in 1969 as a member of the first *Venceremos* (We shall be victorious) Brigade. Afterward, I participated in Cuban solidarity activity for a while with several of the other *brigadistas*. In 1971, I became a member of the Liberation News Service collective and had the opportunity to visit Cuba again to report on the July 26 celebration that year. While I continued to maintain a connection to Cuba's solidarity activity, I was drawn to the movement advocating for non-intervention in Chile a few months before the September 1973 coup. The danger was palpable even here. After the coup, the Chilean solidarity movement quickly and unfortunately degenerated into a sectarian morass, making it very difficult for activists, who wanted no part in the internal disputes, to build a meaningful mass response to the coup and our government's role in the overthrow of Chile's democratically elected Socialist government led by Salvador Allende.

About the same time as the coup, I learned from other Latin American solidarity activists that Ramón Arbona, then a leader of the Puerto Rican Socialist Party (PSP) and an editor of its paper, *Claridad*, had relocated to New York to help establish the U.S. Branch of the PSP. As part of the PSP's plan to build relations with the New York progressive community, Arbona was eager to meet activists in the New York–based Latin American solidarity movements.

I was curious. Alan Howard, my then partner and now husband, and I invited Arbona to dinner at our apartment in late 1973. He and Alan had a mutual Dominican friend who had encouraged us to meet him. The dinner conversation was a Puerto Rican history lesson. I had never heard an analysis of the colonial relationship between the United States and Puerto Rico that was so clear and compelling. Although I had what I would call a "politically correct" position on Puerto Rico, that night Arbona convinced me of the unique role the progressive movement in the United States could and should take in supporting the anti-colonial struggle.

Arbona's explanation of how the colonial experience affected Puerto Ricans living in the United States was evocative. I grew up in the Jewish community of Newark, New Jersey, in the late 1950s and early 1960s. When I entered junior high school with seventh graders from three other elementary schools, I met Puerto Ricans for the first time in my life. These classmates were exotic, particularly when they spoke Spanish to each other or in class when they used Spanish to express what they otherwise could not explain in English. I never understood what they were saying in Spanish—it was not a popular elective. They were marginalized from the social life of the school by their perceived resistance to assimilation, often depicted in the mass media, and by our unfriendliness.

Arbona's lesson swept the cobwebs away. In the space of an hour or so, I grasped the reasons for the mass Puerto Rican immigration, their failure/unwillingness to assimilate (they loved their country first), and their passive reliance on public assistance as a feature of colonial life. I am a child of Holocaust survivors who, like thousands of other survivors, had rapidly assimilated themselves into mainstream U.S. life (learning English, enjoying American culture, and acquiring TVs, washing machines, and cars, and so forth). In my community, the process of becoming "American," particularly the mastery of English, was essential. No one wanted to be a greenhorn. My attendance at a Yiddish folk school was considered odd by my friends, American and foreign-born, and I resented every minute that my parents forced me to attend. This school was not "American." I recall my mother boasting one evening after an elementary school parent/teacher conference that my teacher thought my accent-free, fluent English was so perfect that she was shocked to learn that we had only been in the United States for seven or eight years.

Whereas I did not want to be tagged as a child of Holocaust survivors for the rest of my life, Puerto Ricans were proud of their heritage, culture, and language—an interesting contrast that, in part, compelled me to get involved.

The Committee for Puerto Rican Decolonization, the Puerto Rican Socialist Party, and *Puerto Rico Libre!*

That evening, Arbona described a new organization: the Committee for Puerto Rican Decolonization (CPRD). The CPRD had been set up by the PSP earlier that year to reinforce efforts led by Cuba at the United Nations (UN) to have the discussion of Puerto Rico's colonial status become a general assembly topic and to do educational outreach in the United States. The group needed volunteers.

A few weeks later, I went to my first CPRD meeting at the rectory of St. Mark's Episcopal Church on Second Avenue and Tenth Street. I was immediately pressed into work by the stern, well-organized, and efficient Shelley Karliner, a PSP member who directed the CPRD in a no-nonsense style. Karliner was counterbalanced by the energetic and loquacious Alfredo López, her superior in the PSP, who directed her work.

I was accustomed to the collective approach to leadership and problem solving that had been nurtured and practiced in the anti-war and solidarity movements, so I was a bit rattled by the CPRD's hierarchy. Volunteers included Dana Biberman, David Burd, Bill Henning, Lally Grauer López, and Liz Mestres, among others. We would meet frequently in the evenings to write, edit, and lay out the CPRD's monthly bulletin (sometimes not quite on schedule, to Karliner's chagrin), *Puerto Rico Libre!* (*PRL!*), priced at five cents per issue. It was mailed to several hundred annual subscribers throughout the United States. We also organized testimony at UN hearings and sponsored educational events in the New York metropolitan area.

The CPRD's first board of directors included the Reverends David Garcia and Ben Chavis; Carlos Feliciano, a prominent member of the Nationalist Party; (Mary) Yuri Kochiyama, a Japanese American activist; Michael Locker, a member of the North American Congress on Latin America (NACLA), a progressive Latin American affairs organization that published a highly regarded monthly magazine; PSP leader Alfredo López; and Ruth Reynolds, a North American who had been jailed in Puerto Rico for five years as punishment for her presence at a Nationalist Party demonstration in the early 1950s.

PRL! had quickly become the English-language publication "of record" for news and information about the independence movement in Puerto Rico and the solidarity movement in the United States. Its initial four-page format squeezed in information about U.S. interference with and repression of the independence and labor movements; the struggle against a proposed "Superport"; the U.S. military's use of Puerto Rico's populated offshore islands Vieques and Culebra for live ammunition weapons training; the despoliation of the island's natural resources and environmental damage caused by the lax enforcement of U.S. Environmental Protection Agency (EPA) standards; and incentives given to U.S. corporations to relocate to Puerto Rico.

The Puerto Rican Solidarity Committee (PRSC) took responsibility for publishing *PRL!* after its founding conference in March 1975. By December 1976, the publication's length had increased to sixteen pages. The expansion enabled the PRSC to publish longer articles as well as interviews, essays, and open letters that were informative and well written and deepened the PRSC's discussion of issues that were important to the independence and solidarity movements. A few articles were even suitable for academic journals. Judith Berkan, Ellen Chapnick, Cam Duncan, Paul Schachter, and Mike Withey, members of the National Lawyers Guild (NLG) Puerto Rico Project, were contributors. Members of the national board and the *PRL!* staff also wrote articles.

In addition, the expanded *PRL!* ran articles about Puerto Rican culture, the arts, and poetry and increased the number of historical and topical fact sheets, "Boxes of Facts," it published from its inception. In November 1976, *PRL!*'s appearance changed when artwork, some original, replaced text on the front cover. In later years, to raise funds for programs, the PRSC created a marketplace page selling phonograph records, posters, buttons, and pamphlets and provided a list of suggested reading materials.

If the PRSC's sole purpose was to publish *PRL!*, it would still have made a major contribution to the solidarity movement simply on the basis of its content and continuity. It is now the only extant chronicle of the existence and accomplishments of the solidarity movement that thrived for more than a decade. The first issue of *PRL!* was published in August 1973; the last issue I have in my possession is dated September 1986. In the process of writing this chapter, I asked several former PRSC members, who continued to be active after I resigned my post as Executive Secretary in the spring of 1978, when *PRL!* actually ceased publication and the date, month, and year in which the PRSC dissolved. No one could provide those answers.

El Acto in Madison Square Garden

To our collective surprise, in early 1974, López and Arbona proposed to the CPRD that we assist the PSP in organizing a solidarity rally in October at Madison Square Garden. The capacity of the Garden was twenty thousand. They had no doubt that between the efforts of the CPRD and the nationwide supporters we had developed through *PRL!* and the PSP, which was rapidly setting up chapters in every Puerto Rican community in the country, that it could be done. López would resign from his position as Executive Secretary of the CPRD and become the Executive Secretary of the new organizing structure—the Puerto Rico Solidarity Day Committee (PRSDC)—to direct the planning and organization of the event. The CPRD would continue publishing *PRL!*, keep up its UN activity, and help the PRSDC staff when needed—an exceedingly unrealistic set of tasks. Lally Grauer López; Dana Biberman; Sally Hamann, who was our printer; and I were invited to staff the PRSDC on a full-time, *paid* basis. We were joined by Julie Nichamin, an academician turned activist. A few members of the PSP were assigned to assist the PRSDC. Notable among them was Alice Berger, a good friend from the Venceremos Brigade, our media liaison.

At first, CPRD members were not enthusiastic about El Acto, the name the PSP gave to the mobilization. Several doubted that the CPRD staff could publish *PRL!* at the same time it helped organize for El Acto. Questions arose about whether the solidarity movement would benefit from El Acto. It was possible that this one-day event would consume a lot of human energy and financial resources and have no lasting effect on the growth of the solidarity movement. It could not supplant the steady work of organizing educational activities in new cities and communities, the most fruitful way to expand the solidarity movement. These concerns were for the most part allayed, and the CPRD and the PRSDC inevitably merged staffs.

In late April, two secondhand color printers were installed in the rectory basement for the exclusive use of the PRSDC. The PRSC had taken responsibility for publishing *PRL!* after its founding conference in March 1975. St. Mark's doubled the rent-free space it already provided to the CPRD, and the four-month organizing drive began in earnest, guided by López's frequently distributed "work plans." "Work plans" were novel to many PRSDC volunteers, like me, who came from the ranks of other solidarity groups and the anti–Vietnam War movement and were not accustomed to implementing written directives. But we had a very short period of time within which to organize El Acto, and using work plans quickly made good sense. (Their use became essential in the PRSC's future organizing campaigns.) López's updated work plans set out new tasks and evaluated how much progress we had made toward the ultimate goal: twenty thousand attendees on October 27, 1974, the date attorneys from the NLG had negotiated on our behalf with the Madison Square Garden management.

I believed that I was at the heart of a colossal military-like operation, although I knew nothing about military mobilizations except what I had seen on movie and television screens. Organizers were recruited in New York City, Buffalo, several New England cities, Chicago, St. Louis, Washington, D.C., Philadelphia, and as far west as California. Each local committee pledged to bring a certain number of supporters to the Garden on October 27, 1974, and to organize fundraising and educational events to generate the funds necessary to sustain the national office and publicity campaign, to hire the buses that would transport supporters to the Garden, and to help finance the Garden's rental fee. The admission fee of $3.00 per ticket did not come near to generating all the needed revenue.

As part of the publicity campaign, Mestres, our artist-in-residence, was commissioned to design posters, leaflets, and literature with Maggie Block, another volunteer artist. Squads of supporters plastered the posters all over New York City. I remember riding on a crosstown bus and restraining myself from gasping with surprise when I saw our posters glued on plywood construction walls on Thirty-Fourth Street. Unfortunately, there were no passengers with whom I could share that delightful moment. Thousands of posters were sent out across the country as well and were displayed similarly.

López seemed to never rest. Running from meeting to meeting, this gathering to that gathering, a radio program, an interview, he was a human dynamo who never stopped talking or moving. There never was a dull moment, never a lull; after a few words delivered in López's inimitable rhetorical style, we were ready for the next task. We were all fired up and ready to work late into the night, through the weekends, whatever was required.

Figure 13.1. Angela Davis at National Day of Solidarity with Puerto Rico.

The first official list of public figures and organizations that supported the event was published in June 1974. The September 1974 issue of *PRL!* reported that mobilization committees were in New York City, Chicago, New Jersey, Boston, New Haven, Hartford, Springfield, Los Angeles, and Washington, D.C. That issue also announced the program participants: Juan Mari Brás; Jane Fonda; Angela Davis; American Indian Movement (AIM) leader Russell Means; Virginia Collins from the Southern Conference Educational Fund, a civil rights organization; Congressman John Conyers (D-MI); the Wounded Knee Drum and Singing Group; Miriam Colón; Ray Barreto; Danny Rivera; Lucecita Benítez; Ossie Davis; the Ballet Folklórico en Aztlan; Holly Near; Piri Thomas; and El Grupo Taoné.

Support came from leaders of AIM, Clyde Bellecourt and John Trudell. At a news conference held in San Juan, Puerto Rico, Bellecourt announced that the ninety-seven representatives attending the first International Indian Treaty Council held at Standing Rock had endorsed the October 27 mobilization. Drawing parallels between the conquest of native lands and Puerto Rico by the U.S. government, Bellecourt said, "[In] 1917, Puerto Ricans were made citizens of the United States against their will. In 1924 they'd made us citizens without our consent."[2]

Figure 13.2. Ray Barretto Band playing at National Day of Solidarity with Puerto Rico.

There was significant African American support for the event. A Black Support Committee chaired by Davis included Imamu (later known as Amiri) Baraka, Walter Collins, James Forman, Florynce Kennedy, Gene Locke, and PRSC board member Frances Beal, a leader of the Third World Women's Alliance (TWWA). In total, forty-one individuals and organizations joined the Black Support Committee. On September 11, four members of the Congressional Black Caucus declared their support: Louis Stokes (D-OH), John Conyers (D-MI), William Clay (D-MO), and Yvonne Burke (D-CA).[3]

The groundswell of publicity was abetted by media attention from at least one very unlikely source: in an August 21 editorial, the *New York Daily News* gave El Acto an inadvertent plug when it ridiculed Jane Fonda and Ramsey Clark for supporting Puerto Rico's independence.

PSP leaders from Puerto Rico visited and were treated like diplomats from a sovereign country. Invitations to meet Juan Mari Brás, Carlos Gallisá, and others were coveted. Inclusion at PSP parties on Friday and Saturday nights at a local cultural center, La Casa de las Americas, was a bonus and laid the groundwork for enduring friendships with some members of the PSP for me. We were propelled by a common belief that the political conditions were ripe for a true transfer of power and that Puerto Rico would soon be independent.

The Puerto Rican Solidarity Committee

Energized by the resounding success of El Acto and encouraged by the PSP, several PRSDC board and national staff members, along with El Acto activists, a few of whom had toured Puerto Rico at the invitation of the PSP shortly after the event, decided to transform the PRSDC into a national membership organization. The Founding Conference of the PRSC was held in March 1975.

From its earliest days, the PRSC was a magnet catching the attention of U.S. leftist and progressive organizations. Many of us who had come of political age during the Vietnam War years were without a political anchor or identity. Students for a Democratic Society (SDS), the vibrant, national student organization, had splintered into factions that, in turn, had spawned small, sectarian socialist Maoist and Marxist-Leninist formations that vied with the established Marxist-Leninist parties for recruits. While the great majority of these unaffiliated activists drifted away from organizational alternatives, several hundred became the core of the PRSC. The PRSC offered an international issue to rally around, an inclusionary structure, and the opportunity to work side by side with Puerto Rican *independentistas* in the immediacy of their struggle.

The two-day gathering at Rutgers Law School in Newark, New Jersey, was attended by 125 delegates drawn from our activist ranks. Most of the attendees of the Founding Conference were white, half of whom were women. The conference attracted members of several Marxist and socialist groups, pacifists, students, community activists, academicians, Puerto Ricans, Mexican Americans, African Americans, and Asian Americans.

The conference adopted a political statement and bylaws, gave approval to five 1975 national campaigns, and elected a twenty-member national board, which reassembled most of the members of the CPRD and PRSDC boards and added a few more representatives of the U.S. Left. The board was racially and ethnically diverse, and nearly half of its members were women. López became the PRSC's first Executive Secretary. The PRSC and its predecessors had a penchant for titles, borrowing from the practice of the PSP.

In ten pages, the political statement covered the history of colonialism, the movement against it, and the commitment made by the PRSC to maintain "unequivocal support for the principle of self-determination. Each struggle will develop its own ideology, tactics and strategy . . . and we must respect that fundamental right. We support the independence of Puerto Rico, not any particular group, organization or force."[4]

The delegates agreed that PRSC members would pay annual dues to distinguish it from a coalition of organizations similar to the PRSDC. As one speaker remarked, the conference was convened not to put together another one-day event but to unite individual participants around programs—short and long range—that would empower and advance the solidarity movement's contribution to the struggle for independence. The collection of dues put the PRSC on the road to financial and political independence and, as a precondition of membership, would deter ill-intentioned organizations from packing the PRSC with the goal of usurping its leadership and/or using it as a cadre recruiting ground, a nasty practice that adherents of the Left had at the time. The PRSC could not be bought. (An exception was later created for the World Council of Churches, whose affiliates, the National Council of Churches [NCC] and the Interreligious Foundation for Community Organization [IFCO], made generous and unconditional gifts to the PRSC for programmatic work.)

The conference adopted five campaigns for 1975. In the "can-do" spirit of the moment, the campaigns were for the most part unformulated:

1. Participation in the International Conference in Support of Puerto Rico's Independence that would be convened in Havana in September 1975
2. Support for Puerto Rico's labor movement
3. Support for the struggle against political repression
4. Support for the freedom of all Puerto Rican political prisoners
5. Support for the struggle against genocidal population policies

In addition, the campaigns the CPRD had been engaged in since August 1973 would be absorbed by the PRSC without discussion and without objection. The proverbial plate became a full platter:

1. The campaign against the superport, already well organized in Puerto Rico
2. The campaign underway in Puerto Rico against U.S. environmental and investment policies that tolerated the exploitation of the island's natural resources for profit and little benefit to the people of Puerto Rico
3. The campaign against the U.S. military occupation of Vieques and Culebra

The PRSC also set an organizational goal of doubling the number of chapters from nine to eighteen in one year (a feat accomplished in May 1976). By the Second National Conference in February 1977, there were chapters in Amherst, Atlanta, Boston, Brooklyn, Chelsea (NYC), Chicago, Hartford, Los Angeles, Madison, New Haven, Philadelphia, St. Louis, San Diego, San Francisco, San Jose, Springfield (MA), the Upper West Side (NYC), and Washington, D.C.

In its political statement, the PRSC committed itself to the fight to end the racial and national oppression of Puerto Ricans in the United States. An example of this commitment was the PRSC's participation in the struggle to save Hostos Community College and the Puerto Rican Studies Departments in the New York City and state college systems that were threatened with closure in 1976. In November 1976, the PRSC sponsored a tour for Hostos student leaders, who met and spoke with several hundred students and academic and nonacademic staff at ten New England campuses. It also participated in a May Day march in the Bronx organized by the Community Coalition to Save Hostos.

The PRSC also worked with the Community Coalition to Save Metropolitan Hospital. Because the hospital was located in the East Harlem community, its patients and employees were mostly Puerto Rican. It was convenient and provided medical services to treat diseases and conditions prevalent in the community, such as a high rate of infant mortality, trauma, drug addiction, lead poisoning, hypertension, tuberculosis, and alcoholism. Thanks to activist pressure, the hospital was not shut down. These are two examples of local organizing campaigns in New York City. In the ensuing years, PRSC chapters joined community campaigns in other cities with significant Puerto Rican and Latino populations.

The PRSC flourished during 1975 and 1976. Our nationwide membership was relatively small, about five hundred people, while our activities impressively attracted several times that number. Alfredo López, Lally Grauer López, Dana Biberman, and I traveled extensively. We visited chapters all over the country. Activity was constant.

Demonstrations were held in conjunction with UN activity, the freedom of the five Nationalist Party political prisoners, and events in Puerto Rico. We lobbied against U.S. maneuvers that sought to further entrench or recast the colonial relationship with new, insidious legislation that supposedly supported the decolonization of Puerto Rico. Representatives of the PRSC participated in international forums concerning Puerto Rico's status, including one held in Cuba in 1975. (Another such event occurred in Mexico in 1979.) Other U.S. organizations and solidarity groups frequently asked PRSC members to speak at their events and give organizing advice.

The "Bicentennial Without Colonies" and Beyond

The March 1975 Founding Conference unanimously approved a motion calling on the PRSC "to develop a national project that would relate the colonial case of Puerto Rico to the 1976 bicentennial plan being run by our [U.S.] government."[5] The national board was tasked with developing a plan for the PRSC's participation in the yet-to-be defined project. And, true to its commitment, a little more than one year after El Acto, the organization was preparing for another large anti-colonial demonstration.

In late February 1976, the PRSC announced that it had formed a coalition with the PSP, AIM, and several other national organizations to march in Philadelphia on July 4, where the thirteen U.S. colonies had declared independence from England in 1776. The demonstration would fittingly demand a "Bicentennial Without Colonies" and present a sharp contrast to the official nationwide celebrations. Simultaneous marches and rallies were planned for the West Coast.

The demonstration was organized around six issues: the struggles against imperialism, racism, sexism, repression, unemployment, and cutbacks in essential services in poor and minority communities. The anti-imperialist plank demanded independence for Puerto Rico and sovereignty for Native Americans.

López resigned his position as Executive Secretary of the PRSC and became the leader of the ad hoc organizing committee. I was appointed to take his place as the PRSC Executive Secretary by its national board. A nine-page, single-spaced work plan called "Study Materials for the Bicentennial Campaigns" was sent to all the chapters. It included a timetable and details of how chapters could organize support from disparate constituencies.

An estimated crowd of forty thousand people marched in Philadelphia on July 4. We were accompanied by musicians and street theater performers. The demonstration made its way through several racially mixed, working-class communities and ended in a rally. Another five to seven thousand marched in Los Angeles and San Francisco.

The "Bicentennial Without Colonies" demonstration was the bookend to El Acto. The Puerto Rican solidarity movement never again organized a mass mobilization of that magnitude. No other solidarity organization had the resources and support to even try to organize similar national events. Both were dramatic achievements. In fewer than two years, relying on the organizational skills the PRSC had learned from the PSP and on the PSP itself, supporters were able to mobilize an approximate total of sixty thousand people to publicly demand Puerto Rico's independence. The U.S. government had received notice that its days of maintaining Puerto Rico as a colony were limited—or so the PRSC believed then.

After the exhilaration of achieving another impressive turnout and the publicity that came with it simmered down, we turned to discussing the value of continuing to organize mass mobilizations pell-mell and to make decisions about the future direction of the PRSC. Most of our best organizers had been involved in the Bicentennial effort, and virtually all PRSC activity had been merged into organizing support for Philadelphia. From the start, some PRSC members resisted working on the campaign for the same reasons that activists resisted working on El Acto. Some PRSC members were annoyed because the campaign organizers ignored their evident unease. Others expressed even stronger feelings: they thought the demonstration was a wasteful publicity ploy, and they resented the PSP's almost fanatical drive to make the mobilization successful. The consensus was that the Bicentennial Without Colonies mobilization had depleted the energy of the PRSC membership.

The challenges before the PRSC were twofold: returning to the implementation of the program adopted at the 1975 Founding Conference and restoring the morale of the membership. It met the challenges, in good part, by embracing the campaign to Free the Five; by advocating for the recognition of Puerto Rico's right to independence during the UN discussions on Puerto Rican self-determination; by supporting Puerto Rico's labor movement and the struggles for women's rights and against sterilization abuse; by denouncing the use of the federal grand jury system to repress the independence movement and supporters by criminalizing their activity; and by supporting campaigns against environmental degradation and to get the U.S. Navy out of Vieques. Space considerations limit me from detailing all the work that the PRSC did in the following years, but the next sections provide two such examples.

The Puerto Rican Solidarity Committee
Goes to Washington

The PRSC made its first foray into the U.S. legislative arena after commonwealth leaders submitted a bill to Congress in late 1975 that they purported would clearly restate Puerto Rico's relationship to the United States. The PRSC unquestionably had to react. The bill called for a "Compact of Permanent Union between Puerto Rico and the United States." Independentistas reviled it as the latest of a long string of commonwealth efforts to disguise Puerto Rico's colonial status. In every extant issue of *PRL!* in 1976, the PRSC reported on demonstrations opposing the compact in Puerto Rico, provided the testimony of independence movement leaders who spoke against it at the congressional hearings held in Puerto Rico, and provided analysis of the bill.

PRSC representatives testified at compact hearings of the Senate's Interior and Insular Affairs Committee on February 9 and May 16, 1976. At one of the panel hearings, Washington, D.C., chapter leader Ted Glick took the senators by surprise by shouting from the observer benches and disrupting the proceedings. He was thrown out by U.S. marshals, putting the PRSC in the national and local news that evening.

The differences between commonwealth status and the compact were frequently muddied by its proponents. The Institute for Policy Studies, a D.C.-based liberal think tank, had taken an interest in the proceedings and organized two public seminars to discuss the distinction between the compact and Puerto Rico's current commonwealth status. The compact bill was never enacted.

From its earliest days, the PRSC envisioned working with elected officials to educate the public about Puerto Rican colonialism. "Mainstream" support for Puerto Rico's independence became news when the March 1974 issue of *PRL!* announced that former U.S. attorney Ramsey Clark supported Puerto Rico's self-determination. Clark's action was the first time in the twentieth century that a member, albeit former, of a U.S. president's cabinet had contradicted U.S. policy on Puerto Rico. The only elected member of Congress who had ever spoken in favor of Puerto Rico's independence had been Vito Marcantonio (D-NY), an Italian American, in a speech he delivered on the floor of the House of Representatives in 1936. Marcantonio had introduced legislation calling for independence while he was in office. In 1996, former U.S. senator Eugene McCarthy (D-MN), running as an independent for president, added himself to the short list of public figures who were independence supporters.

Ron Dellums (D-CA) made the first discernible impact. On July 1, 1976, days before the Bicentennial demonstration, he introduced a joint resolution in the U.S. House of Representatives that called for the transfer of powers from the federal government to Puerto Rico. National board member and constitutional law expert Arthur Kinoy had worked closely with him on the bill. Dellums reintroduced the bill on several other occasions while he was a House member, and each time the bill was discussed in committee, the PRSC testified on its behalf.

Working in the legislative arena was a thorny issue for the PRSC and hotly debated at the Second National Conference in February 1977. While common sense dictated that any legislative activity that advocated self-determination for Puerto Rico should be supported, some members feared that working on the passage of the bill might turn the PRSC into a congressional lobby. The fear did not take hold.

The PRSC never withdrew its support for the Dellums Resolution. The bulletin continued to report on and analyze the various iterations and reiterations of the colonial relationship, the contradictions of the pro-commonwealth and pro-statehood parties and their respective resuscitations, and the participation of independence forces in electoral politics. The crucial debate at the PRSC's Third National Conference held in 1979 was whether statehood or commonwealth status posed the greater threat to the independence movement. The prevailing view that emerged at that time was that commonwealth status was the greater danger. Protecting the independence movement from its advancement was a key element of the two-year program that was adopted. The conference affirmed support for any legislation that called for the transfer of powers from the United States to Puerto Rico, when two years earlier some delegates had vilified the Dellums Resolution at the Second National Conference.

Political Prisoners

Some PRSC members believed that the organization's efforts in the freedom campaign were weak. A review of *PRL!* issues from August 1973 through the early fall of 1975 indicates that the freedom of the five Nationalist prisoners was not a high PRSC priority during that period. A short article in the October 1974 issue of *PRL!* announced the formation of the Lolita Lebrón Committee by the TWWA in New York City, and a brief profile of her appeared in an early 1975 women's issue. Coverage of political prisoners had been limited to the arrest, trial, imprisonment, and release of Nationalist Party leader Feliciano. PRSC board member Feliciano had been sentenced to a five-year term in a federal penitentiary in October 1973 for the possession of illegal weapons, although he was initially charged with participating in forty-one New York City bombings. He was represented by civil rights attorney William Kunstler. When the sentence was handed down, two thousand supporters of the United Front to Free Puerto Rican Political Prisoners marched on the White House to demand his release and the release of the five. His support committees in New York City and Washington, D.C., played a major role in securing his early release in July 1975.

By October 1975, the PRSC had begun to work with the national campaign led by an independent group called the Free the Five Nationalist Prisoners Committee. That the PRSC was slow to engage in the campaign was an accurate assessment. Resistance principally came from members who found it difficult to distinguish between supporting the release of the five as political prisoners (i.e., imprisoned for ideas and not deeds) and endorsing their use of weapons and, by inference, armed struggle.

Through internal debate and discussion, the PRSC's support for the prisoners' release was bolstered by arguments that pointed out that their sentences were excessive compared to the shorter terms served by inmates who had committed even more egregious violent crimes, including murder and rape; that denounced the punitive denial of parole; that exposed their deplorable prison living conditions and medical inattention to declining health; and that criticized the denial of visitations by relatives and the prison system's failure to recognize their years of good behavior. It was obvious that, if not for their support of independence, they would have been released many years earlier.

The PRSC joined Free the Five demonstrations at the UN, Chicago, and San Francisco on November 1, 1975. November 1 was the twenty-fifth anniversary of the day that prisoner Oscar Collazo and another Nationalist Party member, who was killed, attacked Blair House, a guest house for dignitaries visiting Washington, D.C. PRSC chapters in San Francisco, San Diego, and Portland organized marches and rallies.

Shortly after the November 1 actions, the PRSC announced that it would participate in a new round of actions planned for March 1, 1976, to mark the twenty-second anniversary of the Nationalist Party's attack on the House of Representatives. The actions included picket lines, visits to the parole offices of the Justice Department in Washington, D.C., and satellite offices in Newark, New York City, San Francisco, Atlanta, Chicago, Boston, Cleveland, Columbus (OH), New Haven, and Minneapolis. Picket lines were set up in Newark, New York City, San Francisco, Atlanta, Chicago, Boston, Cleveland, Columbus (OH), New Haven, and Minneapolis. The largest action was a march on UN headquarters in New York City.

The PRSC joined mass actions on October 3, 1976, which were dedicated to the Nationalist Party–led rebellion in Jayuya, Puerto Rico, in October 1950. Demonstrations were held in Ann Arbor, Madison, and Atlanta and in Springfield, Missouri, at the Federal Prison Medical Facility where Andrés Figueroa Cordero, dying of cancer, was hospitalized. The demonstration

at the prison facility was attended by supporters from Iowa, Kansas, Okla-
homa, Arkansas, St. Louis, Texas, Chicago, and Gary, Indiana. (Figueroa
was released in November 1977 and returned to Puerto Rico, where he died
in March 1979.)

As part of the campaign, and following the Second National Conference, the New York City chapter organized two seminars in 1977 linking
the imprisonment of the five to the repressive role of grand juries, the status
of other U.S. political prisoners, the Chilean coup, and apartheid. In 1978,
the PRSC helped support a regional tour of Zoraida Collazo, the daughter
of Oscar Collazo, who spoke at public events in New York City, Storrs (CT),
Boston, Amherst, New Haven, Newark, and Philadelphia.

Public solidarity with the four remaining prisoners broadened in 1978.
Trade unionists representing the Amalgamated Meat Cutters and Butcher
Workmen of America; the Lake States District of the United Shoe Workers of America; the Fur, Leather and Machine Workers Union Joint Board;
the United Electrical, Radio and Machine Workers of America; and the
International Association of Machinists and Aerospace Workers, District
134, announced their support for their release. Statements of public support
at that time were issued by congressional representatives, state legislators,
Nobel Laureates, and Hollywood activists.

Leaders of the Puerto Rican and U.S. religious community met with
members of President Jimmy Carter's White House staff on December 22,
1978, asking for the president to include the five in an unconditional Christ-
mas amnesty. The group represented the NCC, many Protestant denomi-
nations, one auxiliary Catholic bishop; the American Friends Service
Committee (Quaker), assorted theologians, and Ruth Reynolds, who presented a petition signed by eight thousand people demanding their release.

On September 10, 1979, the four surviving prisoners were released and
reunited at Chicago's O'Hare Airport. The jubilant reunion included family members, attorneys, and supporters who had camped out at the airport,
waiting for their planes to land. Speaking briefly, the freed prisoners reaffirmed their commitment to the independence struggle.

After the five were freed, the National Committee to Free the Five
Nationalist Prisoners announced in January 1980 that it would reconsti-
tute as the United Committee Against Repression (CUCRE) headed by
Nelson W. Canals. A similarly named organization formed in New York.
The CUCRE's board of directors included Rafael Cancel Miranda, Irvin
Flores, Lolita Lebrón, and Oscar Collazo. The Puerto Rican Independence
Party (PIP) and the PSP declined invitations to join, but organizations that
did join included the Communist Party, the Nationalist Party, the Revolu-
tionary Socialist Party, the Popular Socialist Movement, the International
Workers League, and the Puerto Rican Socialist League. The list reflects

the fragmentation of the Puerto Rican independence movement into new organizations and marked the decline of the PIP's and the PSP's influence.

The Second National Conference of the Puerto Rican Solidarity Committee (1977)

After the exhaustive effort of the Bicentennial demonstrations in mid-1976, the quarterly meetings of the PRSC executive board grew increasingly contentious, indicating that the implementation of the program of the PRSC was not resolved. The Second National Conference was convened in February 1977 in Chicago to discuss the issues that were affecting internal cohesion and to adopt a strategy and tactics to respond to evolving conditions in Puerto Rico without going into crisis mode.

The hundred or so PRSC delegates were expected to unite the organization by celebrating the second anniversary of the PRSC and the achievements of the independence movement, reviewing the work of the past two years, and adopting a revised political statement or reaffirming the existing one and programs for the next two years. In the issue prior to the conference, *PRL!* published greetings from twenty national progressive organizations and individuals saluting the PRSC and the independence movement, proof of the widespread respect the PRSC had within the Left. The PRSC's dues-paying membership structure was viewed as a model for other solidarity groups. The ability to organize El Acto and the Bicentennial Without Colonies mobilization were proof of its success.

During the preceding three months, members had hammered out an agenda and procedures and circulated resolutions, including a revised political statement of purpose, which became known as the "first draft." However, ten days prior to the conference, the San Francisco chapter circulated a "second draft," its version of a revised political statement for consideration. Complaints were made from the floor that the "second draft" submission was untimely and that members did not have a sufficient amount of time to compare it with the "first draft" that had been subject to revision and review for three months. The plenary body decided to consider the "second draft" along with the "first draft" to avoid divisive unpleasantness. The debate over the drafts swept away nearly the entire two-day agenda.

The question at the heart of the debate of the competing drafts was how solidarity for Puerto Rico's independence should be built. Could the North American working class be motivated by its economic self-interest to support independence for the same economic self-interest that motivated Puerto Ricans to struggle for independence? The "first-draft" supporters said yes. The other side, supporting the "second draft," said no. To paraphrase their position and to use their words, the North American working class was not a "reliable sector." The "first-draft" supporters maintained that class struggle was the fundamental dynamic that controlled the worldwide struggle for economic justice and national sovereignty, which included Puerto Rico's status. The "second-draft" supporters argued that the dynamic of the struggle between the forces of imperialism and anti-imperialism would determine the fate of the world and, by extension, Puerto Rico's status.

Similar debates were taking place throughout the U.S. Left. It seemed that every faction of the Left was vying to be *the* political organization, grounded in the only correct theory that would lead the struggle for universal peace, justice, and equality. The "first-draft" supporters agreed to certain amendments to their draft, but when the "second-draft" supporters insisted that the political statement include a new section that characterized the North American working class as an "unreliable sector," a motion to end the debate was passed, and the "first draft" identifying class unity as the most viable basis for solidarity was adopted in a 60–30 vote. The bitterness and the disharmony caused by this rift infected the PRSC at least through 1978.

In my opinion, the debate was conducted by polemical arguments with pretensions of erudition and contributed nothing to the implementation of the PRSC program. While the Puerto Rican labor movement was militant, and many argued that independence was the solution to the problems of poor wages, dangerous working conditions, and high rates of unemployment, the PRSC was not seriously poised to organize U.S. labor support for independence on the scale imagined by the "first-draft" supporters. On the other side, the "anti-imperialist" "second-draft" supporters, untethered from reality, covered their ignorance with forceful arrogant bluster and ad hominem attacks on individuals who disagreed with their incoherent interventions.

The conference had time for one more plenary debate about the relationship between the PRSC and the independence movement. A motion was passed that the PRSC as a solidarity organization should have no loyalty to or bias in favor of or against any parties and formations that participated in the anti-colonial struggle. In short, this motion was a compromise that basically restated language that already was in the political statement and the neutrality disclaimer that was printed in every issue of *PRL!* I believe that this motion—which, of course, passed—was designed to address the uneasiness some members had about the PSP's influence in the PRSC and the concern of others that the PRSC was hostile to Puerto Rican independence formations that supported armed struggle. I never shook off the belief that the sponsors of the motion actually wanted the PRSC to endorse the strategy and tactics of those sectors of the independence movement that advocated armed struggle as the only way to achieve

Puerto Rico's independence. Opposition to organizing around the Dellums Resolution was woven into the debate, as were jabs at the PRSC's perceived lackluster support of the five.

A new board was elected that included for the first time representatives from El Comité–MINP, the Workers World Party, the Union of Democratic Filipinos; the Women's International League for Peace and Freedom; the American Friends Service Committee; the Committee to End Sterilization Abuse (CESA); CASA; and Attica NOW! The new board included union activists; scholars Archie Singham and Robert Chrisman; and PRSC activists James Early, Irwin Silber, Fran Beal, Annie Stein, and Arthur Kinoy; and a PSP representative. The new board included more women and African Americans than the first and, for the first time, leaders of political organizations other than the PSP.

Because the debate over the political statement and the neutrality motion took so long, the plenary body decided that the program for the next two years would be decided in committees subject to membership review through internal communications. In the end, no changes were made to the existing programs.

The PRSC almost disbanded at the conference. It survived because of the perseverance of four capable women: chapter leaders Cindy Zucker from Chicago and Dianne Taylor from St. Louis and national board members Fran Beal and Annie Stein. They stepped in to calm emotions and to propose ways forward that everyone could live with, at least through the end of the conference.

The Third National Conference

I did not attend the Third National Conference, which was held in New York City in July 1979. *PRL!* reported that the central debate focused on determining the greater threat to the independence movement in the prevailing political climate in Puerto Rico and the United States: the forces that supported commonwealth status and those that supported statehood. The conclusion was commonwealth. The sixty-five delegates were prepared for plenaries and workshops that had these goals: evaluating the PRSC's work since the 1977 conference, defining a strategy for the PRSC based on protecting Puerto Rico from an entrenchment of commonwealth status, developing a two-year work plan, and electing a new board.

The delegates also discussed the PRSC's role "as an important component of both the solidarity movement and the left forces within the United States."[6] The conference documents stressed that the PRSC "[had] a very important responsibility as an anti-imperialist organization to help combat imperialism at home and abroad."[7] What form that participation should take as a component of the leftist forces combatting imperialism at home was not defined. I believe that this discussion reflected the practical need of international solidarity organizations at the time to support one another in the face of declining memberships and changing political conditions. About this time, *PRL!* opened its pages to articles from other solidarity movements and reports of PRSC engagement in joint mass actions.

The conference urged PRSC members to pay greater attention to the increases in labor and political repression, including the murder of two young independentistas in a police ambush at Cerro Maravilla; to support the release of the four Nationalists who were still in prison; to support the Vieques struggle against the U.S. Navy, which at that time was focused on the arrest of twenty-one demonstrators, including Judith Berkan, the chief attorney for the Vieques demonstrators, and an inquiry into the Florida prison death of Ángel Rodríguez Cristóbal, one of the twenty-one. The new board was a mix of old and new representatives. Several more chapter leaders were added as well as Harvard professor Richard Levins and activists Luis Prado and Judith Berkan.

The PRSC held its Fourth National Conference in New York City in February 1982 and reaffirmed the March 1, 1975, Founding Conference political statement as its basis of unity.

Conclusion

I am proud to have participated during a very short period of time, along with several hundred other people, in organizing two major national mobilizations around an issue that barely had any visibility outside the Puerto Rican community before Arbona came to town. I learned how to organize and lead, and I made lifelong friends and helped put the struggle for Puerto Rico's independence on the agenda of the progressive movement in our country.

As well, I am struck by how much I have forgotten of the detail of the debates and discussions of the time—things that I thought I could never forget. One memory that stays with me clearly is the Second National Conference, because it brought the PRSC to the edge of destruction. Notwithstanding our successes, we made serious mistakes: miscalculating the ability of our government to hold on to Puerto Rico, relying almost exclusively on the PSP's analysis of prevailing conditions, and allowing wrongheaded and misguided individuals and groups an undeserved platform from which to foment internal struggles that undermined outreach programs and alienated many members.

I found being a parent and a leader of the PRSC to be very difficult. I was among the first PRSC activists to have a child. The PRSC and I were not prepared to adopt a work model that combined work and child-rearing responsibilities to the detriment of neither. Although it was never spelled out, I was expected to keep parenting at home. This requirement was not possible because the cost of childcare was prohibitive, as it is today. When I brought my daughter, Diana, to work, I felt as though I were intruding. While I did not expect the staff of the national office to share my childcare responsibilities, I was unnerved, for example, by rolling eyes when I asked someone to watch her for a few moments when I was on an important phone call or needed to step out of the office. I resigned regretfully in mid-1978 and was replaced by Lally Grauer López as Executive Secretary. I believe that when she left in 1981, the position was never filled again. An accommodation to my circumstances and those of other female activists might have, at least, kept me in the PRSC in a leadership position for as long as the political situation required it at that time.

I am not sure what young parents, particularly mothers, do to balance child rearing and volunteer political activity now. I am aware that some nonprofit, progressive organizations provide benefits that include paid parental leave and in-house child care centers. Perhaps my story and those of others have made it easier for women to parent and work with little friction.

Looking back, I believe that my experience is sort of a cautionary tale for younger activists of today, female and male. These are challenges that activists have always faced and that social movements need to address if the struggle for change is to be more successfully and humanely carried out.

After I left the PRSC, I spent approximately two years, off and on, typing briefs at the Center for Constitutional Rights for several attorneys I admired: Doris Peterson, Elizabeth Schneider, Nancy Stearns, and Rhonda Copelon. They inspired me to enroll in Rutgers-Newark Law School, where Center for Constitutional Rights attorney and PRSC board member Arthur Kinoy taught. In 1983, I became a staff attorney at Professional Employees Legal Services, a provider of personal legal services to New York City municipal employees organized by the Civil Service Technical Guild. I retired from my position as director and general counsel in 2011 and now spend time contentedly with my husband, two children, and two grandchildren. A tie of affection and communication remains to old friends in the solidarity movement and to the people of Puerto Rico, who continue their long search for self-determination.

NOTES

1. I wish to thank the following people, who helped me enormously with their recollections: Judith Berkan, Dana Biberman, Maggie Block, James Early, and Liz Mestres.

2. "97 Indian Tribes Support Rican Independence," *Puerto Rico Libre!* 2, no. 3 (August 1974): 5.

3. "Blacks Support Puerto Rico Struggle," *Triple Jeopardy* 4, no. 1 (September/October 1974): 2.

4. "Independence for Puerto Rico! Political Statement of the Puerto Rican Solidarity Committee," the Puerto Rico Solidarity Committee, New York City, March 1975.

5. "National Conference Founds Solidarity Organization," *Puerto Rico Libre!* 2, no. 7 (March 15, 1975): 9.

6. "PRSC Holds 3rd Conference," *Puerto Rico Libre!* 5, no. 4 (September/October 1979): 15.

7. Ibid.

Independentista Politics, Independent Politics

My Years Working with the Puerto Rican Socialist Party

TED GLICK

I Was Not Planning to be a Revolutionary

Growing up, I had no personal contact with individual Puerto Ricans or issues related to Puerto Rico. My first exposure was the Broadway play *West Side Story*. When I was a teenager in the early 1960s in Lancaster, Pennsylvania, my parents brought the family to New York City to see this famous play. A few years later, I worked in a local tobacco warehouse that employed some Puerto Rican men. My memory is of several friendly coworkers, but our interaction was minimal because of the language difference. From these meager connections, I never would have imagined the intense familiarity with the Puerto Rican experience that would later be a part of my life.

The next interaction coincided with my turn to political activity at the age of twenty-one. In 1970, I found myself in federal prison, where I was serving an eighteen-month sentence for my involvement in an anti-war, anti-repression action in Rochester, New York. Late one night, inside an FBI office, seven other pacifists and I had spent five hours cutting up thousands of Selective Service draft files. We had been arrested just as we were about to leave the building with suitcases full of those files.

I spent four of those months in prison in Danbury Federal Correctional Institution. A number of Puerto Rican prisoners were locked up with me, and I recall having conversations with them.

Growing up in Lancaster in the 1950s and 1960s, I was not planning to become a revolutionary, or a burglar of buildings housing the Selective

Service or war corporations or the Federal Bureau of Investigation (FBI) offices, much less spend long months in prison. But in 1967 and 1968, as a freshman at Grinnell College in Iowa, I was exposed for the first time to people who were strongly against the Vietnam War.

I spent time studying up on that war's origins and its reality. As I did so, I became increasingly anti-war, increasingly agitated as I realized that the U.S. government was essentially on the wrong side, propping up corrupt and repressive dictatorships and killing massive numbers of people, Vietnamese and American, in the process.

I was also affected by the civil rights and black freedom movements. My father was active in it locally, and he drove to Selma to take part in the march to Montgomery in 1965. I heard Martin Luther King Jr. speak twice, once in Lancaster and once at Grinnell.

Indeed, the day King was assassinated, April 4, 1968, is the day I became an activist. For the first time in my life, I did something against war and injustice. I posted a petition to Congress that night on the wall of the college mailroom, calling upon representatives to take action to address the conditions of U.S. society that King had been working to change. I sent it off to Washington, D.C., a couple days later with 450 signatures. This action launched me onto a road of progressive activism and organizing that I am still on, fifty years later as I write this essay.

I left college a year later after publicly returning my draft card to my draft board. I refused induction when told to report for it and soon joined the Catholic Left, a network led by Phil and Dan Berrigan and other priests and nuns. This wing of the peace movement was entering draft boards and nonviolently destroying draft files to disrupt the operations of the war machine. Actions were also being taken at war-related corporate offices. For nine months, I participated actively to help get prepared for and then to take part in four such actions, the last one being in Rochester, where I was arrested and sent to prison.

The eleven months I ended up spending in prison were undoubtedly the most educational period of my life. I had had almost no contact with people of color until I went off to college. My friends and classmates all through high school were overwhelmingly white working-class and white middle-class, and Lancaster was a Republican-dominated town. Prison, on the other hand, exposed me to many people of color and to race and class issues in a very up front and personal way. Prison strengthened my commitment to social change as I came to understand how fundamentally unjust, exploitative, and imperialistic the U.S. government and system really were. I continued my progressive/revolutionary activism after prison.

In 1974, I first met a member of the Puerto Rican Socialist Party (PSP), Alfredo López. I was living in Washington, D.C., at the time, making a living by working as a groundskeeper at a cemetery in Landover, Maryland, and in the evenings and on weekends volunteering as a coordinator of the National Campaign to Impeach Nixon. Through that work, I encountered a new group being formed, the National Interim Committee for a Mass Party of the People, initiated by long-time movement lawyer Arthur Kinoy.

Kinoy had written a theoretical and strategic paper, "Toward a Party of the People," forty-four pages covered in very small typeface, that called for

> a strategy which would have as its core the building of a permanent mass-based party of the people. This party would be based upon the fundamental program of taking state power as well as power in every institution and area of American life and placing it into the hands of the people. Just as organization for industrial union-ism was the fundamental strategy of the thirties, so organization for people's power must be the fundamental strategy of the seventies.[1]

Kinoy's paper did not say very much about the Puerto Rican reality, either as a colonized nation or as people forced to come to the United States and finding here extensive racial discrimination and oppression. But Puerto Ricans, "driven to the ghettoes of the mainland by the poverty imposed on their own land by the imperialism of this country,"[2] were considered to be one of the many groups that would make up the strategic alliance necessary to confront the ruling class.

The concept of a strategic alliance was a central aspect of Toward a Party of the People:

> The bankruptcy of the system which has so infected and poisoned every aspect of society has created a situation in which many groups of oppressed people now have, together with the workers, an objec-tive and real stake in the taking of power. In this alliance, from time to time, one or another of the oppressed groupings will assume leadership and surge to the forefront of the struggle. At one historic instant it will be the Black people rising in the urban ghettoes of the North and the rural ghettoes of the South. At another instant it will be the fury of the students. And at another instant it will be the workers in the factories and plants lashing out against the growing economic tensions and the insanity of factory life.[3]

Practically, this goal had to mean a "dualism in organizational and political approach"[4] on the part of a Mass Party toward the black move-ment. That movement had its own dynamics, its own leadership, and its own processes, and these had to be respected and followed—the principle of self-determination; at the same time, black people who agreed with the Mass Party strategy had to be fully involved within it at all levels.

This approach also applied to other nationally oppressed peoples—Native Americans, Chicanos, Puerto Ricans, and Asian Americans. It was similar, although by no means the same, with respect to the women's movement, a distinct movement that had its own particularities and dynamics and whose demands had to be actively supported by the party: "The failure to analyze scientifically the role of women as an 'agency for social change' has been a serious and often fatal weakness in the thinking of the left in this country and abroad."[5]

A new party must be genuinely and deeply rooted in the masses of the people:

> Essential to the survival and success of such a mass party of the people is that programmatic proposals to meet the central problems of each of these sections of the people must be derived from them. A party of the people must learn from the people, appreciate that the people make the history—not a party, and not individual leaders, no matter how brilliant and creative they may be. Respect and equality rather than domination and direction [must be the day-to-day way of working].[6]

Electoral activity had to be a part of the work:

> A party of the people must be prepared to enter fully and energetically into the struggle in every available arena, including participation in electoral struggles in every form and on every level. The determining factor would always be whether participation in that particular struggle would or would not advance the level of understanding, the morale, the fighting spirit of the people involved.[7]

And such a party must conduct its decision making through an

> open process, open to the members and open to those affected by the decisions. Built in this spirit, the party can win the respect of the millions of people necessary to the achievement of its central goal. More than this—the building of a party in this spirit would reach for the essential: the building of the new within the womb of the old.[8]

In the summer of 1974, this Mass Party effort held a national organizational meeting in Washington, D.C. I knew Kinoy—I had met him in 1972 and had told him about my interest in this initiative—and I was invited to attend. I was impressed with the discussion, believed that it was a group for me, and began to work with others to form a local group in D.C.

Connecting with the Puerto Rican Socialist Party

I was also impressed with Alfredo. I do not remember what he said at that Mass Party meeting, but I remember him being a combination of passionate, articulate, clear, and nothing like the leaders of other groups that called themselves Marxist-Leninist whom I had begun to meet in the course of my impeachment work. I know that Alfredo spoke about the Puerto Rican Solidarity Committee (PRSC) and the upcoming October 27, 1974, demonstration at Madison Square Garden in support of "the December, 1973, history-making United Nations' resolution recognizing 'the inalienable right of the people of Puerto Rico to self-determination and independence,'" as expressed on a brochure I still have. For years to come, these two causes— the building of an independent mass party of the people and support for Puerto Rican independence—were top personal priorities.

It was not hard for me to become active with the PSP through the PRSC. I had told Alfredo at the Mass Party meeting that I was interested in helping in whatever way I could. I knew very little at the time about Puerto Rico, but I considered myself to be an anti-racist, had spent years of my life fighting to stop the imperialist war in Vietnam, and fully understood that I had a responsibility as a U.S. citizen to do all that I could to end U.S. colonial domination.

Within a month of the meeting, Alfredo came to Washington, D.C. He stayed in the small apartment with me and my then-wife, Peg Averill, sleeping on a mattress we put on the floor of our living room.

Alfredo was a good organizer. He was easy to talk to. We enjoyed putting him up.

A meeting had been set up with Congressman Ron Dellums, and Alfredo took me with him to that meeting. I think he was the first U.S. congressional representative I ever met. The one thing that stands out about what he said was his statement early on in the meeting: he supported the right of Puerto Rico to self-determination and independence and viewed this support as very basic to his political beliefs. He followed up on this statement in 1976 by introducing a resolution in Congress in support of Puerto Rican independence.

Alfredo also spoke at a meeting that led to the creation of the D.C. Committee to Support Puerto Rican Independence. I was chosen to be a cochair along with a Puerto Rican man, Antonio Rosa, whom I had not known before that meeting. We were soon actively working to fill a bus to go to the big October 27 Madison Square Garden rally.

In an outreach letter we cosigned toward that end, we referred to the December 1973 United Nations (UN) General Assembly resolution supporting the independence of the island and said, "The firm and massive rejection by the people of this country of that illegal and immoral occupation becomes crucial. The millions of people who opposed this policy in Vietnam must again be mobilized and their ranks grow to assure that our voices join the voices of the world in denouncing U.S. colonialism in Puerto Rico."[9]

As I learned more about Puerto Rico and the PSP, I became more impressed. In an unpublished piece I wrote around this time, I quoted Ramón Arbona, a PSP leader, referring to Marxism as "a guide to action, and the only successful Marxists have been those capable of applying it as a tool for analysis and a guide, in a creative and dynamic way, to the particular circumstances of their place and their time."

In a letter I sent to a friend I was corresponding with about political strategy, I wrote, "Study their organization. Get 'The Socialist Alternative' from NACLA [North American Congress on Latin America] of a couple of months ago. PSP is the vanguard of the left in the U.S. at this moment in history, and I only wish they were taking a more active role in building the united front which is so necessary for this period."[10] To another friend I wrote, "The most dynamic organization in the United States today is the Puerto Rican Socialist Party."[11]

The successful initiative to fill Madison Square Garden on October 27 was the concrete manifestation of this belief. It had been decades since the Left had done such a thing, and it has happened rarely ever since. The only comparable time I can remember was during the Green Party's Ralph Nader/Winona LaDuke presidential campaign in 2000. It was energizing to be part of the event in New York City in 1974. It was a full house, twenty thousand people, according to the organizers. There was lots of energy in the crowd, particularly from the many thousands of Puerto Ricans who were there.

In an article about the rally that appeared in the November 1974 issue of *Puerto Rico Libre!*, the publication of the Committee for Puerto Rican Decolonization (CPRD), PSP leader Juan Mari Brás was quoted in reference to the planned 1976 Bicentennial activities in the United States. He called it "a magnificent historical opportunity to convert the celebration planned by imperialists into a great movement" that would not only push forward the independence of Puerto Rico but also develop "the struggle for the liberation of all the oppressed sectors here."[12]

The article went on to report that "an estimated six thousand people travelled from over 25 major cities throughout the United States to join the thousands of Puerto Ricans, Dominicans, Haitians, Afro-Americans, Asians, Indians and white North Americans from the New York area."[13]

A Delegation to Puerto Rico

A month or two later, I was very honored to be invited by the PSP to be part of a delegation of U.S. solidarity activists on a ten-day tour of Puerto Rico, which took place in January 1975. Seven or eight of us went on the trip, from New York and several other localities.

We traveled all over the island. Localities we visited included San Juan, Ponce, Guayanilla, Lares, Utuado, and Mayagüez. We learned about the PSP's basic organizational structure. We learned about the "pillars" of its strategy, which emphasized a focus on the working class and its struggles and unity with other socialists in Puerto Rico as well as unity with non-aligned countries and socialists in other countries.

We met with leaders of the labor movement. We learned that about half of the unions were independent, and half were affiliated with the American Federation of Labor and Congress of Industrial Organizations (AFL-CIO). We were given a history of the union movement going back to 1930. We met with a leader of the Puerto Rican Independence Party (PIP), who presented his party's perspectives on the fight for independence, which did not sound to me at the time a great deal different than those of the PSP. It seemed that a major difference was that the PIP was much more of an electoral party than was the PSP. Carlos Gallisá, a PSP member and former PIP leader who had been elected to the colonial Congress, explained that his primary job was to educate people that their problems could not be solved with legislation because of colonial control, which prevented the kinds of basic changes needed.

On my return, I wrote an article about Puerto Rico that was printed in the bulletin of the Mass Party group. I quoted from the PSP's "Political Theses of the Puerto Rican Socialist Party: The Socialist Alternative," which stated:

> If Puerto Rican independence is an essential element for the transformation of North American society, as a tremendous blow to the power of the imperialist bourgeoisie and to the very system that determines the relations of production within U.S. borders, our struggle is intimately linked to the highest interests of U.S. workers. . . .
>
> For Puerto Ricans living in the United States, the construction of socialism in that country is also a primary task. The effective participation of Puerto Rican workers in the radical struggles of United States society will be an important contribution to the class struggle there.[14]

Throughout 1975, I continued to deepen my work with the PSP in several different arenas.

The Founding Conference of the Puerto Rican Solidarity Committee

In early March 1975 the PRSC held a national founding conference at Rutgers University in Newark, New Jersey. One hundred people from around the country attended. This conference was organized as a way to build upon the momentum from the successful Madison Square Garden event and generate energy for ongoing work and outreach. The discussion document put together for this event stated that we would be "building a permanent organization, with ongoing activities, actions and educational programs and campaigns; that the primary goal around which the Committee will be organized is support for the national liberation of Puerto Rico and the self-determination of the Puerto Rican people."[15]

Five "more short-range" goals were put forward: (1) "concrete support for the Puerto Rican movement's demand for independence"; (2) "support for the workers' struggles in Puerto Rico"; (3) "struggle against repression"; (4) "involv[ing] ourselves in concrete support for the struggles of Puerto Rican people in the US"; and (5) "oppos[ing] the genocidal population policies of the US imperialists in Puerto Rico, whose two chief forms are forced emigration and sterilization".[16]

> Every opportunity must be taken to expose the rhetoric of the U.S. government about Puerto Rico and show how the government's strategy in Puerto Rico also affects North Americans. People can and will understand that the Puerto Rican struggle will profoundly affect objective and subjective conditions in this country, and that the liberation of Puerto Rico will signify a tremendous step on the road to basic social and economic change in this country.[17]

I returned to Washington, D.C., charged up to keep working. Our committee worked on two activities for May. One was to support several members of the Community Union, who came to D.C. to picket the then-governor of Puerto Rico, Rafael Hernández Colón, who was speaking on May 15. The Community Union was a group of thousands of landless Puerto Ricans who had laid claim to unused government land and built their own communities on it. In response, the Puerto Rican colonial government had used bulldozers to level homes and push out families. For ten days, the families had been conducting a round-the-clock picket of La Fortaleza, the governor's palace, demanding a meeting with him, which he had not agreed to.

We also organized two days of activities in D.C. at the end of May for Pedro Grant, the Secretary-Treasurer of the Boilermakers Union and coordinator of the United Workers Movement (MOU). The MOU comprised one hundred local unions representing fifty thousand workers, 20 percent of all organized labor in Puerto Rico. The national PRSC organized a two-week tour for Grant, and we were the last stop on the tour. We organized a number of events: at the National Press Club, with a leader of the American Federation of State, County and Municipal Employees (AFSCME), radio interviews, a meeting with members of the D.C. Central Labor Council, a large public meeting at All Souls Church, and other activities. For the meeting at All Souls Church, I prepared a slideshow with pictures from my trip to Puerto Rico in January. I remember Grant complimenting me publicly for what I had produced after it was shown.

Mass Party Organizing

Later in 1975, I became actively involved, representing the Mass Party group, on an organizing committee for a national Hard Times Conference, which was to take place at the end of January 1976. This conference was for the anti-imperialist Left, and the organizing committee included a pretty broad cross-section of group representatives who shared these politics, including José E. Velázquez of the PSP. I got to know Velázquez in the period leading up to the conference, and my affinity with PSP politics was reaffirmed, as he and I were often in vocal agreement on issues that arose during contentious discussions. This synchronicity was fortunate, as this assembly of activists was complex, and creating a firm base of unity was not easily achieved.

In a memo to the others on the committee in late November, I wrote:

> The reality is that our movement is divided and fractured. We have not worked together, many of us do not even know one another, and I do not think people will be ready to commit themselves to a program coming out of the conference unless the conference provides a beginning opportunity for democratic discussion among the participants about what that program should be. I can't emphasize enough the dangers of underestimating the fragmentation and [praiseworthy] deep commitment to democratically helping to shape decisions, which is so much the case on the left.[18]

I do not recall the response to my view from fellow activists, but my general recollection of this conference more than forty years later is that it was of value. Several thousand or so people attended, a multiracial mix. Some very good speakers addressed the crowd. I remember that Velázquez and the PSP brought to the conference their call for a "Bicentennial Without Colonies" campaign, which would culminate in a mass demonstration in Philadelphia, Pennsylvania, on July 4, and that this call was well received.

Another idea with which the Mass Party group was involved received less support, an initiative of the National Black Political Assembly (NBPA) to run an African American leader on a third-party ticket in the 1976 presidential elections. For many at the Hard Times Conference, full-scale engagement in an electoral campaign, even for an independent party, was not on their list of priorities. I remember at the Sunday closing plenary, a speaker from the NBPA presented the organization's case as one of several main speakers, and the response was disappointing.

Through the last half of 1974 and all of 1975, I had played an active role in the Mass Party Organizing Committee (MPOC) effort, which was the name our group eventually adopted. It had not been easy work. In Washington, D.C., where I was living, a core group had continued to meet throughout this time. We had organized several forums on issues of concern, such as D.C. statehood, and taken part in coalitions with other groups in various action campaigns. In other localities, such as Chicago, Hartford, and New York City, we had local groups very much involved in the urban crises of the day. We were all searching for ways to put the Kinoy strategic perspective into effect yet had very limited results.

As 1975 turned into 1976, two main focuses emerged for the MPOC: the PSP-initiated July 4th Coalition (J4C) and the NBPA's effort to forge a multiracial coalition, including the PSP, to run a black leader for president in 1976 as an independent. The MPOC's decision to make these our top priorities was very consistent with our politics, as reflected in Kinoy's original theoretical paper. Both were initiatives being led by people of color in the United States. Both involved efforts to join constituencies and sectors of the population into a mass movement for fundamental social change. One was the tactic of mass action in the streets; the other was electoral.

In November 1975, I moved to New York City to work in the national office of the MPOC. For the next eight months, my primary work was on these two major projects.

The July 4th Coalition

The J4C put forward three overall demands: (1) a "Bicentennial Without Colonies," which included freedom for all oppressed nations; (2) jobs and a decent standard of living; and (3) full democracy and equality. The organizing effort was launched at a National Conference for a People's July 4th in New York City on March 27–28. Attendees included 225 representatives from 102 organizations, 53 cities, and 27 states.[19]

In a "July 4th Bulletin" reporting on the results of the conference, José Alberto Álvarez, the First Secretary of the U.S. Branch of the PSP, was quoted as saying, "We are here today because we see that this coalition has

Figure 14.1. Bicentennial Without Colonies.

the potential to represent all of our struggles; because we see the possibility of advancing our struggles through unitary action. We can say that almost every question which must be raised about the system which dominates this country is present in this room."[20]

Several months later, in response to an editorial critique of the J4C by the *Guardian*, a national weekly newspaper for the radical Left, Alfredo, as director of the coalition, argued that the J4C approach was appropriate for the anti-imperialist Left:

No matter what criticisms can be raised, everyone reading my words can look at the 200 national organizations and well over 500 local organizations supporting this activity to understand its incredible breadth. . . . May I personally and humbly offer a lesson learned from the arduous task of building the Puerto Rican Socialist Party [PSP]. Our party was built through the sharpening of political focus, *inside a mass movement*. It was through the practice of mass struggle that we learned to analyze, to construct strategy and to hammer out political consensus. The building of that kind of movement in this country is a task of great priority to virtually everyone in the coalition and for good reason—it is essential to our survival against the forces of the right, and it provides one of the best opportunities for practice in articulation of a mass, anti-imperialist line. If the *Guardian* is so critical of the inability of the left to "focus" a coalition how does it expect the left to focus a party without more mass work? (original emphasis)[21]

The organizing toward July 4 in Philadelphia, and sister actions in San Francisco and Los Angeles on the same day, was successful. Fifty thousand people turned out in Philadelphia. I remember marching through the streets of Philadelphia, through working-class and people of color's neighborhoods to the park where the rally with too many speakers, as usual, was held. I remember the feeling of empowerment to see the mix of races and nationalities making up the big crowd on a hot and humid day. I remember the abrupt ending of the rally as the dark rain clouds rolled in and Mari Brás's speech, passed out through the crowd in advance, was halted by very strong thunderstorms that went on for a long time and that drenched us all.

And I remember the extensive and generally okay press coverage received from the mass media. The decision to stage this event on July 4 in Philadelphia, a main site for official government celebrations of the two hundredth anniversary of the Declaration of Independence, had been sound. For this one day, the Left was visible, a reality, to tens of millions of Americans. As importantly, a basis had been laid for ongoing communications, coordination, and unity in action.

A Black-Led Independent Presidential Campaign

Discussions about running an African American leader for president had begun in 1975. In March of that year, the MPOC joined with Amiri Baraka and the Congress of Afrikan People to organize a national meeting to discuss this idea. Present at the meeting, held in Newark, New Jersey, were representatives of about forty organizations, most from the east coast—a mix of socialist and Marxist-Leninist groups, people of color–based organizations, third-party groups, and community organizations.

The organizers adopted a statement at the end of the meeting, but only eleven groups supported it. All but two of the other organizations either abstained or were not present when the vote was taken on the second day.

In the words of the statement, supporters "agreed, in principle, with the need for an explicitly anti-capitalist and implicitly socialist mass movement electoral campaign in 1976."[22] After various steps to move this process forward were approved, a National Coordinating Committee for Strategy 76 was established.

That spring, discussions were also taking place within the leadership of the NBPA about this idea. As stated by Mtangulizi Sanyika in a document adopted by the NBPA's Task Force on 1976 Political Strategy on April 23, "[we have a] unique opportunity to translate [our] concept of 'New Black

Politics' into a tangible form which the masses of people can identify with, given the deep social crisis of the capitalist system, and the lack of leadership of the one party system (both branches)."[23]

Such a campaign, "because the Assembly is still an embryonic political organization," should

> use the national election to organizationally strengthen existing state and local assemblies, popularize "New Black Politics" among the masses, establish the Assembly as a progressive popular Black alternative to one party (two branches) capitalist leadership, influence policy outputs of any structures which make decisions affecting Black well-being, educate Black people to the need for an alternative social system based on human needs, democracy and self-determination, and support state-local Assembly approved candidates in conjunction with the presidential campaign.[24]

Sanyika's document went on to say:

> It should be clear that of necessity we will interface with other groups and institutions whose immediate agendas may touch our own. The objective social conditions might suggest the need for new political relationships. In the profound language of the Gary Preamble [the historic Gary, Indiana, National Black Political Convention in 1972 out of which the NBPA had developed], "The crises we face as Black people are the crises of the entire society. They go deep to the very bones and marrow, to the essential nature of America's economic, political and cultural system."[25]

By the fall of 1975, representatives of the National Coordinating Committee for Strategy 76, including the MPOC, had met with representatives of the NBPA. The NBPA presented in some depth its plans and progress on its campaign plans for 1976, and we MPOC members felt encouraged.

The key to this strategy was the willingness of a progressive, nationally known, black leader to be willing to essentially be drafted by the NBPA and its allies to run for president. Potential candidates who were considered and/or wooed included Julian Bond, Dick Gregory, Richard Hatcher, John Conyers, and Ron Dellums. The NBPA scheduled a national gathering for Cincinnati, Ohio, in March 1976 to make its decision. Just before that gathering, Bond decided that he was not willing to undertake such an effort. All attention and pressure then focused on Dellums. In the end, although Dellums attended the Cincinnati meeting, he also decided not to accept the offer. Later that spring, a lesser-known black leader, Reverend

Frederick Douglass Kirkpatrick, agreed to accept, but the campaign never really materialized.

This campaign was an electoral setback for the Left in the United States in 1976. The PSP suffered a setback of its own later that year when its first-ever full-scale campaign for governor in Puerto Rico, with Mari Brás as the candidate, ending up receiving less than 1 percent of the vote, far below what was expected.

However, in retrospect, it strikes me as realistic to view these electoral setbacks as part of the process that led, starting in 1979, to positive electoral results for candidates who were connected to the Left in key cities, such as New York, Boston, and Chicago. In all three localities, African American and working-class white, progressive candidates for mayor ran strong campaigns, undoubtedly inspiring Jesse Jackson to decide to run for president in 1984.

The Peoples Alliance, 1977–1980

Following the J4C demonstrations, meetings were held with the groups that had worked with the PSP to organize them. The meetings were not always easy. As Kinoy wrote in an MPOC document published at the beginning of 1977, "We have all discussed over the past months many of the weaknesses and mistakes made in the organizing days and in the demonstrations themselves. We must continue to learn from these discussions. But in the perspective of history the central characteristic of the demonstrations of 60,000 people on July 4th was its success, its power and its strength. This is a fact increasingly acknowledged even by government agencies."[26]

No one else on the Left in the United States was doing what the PSP, the MPOC, and the many other member groups in the J4C were doing: "Out of the painfully developing unity was emerging the very first glimmerings of the vision of a strategic alliance which opens up the road to victory and final liberation, the alliance of working women and men and the oppressed nations and nationalities against their common energy, the industrial and financial rulers and the state they control—the U.S. imperialist state."[27]

These meetings developed sufficient unity and momentum for participants to move forward together, and the first thing that we agreed to organize was a National Conference to Build a Peoples Alliance. This conference was held in Washington, D.C., and it was a big success. We formed the Peoples Alliance over the weekend of May 28–30, 1977. Nearly 200 people were in attendance from 85 organizations, 20 states, and 47 cities and towns. This number included representatives from eight local J4C groups.

The conference passed a document putting forward various programmatic demands and action focuses that emerged out of workshops held in the areas of jobs, cities, international, repression, anti-nuclear, and communications. A basic organizational structure was adopted that mandated the formation of a broad National Committee, which would establish a smaller Executive Committee and hire staff. It was understood that local alliances were desirable, and a mechanism was created to figure out how those could be developed and affiliated.

Five organizations composed a Temporary Executive Committee, authorized to take the overall program and come up with a proposal for how to prioritize and advance it as well as to draft a more in-depth organizational proposal. The five groups were the PSP, the MPOC, the American Indian Movement (AIM), the Black Panther Party (BPP), and casa/General Brotherhood of Workers. Andrés Torres represented the PSP, which proposed three priority campaigns: an immediate campaign to stop FBI harassment and intimidation of the people's movement; taking on the struggle in support of the concept of affirmative action, now under attack in the *Bakke* legal case; and the organization of a week of activities occurring nationally around the theme of "Human Rights Begin at Home."

At the first meeting of the new alliance's National Committee on July 16–17, these three proposals were adopted, with some amendments, as were two others: support the efforts of the women's movement in responding to the attacks on women's right to control their own bodies and develop an analysis of President Jimmy Carter's energy plan and its relationship to the spread of nuclear weapons and technology.

An Executive Committee was elected that included Akil Al-Jundi, José Alberto Álvarez Febles, Vernon Bellecourt/Jimmie Durham, Bob Brown, Elaine Brown, Leslie Cagan, Marilyn Clement, Slim Coleman, Dave Dellinger, Ann Gael, Arthur Kinoy, Sara Nelson, Bruce Occena, Antonio Rodríguez, Liz Stewart, and Sharon Tracy.

The alliance continued to develop in 1978. In a preparatory document for the second National Committee meeting in mid-February, it was projected that

> the one, major, most important development since that first meeting has been a deepening of the unity, a steady movement forward of the "learning process" which began to develop in May and July. The national meetings of the Executive Committee, the meetings of the various program task forces, the discussions between Alliance organizations and members outside of the context of the actual Alliance organizational work . . . all have contributed to this process.[28]

At that February meeting, it was decided that the alliance should set up a National Full Employment/Jobs Strategy Committee to develop a plan for how we could work together on the jobs issue. This focus was not the only decision made—there were a number of others—but it was agreed that the jobs issue was of utmost importance. A working paper on jobs and unemployment was produced, and discussions were held about how best to move forward. One approved focus was the organization of local conferences around this issue. The second, and what became more significant, was the opening of the question of independent electoral work in connection with the work around jobs.

Just prior to the February meeting of the alliance, I testified at the confirmation hearings in the U.S. Senate when William Webster had been nominated to be the new director of the FBI. This type of work was one example of what we were doing on the issue of the FBI and the Central Intelligence Agency (CIA). In my testimony, I reported on a number of specific cases of government repression that members of the alliance had experienced or knew about. On behalf of the alliance, I called for specific commitments to be made by Webster, including an end to all politically motivated surveillance; the revelation and removal of all informers and paid provocateurs in trade unions, women's organizations, third-world organizations, and political, gay, church, peace and community organizations; and the complete and public exposure of all covert FBI activities directed against the peoples of this country. I was pressed by Senators Howard Metzenbaum and Dennis DeConcini regarding whether the alliance thought Webster should be confirmed. I said that our members thought not, but our view was not accepted, and Webster was confirmed.

Later that year, the alliance took note of several developments within the labor movement. We published a special edition of our "Organizers' Bulletin" in the fall of 1978 that carried statements from the United Auto Workers president Douglas Fraser and the International Association of Machinists (IAM) president William Winpisinger and a resolution from the United Electrical, Radio and Machine Workers of America (UE).

Fraser commented on his previous resignation from a labor management group he had been part of:

> The leaders of industry, commerce and finance in the United States
> have broken and discarded the fragile, unwritten compact previ-
> ously existing during a past period of growth and progress. . . . I
> believe leaders of the business community, with few exceptions, have
> chosen to wage a one-sided class war today in this country—a war
> against working people, the unemployed, the poor, the minorities,
> the very young and the very old, and even many in the middle class
> of our society.[29]

At an Industrial Union Department Conference on the Radical Right Wing, Winpisinger described a

> right-wing attack against working people aimed not [just] at union members alone. This is not a case of malice toward some, but malice toward all. The wrath of the right wing is directed against every American who works for wages. . . . Anyone who thinks America doesn't have its own aristocracy of great wealth is either naïve or has been brainwashed by big business propaganda.[30]

At a national convention in September, the UE adopted a resolution that said:

> There is no fundamental difference between the two dominant parties in American political life. The anti-working class nature of the two major parties has rarely been more evident than during the past two years. Despite a Democratic administration, together with an overwhelmingly Democratic Congress, Republicans and Democrats teamed up to attack the union programs. There is no solution to the political bind in which we find ourselves except the formation of a labor party—a party which unites workers, blacks, Hispanics and other minorities, the women's movement, senior citizens, farmers, consumers, progressive intellectuals and others who are fed up with what is happening to our economic and political life.[31]

These developments, coming on top of everything else with which the alliance was connected, were a clear sign that at the grass roots of U.S. society, political changes were happening, and progressive ideas and analyses were growing.

We responded by initiating work toward what became, in November 1979, a National Conference on a Strategy for Independent Political Action in the 1980s. A proposal for such a conference was put together for a January 1979 meeting of the Executive Committee. It suggested three areas of focus: (1) "Strategy" (addressing the question of a third party and independent local electoral work relating to the 1980 and 1984 national elections, building mass organizations, developing a program for the meeting of people's needs and for people's power, and so forth), (2) "Nuts and Bolts/ Organizing Skills" (principles of mass organization—recruitment, political education, finances, building tactical alliances, running candidates, fundraising, communications, and so forth), and (3) "Programmatic Issues" (affirmative action, nuclear power and weaponry, jobs and unemployment, urban crisis/master plans, abortion rights/sterilization abuse, government repression, and international concerns).

A call to the meeting stated:

Something new is taking shape, emerging, struggling to be born. We see it being forged in the heat of principled commitment. We see it taking a tough and practical shape, emerging through organizations and groups all over the country [on a wide range of issues and among a range of constituencies and sectors]. These developing forces are generally rooted in localized struggle. The mass media may advertise the 1970s as barren of any sort of mass movement, but we know different. There is probably more going on today at the grassroots level in the United States than at any time in the last 40 years.[32]

About sixty organizations were represented at the national conference, held in Nashville, Tennessee, on November 9–11, 1979. One hundred people registered, from sixteen states and Puerto Rico and from thirty-six cities and towns. Major speakers included José Alberto Álvarez Febles of the PSP; Lorelei Means of the AIM; Charlie Young of the Bois d'Arc Patriots in Dallas, Texas; Arturo Vásquez of CASA/General Brotherhood of Workers; Fred Taylor of the Southern Christian Leadership Conference; Ron Whitehorn of the Philadelphia Workers Organizing Committee; Jack Russell of the Detroit Alliance for a Rational Economy; Helen Shiller of the Organization for Justice, Democracy, and Unity in Chicago; Arthur Kinoy of the MPOC; Mel King, a member of the Massachusetts State House of Representatives and candidate for mayor of Boston in 1979; Leslie Cagan from the socialist/feminist movement; Lucius Walker of the Citizens Party and the Interreligious Foundation for Community Organization (IFCO); and Dave Dellinger, peace movement leader. The conference affirmed that:

We must see the necessity of consciously building toward an independent political party that breaks with the two-party system. The people need a political party of their own which fights against their common enemy: big business, the multi-national corporations, the banks, the government they control and the oppressive culture. It must be built from the ground up. We must work with and help to build local, grass roots, mass independent political movements and formations.[33]

A follow-up meeting was held in December. The notes of that meeting report that "the major point of discussion was the Democratic Convention and how we saw possible activities around it, a two-pronged approach as far as what should take place there [there being New York City on August 11–14]. One would be some kind of people's convention leading to the emergence of a people's program. The other would be a major demonstration bringing together all of the constituencies."[34]

A meeting to advance this work was planned for mid-March 1980, in Youngstown, Ohio. Youngstown was a place where we had developed good relationships with Ed Mann, the president of Steelworkers Union Local 1462, and Ron Daniels, the leader of the NBPA.

In the call for the meeting, which would discuss ideas for a People's Convention and March, we concluded with this explanation of why Youngstown was the ideal site:

> Youngstown was chosen for the conference site because of the important struggle now being waged by rank and file steel workers against the U.S. Steel Company, which is threatening to close down two plants currently employing 4,000 workers. By coming to Youngstown we will be expressing our solidarity with the steelworkers whose bold and courageous actions are an inspiration to us and clearly a matter of survival for themselves and the people of their city.[35]

The People's Convention in the South Bronx

The meeting was a success. There was broad-based representation of groups, and there was full agreement on moving forward with plans for a People's Convention on August 8–10 and a march right before the Democratic National Convention, which was to take place at Madison Square Garden.

A significant development for the eventual success of these actions was the presence of José Rivera, a long-time community and labor activist and the leader of the group United Tremont Trades (UTT) in the Bronx. The UTT was an organization of black and Latino working-class people who engaged in direct action and other organizing to get jobs for the unemployed. The PSP had talked with Rivera about our discussions and had brought him to Youngstown. He wanted the People's Convention to take place in the South Bronx on Charlotte Street, the devastated area where President Carter had issued his hollow promise to fund the rebuilding and revitalization of America's inner cities. Consensus at the meeting strongly suggested that this was a great idea. We called the new organizing network the Coalition for a People's Alternative (CPA).

For the next five months, we held regular meetings of the CPA leadership, established task forces, began fundraising, hired staff, reached out to the mass media, and issued a Call to the People's Convention and March on the Democratic Convention. By May, we had come up with a basic slogan: "Too Many Years of Broken Promises, Now We Will Be Heard."

We decided that the People's Convention would be held in a big circus tent and that we would clear away the rubble on enough of the huge, ten-square-block abandoned area on Charlotte Street to allow this staging to happen. On July 4, we organized a Charlotte Street cleanup party. Despite the serious summer heat, about a hundred activists and volunteers showed up, including a reporter for CBS Radio. A few days later, the story was carried in the media. The buildup had begun in earnest.

On June 24, a sidewalk press conference was held outside Madison Square Garden. A statement signed by José Alberto Álvarez Febles, Reverend Hubert Daughtry of the Black United Front, Dave Dellinger, Flo Kennedy from Black Women United for Political Action, Arthur Kinoy, Bobby Seale, and members of the Love Canal and Three Mile Island protest groups declared:

> The urgent needs of the majority of Americans have been virtually ignored by the two major political parties. The Democratic Party has long claimed—at times with some credibility—to represent the interests of working people, minorities, women and others who have not shared equally in the fruits of our society. In the case of the Republican Party, few of us have ever harbored such illusions. We cannot stand by and silently endorse this failure of the democratic process.[36]

Finally, the big days arrived. Several thousand people gathered on August 8–9 on Charlotte Street, where a big circus tent was indeed set up. Workshops were held in smaller tents scattered around the site. Endorsing groups set up tables with their materials. The weather was hot but dry, with no rain on either day. A unity statement, "The Declaration of Charlotte Street," had been put together prior to the convention, and it was the focus of discussion in the big tent. The process was not the smoothest, but a spirit of unity prevailed, and eventually an amended document was adopted with strong support.

Issue workshops were held in twenty areas. An open mic on the first morning allowed people to express "why we are here." One evening, former political prisoner Lolita Lebrón spoke, a definite highlight. Plenary sessions were held on the economic crisis; war, militarism, and liberation struggles; and struggles for democratic rights.

On Sunday morning, a prayer service was held, with celebrants singing the hymn "The Lord Hears the Cry of the Poor." People then left to gather on Central Park West next to Central Park. Numerous contingents from all sorts of movements and communities (tenants, the South Bronx, religious, labor, third world, peace, women, and others) showed up. In early afternoon, the march began, descending Seventh Avenue and ending at a stage set up in the middle of the street, right next to Madison Square Garden. Fifteen thousand people were present, as was the media, not losing an opportunity to cover a pre-convention event that was critical of the Democratic Party.

Participating speakers and musicians included Ella Baker, Ted Means, Rafael Cancel Miranda, Audre Lorde, Leslie Cagan, Roy Brown, William Winpisinger, José Rivera, Maggie Kuhn, and the Palestine Liberation Organization's (PLO's) UN representative.

The three days' activities received a great deal of press coverage. I remember hearing from a friend that the march was announced the day before on CBS national TV news. All the major New York City papers had big stories about it, as did the *Boston Globe*. The Associated Press also covered it.

The *Guardian*'s story reported that Winpisinger of the IAM "received some of the loudest cheers of the afternoon when he told the rally that President Jimmy Carter was a 'deceitful little hypocrite.' He got more cheers when he said, 'This country doesn't have two parties but one giant ideological party that feeds at the corporate troughs and gets fat on the misery and agony of those forced to carry the burden in this "free enterprise" system.'"[37]

Post-People's Convention, 1980–1982

The National Committee of the CPA, which had organized these events, met about a month later. In the evaluation of the three days of activities, "almost everyone felt that the Convention and Demonstration were successful actions, which furthered the unity of our movements. A consensus emerged that people want the Coalition to continue as a form in which progressives can work together on periodic mass actions and discuss political questions."[38] And for the next several years, that is what the CPA did.

One of the major actions that we became involved with was a mass mobilization to the Pentagon on May 3, 1981, in connection with the then-escalating U.S. role in the civil war in El Salvador. The newly elected Ronald Reagan administration was militarily supporting the repressive and brutal government there. Upwards of one hundred thousand people attended.

We supported Rivera in an independent electoral campaign (although running within the Democratic Party, he was going up against the party machine) for a city council at-large seat in the Bronx. This initiative was connected with a progressive insurgent campaign for mayor of New York City of Frank Barbaro, a state assemblyman with a lot of labor support.

Despite being outspent by an eight-to-one margin, Barbaro received 36 percent of the vote in a September Democratic primary election, running against incumbent mayor Ed Koch. As was written in a CPA newsletter, "Relying on people power and the efforts of a broad progressive coalition put together in the preceding months, Barbaro's victory testified to the growing strength and unity of the people's movement in this city. Not since last year's People's Convention and March on the Democratic Convention has it demonstrated such power."[39]

Barbaro also ran on an independent line, the Unity Party, for the general election, as he had pledged to do prior to the primary. With a lot fewer resources than the primary campaign, he received 13 percent of the vote.

Building on this developing momentum, we convened a meeting of forty organizations at the national headquarters of the IAM in Washington, D.C., in late April 1982. At that meeting, the role of electoral work in the process of building broad alliances on local levels around issues was the focus of much discussion. Several people emphasized the need for an ongoing organization or movement to work with candidates and candidates elected to office. A nine-point proposal was adopted to advance this process. Over the course of the year, an orientation toward what could be done evolved so that, in the 1984 presidential election year, we could have a political impact.

The year 1982 also saw the victory of Rivera in a campaign within the Democratic Party for state assemblyman. A number of CPA-related New Yorkers worked on Rivera's campaign. As described in the CPA newsletter:

> José's campaign was probably the only campaign that was fully multi-racial. Blacks, Latinos and whites worked together and worked together well. The public theme of the campaign was: José Rivera, the Candidate of All the People. Though there was a focus of work in the 75% of the district that was Black and Latino, the 25% that was white was also worked by campaign organizers.[40]

Harold Washington, Mel King, and Jesse Jackson

The mayoral election in Chicago in late February 1983 brought a huge win for progressives: the victory of Harold Washington in the Democratic primary and then in the general election. A mass movement in the African American community combined with serious divisions within the white and big business–dominated Chicago machine were the two principal reasons for this victory. Also key was the forging of a "Rainbow Coalition" type of campaign bringing together black people, Puerto Ricans, Chicanos, and progressive white people.

Something similar was happening in Boston. State Assemblyman Mel King, someone who had supported and attended meetings of the CPA, was running for mayor, bringing together what was being called a Boston Rainbow Coalition. In the first election in the fall, he came in first. Although he then lost in the November runoff between him and Ray Flynn, the second-highest vote getter, the successes of his campaign were inspiring.

Without question, the electoral victories of Washington and King had an impact on Jesse Jackson, who by the summer of 1983 was openly considering whether he should run for president in 1984. At a huge, 250,000-person rally in Washington, D.C., on August 28, on the twentieth anniversary of the 1963 march on Washington, it was clear when he spoke that many in the crowd were very excited about the prospect of his doing so.

In the fall of that year, a number of CPA leaders signed a letter to Jackson, encouraging him to run. We also began organizing for what became a February 11–12, 1984, conference at Howard University in Washington, D.C., to form a National Committee for Independent Political Action (NCIPA). Among the signers of the call for that conference were Digna Sánchez of the PSP, Clark Johnson of the IAM, Mel King, Arthur Kinoy, Carlotta Scott, an aide to Congressman Ron Dellums, and Congressman John Conyers.

In his keynote speech to the NCIPA Founding Conference, Kinoy said, "In this time of crisis the people are ready to move—in political and electoral struggles and upon the streets. The issue before this conference is how to build the movement both during the Jesse Jackson campaign and after it is over. We must here set up an organization national in scope and permanent in form, dedicated to building the unity and strength of the Rainbow Coalition."[41]

And the rest is history. The NCIPA continued on for many years, but the big new development was Jackson's electoral successes in 1984 and 1988 and the emergence of the National Rainbow Coalition.

Conclusion

As of this writing (June 2020), the United States has experienced two historic presidential campaigns led by Vermont senator Bernie Sanders. Although he will not win in 2020, these campaigns have dramatically brought to the surface and expanded a mass constituency of tens of millions for strong progressive, even socialist politics. Also, massive protests throughout the country have risen against the killings of innocent black men and women, laying bare a long history of racial injustice and police violence against black and brown people. We hear the cry throughout the country and around the world that "Black Lives Matter." The Left is on the upswing, leading the resistance against the regressive, reactionary, destructive Donald Trump presidency and the Trumpist Republican Party. A broadly based, electoral, issue-oriented, and activist independent progressive movement is very much alive and well.

Without a doubt, the work and the experiences of those who were part of the various Left unity efforts that the PSP was so central to from 1974 to the early 1980s were essential building blocks. They unquestionably plowed the hard ground and planted the tender seeds that keep growing and developing. *La lucha continúa* (The struggle continues).

NOTES

1. Arthur Kinoy, "Toward a Party of the People," 1975, 1, personal files of Ted Glick.
2. Ibid., 23.
3. Ibid., 15.
4. Ibid., 18.
5. Ibid., 31.
6. Ibid., 7.
7. Ibid., 9.
8. Ibid., 10.
9. Outreach letter by Antonio Rosa and Ted Glick, December 1973, personal files of Ted Glick.
10. Letter, personal files of Ted Glick.
11. Letter, personal files of Ted Glick.
12. "20,000 Demand Independence," *Puerto Rico Libre!* (November 1974): 1.
13. Ibid.
14. "Political Thesis of the Puerto Rican Socialist Party: The Socialist Alternative," North American Congress on Latin America, 1975, 46.
15. Political Statement and Discussion Document for Founding National Congress of the Puerto Rican Solidarity Committee, March 1–2, 1975, 11, personal files of Ted Glick.
16. Ibid., 11–12.
17. Ibid., 12.
18. Memo from Ted Glick to members of the Board of the Hard Times Conference, "The Proposed Agenda for the Hard Times Conference," personal files of Ted Glick.
19. "After 200 Years We Are Still Fighting for Our Freedom . . . ," July 4th Bulletin, April 1976, 1, personal files of Ted Glick.
20. Ibid.
21. "Criticizes Guardian July 4 position," *Guardian*, June 30, 1976. This article was written by Alfredo López for the *Guardian* but appears without a title. The *Guardian* editors headed the piece as appears here.
22. "Proposal Adopted at March 3–4, 1975, Meeting to Discuss a '76 Campaign," personal files of Ted Glick.
23. "Toward a Strategy for the National Election of 1976 as Amended and Adopted by the Task Force on 1976 Political Strategy," Mtangulizi Sanyika, Washington, D.C., April 25, 1975, 1, personal files of Ted Glick.
24. Ibid.
25. Ibid.

26. "Some Further Thoughts on the Road Ahead," Arthur Kinoy, early 1977, personal files of Ted Glick.

27. Ibid.

28. "Entering 1978: Taking Stock, Setting Direction," Peoples Alliance, 4, personal files of Ted Glick.

29. "Letter of Resignation Sent to Members of Labor-Management Group, by Douglas Fraser, President of United Auto Workers," Peoples Alliance *Bulletin*, Special Edition (October/December 1978), personal files of Ted Glick.

30. "Remarks by William W. Winpisinger, International President International Association of Machinists and Aerospace Workers at the IUD Conference on the Radical Right Wing, August 29, 1978," Peoples Alliance *Bulletin*, Special Edition (October/December 1978), personal files of Ted Glick.

31. "Independent Political Action Resolution Adopted by National Convention of United Electrical Workers Union, September 1978," Peoples Alliance *Bulletin*, Special Edition (October/December 1978), personal files of Ted Glick.

32. "Call for a Conference," personal files of Ted Glick.

33. "Movement and Party," published by the Peoples Alliance, 53, personal files of Ted Glick.

34. Notes of a meeting of the Peoples Alliance, December 1979, personal files of Ted Glick.

35. "An Invitation to a National Conference to Develop a Plan of Action at the Democratic Convention in New York City in August," personal files of Ted Glick.

36. June 24 statement of the Peoples Alliance, personal files of Ted Glick.

37. *The Guardian*, August 20, 1980, page not available, personal files of Ted Glick.

38. Notes on an evaluation of the People's Convention, personal files of Ted Glick.

39. Coalition for a People's Alternative Newsletter, November/December 1981, personal files of Ted Glick.

40. Coalition for a People's Alternative Newsletter, November/December 1982, personal files of Ted Glick.

41. "Weekend Conference Launches National Committee for Independent Political Action," personal files of Ted Glick.

From March to Movement?

The Bicentennial Without Colonies
and the Peoples Alliance

ALYSSA RIBEIRO

n the summer of 1976, public officials warned of "extremist minorities" and "terrorists" who could potentially disrupt Bicentennial celebrations.[1] They were referring to a coalition spearheaded by the Puerto Rican Socialist Party (PSP), which drew fifty thousand supporters to a Philadelphia rally. Demonstrators gathered there to share their left-leaning visions for the country and belie the notion that they were "divided and weak."[2] Yet unlike major demonstrations in previous years, the Bicentennial protest and the subsequent effort to sustain its energy have attracted scant attention from scholars.[3]

While the July 4th Coalition (J4C) succeeded in drawing supporters to its "Bicentennial Without Colonies" event, it suffered from reactionary responses by elected officials, limited coverage by mainstream media, and festering divisions within its own ranks. Attempts to turn the coalition into a more permanent Peoples Alliance foundered. Drawing upon archival research and press coverage, this chapter illuminates the constraints that this coalition encountered. I argue that the J4C encountered challenges in two key areas: first, state and mainstream media efforts substantially diminished the coalition's legitimacy in the public sphere. Second, the coalition struggled to formulate an agenda acceptable to all stakeholders and an executable program.

Bicentennial Visions

While planners in Philadelphia had earlier envisioned grand celebrations that would draw tens of millions of visitors to key sites, local controversy swirled over the expense, scale, and location of the city's official events. Ultimately, the city held a relatively muted official Bicentennial observance.[4]

Juan Mari Brás initiated the call for a "Bicentennial Without Colonies" in front of an audience of twenty thousand at the October 1974 National Day of Solidarity with Puerto Rico held in Madison Square Garden. In January 1976, representatives from thirty-five organizations gathered at a conference to call for a mass demonstration in Philadelphia to "observe the bicentennial in protest and celebrate our unity in struggle." Three particular areas of concern were labor rights, political rights, and U.S. foreign policy, and the group hoped to gather "the widest possible spectrum of forces in this country who are concerned about U.S. domestic and foreign policy."[5] Even more pointedly, they hoped to build "a national coalition with a broad enough base to bring hundreds of thousands of people to Philadelphia on the fourth." Organizers believed that "high priority should be given to labor unions, churches, women's groups and Afro-American organizations and other national organizations." At the regional level, membership would be open "to any group that agrees with the general thrust of the call." Critically, early organizers recognized that the composition of the coalition would in many ways determine its legitimacy. Numbers and political orientation mattered. They noted "the higher proportion of grassroots groups with some kind of a social base to 'left' political organizations, the healthier the coalition and the greater its mobilizing potential."[6]

The demonstration was intended to reestablish the progressive Left as a force to be reckoned with amid many white Americans' political migration to the Right. Organizers recalled the power of demonstrations like those in the 1960s to "give strength to people's work and . . . focus the diverse problems of all of us" and called them "an effective means of [political] pressure."[7] Such action was again necessary because "the government sees us as divided and weak. But tens of thousands of us will march in Philadelphia on July 4th to show that we are outgrowing our divisions; that our many struggles are part of a powerful movement for change in this country and the world; and to show that only a unified response can defeat these attacks."[8]

PSP representatives quickly set about reaching out to progressive individuals and organizations to ask for endorsements.[9] After the largest cities, they planned to make contact in "Boston, Chicago, New Haven, Newark, Pittsburg[h], Hartford, Buffalo, Atlanta, Milwaukee, [and] Madison, among others."[10] Such locations were home to substantial black, Latino, and/or student populations, which the PSP envisioned as its target audience. Some PSP cadre were shifted from other party priorities entirely to plan and execute the demonstration as the event drew nearer. As PSP leader José E. Velázquez observed, the party had quickly become an organization with an unmatched ability to mobilize the masses and get the unwieldy U.S. Left to collaborate, if only briefly.[11]

Sound the Alarm

In mid-May 1976, *Washington Post* columnist Jack Anderson sounded the alarm about terrorist disruptions of Bicentennial celebrations. Citing law enforcement documents, Anderson captured readers' attention with the prospect of a Trojan horse–style tanker truck. While appearing normal on the outside, such a vehicle's tank would house "a terrorist office, dormitory and arsenal."[12] Anderson warned that the militant Fuerzas Armadas de Liberación Nacional (FALN) "may work with the [PSP], controlled by Fidel Castro, to disrupt the bicentennial."[13] The PSP vehemently objected to its peaceful aims being portrayed as connected to the FALN, a group that had claimed responsibility for bombings in the United States the previous year.

Congressional hearings followed in June to assess "Threats to the Peaceful Observance of the Bicentennial." Such witnesses as William R. Kintner, a political science professor at the University of Pennsylvania, again tied the PSP to the FALN as well as to the Prairie Fire Organizing Committee and the Weather Underground. He also pointed the finger at "radical groups, ranging from the Communist Party, Socialist Workers Party, Guardian, Workers World Party, and the Yippies [the Youth International Party], to an array of violence prone organizations like the Black Panthers, the American Indian Movement, and the Palestinian Solidarity Committee."[14] And especially worrisome was the fact that the coalition was headed by the PSP's Alfredo López, who Kintner claimed had been "formerly identified with the pro-terrorist tendency in the Socialist Workers Party." Kintner even went so far as to infer that the PSP was controlled by the Cuban intelligence service.[15]

For some policy makers, the J4C seemed to signal that radical and leftist groups were successfully building coalitions and would potentially present more formidable opposition. These officials were especially unnerved by large-scale meetings and rallies because they feared disorder, property destruction, and physical violence. Such gatherings as the Revolutionary Peoples Constitutional Convention of 1970 had been going on for years, but they were much less frequent by the mid-1970s. In 1974, the PSP had sponsored a solidarity rally at Madison Square Garden that included such speakers as Angela Davis, Jane Fonda, and Russell Means of the American Indian Movement (AIM).[16] In early 1976, the Hard Times Conference had brought about 2,500 activists, including representatives from the PSP, AIM, and the World Workers Party, to Chicago.[17] According to Kintner, "One of the most important actions taken by the [Hard Times] conference was the approval of a proposal by the Puerto Rican Socialist Party for a militant mass demonstration in Philadelphia on July 4th."[18]

The J4C quickly drew the interest of the Federal Bureau of Investigation (FBI). Prominent activists in the PSP, the African People's Socialist Party, and the J4C's local Philadelphia office reported being visited and harassed by federal agents.[19] Two members of the PSP were even subpoenaed by a New York grand jury attempting to link them to the FALN.[20]

Best-Laid Plans

Coalition forces beyond Philadelphia set about coordinating logistics for the event, including transportation, security, and legal representation. The J4C gathered representatives from sixty participating organizations at a national conference in late March to plan the event's themes and speakers.[21] Discussions at this meeting highlighted some of the tensions within the coalition, such as a three-hour conversation on how and whether the American flag should be displayed at the protest. Ultimately, a majority of the planners rejected its use because they saw it as a symbol of oppression.[22] The resulting program centered primarily around the twin priorities of Puerto Rico's independence and pressing domestic struggles, making relatively brief reference to broader movements for third-world liberation.[23] By June, the J4C had collected nearly $17,000 in contributions and taken out $28,000 in loans to help finance the event.[24] Funding was critical for publicity efforts, including a full-page ad in the New York Times, which alone cost more than $15,000.[25] Requests for $10 donations from endorsing individuals and institutions could not hope to match expenses.[26]

The New York headquarters reserved eighty buses to carry demonstrators from New York to Philadelphia at a cost of $7 round-trip per passenger. Demonstrators were advised to leave early if they were driving and to bring a lunch that would not spoil.[27] In Ohio, Dayton organizers had a rally in June to promote the Philadelphia demonstration.[28] In California, Bay Area J4C organizers held parties, dances, and concerts to fundraise for the effort.[29] One such event reportedly drew a crowd of twelve hundred strong.[30] As the date drew nearer, the PSP's newspaper Claridad posted a list of locations, including Boston, Hartford, and Chicago, where demonstrators could join the "people's caravans" to travel the rest of the way to Philadelphia.[31]

Back in Philadelphia, local planning was an uphill battle. The coalition faced opposition from multiple fronts. It was difficult to secure approval from city officials. Permits for the event came only at the end of a protracted battle with the city of Philadelphia. Fairmount Park Commission initially denied an event permit because it claimed the park was "reserved for the people" and that city services would be absorbed by the expected two million visitors to the Independence Hall area.[32] Confusion between the J4C and another group called Rich Off Our Backs—July 4th Coalition further clouded the process.[33]

Community outreach was another concern; some black community leaders were wary of an effort initiated by outsiders. The J4C used a local member organization, the Black Anti-Bicentennial Action Committee, to reach out to residents of North Philadelphia. Although its members canvassed and leafletted the neighborhood, the group apparently "failed to touch base with the establishment of North Philadelphia." Black leader Cecil Moore therefore threatened to block the march any way he could because he was insulted that the local community had not been consulted about the march's route. A local church and the Philadelphia Welfare Rights Organization also expressed concern.[34] Hundreds of residents went so far as to sign a petition asking the city to reject the J4C's permit. Charles Bowser emphasized that "neighborhood objections were based on crowds, traffic and trash problems—not on philosophic difference with the July 4th protestors."[35] Additionally, many residents mistakenly believed that the city was "dumping" the demonstration on their neighborhood to protect downtown areas.[36]

These concerns prompted new negotiations between the city and the J4C. While organizers had originally proposed to march from Thirty-Third Street to Fairmount Park along Diamond, they shifted the route through North Philadelphia considerably after conferring with local residents.[37] With this compromise, local leaders endorsed the march. By late June, the North Philadelphia community was "ready to embrace the July Fourth Coalition."[38] Some residents understandably remained apathetic; Doris Walker told reporters, "That parade thing going up and down the street won't mean anything to a lot of people. Instead of that parade stuff they ought to give me more money in my check."[39]

Publicity was also a problem due to the mainstream media's refusal to advertise the event. The J4C threatened to complain to the Federal Communications Commission because major stations in New York, Boston, and Washington, D.C., declined to sell it time for announcements. Local Philadelphia channels also denied the coalition ad time but allowed representatives to express their views on local programs.[40]

As the date approached, Philadelphia mayor Frank Rizzo requested fifteen thousand federal troops to better handle demonstrations that he feared would spiral out of control.[41] Even organizations unaffiliated with the J4C strongly objected to this prospect of militarization.[42] Rizzo's call for troops to be armed with sidearms as opposed to rifles mattered little. When federal officials declined to supply soldiers, Rizzo next tried for state National Guard reinforcements, also unsuccessfully.[43] Rizzo told a local newspaper that "the Federal Government is playing politics with people's lives and, if there are disturbances in Philadelphia on July 4th, the blood is on their hands."[44] Resigned to handle any Bicentennial disruptions with local law enforcement, the mayor ultimately warned people away from Philadelphia entirely. Rizzo's grandstanding, not coincidentally, occurred just as a recall campaign to remove him from office was getting started.[45]

A Fragile Coalition

The J4C was an ambitiously broad coalition that attempted to include "just about every political persuasion to the left of Jimmy Carter."[46] Concerned that the political establishment would paint it as radical, the coalition consciously sought to demonstrate wide appeal. The imprint of major organizations and a lengthy list of affiliates were thus desirable.

Somewhat disingenuously, by using individuals' organizational affiliations in their promotional materials "for identification purposes," the coalition also implied endorsement by larger organizations. A partial list of supporters published in *Claridad*, for instance, included affiliates of the National Lawyers Guild, the *Philadelphia Tribune*, and the Democratic Party of New York. Some organizations unsurprisingly pushed back, hasty to avoid association with a coalition that seemed politically risky. Ed Nakawatase of the American Friends Service Committee (AFSC), for instance, sought to clarify that he and colleagues endorsed the event solely "as individuals."[47] Other AFSC administrators ultimately decided not to publicly affiliate because the coalition's positions were not "altogether congruous" with those of the AFSC.[48] One AFSC official eventually fired off a letter to the J4C, asking it to remove any mention of the AFSC from the coalition's letterhead due to avoid false assumptions about the larger organization's support.[49] There were plenty of other names to go around, though. A partial list of supporters contained 141 names and stretched nearly four pages long.[50]

Meanwhile, others worried that the J4C's specific stance on too many issues inherently limited its base of support. David McReynolds of the War Resisters League opined, "The Philadelphia [call to action] is too specific, too abrasive, too militant. Too . . . should I use the word? . . . revolutionary." The J4C was in the difficult position of trying to reconcile "pacifists and Marxists and Puerto Rican nationalists."[51]

Some members quickly grew disenchanted. Reverend Muhammad Kenyatta, a black leader from Philadelphia, resigned from the national board and implied that white radicals were manipulating the Puerto Rican community for their own aims. Wilfredo Rojas, a former member of the Young Lords and Philadelphia point person for the J4C, dismissed the accusations as "an insult" and downplayed the resignation's effects on the march.

Kenyatta further betrayed the J4C by testifying in U.S. district court that the demonstrations might turn violent.[52]

Overall, though, many nationally recognized figures supported the effort through to the end. Southern Christian Leadership Conference (SCLC) head Ralph Abernathy, for instance, telegrammed Father Paul Washington in Philadelphia to express support for the march and say, "We join you in this call for support from the black community."[53] Arthur Kinoy, an attorney known for his work in civil liberties cases like that of the Chicago Seven, promoted unity among the activists. He was the author of the "Kinoy paper," an eighty-page proposal circulated in 1973 setting forth principals for a progressive political party that would steer through the Left's previous vacillations between electoral and revolutionary strategies. In the following years, he served as "spiritual and intellectual leader" of the Mass Party Organizing Committee (MPOC).[54] Kinoy also helped broker compromise in person. Black leader Saladin Muhammad recalled that during the Bicentennial campaign, "When some 'white left' forces tried to attack and isolate Revolutionary Black Nationalist forces after we had won the right for the coalition to march, telling the Native Americans that Black people wanted to lead the march through our community and in front of the Native Americans, Kinoy helped to arrange a meeting between AIM leader Vernon Bellecourt and myself. The African Americans and Native Americans walked together side-by-side leading the massive march."[55]

The coalition stressed different grievances to various member constituencies, depending on geography and social identity. New York activists criticized the closure of daycares and hospitals, layoffs, and the lockout of City University of New York (CUNY) students and faculty amid the fallout of the city's fiscal crisis.[56] References to the Bicentennial protest even popped up at a relatively small demonstration by New York parents against school closures.[57] In Dayton, organizers critiqued Ohio welfare cuts and tuition hikes.[58] Other brochures targeted particular demographics. For instance, "A Call to the Women of America" criticized the anti-abortion movement, affirmative-action losses, unemployment, daycare closures, and welfare cutbacks.[59] A separate brochure aimed at African American audiences proclaimed, "We will not accept another two hundred years of inferior education, house-bombings, poverty, urban cutbacks, unemployment and FBI-CIA destruction of our beloved leaders." To attract workers, the J4C emphasized "unemployment, inflation, speed-ups and union-busting that is pushing our back to the wall."[60]

In Philadelphia, the coalition found solidarity among an array of community groups. DYKETACTICS, a multiracial lesbian political group, joined in larger protests while also coordinating some of its own activities.[61] Members of the national coalition credited the Afrikan People's Party with mobilizing black communities in Philadelphia.[62]

The Fourth of July

On the day of reckoning, demonstrators opened the morning with an inter-faith religious service at the Church of the Advocate.[63] Upon emerging, they found a heavy police presence, including approximately three hundred offi-cers on the ground and helicopters overhead. At the coalition's request, the police removed sharpshooters from North Philadelphia rooftops.[64] Desig-nated coalition marshals worked to ensure that the protest remained non-violent and that demonstrators were not subject to physical attack.[65]

Across town, President Gerald Ford spoke at Independence Hall. There, a separate police presence, including "officers, vans, dogs, horses, buses, spare barriers and weapons" stood between protestors and official ceremo-nies in a "deliberate, rational and strategic" attempt to contain any disrup-tion.[66] Despite the heavy police presence, the march and rally proceeded so peacefully that the many lawyers mobilized to provide legal aid for demon-strators had little work to do.[67] Even the conservative *Philadelphia Inquirer* admitted that there was not "a single arrest or disturbance."[68]

Turnout was strong. Estimates ranged from ten thousand to sixty thousand, with most sources settling on around twenty thousand to forty thousand participants.[69] The gathering was called "probably the largest mul-tiracial political demonstration in many years" and the "largest political demonstration of any sort" since the end of the Vietnam War.[70]

Enough folks joined the march that the column stretched twelve blocks long. Along the route, marchers covered thirty-two blocks, or approximately two miles, of North Philadelphia neighborhoods.[71] They were greeted by "raised fists and Black liberation flags which hung from the windows of many of the tenements."[72] According to columnist Harry Amana, "My beautiful Black Brothers and Sisters from North Philly and elsewhere came out in droves, picked up the chants, participated in the parade for blocks at a time and sold soft drinks and food to the marchers."[73]

The crowd was diverse, including "domestic workers . . . poor rural white . . . child care activists . . . prisoners rights organizers . . . [and] farm workers" from across the nation.[74] More than four hundred organizations sent representatives.[75] And the assembly held far more meaning for its par-ticipants than "dilly[ing] around a cracked bell with no significance to grassroots people."[76]

The *New York Times* described the rally as "an echo of the protest days of the 1960s."[77] A *Philadelphia Tribune* columnist called it a "people's victory" that resembled the Poor People's Campaign of 1968.[78] Speakers included

Figure 15.1. Bicentennial Without Colonies.

Elaine Brown of the Black Panthers and Karen Crow, the president of the National Organization for Women. They were joined by major civil rights figures, such as Ella Baker and former Attica inmate Frank "Big Black" Smith. Altogether about thirty speakers engaged the crowd for three hours and stopped then only due to rain.[79]

Across town, official celebration activities were muted. One observer estimated that only thirty-five thousand of the scheduled seventy-five thousand participants showed up for the city's parade, suggesting that the J4C managed to attract a larger crowd.[80] This fact, of course, was left out of most mainstream media portrayals.

Overall, though, many people avoided Philadelphia altogether. Rizzo's warnings about violent threats combined with concerns about congestion discouraged potential visitors. Hotels, which had originally worried about being able to supply enough rooms for Bicentennial crowds, ended up with a 25 percent vacancy rate.[81] The J4C staged smaller demonstrations in San Francisco, San Antonio, Seattle, and Los Angeles as well,[82] but those received paltry attention compared to the main parade and rally in Philadelphia.

Alliance in the Aftermath?

After the Bicentennial, the J4C's national board worked to assemble a more durable "Peoples Alliance" by calling a national conference. Organizers perceived "a moment of great opportunity to the progressive forces of this country." They rightly realized that building a more permanent coalition would be more difficult but felt compelled to try to take the "second step" after the Bicentennial protest.[83]

Aside from Puerto Rican independence, organizers believed that their political messages had been lacking. The long list of speakers further diffused messages, and rain cut the program short. They also regretted the "relative under-representation of white working-class people as well as Black people." They reflected that "too much ideological purity" surrounding anti-imperialism might "exclude important sectors" of the larger progressive movement. Rather than positioning themselves as merely "anti-racist, anti-sexist, [and] anti-imperialist," the alliance needed to express a more "positive articulation" of alternatives. Remaining debt of $29,000 was another concern, and the Continuations Committee appealed to local coalitions to help pay it off as a shared burden.[84]

A working paper noted that Philadelphia had offered "a glimpse of the potential power and strength of combined and unified action. Our problem has been how to translate this bare beginning understanding into a continuing, growing, and developing reality in the face of the most intense internal and external obstacles to moving along the path to victory."[85] Things proceeded slowly. Organizers reflected, "We were unable to follow up on that massive mobilization because of vague and impractical objectives and a lack of explicit political consensus on what issues to concentrate coalition effort."[86]

Compounding their difficulty, the Bicentennial action had been neglected by mainstream media. A study of eighteen major newspapers found no front-page stories; what coverage it got was buried between snippets about other events. By largely ignoring the "Bicentennial Without Colonies" protest, the press managed to "turn an event attended by tens of thousands of people gathered from all corners of the United States into a nonevent."[87] Therefore, the J4C could not even fully capitalize on a wave of publicity surrounding a successful demonstration.

It took many months to come together, but the coalition finally held an organizing conference in May 1977. Five guiding themes surrounded employment, urban life, U.S. imperialism, government repression, and nuclear threats. Attendees likened the political moment to the Great Depression, claiming that more people were open to change.[88] Ted Glick acknowledged that the meeting included "open discussion and frank disagreement" but added that the resulting program was adopted "almost unanimously."[89]

In addition to ideological skirmishes, competing geographic scales presented a formidable challenge. Many groups that had been active in the Bicentennial campaign wanted to remain focused on the local concerns most immediate to their base. Other leaders stressed the necessity of national action. And a third, smaller contingent remained more committed to broad linkages with liberation movements in the third world.

Such tensions contributed to the PSP's relinquishing its leadership role in the Peoples Alliance. By reducing the organization's participation to better reflect Puerto Ricans' relatively small demographic representation in the United States, PSP representatives believed that they could focus more fully on liberating the island and tending to workers' concerns.[90] Without continued coordination from the PSP, though, the Peoples Alliance withered.

Ultimately, it proved difficult to convert the energy from the Bicentennial into a more permanent coalition, and the effort slowly receded. In part, planning sapped organizational capacity. Meanwhile, groups felt torn between local concerns, national action, and transnational solidarity. Overall, the "Bicentennial Without Colonies" event offered a sense of possibility for progressive mobilization in the mid-1970s while also outlining the challenges of sustaining broad and unwieldy coalitions. It was also a prime example of how quickly growing Latino populations, who still play a minor role in most historical accounts, influenced national politics in an era of intractable social, political, and economic strains.

NOTES

1. William Kintner, quoted in *Threats to the Peaceful Observance of the Bicentennial: Hearing before the Subcommittee to Investigate the Administration of the Internal Security Act and Other Internal Security Laws of the Committee on the Judiciary, United States Senate, 94th Cong., 2d Sess., June 18, 1976* (Washington, DC: Government Printing Office, 1976), 9, 11.

2. July 4th Coalition, "What's to Celebrate?" 1976, Box 4, Folder 22, M2001-024 Anne Farrar Papers, Wisconsin Historical Society, Madison, Wisconsin (hereafter Farrar Papers).

3. For existing coverage, see José E. Velázquez, "Coming Full Circle: The Puerto Rican Socialist Party, U.S. Branch," in *The Puerto Rican Movement: Voices from the Diaspora*, ed. Andrés Torres and José E. Velázquez (Philadelphia: Temple University Press, 1998), 54–60; John Bodnar, *Remaking America: Public Memory, Commemoration, and Patriotism in the Twentieth Century* (Princeton, NJ: Princeton University Press, 1992), 236–237; Christopher Capozzola, "'It Makes You Want to Believe in the Country': Celebrating the Bicentennial in an Age of Limits," in *America in the Seventies*, ed. Beth Bailey and David Farber (Lawrence: University Press of Kansas, 2004), 41–43; Meg Starr, "'Hit Them Harder': Leadership, Solidarity, and the Puerto Rican Independence Movement," in *The Hidden 1970s: Histories of Radicalism*, ed. Dan Berger (New Brunswick, NJ: Rutgers University Press, 2010), 143; Aaron J. Leonard and Conor A. Gallagher, *Heavy Radicals: The FBI's Secret War on America's Maoists* (Winchester, UK: Zero Books, 2014), 195–200; Pat Lauderdale and Rhoda E. Estep, "The Bicentennial Protest: An Examination of Hegemony in the Definition of Deviant Political Activity," in *A Political Analysis of Deviance*, ed. Pat Lauderdale (Minneapolis: University of Minnesota

Press, 1980), 72–91; and Lorrin Thomas and Aldo A. Lauria-Santiago, *Rethinking the Struggle for Puerto Rican Rights* (New York: Routledge, 2019), 143.

4. Andrew Feffer, "Show Down in Center City: Staging Redevelopment and Citizenship in Bicentennial Philadelphia, 1974–1977," *Journal of Urban History* 30, no. 6 (2004): 800.

5. Mario Torres, "Bicentennial Demo Planned for Phila.," *Claridad*, February 1, 1976, Wisconsin Historical Society Microforms (all *Claridad* articles from Wisconsin Historical Society Microforms).

6. "Bulletin of the July 4th Interim Committee," 1976, 2, M325 Centro de Acción Social Autónomo, Box 32, Folder 5, Special Collections, Stanford University (hereafter CASA).

7. Ella Baker and Noam Chomsky to friend, 1976, Box 191, Folder 31, Collection 1083, Southern Christian Leadership Conference, Manuscript, Archives, and Rare Book Library, Emory University (hereafter SCLC).

8. July 4th Coalition, "What's to Celebrate?"

9. Maritza Arrastía to Ed Nakawasake, January 27, 1976, CRD Administration 1976, Committees and Organizations, July 4th Coalition, Folder 2921, American Friends Service Committee Archives, Philadelphia (hereafter AFSC).

10. "Bulletin of the July 4th Interim Committee," 3.

11. Velázquez, "Coming Full Circle," 56–57.

12. Jack Anderson, "Terrorist 'Fish' in a Sea of Tourists," *Washington Post*, May 16, 1976.

13. Ibid.

14. *Threats to the Peaceful Observance of the Bicentennial*, 11; "Senators Warned of July 4 Strife," *New York Times*, June 19, 1976, CRD Administration 1976, Committees and Organizations, July 4th Coalition, Folder 2921, AFSC.

15. *Threats to the Peaceful Observance of the Bicentennial*, 20.

16. Ibid., 21.

17. Ibid., 15; "Conference Supports Phila. Demo," *Claridad*, February 8, 1976.

18. *Threats to the Peaceful Observance of the Bicentennial*, 15.

19. Margot Hornblower, "FBI Probes Coalition," *Washington Post*, May 16, 1976.

20. Laura Murray, "The Radicals Are Coming July 4!" *Philadelphia Daily News*, June 29, 1976, July 4th Coalition, Bulletin Clippings, Special Collections Research Center, Temple University Libraries (hereafter SCRC).

21. "Conference Will Map July 4 Plans," *Claridad*, March 7, 1976; Tamara Ferrer, "Calls US Conference on Bicentennial," *Claridad*, March 28, 1976.

22. Ed Nakawatase to Barbara Moffett, "July 4th Coalition," July 22, 1976, 2, CRD Administration 1976, Committees and Organizations, July 4th Coalition, Folder 2921, AFSC.

23. "After 200 Years We Are Still Fighting for Our Freedom," *July 4th Bulletin*, April 1976, Box 191, Folder 31, SCLC.

24. "Financial Report—July 4th Coalition, Totals: January–June 1976," n.d., CRD Administration 1976, Committees and Organizations, July 4th Coalition, Folder 2921, AFSC.

25. Dave Dellinger et al. to friend, June 22, 1976, Box 191, Folder 31, SCLC.

26. Barbara Webster to friend, June 24, 1976, Box 191, Folder 31, SCLC.

27. July 4th Coalition, "What's to Celebrate?"

28. Dayton July 4th Coalition, "Press Release," June 1976, Box 4, Folder 22, Farrar Papers.

29. "Benefit Party for July 4th Coalition," 1976, Box 4, Folder 22, Farrar Papers; "A Calendar of Upcoming Events," 1976, Box 4, Folder 22, Farrar Papers; "A Boogie / Un Baile," 1976, Box 4, Folder 22, Farrar Papers.

30. "July 4th Coalition Benefit Concert Successful," *The Black Panther*, July 3, 1976.

31. "Join the People's Caravans," *Claridad*, July 6, 1976.

32. "Coalition Rally Nixed for July 4," *Philadelphia Daily News*, April 14, 1976, General Administration 1976, Committees and Organizations, July 4th Coalition, Folder 3945, AFSC; "The Right to Disagree," *Philadelphia Inquirer*, April 14, 1976, General Administration 1976, Committees and Organizations, July 4th Coalition, Folder 3945, AFSC.

33. *We've Carried the Rich, etc. v. City of Philadelphia*, 414 F. Supp. 611 (1976).

34. John T. Gillespie and Joe Sharkey, "Cecil Moore Threatens to Block July 4th Parade," *Philadelphia Evening Bulletin*, June 25, 1976, SCRC.

35. Gunter David and Harmon Y. Gordon, "N. Phila. Groups Ask Rejection of Coalition Parade Permits," *Philadelphia Evening Bulletin*, June 6, 1976, SCRC.

36. Murray, "The Radicals Are Coming July 4!"

37. Gillespie and Sharkey, "Cecil Moore Threatens to Block July 4th Parade."

38. Laura Murray, "March Route OKd for Rebel Group," *Philadelphia Daily News*, June 29, 1976.

39. Joe Davidson and Lou Antosh, "Blacks Say North Phila. Decay Cramps Their July 4th Spirit," *Philadelphia Evening Bulletin*, June 27, 1976, SCRC.

40. "Suit Threatened," *Philadelphia Evening Bulletin*, July 2, 1976, SCRC.

41. "U.S. Bars Troops for Philadelphia," *New York Times*, June 22, 1976, CRD Administration 1976, Committees and Organizations, July 4th Coalition, Folder 2921, AFSC.

42. July 4th Coalition, "Coalition to Continue After July 4th, Blasts Media Coverage of Bicentennial Events," July 9, 1976, General Administration 1976, Committees and Organizations, July 4th Coalition, Folder 3945, AFSC.

43. "U.S. Bars Troops for Philadelphia."

44. Quoted in Lauderdale and Estep, "The Bicentennial Protest," 80.

45. Frank J. Donner, *Protectors of Privilege: Red Squads and Police Repression in Urban America* (Berkeley: University of California Press, 1990), 236–237.

46. Murray, "The Radicals Are Coming July 4!"

47. Ed Nakawatase to Lou Schneider, "July 4th Coalition," May 5, 1976, 2, General Administration 1976, Committees and Organizations, July 4th Coalition, Folder 3945, AFSC.

48. Lou Schneider to General Consultative Group, "July 4th Coalition," May 28, 1976, General Administration 1976, Committees and Organizations, July 4th Coalition, Folder 3945, AFSC.

49. John A. Sullivan to July 4th Coalition, June 23, 1976, General Administration 1976, Committees and Organizations, July 4th Coalition, Folder 3945, AFSC.

50. "Partial List of Sponsoring Individuals—July 4th Coalition," 1976, Box 191 Folder 31, SCLC.

51. David McReynolds to Ted Howard, May 18, 1976, Folder 2921, July 4th Coalition, CRD Administration, 1976, AFSC.

52. Murray, "The Radicals Are Coming July 4!"

53. Ralph Abernathy to Paul Washington, Mailgram, June 28, 1976, Box 191, Folder 31, SCLC.

54. Brian Lloyd, "The Kinoy Paper and the Passing of 1960s Radicalism," *Science and Society* 67, no. 4 (Winter 2003/2004): 431, 435–436; Ted Glick, "A 'Party of the People,'"

New York Beacon, October 20, 2005; see also Kinoy's autobiography, Arthur Kinoy, *Rights on Trial: The Odyssey of a People's Lawyer* (Cambridge, MA: Harvard University Press, 1983).

55. Saladin Muhammad, "I First Met Arthur in 1975," *Independent Politics News: A Publication of the Independent Progressive Politics Network* 7, no. 4 (January 2004): 13.

56. July 4th Coalition, "What's to Celebrate?"

57. "Community Backs July 4th Demo," *Claridad*, April 18, 1976.

58. Dayton July 4th Coalition, "Press Release."

59. July 4th Coalition, "A Call to the Women of America," 1976, Box 4, Folder 22, Farrar Papers.

60. July 4th Coalition, "Brothers and Sisters, Workers throughout the Land," 1976, Box 4, Folder 22, Farrar Papers.

61. Paola Bacchetta, "Dyketactics! Notes toward an Un-Silencing," in *Smash the Church, Smash the State! The Early Years of Gay Liberation*, ed. Tommi Avicolli Mecca (San Francisco: City Lights Books, 2009), 218.

62. "July 4th Organizer's Bulletin," March 7, 1977, 3, CASA.

63. "Bicentennial ithout Colonies," *Claridad*, June 27, 1976; "A Community Celebration of Struggle and Hope," July 4, 1976, Box 191, Folder 31, SCLC.

64. Gunter David, "30 Talk at Rally in Park," *Philadelphia Evening Bulletin*, July 5, 1976, SCRC.

65. Ibid.

66. Neil Smith, "Symbol, Space and the Bicentennial," *Antipode* 9, no. 2 (1977): 77.

67. "Lawyers at Protests Had Little to Do," *Philadelphia Evening Bulletin*, July 7, 1976, SCRC.

68. Mike Zielenziger and Rod Nordland, "Radical Groups March Peacefully," *Philadelphia Inquirer*, July 5, 1976, CRD Administration 1976, Committees and Organizations, July 4th Coalition, Folder 2921, AFSC.

69. Nakawatase to Moffett, 1; David, "30 Talk at Rally in Park."

70. Nakawatase to Moffett, 1.

71. David, "30 Talk at Rally in Park."

72. Zoraida Santiago, "Community Welcomes Marchers," *Claridad*, July 11, 1976.

73. Harry Amana, "Bicen Protest Resembles 'Poor People's March,'" *Philadelphia Tribune*, July 1976, CRD Administration 1976, Committees and Organizations, July 4th Coalition, Folder 2921, AFSC.

74. Ibid.

75. Nakawatase to Moffett.

76. Amana, "Bicen Protest Resembles 'Poor People's March.'"

77. John Kifner, "2 Counterrallies in Philadelphia," *New York Times*, July 5, 1976.

78. Amana, "Bicen Protest Resembles 'Poor People's March.'"

79. David, "30 Talk at Rally in Park"; "Bicentennial Without Colonies."

80. Amana, "Bicen Protest Resembles 'Poor People's March'"; July 4th Coalition, "Coalition to Continue after July 4th," 2.

81. Scott Heimer, "Fear of Violence Hurting Hotels," *Philadelphia Daily News*, June 29, 1976; Stanley Carr, "Notes: Room at the Inn, after All," *New York Times*, July 4, 1976.

82. "July 4th Coalition Denounces Federal Harassment," *Black Panther*, July 3, 1976.

83. "A Call to a National Conference to Build a People's Alliance," 1976, CRD Administration 1976, Committees and Organizations, July 4th Coalition, Folder 2921, AFSC.

84. "Report of Continuations Committee Meeting," July 22, 1976, 2, CRD Administration 1976, Committees and Organizations, July 4th Coalition, Folder 2921, AFSC.

85. "A Working Paper: A Perspective on Building the Alliance," February 1977, 3, CASA.

86. "July 4th Organizer's Bulletin," March 7, 1977, 1.

87. Lauderdale and Estep, "The Bicentennial Protest," 73.

88. "July 4th Organizer's Bulletin," May 1, 1977, 3, CASA; "Call for a National 'People's Alliance,'" *Black Panther*, June 18, 1977; "July 4th Coalition Appeal to Black Communities," *Black Panther*, June 26, 1976.

89. Judy MacLean, "July 4th Coalition Forms Alliance," *In These Times*, June 8, 1977.

90. "Informe Político, Comité Seccional, Reunión Del 14 y 15 de Mayo, 1977," May 15, 1977, 7, Partido Socialista Puertorriqueño, personal collection of Andrés Torres.

IV

Conclusion

Conclusion

José E. Velázquez, Carmen V. Rivera,
and Andrés Torres

In Retrospect: Achievements, Contributions, and Mistakes

This book discusses how a renewed Puerto Rican Left emerged in the United States in the late 1960s. A revitalized radicalism served as a reaffirmation of Puerto Rican identity, particularly among second-generation Boricuas. The Puerto Rican Socialist Party's (PSP's) U.S. Branch (*Seccional*) became the largest of these new formations and the one that endured the longest. At its peak, in the 1970s, it established and sustained a broad presence in the Puerto Rican diaspora, organized in forty-nine chapters (*núcleos* or nuclei) across eleven states in the Northeast, the Midwest, and the West Coast. A decline in membership and reach began in the early 1980s, ending with its eventual dissolution in 1993. The impact and contributions of its members and organizing efforts are still felt to this day within the Puerto Rican community and movements for social change in the United States.

The PSP merged a national liberation movement with socioeconomic struggles where Puerto Ricans lived and worked, organizing Puerto Rican workers in major U.S. cities, in the steel plants of Gary, Indiana, and migrant workers in the fields of the Northeast through the Asociación de Trabajadores Agrícolas (Association of Agricultural Workers [ATA]). It played important leadership roles for tenants' rights in New York and Chicago; for education and cultural programs across several cities; in the student and community movement to save Hostos Community College in the Bronx; in the housing struggles in Boston that gave birth to Villa Victoria in the South

End; in the struggles against proposals to barricade the Puerto Rican community in Hartford, Connecticut; against displacement and gentrification
in Chicago; against police brutality in New York, Chicago, Connecticut, and
New Jersey; in leading the September 1974 uprisings in Newark, New Jersey;
and against the sterilization abuse of Puerto Rican women.

Campaigns and mass mobilizations were built to form alliances and
coalitions with other progressive and leftist formations beyond the Puerto
Rican community. Two of the most significant efforts included the National
Day of Solidarity with Puerto Rico's Independence, on October 27, 1974,
when twenty thousand people gathered in Madison Square Garden in New
York City, and the "Bicentennial Without Colonies" protest on July 4, 1976,
in Philadelphia with more than forty thousand marchers. Major efforts to
build unity among the North American Left included the Hard Times Conference in 1976, the People's Coalition in 1980, and independent electoral
efforts for Frank Barbaro in New York City.

As should be expected of any social movement, mistakes were made,
and lessons were learned. The PSP was an ambitious effort to bring Puerto
Rico's national liberation movement to the "belly of the beast" *and* link it to
the revolutionary transformation of North American society. The chapters
in this book present a firsthand account of these struggles and lessons.

The top leadership of the PSP in Puerto Rico, beginning with Juan Mari
Brás, presented a compelling case for revolutionary action. This vision
was grandiose, by modern lights, but the historical conjuncture encouraged such a view. The emergence of La Nueva Lucha (the New Struggle) led
Puerto Rican revolutionaries to incorrectly project that victory was "right
around the corner." In the United States, especially among the New Left,
many believed that radical change was on the horizon. This feeling was
abetted by such expressions as the civil rights movement, third-world struggles in the United States, and the women's movement. Present as well was
the sense of an impending defeat of U.S. imperialism in Vietnam.

Given the distance from Puerto Rico and less familiarity with island history and current events, militants in the Seccional often lacked the information to assess the capacity of the national PSP (in Puerto Rico) to achieve the
group's strategic goals. They generally acquiesced to the national leadership.
Deference to a charismatic and male-dominated leadership perpetuated a
style of *caudillismo* (charismatic, often autocratic leadership), *machismo*
(exaggerated masculinity inducing subservience and dominance), and sexism (discrimination or prejudice based on gender or sex and the belief that
men are superior to women).

The *Comité Seccional* (U.S. Branch Central Committee) often functioned as a rubber stamp for the decisions of the national Political Commission and Central Committee, for which PSP members had great respect

and confidence until certain questions arose in the early 1980s. This latter problem can also partly be attributed to Stalinist-type structures that impeded broader decision-making practices. The national PSP's firm control reflected a concern that the Seccional might give too much weight to local diaspora issues, at times labeled "reformist." Such an approach was seen as distracting from the solidarity work that was indispensable for Puerto Rican independence.

After the PSP articulated important theoretical and strategic conceptions in its 1973 Political Declaration, *Desde Las Entrañas*, the following years witnessed the organization's failure to make adjustments that might have steered it toward renewal. Internal debates over strategy persisted into the early 1980s, leading to a painful, slow denouement. Certainly, egos of leaders got in the way, violations of democratic practice negated reasoned debate, and the forces of repression were active. But in the end, the failure to reach a solid consensus on strategy—and to stick to any strategy that was chosen—was the organization's Achilles' heel. Beyond these problems was the general incapacity of the independence and socialist movements of the day to convince the masses of Puerto Rican people that fighting U.S. domination was either feasible or in their best interests.

The National Question: Then and Now

Central to the internal debates throughout the years was the PSP's view on the "national question," first articulated in *Desde Las Entrañas*. It summarized its views on the characteristics of Puerto Ricans in the United States and the nature of its struggle in this country. Its central thesis was that Puerto Ricans in the United States had a dual role: fighting for independence and socialism in Puerto Rico and working for revolutionary and socialist transformation in the United States. In characterizing the struggle in the United States, it rejected the traditional Left formulation of "national minority," instead arguing that Puerto Ricans were part of the Puerto Rican nation and therefore could be organized by a party directed from Puerto Rico.[1]

Although the debate over the national question was initially an argument within the North American Left, it also became a focus of the Puerto Rican Left, when the view that Puerto Ricans in the diaspora actually constituted a "national minority" won a following among some organizations. By 1973–1974, two positions had taken hold: (1) that the diaspora was part of the Puerto Rican nation or (2) that its members composed a national minority within the United States. These opposing formulations had meaning when it came to describing the nature of the Puerto Rican community and for defining strategic, tactical, and organizational concepts for the Left.

The PSP pointed to several features of the diaspora as consistent with the part-of-the-nation concept: the constant migratory flow, intense communication between the two sites, similar processes of cultural aggression and capitalist superexploitation, similar processes of proletarianization, and social and political alienation (ghettoization) from U.S. society. There was no question, according to the PSP, that Puerto Rico was a nation, with its own national territory, language, culture, and history of colonialism and racism. Furthermore, there was no question that mass migration and settlement in the United States represented a new *extension* of that nation, not the *creation* of a new people, in the form of a national minority.[2]

Desde Las Entrañas also projected a sequence of stages in the evolution of the diaspora, stating that the

> majority of Puerto Ricans residing in the United States . . . have plans of returning to Puerto Rico. . . . At least 10 more years are required before the so-called "second generation" has sufficient impact to be able to change the objective characteristics of our community. . . . The constant interrelation that presently exists between Puerto Ricans in the United States and those on the island will be significantly interrupted when the independence of Puerto Rico is obtained. At that time, it will be possible for the portion of our people that stays in the United States to develop its own characteristics. It is then that Puerto Ricans in the United States may begin to be different from Puerto Ricans on the island, although they will still be struggling against North American cultural aggression. Only then will we be able to speak of Puerto Ricans in the United States as a national minority in this country.[3]

The document also depicted how independence would be a force for radical change in the metropolis:

> Independence . . . will be a deadly blow to the power of the imperialist bourgeoisie and to the very system on which the relations of production in this country are based. . . . [B]ringing the Third World's war of liberation to the very heart of North American cities . . . [is] the greatest contribution we can make to . . . the revolutionary transformation of this society.[4]

The rearview mirror of historical perspective reveals that these assertions were way off base, understandable now in the context of the belief at the time of imminent independence. Moving from this analysis, the struggle for democratic rights was often viewed as "reformist," and the priority became building solidarity for the upcoming revolution.

People misread the actual historical juncture. The PSP also theorized that the qualitative change in the sociological and cultural composition of the Puerto Rican community would not occur until independence. But in reality, the transforming impact from generational change was already happening, not waiting for national liberation.

Today, two and three generations later, we note a fundamental evolution and differentiation in the characteristics of Puerto Ricans in both localities. In the diaspora, we have seen continued rise in interracial marriages, a larger middle-class and suburban population, increasing loss of Spanish-language use, and a new generation of hundreds of thousands who recently migrated in the aftermath of Hurricane María, among other trends. Activism among youth is linked to broader multiracial social movements and at some level with Puerto Rican organizations. Nevertheless, efforts continue to link Puerto Ricans to supporting independence. The question is, how much of this push is fostered primarily by an older generation of movement radicals and others more closely tied to the island, such as those who are recently relocated Puerto Ricans affected by Hurricane María?

This question does not mean that Boricuas are dissociated from Puerto Rico or the Puerto Rican identity—far from it. But it does suggest that being "Puerto Rican" means different things in the diaspora and on the island, which may suggest different political and cultural consequences.[5]

Nevertheless, the PSP was at its best, especially in the mid-1970s, when many Puerto Ricans joined the party as it led democratic rights struggles, linking them to the colonial situation of Puerto Rico as well as the class struggle in the United States. The PSP should have more effectively linked this struggle with the overall national liberation movement and the movement for radical change in the United States, but this connection proved unsustainable over the long haul. Ultimately, the party fell short at both tasks.

Yet these assertions inspired much creative activism and many positive contributions. They also served as the basis for the PSP's actual practice: an agenda of constant mobilization for solidarity work, accompanied by an undaunted effort to link these mobilizations to democratic rights and labor work. The attempt at realizing the dual role ultimately led to much confusion and internal criticism for the demands it imposed on a committed but tiring membership base. The result was diminishing returns to the work around democratic rights in the United States and eventual abandonment of work with the North American Left, itself in decline.

Several explanations, articulated throughout this book, may be offered: the sheer pace of work expected by national and U.S. Branch leadership; the inability to further develop the analysis on the national question; the confusion and lack of consensus on the concept of democratic rights, especially in its revolutionary potential; a rigid application of Marxism-Leninism and democratic centralism; and a class composition in the national PSP leadership, and to a lesser extent in the U.S. Branch, that privileged the focus on independence over attention to labor and community. The particular weight attributable to each factor and the possible connection among these factors are other aspects to consider. However, as an integral part of an organization from Puerto Rico, the ideological and leadership conflicts emanating from the island ultimately determined the future of the organization. The internal conflicts and dissolution of the PSP in Puerto Rico put an end to any possibility of a continuation of the U.S. Branch. These are factors, the editors note here, over which the PSP *could have had effective control.*

Lurking beyond were greater obstacles over which the PSP had much less effective control: the tremendous power differential between the colonizer and the colonized and the global decline of socialism, starting in 1989 with the fall of the Berlin Wall. On this last point, it is the editors' view that the versions of socialism represented by the Soviet Bloc, the People's Republic of China, and other centers of socialism raised serious questions about the socialist models of the day. In any case, the PSP's internal discussions at the time were subordinated to the larger purpose of gaining solidarity with our national liberation movement, as opposed to articulating a critical analysis of the socialist bloc.

Although the PSP Branch in the United States certainly experienced attempts at repression, little evidence suggests that counterintelligence programs (COINTELPRO) and activities were the key factor in the demise of the organization. Attempts at infiltration and other repressive tactics were limited by effective counterintelligence. More harmful was the Stalinist-like application of democratic centralism that created a hierarchical organization that in the later stages was dominated by a small, inbred Political Commission.[6] What cannot be underestimated is how the repressive measures on the PSP in Puerto Rico affected the public support for the party in the U.S. Puerto Rican communities.

Puerto Rico Today: The Status Question

We have seen new efforts to rebuild Puerto Rico and to advocate for political and economic change in the relationship between the United States and Puerto Rico. The challenge for the independence movement continues to be convincing the Puerto Rican people of the need for and possibility of independence and creating a mass movement and alliances in that direction. Although support for statehood has increased over the last few decades, its claim to be a majority view is not supported by recent elections and plebiscites. Support for independence has stagnated, although its potential to build effective alliances has been demonstrated in the struggle for Vieques, freedom campaign for Oscar López Rivera, support for the elimination of the Jones Act, and the election of Puerto Rican Independence Party (PIP) representatives to the legislature. New political developments include support for third-party candidates and increasing support for the concept of true Free Association (Libre Asociación), which, although not outright independence, pushes sentiment toward sovereignty.

The support for sovereignty by those calling for complete independence or free association may be a basis for future political alliances. Yet another potentially positive force is the Movimiento Victoria Ciudadana (Citizens' Victory Movement [MVC]), an independent political formation with electoral aspirations. Alexandra Lúgaro, an independent candidate for governor in the 2016 election and now a part of the MVC, won 11 percent (175,831) of the vote, well more than the *independentista* candidate in any previous election since the 1950s. In its orientation toward social justice and independent political action, the MVC seems similar to other movements, such as Syriza (Greece) and Podemos (Spain).[7]

In building support for independence, the questions of economic sustainability and U.S. citizenship are big concerns. Those who argue for sovereignty and economic sustainability point to the potential for developing a mixed economy, based on nationalization of major industries, development of small businesses, and support for agro-industrial complexes and fishing industries. Supporters agree on the need for a moratorium on the debt and a transitional relationship with the United States, including the maintenance of U.S. citizenship and acceptance of dual-citizenship agreements, even among pro-independence sectors.

Free Association advocates call for the elimination of the territorial clause and federal laws, delegation of certain powers to the United States, annual financial support of $5.6 billion, and reparations for a period of twenty-five years. Pro-independence forces call for a constitutional assembly to define the relationship with the United States from a position of sovereignty. Whatever one may say about the limitations of decolonization efforts in the past, lack of proposals for a self-sustaining and self-determining Puerto Rico of the future is not one of them. Beyond the printed page on which these proposals have appeared is the greater challenge of convincing the Puerto Rican people that they are capable of concretizing these ideas. Of course, the colonizer has its own agenda for continuing to reap profits for North American corporations under continued territorial status.[8]

Over the past two decades, the U.S. Congress and the White House have discussed different status options: President Bill Clinton's Task Force in 2000, President Barack Obama's Task Force on Puerto Rico's Status in 2011, and the Young Bill of 2017–2018. None of these has resulted in any action concerning status change. A "Statehood, Yes or No?" plebiscite for the November 2020 elections was passed by the PNP-controlled legislature, but its support by the Donald Trump administration was unclear at the time of this writing. Conservatives in Congress have usually required that statehood come with the acceptance of English in public schools and government functions, along with economic development that does not depend on federal funds. Despite these various proposals, any status change seems not to be a matter for serious, much less urgent, consideration by the U.S. Congress. The Puerto Rican people must make a convincing case, through mobilization, self-organization, and demands for change.[9]

Puerto Rico Today: Austerity, Hurricane María, and the People's Response

The U.S. press has given much attention to Puerto Rico as a result of the devastating effects of Hurricane María in September 2017. It is estimated that Puerto Rico suffered up to four thousand deaths and more than $130 billion in damages. Before María, the island was already on the path of serious economic decline, as models for economic growth had been failing for years, resulting in a total debt of more than $72 billion in 2016. As a result of federal-tax loopholes, the Puerto Rican colonial government and its public corporations have accumulated immense amounts of debt through the issuance of bonds, leading to failing credit ratings, even while trying to cut services and raise taxes. A long sequence of problems has converged to bring Puerto Rico to a breakdown: the phasing out of the Section 936 corporations, the continued expense of the Jones Act, the doubling of oil prices, a banking and credit crunch, the "great recession" of 2008, and spiraling unemployment and emigration.

A 2015 report by Anne O. Krueger, Ranjit Teja, and Andrew Wolfe points to these problems and calls for neoliberal solutions of fiscal oversight and austerity. In 2016, the U.S. Congress imposed the Puerto Rico Oversight, Management, and Economic Stability Act (PROMESA), creating a seven-person Financial Oversight and Management Board, with a $370 million price tag for its operations to be paid by Puerto Rican taxpayers. PROMESA was charged with the power to oversee and approve all local economic decisions and to maximize debt repayments by cutting pensions, public services, health care, school systems, and the University of Puerto Rico's budget.

Eyeing opportunity in crisis, bankers, real-estate developers, and cryptocurrency traders envision transforming Puerto Rico into a "visitor economy," with fewer Puerto Ricans living on the island, to be replaced by foreign investors lured by tax breaks and resort lifestyles. In the coming years, Puerto Ricans living in the continental United States are expected to increase to 66 percent of the total Boricua population. Some believe that the U.S elite would prefer that skilled Puerto Ricans migrate to the United States and make available their labor power than to remain on the island, unemployed and reliant on federal funds. As one *independentista* commentator said, "It seems the North Americans are not so interested in the bird, they're interested in the cage."[10]

Puerto Ricans are forging an agenda of struggle in Puerto Rico and the diaspora, questioning the legality of this enormous debt. Aside from support efforts immediately after Hurricane María, opposition has developed to challenge the vulture funds, federal abandonment, and debt obligation. Many argue that the debt is illegal and unsustainable, pointing to the tens of billions of dollars in profits reaped annually by foreign corporations, and that political subordination prevents Puerto Rico from making sovereign decisions to attend to its problems.[11] Popular pushback has generated a series of People's Assemblies (Asambleas de Pueblo) throughout the island and the diaspora in which communities attempt to audit the true debt level and to develop alternative strategies for the future. Others have supported PROMESA, saying that at least it provides for restructuring of the debt and that the alternative would be further crisis. Policy forums in the diaspora, such as the National Puerto Rican Agenda's "Summits" hosted by the Center for Puerto Rican Studies, have sought to create a space for analysis of the crisis and potential solutions.[12]

The struggle against PROMESA and the imposition of the Fiscal Control Board (FCB) took a new turn in the summer of 2019, when Puerto Ricans rose in an unprecedented civil disobedience movement to topple pro-statehood Governor Ricardo Rosselló. For several weeks prior, the media had reported on almost nine hundred pages of private chats between Rosselló, cabinet members, contractors, and lobbyists. Their comments attacked in misogynist and threatening fashion all of civil society and even joked about the dead victims of Hurricane María. Several members of Rossello's cabinet had already resigned on charges of corruption, and the administration was reeling.

For many who were struggling to survive an economic depression and the FCB's policies, revelation of the chats was the final straw. Spontaneous protests filled the streets of Old San Juan over a twelve-day period, culminating on July 22, when a massive march on the Las Americas highway took place. The march, estimated at almost one million people, called for the governor's resignation. Rosselló stepped down on August 2, 2019. He tried to install as his replacement Pedro Pierluisi, a New Progressive Party

(PNP) leader and attorney representing the FCB, but this step was declared unconstitutional. A week later, Wanda Vázquez Garced became the new governor. As Puerto Rico's secretary of justice, Vázquez Garced was next in the line of succession in the absence of a secretary of state.[13]

The anger and rage manifested in this popular opposition had its roots in much that had gone wrong in recent years. But few things were as powerful as the demeaning behavior of President Trump in the aftermath of Hurricane María. Not many Puerto Ricans will forget his tossing of paper towels to the public, supposedly in a gesture of humanitarian aid in a visit to Puerto Rico in October 2017.

Meanwhile, on August 23, 2019, in the middle of preparations for Tropical Storm Dorian, it was reported that in 2018, President Trump had joked about exchanging Puerto Rico for Greenland. In further tweets, he described Puerto Rico as one of the most corrupt places on Earth; denounced San Juan mayor Carmen Yulín Cruz; stated that he was the best thing that has happened to Puerto Rico; and repeated the false claim that the United States gave Puerto Rico $92 billion after Hurricane María. The National Association for the Advancement of Colored People (NAACP), LatinoJustice PRLDEF, the National Puerto Rican Agenda, Power4PR, Congresswoman Alexandria Ocasio-Cortez, and many others in the Puerto Rican diaspora roundly denounced Trump's remarks.

More than two years after Hurricane María, estimates are that Puerto Rico has received only a fraction of the promised federal relief and recovery aid. Much of that aid was funneled back to American corporations, at the expense of local development.[14] Two other events have complicated the economic picture: major earthquake activity and the 2020 coronavirus pandemic. In December 2019, seismic activity shocked southern Puerto Rico, culminating in a 6.4-magnitude earthquake on January 7, 2020. Hundreds of homes were devastated, causing thousands to flee their homes in fear and resulting in economic damages estimated in the millions.[15]

Puerto Rico also reported its first confirmed case of coronavirus (SARS-CoV-2) in early March 2020 and imposed an economic lockdown, except for essential services, and a curfew on March 15, 2020. The economic shutdown has battered the already flailing economy, leading to an estimated $4 billion in losses, a projected unemployment rate of 37 percent, and an increase in childhood poverty to 57 percent. A recent research study estimates another projected migration wave of hundreds of thousands to the United States.[16]

With Puerto Ricans' ever-increasing loss of confidence in the colonial government, it remains to be seen what political and economic repercussions Hurricane María, earthquakes, and the coronavirus pandemic will have on the social, political, and economic future of the country.

And the Puerto Rican Left in the Diaspora?

The experience of the PSP should be viewed as part of the international movement for reimagining the socialist project for the twenty-first century. There is real concern not only about "independence in our lifetime" and other possible transitional phases but also about identifying a socialist model as a realistic project to define a transition from capitalism to socialism. This challenge faces the movement in Puerto Rico and the Left in the United States. Participation by the PSP in the North American Left helped build unity beyond solidarity efforts with Puerto Rico. Especially relevant was the efforts to go beyond traditional Marxist-Leninist organizations, which often reflected dogmatic formulations, to develop alliances with anti-imperialist and progressive forces that aimed to radically transform North American society.

In the first half of the twentieth century, Puerto Rican radicals in the diaspora were largely incorporated into the North American Left. The Nationalist Party and the PIP had a presence but were engaged primarily in solidarity work. From the early 1960s onward, new organizations arose, such as the *Movimiento Pro Independencia* (MPI), which became the PSP; the Young Lords Organization (Chicago); the Young Lords Party–Puerto Rican Revolutionary Workers Organization (New York); the Puerto Rican Student Union (PRSU); El Comité–MINP; the Federación Universitaria Socialista Puertorriqueña (FUSP); the Movimiento de Liberación Nacional (MLN); and the Fuerzas Armadas de Liberación Nacional (FALN).

With the passing into history of these organizations, the Puerto Rican Left entered a phase of dispersion and relative inactivity. Today, it is difficult to generalize about a set of common characteristics among the individuals and organizations that espouse independence and socialism. If by "Puerto Rican Left" we mean a collection of groups and individuals who—despite differences in ideology—are capable of pursuing a common goal, we might very well question whether such an entity exists. This state of affairs is regrettable.

We can find positive signs in the upsurge of labor, student, multiracial, and multinational social justice movements throughout the United States in which Boricua activists are playing an important role, especially women, the young, and lesbian, gay, bisexual, transgender, and queer/questioning (LGBTQ) communities. We can applaud the formation of new Puerto Rican networks and groups that focus on Boricua democratic rights and decolonizing projects. We can celebrate the fact that many men and women of past radical organizations are leaders in the political, cultural, and social structures of the Boricua community and in mainstream U.S. institutions as well. We can be inspired by the powerful, yet still insufficient, response to the crisis conditions in Puerto Rico. However, we wonder whether the activists who are the backbone of these organizing efforts constitute a conscious collectivity, forging and leading a new Left.

A number of questions require serious consideration if a revival of the Left is to take place. What should be the relationship between *independentistas* and *socialistas* in Puerto Rico and the diaspora? What should be the role of the diaspora in Puerto Rico's future, especially given the now well-known fact that about two out of every three Boricuas reside in the United States? How should radical Boricuas define their role in a socialist project for the United States?

This book's contributors—and readers—may agree or disagree with the conclusions and questions posited here by the editors. It is our hope that *Revolution Around the Corner* generates further discussion about the PSP experience and its relevance to the contemporary situation. Let the conversation proceed.

NOTES

1. *Desde Las Entrañas, Political Declaration of the Puerto Rican Socialist Party U.S. Branch*, April 1, 1973. See the section on "Strategic and Organizational Objectives."

2. In the almost fifty years since, much history has transpired, and much research and scholarship have been dedicated to a discussion and debate of this view. A full treatment of this topic is beyond the scope of this book.

3. *Desde Las Entrañas*, Part 1, 9, 17.

4. Ibid., Part 1, 18.

5. The work of the late James Blaut, a member of the PSP, offers a vision slightly at variance with this interpretation. He argues that Puerto Ricans in the diaspora were subject to a process not of "acculturation" but of "ghettoization." In other words, second- and third-generation Boricuas were not dissolving into mainstream America (white or black, Latino or Anglo) but rather becoming economically and culturally isolated. Whether this distinction made a difference for the PSP's strategic vision at the time remains a matter of debate. See Chapter 1 by Andrés Torres and Chapter 2 by José F. Velázquez Luyanda in the present volume for more on this issue. Two key writings on this topic include James Blaut, "Are Puerto Ricans a National Minority?" *Monthly Review* 29, no. 1 (1977): 35–55; and James Blaut, *The National Question: Decolonizing the Theory of Colonialism* (London: Zed Books, 1987).

6. At one point in the late 1970s, the seven-member Political Commission replaced members who had resigned with others who were clearly sympathetic to the current leadership. Also by 1980, the commission included two married couples. Although each person had started out as unattached individuals, they became two pairs of spouses. This situation led to the complaint by some members that the Political Commission was dominated by "*matrimonios políticos*" (political marriages).

7. Movimiento Unión Soberanista, *Resumen Ejecutivo: Tratado de Libre Asociación Entre el Estado Soberano de Puerto Rico y Los Estados Unidos de America* (San Juan, Puerto Rico: August 30, 2016).

8. Partido Socialista Puertorriqueño, *Programa Socialista* (San Juan, Puerto Rico: 1975); Manuel Rodríguez Orellano, *Por Senderos de la Descolonización: Autoretratos*

(Puerto Rico: Edición Patria, 2011), 175–189; Rubén Berríos Martínez, Francisco Catalá Oliveras, and Fernando Martín García, *Puerto Rico: Nación Independiente, Imperativo del Siglo XXI* (Puerto Rico: Editora Corripio, April 2010), 21–32, 72–98, 101–168; and Juan Mari Brás, "Nuevo Curso Estratégico del Independentismo," in *Memorias de Un Ciudadano* (Puerto Rico: Editorial Barco de Papel, 2006), 352–360.

9. White House, *Report by the President's Task Force on Puerto Rico's Status* (Washington, DC: March 2011).

10. Naomi Klein, "Puerto Ricans and Ultrarich 'Puertopians' Are Locked in a Pitched Struggle Over How to Remake the Island," *The Intercept*, March 20, 2018, available at https://theintercept.com/2018/03/20/puerto-rico-hurricane-maria-recovery/File:// localhost/staff/naomi-klein; Dara Lind, "Puerto Rico's Debt Crisis, Explained in 11 Basic Facts," *Vox*, August 3, 2015, available at https://www.vox.com/2015/7/10 /8924517/puerto-rico-bankrupt-debt; Anne O. Krueger, Ranjit Teja, and Andrew Wolfe, "Puerto Rico: A Way Forward," Puerto Rico Government Development Bank, June 29, 2015, available at https://bae2008.files.wordpress.com/2015/07/puerto-rico-a -way-forward.pdf; Alexandra Tempus, "Puerto Rico: I Know There's a Path," *Portside* https://portside.org/2019-03-08/puerto-rico-i-know-theres-path, March 8, 2019, available at https://portside.org/2019-03-08/puerto-rico-i-know-theres-path; and Rubén Colón Morales, "Capitalismo, colonialismo, deuda y la desaparición de Puerto Rico," *80 Grados Prensasinprisa*, June 1, 2018, available at http://www.80grados.net/capitalismo -colonialismo-deuda-y-la-desaparicion-de-puerto-rico/ (Velázquez's translation).

11. José Nicholás Medina Fuentes, *La deuda odiosa y la descolonización de Puerto Rico* (San Juan: Publicaciones Libre Pensado, 2018); Ed Morales, *Fantasy Island: Colonialism, Exploitation, and The Betrayal of Puerto Rico* (New York: Bold Type Books, 2019); and Naomi Klein, *The Battle for Paradise* (Chicago: Haymarket Books, 2018).

12. Nydia Velázquez, "Floor Statement on PROMESA," U.S. House of Representatives, June 9, 2016; Nelson Torres-Ríos, "Is Puerto Rico's Debt Illegal? Exploring the Application of Litchfield v. Balley," Institute for Puerto Rican Policy Network, October 27, 2015; and A Call to Action on Puerto Rico, "Forging an Agenda of Struggle within the Puerto Rican Diaspora," October 12, 2015.

13. Patricia Mazzei and Frances Robles, "Ricardo Rosselló, Puerto Rico's Governor, Resigns after Protests," *New York Times*, July 24, 2019. For a detailed account of events leading up to and after the resignation, see José E. Velázquez, "Checkmate: Days That Changed the History of Puerto Rico," Parts 1 and 2, in *Temporal*, August 31 and October 12, 2019, available at http://www.temporalpr.cemipress.com.

14. Arelis R. Hernández, "Puerto Ricans Still Waiting on Disaster Funds as Hurricane María's Aftermath, Earthquakes Continue to Affect Life on the Island," *Washington Post*, January 19, 2020.

15. Erica Werner, "Hit by Devastating Earthquakes, Puerto Rico Still Waiting on Billions for Hurricane Relief," *Washington Post*, January 9, 2020.

16. "Puerto Rico Coronavirus Case Count," *New York Times*, May 23, 2020; Keila Alicea, "Wanda Vázquez decreta toque de queda para todo Puerto Rico para contener el coronavirus," *El Nuevo Dia*, March 15, 2020; Ricardo Cortes Chico, "Dramática alza en el desempleo," *El Nuevo Dia*, April 27, 2020; Christian Ramos Segarra, "Coronavirus disparara migración en la Isla," *El Vocero*, May 25, 2020.

Interviews

All interviews were conducted by Carmen V. Rivera and José E. Velázquez, except for those of Rafael Baerga and Dixie Bayó, which were conducted by Digna Sánchez. Focus groups were facilitated by Teresa Basilio Gaztambide.

Baerga, Rafael "Rafín": Puerto Rico, November 25, 2016
Barreto, Hilda: Puerto Rico, December 7, 2015
Barreto, Ismael: Puerto Rico, December 7, 2015
Bayó, Dixie: Puerto Rico, November 30, 2015
Blais Alemany, Emily: Puerto Rico, July 15, 2017
Capote, Jorge E.: Puerto Rico, July 15, 2015
Cruz, William: Puerto Rico, December 5, 2015
Delgado, Eduardo "Tito": New York City, September 8, 2015
Domenech, Armengol: Puerto Rico, July 24, 2017
Maldonado LaFontaine, Mariesel: Puerto Rico, July 15, 2017,
Matos, Graciano: New York City, February 6, 2018, and October 22, 2019
Medina Cruz, Pablo: Puerto Rico, July 15 and 16, 2017
Morales, Milga: New York City, October 6, 2015
Nadal, Antonio "Tony": New York City, October 6, 2015
Reyes, Pedro: New Jersey, November 22, 2015
Ríos, Elsa: New York City, October 7, 2015
Rodríguez, Freddie: Puerto Rico, July 17, 2017
Rodríguez, Sandra: Puerto Rico, December 9, 2015
Sorrentini, América "Meca": Puerto Rico, December 4, 2015

Focus group with children of the Puerto Rican Socialist Party (PSP) in New York City, October 29, 2017: Karim López, Lenina Nadal, and Orlando Torres
Focus group with children of the PSP in New York City, May 6, 2018: Jessica Colón, Camilo Matos, Graciano Emil Matos, and Rachel Torres

Bibliography

Abramson, Michael. *Palante: Young Lords Party*. Chicago: Haymarket, 1971.

Acosta-Belén, Edna, and Carlos E. Santiago. *Puerto Ricans in the United States: A Contemporary Portrait*. 2nd ed. Boulder, CO: Lynne Rienner Publishers, 2018.

Agosto, Ángel M. *Lustro de Gloria*. Rio Grande, Puerto Rico: LaCasa Editora de Puerto Rico, 2009.

Alamo-Pastrana, Carlos. *Seams of Empire: Race and Radicalism in Puerto Rico and the United States*. Gainesville, FL: University of Florida Press, 2016.

Álvarez Febles, José Alberto. *Proyecto de País vs. Proyecto de Estado*. Puerto Rico: Editorial Luna Llena, 2016.

Amy Moreno de Toro, Ángel A. "An Oral History of the Puerto Rican Socialist Party in Boston, 1972–1978." In *The Puerto Rican Movement: Voices from the Diaspora*, edited by Andrés Torres and José E. Velázquez, 246–259. Philadelphia: Temple University Press, 1998.

Aponte-Parés, Luis. "Lessons from El Barrio—The East Harlem Real Great Society/Urban Planning Studio: A Puerto Rican Chapter in the Fight for Urban Self-Determination." In *Latino Social Movements: Historical and Theoretical Perspectives*, edited by Rodolfo D. Torres and George N. Katsiaficas, 399–420. New York: Routledge, 1999.

Arnau, Ariel. "The Evolution of Leadership within the Puerto Rican Community of Philadelphia, 1950s–1970s." *Pennsylvania Magazine of History and Biography* 136, no. 1 (2012): 53–81.

Ayala, César J., and Rafael Bernabé. *Puerto Rico in the American Century: A History since 1898*. Chapel Hill: University of North Carolina Press, 2007.

Bacchetta, Paola. "Dyketactics! Notes toward an Un-Silencing." In *Smash the Church, Smash the State! The Early Years of Gay Liberation*, edited by Tommi Avicolli Mecca. San Francisco: City Lights Books, 2009.

Berger, Dan, ed. *The Hidden 1970s: Histories of Radicalism*. New Brunswick, NJ: Rutgers University Press, 2010.

Blake, John. *Children of the Movement: The Sons and Daughters of Martin Luther King, Jr., Malcolm X, Elijah Muhammad, George Wallace, Andrew Young, Julian Bond, Stokely Carmichael, Bob Moses, James Chaney, Elaine Brown, and Others Reveal How the Civil Rights Movement Tested and Transformed Their Families*. Chicago: Lawrence Hill Books, 2004.

Blaut, James. "Are Puerto Ricans a National Minority?" *Monthly Review* 29, no. 1 (1977): 35–55.

———. *The National Question: Decolonizing the Theory of Colonialism*. London: Zed Books, 1987.

Bodnar, John. *Remaking America: Public Memory, Commemoration, and Patriotism in the Twentieth Century*. Princeton, NJ: Princeton University Press, 1992.

Brown, Autumn, and Maryse Mitchell-Brody. *Healing Justice Practice Spaces: A How-To Guide*. Just Healing Resource Site, December 18, 2014. Available at https://justhealing.files.wordpress.com/2012/04/healing-justice-practice-spaces-a-how-to-guide-with-links.pdf.

Cabán, Pedro A. *Constructing a Colonial People: Puerto Ricans and the United States, 1898-1932*. Boulder: Westview Press, 1999.

Capozzola, Christopher. "'It Makes You Want to Believe in the Country': Celebrating the Bicentennial in an Age of Limits." In *America in the Seventies*, edited by Beth Bailey and David Farber, 41–43. Lawrence: University Press of Kansas, 2004.

Center for Puerto Rican Studies, Puerto Ricans in Illinois, the United States, and Puerto Rico (New York: Center for Puerto Rican Studies, Centro DS2016US-9, April 2016).

Colón, Jesús. *A Puerto Rican in New York*. New York: Mainstream Publishers, 1961.

Colón López, Joaquín. *Pioneros Puertorriqueños en Nueva York, 1917-1947*. Houston: Arte Público Press, 2002.

Cruz, José E. *Identity and Power: Puerto Rican Politics and the Challenge of Ethnicity*. Philadelphia: Temple University Press, 1998.

———. *Liberalism and Identity Politics: Puerto Rican Community Organizations and Collective Action in New York City*. New York: Centro Press, 2017.

———. *Puerto Rican Identity, Political Development, and Democracy in New York, 1960-1990*. Lanham, MD: Lexington Books, 2017.

———. "Pushing Left to Get to the Center: Puerto Rican Radicalism in Hartford, Connecticut." In *The Puerto Rican Movement: Voices from the Diaspora*, edited by Andrés Torres and José E. Velázquez, 69–87. Philadelphia: Temple University Press, 1998.

Cruz, Wilfredo. *Puerto Rican Chicago*. Chicago: Arcadia Publishing, 2004.

Delgado, Linda C. "Jesús Colón and the Making of a New York City Community: 1917–1974." In *The Puerto Rican Diaspora: Historical Perspectives*, ed. Carmen Theresa Whalen and Victor Vázquez-Hernández, 68–87. Philadelphia: Temple University Press, 2005.

Denis, Nelson A. *War against All Puerto Ricans: Revolution and Terror in America's Colony*. New York: Nation Books, 2015.

Donner, Frank J. *Protectors of Privilege: Red Squads and Police Repression in Urban America*. Berkeley: University of California Press, 1990.

Duany, Jorge. *The Puerto Rican Nation on the Move: Identities on the Island and in the United States*. Chapel Hill: University of North Carolina Press, 2002.

Early, James. "An African American–Puerto Rican Connection." In *The Puerto Rican Movement: Voices from the Diaspora*, edited by Andrés Torres and José E. Velázquez, 316–328. Philadelphia: Temple University Press, 1998.

Early, Steve. "From the Old Left to the New: Perils of Progressive Parenting." *Monthly Review*, October 22, 2017. Available at https://mronline.org/2017/10/22/from-the-old-left-to-the-new-perils-of-progressive-parenting.

Feffer, Andrew. "Show Down in Center City: Staging Redevelopment and Citizenship in Bicentennial Philadelphia, 1974–1977." *Journal of Urban History* 30, no. 6 (2004): 791–825.

Fernández, Johanna. "The Young Lords and the Social and Structural Roots of Late Sixties Urban Radicalism." In *Civil Rights in New York City: From World War II to the Giuliani Era*, edited by Clarence Taylor, 141–160. New York: Fordham University Press, 2011.

———. *The Young Lords: A Radical History*. Chapel Hill: The University of North Carolina Press, 2020.

Fernández, Lilia. *Brown in the Windy City: Mexicans and Puerto Ricans in Postwar Chicago*. Chicago: University of Chicago Press, 2012.

Fernandez, Ronald, Serafín Fernandez, and Gail Cueto. *Puerto Rico Past and Present: An Encyclopedia*. Westport, CT: Greenwood Press, 1998.

Fitzpatrick, Joseph P. *Puerto Rican Americans: The Meaning of Migration to the Mainland*. 2nd ed. Englewood Cliffs, NJ: Prentice-Hall, 1987.

Gerena Valentín, Gilberto. *Gilberto Gerena Valentín: My Life as a Community Organizer, Labor Activist, and Progressive Politician in New York City*. New York: Center for Puerto Rican Studies, 2013.

———. *Soy Gilberto Gerena Valentín: Memorias de un Puertorriqueño en Nueva York*. New York: Center for Puerto Rican Studies, 2013.

Glick, Ted. *Burglar for Peace: Lessons Learned in the Catholic Left's Resistance to the Vietnam War*. Oakland, CA: PM Press, 2020.

González, Juan. "The Turbulent Progress of Puerto Ricans in Philadelphia." CENTRO *Journal* 2, no. 2 (Winter 1987/1988): 34–41.

Gutiérrez, Luis. *Still Dreaming: My Journey from the Barrio to Capitol Hill*. New York: Norton, 2013.

Immerwahr, Daniel. *How to Hide an Empire: A History of the Greater United States*. New York: Farrar, Straus and Giroux, 2019.

Jeffries, Judson. "From Gang-Bangers to Urban Revolutionaries: The Young Lords of Chicago." *Journal of the Illinois State Historical Society* 96, no. 3 (2003): 288–304.

Jiménez, Ramón J. "Hostos Community College: Battle of the Seventies." CENTRO *Journal* 15, no. 1 (Spring 2003): 99–111.

Kinoy, Arthur. *Rights on Trial: The Odyssey of a People's Lawyer*. Cambridge, MA: Harvard University Press, 1983.

Klein, Naomi. *The Battle for Paradise*. Chicago: Haymarket Books, 2018.

Laó-Montes, Agustín, and Arlene Dávila, eds. *Mambo Montage*. New York: Columbia University Press, 2001.

Larson, Eric. "José Soler: A Life Working at the Intersections of Nationalism, Internationalism, and Working-Class Radicalism." *Radical History Review*, no. 128 (2017): 63–76.

Lauderdale, Pat, and Rhoda E. Estep. "The Bicentennial Protest: An Examination of Hegemony in the Definition of Deviant Political Activity." In *A Political Analysis of Deviance*, edited by Pat Lauderdale, 72–91. Minneapolis: University of Minnesota Press, 1980.

Lee, Sonia S., and Ande Diaz. "'I Was the One Percenter': Manny Diaz and the Beginnings of a Black-Puerto Rican Coalition." *Journal of American Ethnic History* 26, no. 3 (Spring 2007): 52–80.

Leonard, Aaron J., and Conor A. Gallagher. *Heavy Radicals: The FBI's Secret War on America's Maoists*. Winchester, UK: Zero Books, 2014.

Lewis, Gordon K. *Puerto Rico: Freedom and Power in the Caribbean*. New York: Harper Torchbooks, 1968.

Lloyd, Brian. "The Kinoy Paper and the Passing of 1960s Radicalism." *Science and Society* 67, no. 4 (Winter 2003/2004): 429–451.

Mari Brás, Juan. *The New Struggle for Puerto Rico's Independence*. Boston: New England Free Press, 1969.

Martínez, Miranda J., and Alan A. Aja. "Democratic Rights and Nuyorican Identity in the Partido Socialista Puertorriqueño." *Latino(a) Research Review* 8, nos. 1–2 (2011/2012): 101–123.

Martínez, Rubén Berríos, Francisco Catalá Oliveras, and Fernando Martín García. *Puerto Rico: Nación Independiente Imperativo del Siglo XXI*. San Juan, Puerto Rico: Editora Corripio, 2010.

Mattos Cintrón, Wilfredo. *Puerta Sin Casa: Crisis del PSP y encrucijada de la Izquierda*. San Juan: Ediciones La Sierra, 1984.

McCaffrey, Katherine T. *Military Power and Popular Protest: The U.S. Navy in Vieques, Puerto Rico*. New Brunswick, NJ: Rutgers University Press, 2002.

Meléndez, Edgardo. "Vito Marcantonio, Puerto Rican Migration, and the 1949 Mayoral Election in New York City." CENTRO *Journal* 22, no. 2 (Fall 2010): 198–234.

Meléndez, Edwin, and Edgardo Meléndez, eds. *Colonial Dilemma*. Boston: South End Press, 1993.

Meléndez, Miguel. *We Took the Streets: Fighting for Latino Rights with the Young Lords*. New York: St. Martin's Press, 2003.

Merced, Florencio. *One Nation, One Party*. New York: Ediciones Puerto Rico, 1975.

Meyer, Gerald. "Save Hostos: Politics and Community Mobilization to Save a College in the Bronx, 1973-78." CENTRO *Journal* 15, no. 1 (Fall 2003): 73–97.

———. *Vito Marcantonio: Radical Politician, 1902–1954*. Albany: State University of New York Press, 1989.

Morales, Ed. *Fantasy Island: Colonialism, Exploitation, and the Betrayal of Puerto Rico*. New York: Bold Type Books, 2019.

Morales, Iris, ed. *Latinas: An Anthology of Struggles and Protests in 21st Century USA*. New York: Red Sugarcane Press, 2018.

———. *Through the Eyes of Rebel Women: The Young Lords: 1969–1976*. New York: Red Sugarcane Press, 2016.

———, ed. *Voices from Puerto Rico: Post-Hurricane María*. New York: Red Sugarcane Press, 2019.

Movimiento Pro Independencia (MPI). *La Hora de la Independencia de Puerto Rico*. San Juan, Puerto Rico: Misión Nacional del MPI, 1963.

———. *Presente y Futuro de Puerto Rico*. Rio Piedras, Puerto Rico: Misión Nacional del MPI, 1969.

———. *Proyecto de Declaración General*. New York: MPI, 1970.

Muhammad, Saladin. "I First Met Arthur in 1975." *Independent Politics News: A Publication of the Independent Progressive Politics Network* 7, no. 4 (January 2004).

Muzio, Rose. *Radical Imagination, Radical Humanity*. Albany: State University Press of New York, 2017.

Nieto, Sonia. "The BC 44, Ethnic Studies, and Transformative Education." In *Latino Civil Rights in Education: La Lucha Sigue*, edited by Anaida Colón-Muñiz and Magaly Lavadenz, 72–87. New York: Routledge, 2016.

Nieves Falcón, Luís, ed. *Oscar López Rivera: Between Torture and Resistance*. Oakland, CA: PM Press, 2013.

Nuñez, Louis. "Reflections on Puerto Rican History: Aspira in the Sixties and the Coming of Age of the Stateside Puerto Rican Community." CENTRO *Journal* 21, no. 2 (Fall 2009): 332–347.

Nuñez, Victoria. "Remembering Pura Belpre's Early Career at the 135th Street New York Public Library: Interracial Cooperation and Puerto Rican Settlement during the Harlem Renaissance." CENTRO *Journal* 21, no. 1 (Spring 2009): 36–51.

Opie, Frederick Douglass. *Upsetting the Apple Cart*. New York: Columbia University Press, 2015.

Padilla, Felix M. *Latino Ethnic Consciousness*. Notre Dame, IN: University of Notre Dame Press, 1985.

———. *Puerto Rican Chicago*. Notre Dame, IN: University of Notre Dame Press, 1987.

Pantoja, Antonia. *Memoirs of a Visionary*. Houston: Arte Público Press, 2002.

Pérez, Gina M. *The Near Northwest Side Story: Migration, Displacement, and Puerto Rican Families*. Berkeley: University of California Press, 2004.

Pérez Soler, Ángel. *Del Movimiento Pro Independencia Al Partido Socialista Puertorriqueño*. San Juan, Puerto Rico: Publicaciones Gaviota, 2019.

Power, Margaret. "Puerto Rican Nationalism in Chicago." CENTRO *Journal* 28, no. 2 (Fall 2016): 36–67.

Puerto Rican Socialist Party, U.S. Branch. *Desde Las Entrañas*. New York: Puerto Rican Socialist Party, 1973.

Ramos-Zayas, Ana. *National Performances: The Politics of Class, Race, and Space in Puerto Rican Chicago*. Chicago: University of Chicago Press, 2003.

Rivera, Carmen V. "Our Movement: One Woman's Story." In *The Puerto Rican Movement: Voices from the Diaspora*, edited by Andrés Torres and José E. Velázquez, 192–209. Philadelphia: Temple University Press, 1998.

Rivera, Raquel Z. *New York Ricans from the Hip Hop Zone*. New York: Palgrave Mac-Millan, 2003.

Rodriguez, Clara E. *Puerto Ricans: Born in the U.S.A.* Boulder, CO: Westview Press, 1991.

Rodríguez, Victor M. "Boricuas, African Americans, and Chicanos in the 'Far West': Notes on the Puerto Rican Pro-Independence Movement in California, 1960s–1980s." In *Latino Social Movements: Historical and Theoretical Perspectives*, edited by Rodolfo D. Torres and George N. Katsiaficas, 79–109. New York: Routledge, 1999.

Rodríguez-Morazzani, Roberto P. "Linking a Fractured Past: The World of the Puerto Rican Old Left." *Centro Boletin* 7, no. 1 (Winter 1994/Spring 1995): 20–30.

———. "Puerto Rican Political Generations in New York: Pioneros, Young Turks, and Radicals." CENTRO *Journal* 4, no. 1 (1991/1992): 97–116.

Rúa, Merida M. *A Grounded Identidad*. Oxford: Oxford University Press, 2012.

Sánchez Korrol, Virginia E. *From Colonia to Community: The History of Puerto Ricans in New York City*. 2nd ed. Berkeley: University of California Press, 1994.

Santiago-Irizarry, Vilma, and Pedro Cabán, "Puerto Ricans." In *The Oxford Encyclopedia of Latinos and Latinas in the United States*, edited by Suzanne Oboler and Deena J. González, 506–515. Oxford: Oxford University Press, 2005.

Serrano, Basilio. "¡*Rifle, Cañón, Escopeta!* A Chronicle of the Puerto Rican Student Union." In *The Puerto Rican Movement: Voices from the Diaspora*, edited by Andrés Torres and José E. Velázquez, 124–143. Philadelphia: Temple University Press, 1978.

Smith, Neil. "Symbol, Space and the Bicentennial." *Antipode* 9, no. 2 (1977): 76–83.

Song-Ha Lee, Sonia. *Building a Latino Civil Rights Movement.* Chapel Hill: University of North Carolina Press, 2014.

Starr, Meg. "'Hit Them Harder': Leadership, Solidarity, and the Puerto Rican Independence Movement." In *The Hidden 1970s: Histories of Radicalism*, edited by Dan Berger, 135–154. New Brunswick, NJ: Rutgers University Press, 2010.

Thomas, Lorrin. *Puerto Rican Citizen.* Chicago: University of Chicago Press, 2010.

———. "Resisting the Racial Binary? Puerto Ricans' Encounter with Race in Depression-Era New York City." *CENTRO Journal* 21, no. 1 (Spring 2009): 4–35.

Thomas, Lorrin, and Aldo A. Lauria-Santiago. *Rethinking the Struggle for Puerto Rican Rights.* New York: Routledge, 2019.

Torres, Andrés. "Introduction: Political Radicalism in the Diaspora—The Puerto Rican Experience." In *The Puerto Rican Movement: Voices from the Diaspora*, edited by Andrés Torres and José E. Velázquez, 1–22. Philadelphia: Temple University Press, 1998.

———. *Signing in Puerto Rican: A Hearing Child and His Deaf Parents.* Washington, DC: Gallaudet University Press, 2009.

Torres, Andrés, and José E. Velázquez, eds. *The Puerto Rican Movement: Voices from the Diaspora.* Philadelphia: Temple University Press, 1998.

Torres, Zoilo. *Leoncio: The Healing of a People.* Pittsburgh, PA: RoseDog Books, 2013.

Trías Monje, José. *Puerto Rico: The Trials of the Oldest Colony in the World.* New Haven: Yale University Press, 1997.

U.S. Commission on Civil Rights. *Puerto Ricans in the Continental United States: An Uncertain Future.* Washington, DC: U.S. Commission on Civil Rights, 1976.

U.S. Committee on the Judiciary. TERRORISTIC ACTIVITY: *The Cuban Connection in Puerto Rico; Castro's Hand in Puerto Rican and U.S. Terrorism.* Washington, DC: U.S. Government Printing Office, July 30, 1975.

Vazquez, David J. "Jesús Colón and the Development of Insurgent Consciousness." *CENTRO Journal* 21, no. 1 (Spring 2009): 78–99.

Velázquez, José E. "Coming Full Circle: The Puerto Rican Socialist Party, U.S. Branch." In *The Puerto Rican Movement: Voices from the Diaspora*, edited by Andrés Torres and José E. Velázquez, 48–68. Philadelphia: Temple University Press, 1998.

Whalen, Carmen Theresa. "Colonialism, Citizenship, and the Making of the Puerto Rican Diaspora." In *The Puerto Rican Diaspora: Historical Perspectives*, ed. Carmen Theresa Whalen and Victor Vázquez-Hernández, 1–42. Philadelphia: Temple University Press, 2005.

———. *From Labor Migrants to the Underclass: Puerto Ricans in Philadelphia.* Philadelphia: Temple University Press, 2000.

Whalen, Carmen Teresa, and Victor Vázquez-Hernández, eds. *The Puerto Rican Diaspora: Historical Perspectives.* Philadelphia: Temple University Press, 2005.

Contributors

Maritza Arrastía is a Cuban–Puerto Rican liberation activist and writer of liberatory prose and poetry.

Teresa Basilio Gaztambide is a Puerto Rico native living in New York City. As a media organizer, filmmaker, and educator, she is committed to building a world where our people are free.

Rosa Borenstein retired in 2011 as the director and general counsel of a municipal employees' legal services program after twenty-eight years of practice. She is still active in progressive politics.

Ted Glick is a long-time progressive activist and organizer. His book *Burglar for Peace* (2020) recounts his Vietnam War resistance activities. He has been a climate-crisis activist since 2003.

The late **Ramón J. Jiménez**, a graduate of Harvard Law School, taught at Hostos Community College. He was a community activist for many years and a leader of the South Bronx Community Congress.

Alfredo López is a founder and leader of May First Movement Technology. He has been a revolutionary activist for a half century and is a journalist and author.

Pablo Medina Cruz, a leader of the Federación Universitaria Socialista Puertorriqueña (FUSP) and the Puerto Rican Socialist Party (PSP) in Chicago, remains active in the struggle for social justice and national liberation.

Lenina Nadal is a multimedia artist, activist, and mom from Brooklyn, New York. She has worked with several organizations and movements developing strategies to engage people in transforming their lives and their society.

José-Manuel Navarro, is a former college administrator and professor of U.S., Latin American, and Puerto Rican history at colleges and at a bilingual high school. He lives and writes in Philadelphia, Pennsylvania.

Alyssa Ribeiro is a historian of race and ethnicity in late-twentieth-century U.S. cities and teaches at Allegheny College.

Carmen V. Rivera has centered her activism on women's rights, national liberation, and social justice movements. One of her personal passions is documenting the history of Puerto Rican political activism in the United States from the 1960s to early 1990s. She directs the ¡Despierta Boricua! Recovering History Project and its archival collection on the Puerto Rican Socialist Party in the United States.

Olga Iris Sanabria Dávila has worked in the Puerto Rican pro-decolonization/independence movement for decades, including internationally and in the United States. She has a bachelor's degree in journalism and a Juris Doctor.

Digna Sánchez was born in Arecibo, Puerto Rico, in 1947. In 1950, her family arrived in New York City, where she later became a progressive activist. After retiring in 2014, she returned to Puerto Rico.

América "Meca" Sorrentini was born in Cabo Rojo, Puerto Rico. She is a member of the Movimiento Independentista Nacional Hostosiano (MINH) and the Fondo Puertorriqueño de Arte y Cultura and is a promoter of Puerto Rico's inclusion in the United Nations Educational, Scientific and Cultural Organization (UNESCO).

Andrés Torres is a retired Distinguished Lecturer from Lehman College, City University of New York. Previously, he was a Professor at the University of Massachusetts, Boston. He is the author or editor of Between Melting Pot and Mosaic: African Americans and Puerto Ricans in the New York Political Economy, The Puerto Rican Movement: Voices from the Diaspora, and Latinos in New England (all Temple). He is also the author of the memoir Signing in Puerto Rican: A Hearing Son and His Deaf Family.

Zoilo Torres is a life-long community, labor, and political organizer. He is an independent consultant and lecturer on community empowerment. Torres is the author of a historical novel, Leoncio: The Healing of a People.

José E. Velázquez is a lifelong activist for social justice in the United States and for Puerto Rican independence, and is coeditor, with Andrés Torres, of The Puerto Rican Movement: Voices from the Diaspora (Temple). His opposition to the Vietnam War in the early 1970s resulted in the important legal case United States v. José Emiliano Velazquez. José is a retired educator and curriculum writer from the Newark Public Schools. A presenter at the founding of the Amistad Commission of New Jersey, he often lectures on Afro-Latino issues.

Index

LaBelle, Pattie, 101
labor movement, Puerto Rico: MPI-PSP and,
26, 65, 82, 93; in Puerto Rico, 295, 301, 304,
310, 321, 322–323; repression against, 312
labor movement, U.S.: changing composition,
199; electoral participation and, 288; the
Left and, 8, 310, 341; AFL-CIO, 8, 65, 321;
AFSCME; 285, 323; Amalgamated Meat
Cutters and Butcher Workmen of America,
308; American Clothing and Textiles
Workers Union, 285; D.C. Central Labor
Council, 323; Fur, Leather and Machine
Workers Joint Board, 308; Hospital Work-
ers Union (1199), 10, 73, 106, 202, 285–286;
Hotel & Club Employees Union (Local 6),
74, 111, 256; International Association of
Machinists (District 134), 308, 330; Inter-
national Furniture Workers of America, 73;
Steelworkers Union Local (1462), 333; Taxi
Workers Alliance, 208; Teamsters, 285;
United Auto Workers, 330; United Auto
Workers (District 65), 8, 286; Unite Latino
Labor/Civil Rights Conference of the East
Coastd Electrical, Radio, and Machine
Workers Union, (UE), 308, 330–331, 335;
United Federation of Teachers, 285; United
Shoe Workers of America, 308. See also
Asociación de Trabajadores Agrícola
(ATA); class; Hispanic Labor Committee
(AFL-CIO); Puerto Rican Socialist Party
(PSP), labor; workers
LaDuke, Winona, 320
La Luz, José, 52, 94n68, 95n87, 128, 276
La Taóna, 236
Latin American Defense Organization, 121
Latino Labor/Civil Rights Conference of the
East Coast, 286
Latinx diaspora, 16, 208, 211–212
Lauria-Santiago, Aldo A., 19n2
Lausell, Luis, 82
Laviera, Tato, 208
Lebrón Sotomayor, Lolita, 75, 118, 238, 259,
260f, 306, 308, 334. See also nationalist
prisoners
Left-wing movements in the United States,
7–8, 10, 47, 52, 62, 77, 112–114, 121–123,
127–128, 191, 195–200, 207, 210–211, 279,
287, 289, 300–301, 309–312, 316, 318–319,
323, 325–326, 328, 337–338, 341–342, 345–
347, 350, 358–359, 361, 367–368; American
Friends Service Committee, 308, 311, 345;
American Labor Party, 7, 8; Bois d'Arc
Patriots, 332; Citizen's Party, 332; Communist Party (USA), 7, 73, 47, 73, 127, 174, 207,

212, 342; Democratic Socialists of America,
211; Green Party, 320; International Workers League, 308; Mass Party Organizing
Committee (MPOC), 18, 317–319, 321,
323–329, 332, 346; People's Alliance, 18,
328–333, 335–337, 340, 348–350; Prairie
Fire, 342; Progressive Labor Party, 35; Revolutionary Communist Party, 207; Revolutionary Socialist Party, 308; Socialist Party,
7; Socialist Workers Party, 47, 342; War
Resisters League, 193, 345; Weather Underground, 342; Worker's World Party, 47, 311,
342; Youth International Party (Yippies),
342. See also coalitions and alliances; Glick,
Ted; Puerto Rican Socialist Party (PSP),
and the Left
Lenin, Vladimir, 43, 74, 201, 204, 259
Levins, Richard, 93n49, 312
Levy, Richard, 104. See also United States v.
José E. Velázquez
LGBTQ+ issues. See gay rights issues
Liberation News Service, 293
liberation theology, 83, 144, 267
libre asociación. See free association
Liga Anti-imperialista, 7
Liga Antillana, 6
Linares, Guillermo, 289
Lincoln Hospital (The Bronx, NYC), 51, 58
Little Anthony and the Imperials, 101
Locker, Michael, 295
Loisaida, 235
López, Ada, 131
López, Alfredo, 12–13, 37f, 92n38, 95n87, 139–
140, 186–200, 316, 379; and the bicentennial
campaign, 342; and Claridad bilingüe, 147,
149, 151–152; and Madison Square Garden,
319–320; and the PRSC, 260–261, 276,
295–298, 303
López, Jesús, 37f, 92n38
López, Karim, 154, 157–158, 160, 164, 167–
168, 199, 371
López Rivera, José, 122, 125, 134. See also
Chicago
López Rivera, Oscar, 114, 119–120, 133, 211,
251, 363. See also political prisoners
Lorde, Audre, 335
Los Angeles, 247, 270, 272, 274–276; bicenten-
nial campaign in, 261, 277–279, 304; Com-
mittee against Police Abuse, 278; PRSC in,
299, 302; Watts riots, 276. See also Puerto
Rican Socialist Party (PSP), California
Watts riots
Los Pleneros de la 23 Abajo, 122
Love Canal, 334